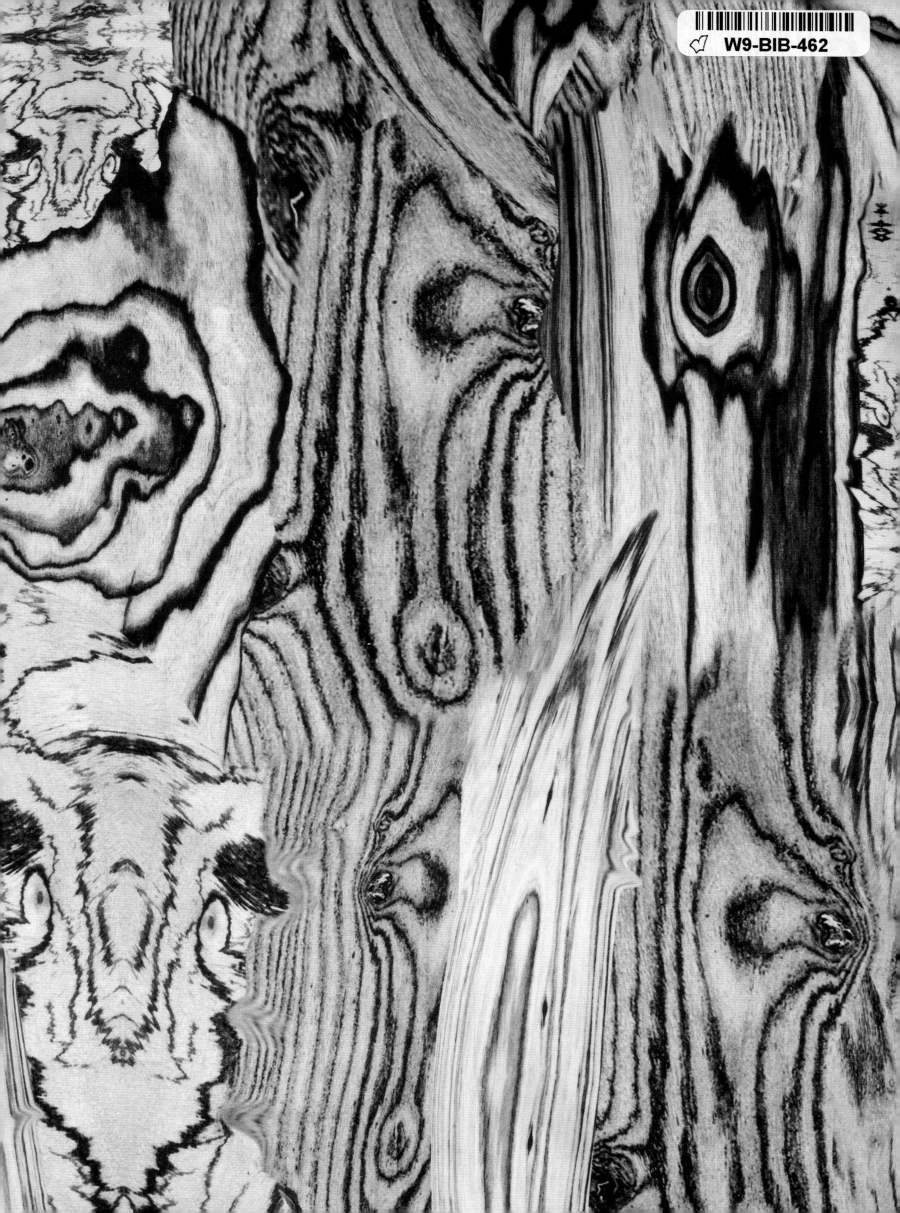

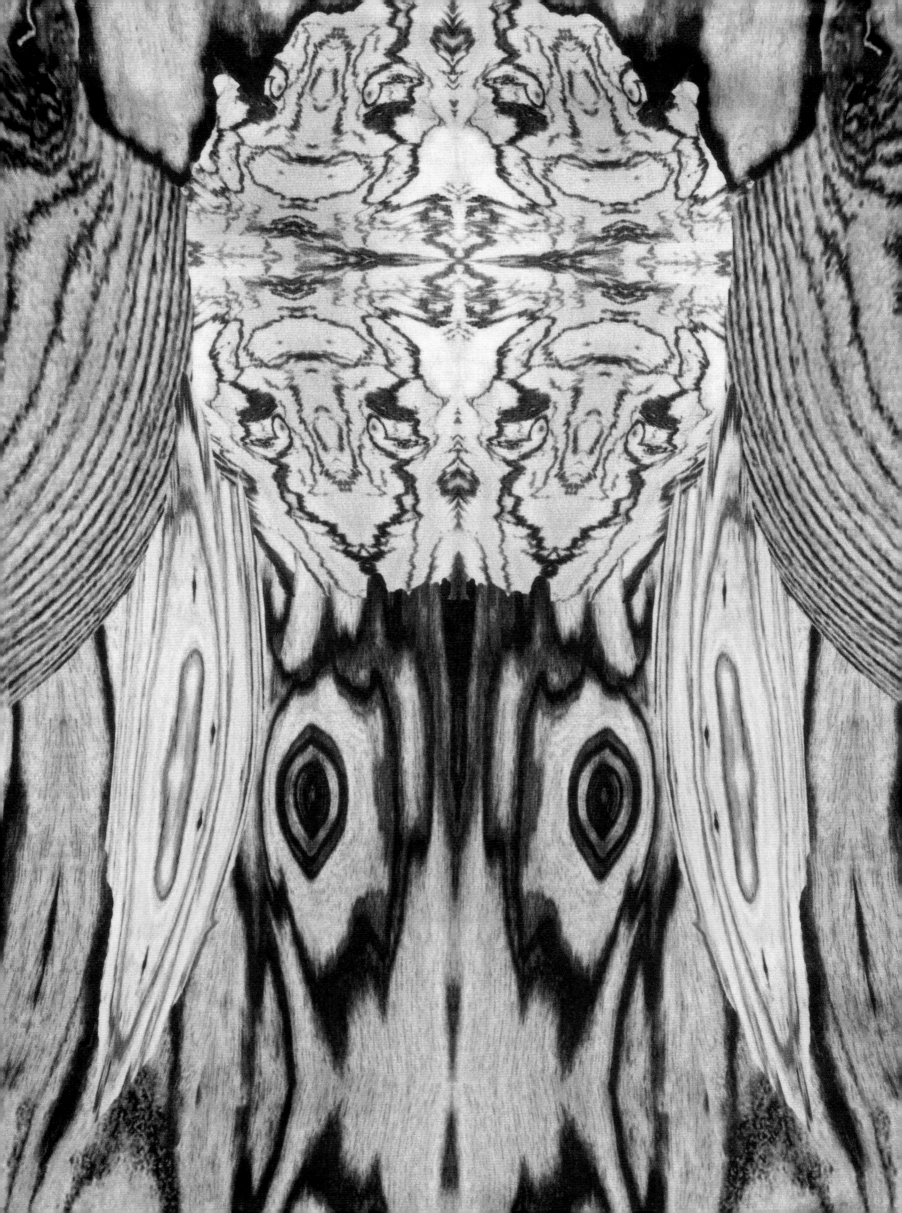

ALEXANDER McQUEEN

SAVAGE BEAUTY

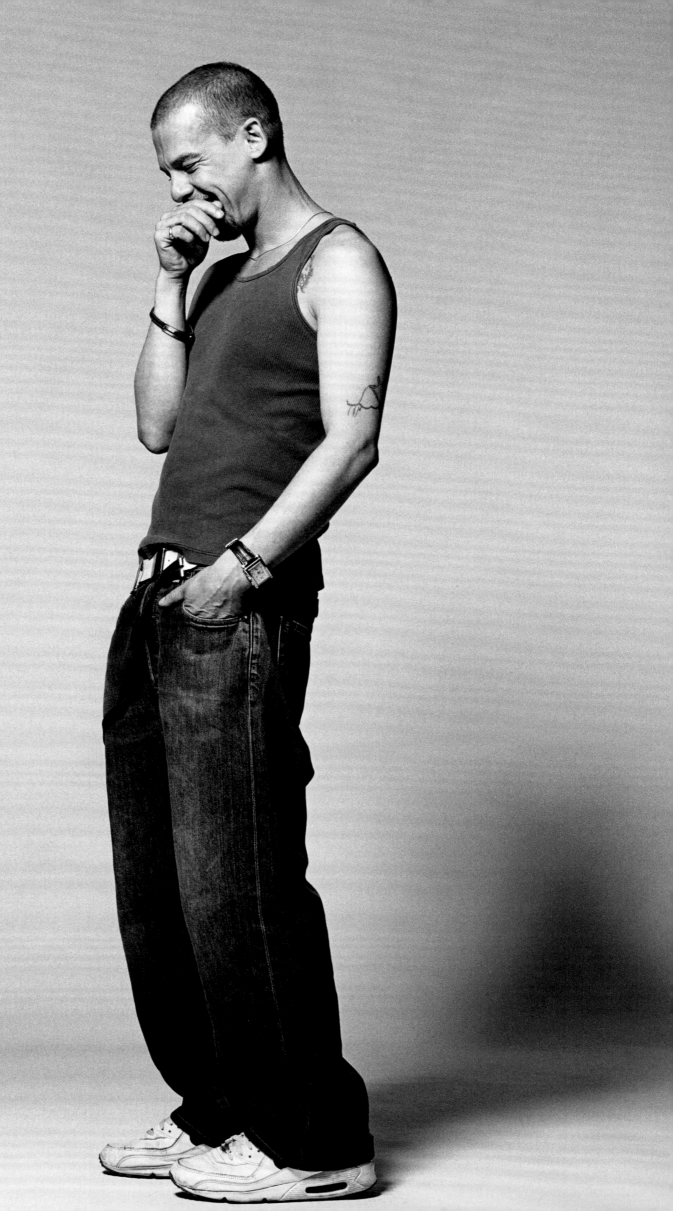

ANDREW BOLTON

WITH CONTRIBUTIONS BY SUSANNAH FRANKEL AND TIM BLANKS

PHOTOGRAPHY BY SØLVE SUNDSBØ

ALEXANDER McQUEEN
SAVAGE BEAUTY

THE METROPOLITAN MUSEUM OF ART, NEW YORK

DISTRIBUTED BY YALE UNIVERSITY PRESS, NEW HAVEN AND LONDON

This catalogue is published in conjunction with the exhibition "Alexander McQueen: Savage Beauty," on view at The Metropolitan Museum of Art, New York, May 4– July 31, 2011.

The exhibition is made possible by

ALEXANDER
MCQUEEN

Additional support is provided in partnership with

AMERICAN EXPRESS   CONDÉ NAST

Sølve Sundsbø Studio:

Photography Assistants: Karina Twiss, Ashley Reynolds, and Myro Wulff

Production by Paula Ekenger, Sally Dawson, and Alex Waitt

Alexander McQueen Studio:

Creative Coordinator: Trino Verkade

Assistant to Creative Coordinator: Laura Kiefer

Archivist: Olivier Van de Velde

Archive Assistants: Natalya Bezborodova, Chi Lael, and Rachel J. Vick

Casting by Sidonie Barton

Makeup by Gina Kane @ Caren

Assisted by Yumiko Yamamoto, Kaori Mitsuyasu, Clare Read, Misaki, and Elizabeth Hsieh

Still-life styling by Johanne Mills

Models:

Polina Kasina at Women Management Milan

Katerina Smutok at Premier Models

Lyza Onysko at Storm Model Management

Uliana Tikhova at Storm Model Management

Retouching by Digital Light Ltd.

Special thanks to the retouching team: Dan Moloney, Phil Crisp, Jayden Tang, Patrick Horgan, Jim Alexandrou, Jake Hickman

www.digitallightltd.com

Cover photography and artwork by Gary James McQueen, originally produced for the invitation to NATURAL DIS-TINCTION UN-NATURAL SELECTION (spring/summer 2009)

Catalogue photography © Sølve Sundsbø/Art + Commerce

Portraits of Alexander McQueen:

Frontispiece: Photo © David Bailey

Pages 28–29: © Don McCullin/Contact Press Images, originally photographed for Harper's Bazaar

Page 224: © Tim Walker/Art + Commerce

Published by The Metropolitan Museum of Art, New York

Mark Polizzotti, Publisher and Editor in Chief

Gwen Roginsky, Associate Publisher and General Manager of Publications

Peter Antony, Chief Production Manager

Michael Sittenfeld, Managing Editor

Elisa Urbanelli, Editor

Takaaki Matsumoto/Matsumoto Incorporated, New York, Designer

Typeset in Adobe Garamond Pro

Printed on 130 gsm Gardapat Kiara

Printed and bound by Conti Tipocolor S.p.A., Florence, Italy

Lenticular cover produced by Graphicom S.r.l., Verona, Italy

The Metropolitan Museum of Art

1000 Fifth Avenue

New York, New York 10028

www.metmuseum.org

Distributed to the trade by

Yale University Press

P.O. Box 209040

New Haven, Connecticut 06520-9040

www.yalebooks.com

Cataloging-in-Publication Data is available from the Library of Congress.

ISBN 978-1-58839-412-5 (hc: The Metropolitan Museum of Art)

ISBN 978-0-300-16978-2 (hc: Yale University Press)

CONTENTS

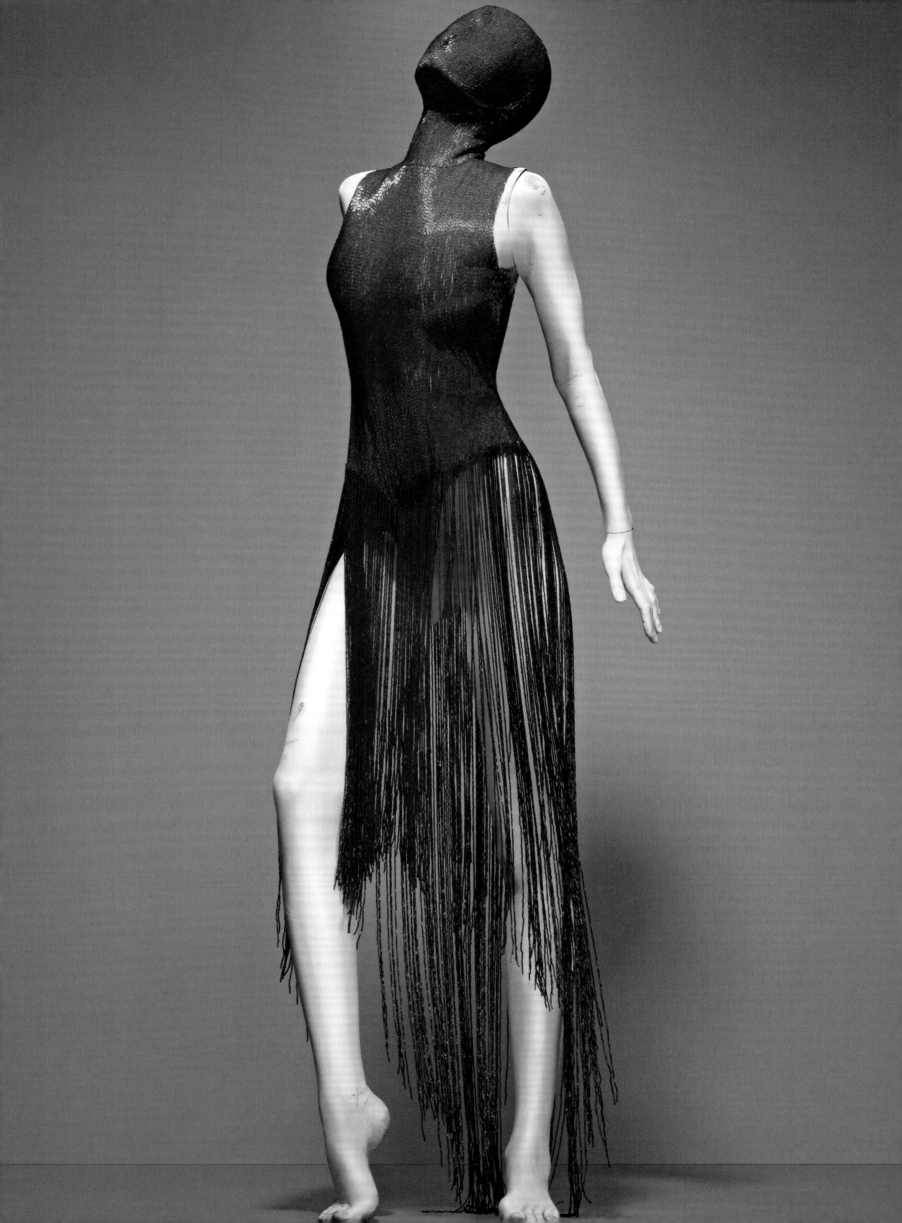

The house of Alexander McQueen is honored that The Costume Institute of The Metropolitan Museum of Art is recognizing Lee Alexander McQueen's extraordinary body of work in its spring 2011 exhibition, *Alexander McQueen: Savage Beauty*.

The exhibition celebrates McQueen's remarkable vision and creativity, showcasing his ingenious fashions as works of art. Comprising approximately one hundred designs—including many rare examples of his early work—the exhibition's selection largely draws upon the extensive Alexander McQueen Archive in London.

As a house, Alexander McQueen has always emphasized the importance of imagination and free expression—and we truly appreciate this recognition of the cultural impact of Lee's inspired designs and his contribution to the fashion community.

Along with American Express® and Condé Nast, the house is delighted to sponsor *Alexander McQueen: Savage Beauty*, preserving Lee Alexander McQueen's incredible legacy for future generations.

Jonathan Akeroyd
Chief Executive Officer, Alexander McQueen

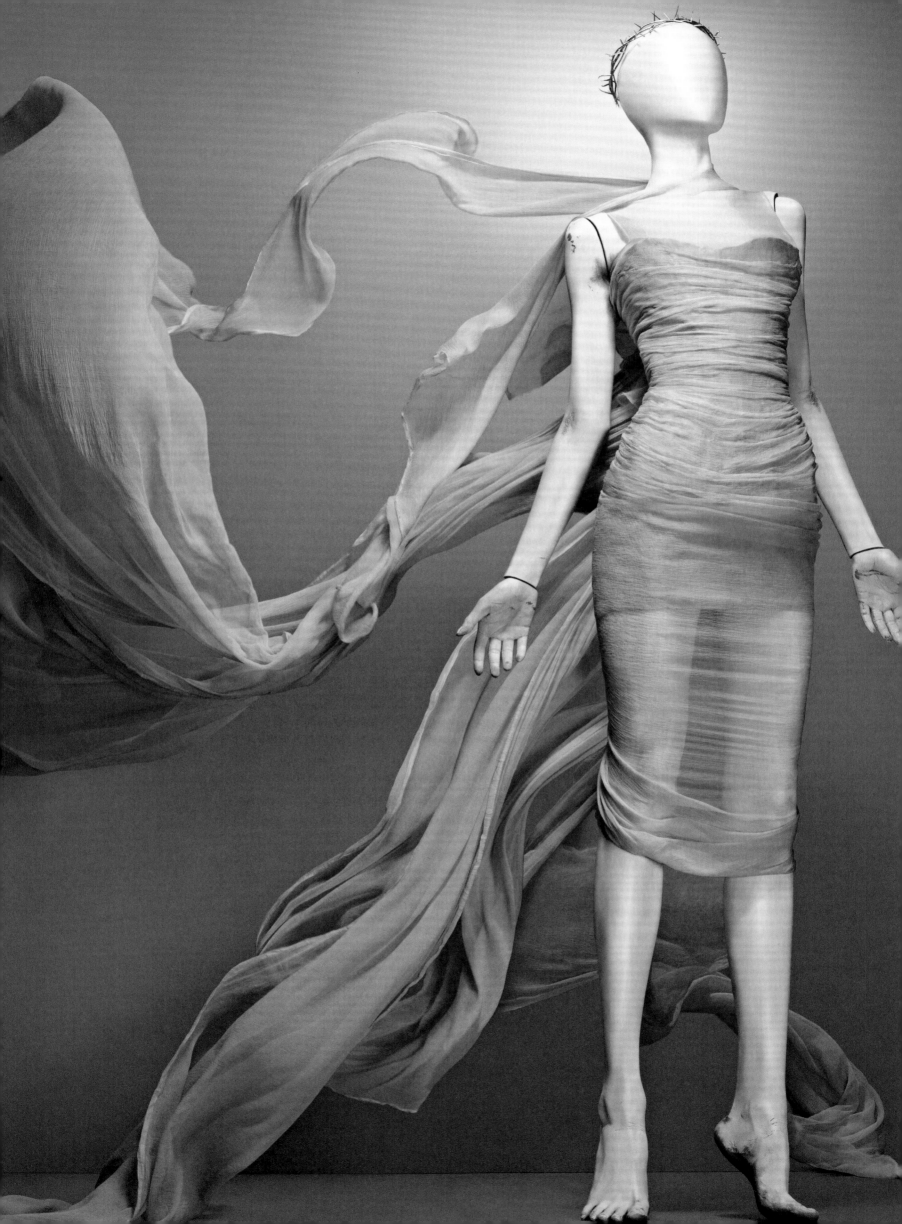

There are any number of fashion designers with the creative distinction to warrant a presentation of their work in an art museum. But I can think of few whose careers fit as easily within the language and methodologies of art history as that of Alexander McQueen. As seen in this catalogue, which accompanies an exhibition at the Metropolitan Museum, McQueen's designs address themes normally beyond the ambitions of fashion. From his prescient student work to his final elegiac collection, his most compelling designs are imbued with recurring narrative, aesthetic, and technical leitmotifs. And yet, his work never devolves into predictability.

Curator Andrew Bolton's examination of McQueen's career reveals the nuanced sophistication behind the designer's dark sensibility. Mythic images of chivalry, brutality, and romance, ideals of heroic women, beauty in the unconventional—these ideas infused McQueen's designs with an unparalleled emotional depth and challenged us to embrace new ideas about gender, history, and nature.

This project has benefited from the generosity of many of the people closest to the late designer. They have not only shared their memories of McQueen but also lent pieces from their wardrobes, including rare surviving examples from his earliest collections. I would particularly like to thank Sarah Burton, creative director of Alexander McQueen, and her staff for their extraordinary efforts on our behalf. We are pleased to include in this book the insightful contributions of fashion journalists Susannah Frankel and Tim Blanks. Sølve Sundsbø's beautiful photographs convey the elegance of McQueen's designs and provide a lasting tribute to the artist.

The exhibition and this accompanying publication are made possible through the generosity of Alexander McQueen™. We would also like to extend our sincere gratitude to American Express® and Condé Nast for their important commitment to this project.

Lastly, I want to thank Anna Wintour for her dedication to the Museum and support of The Costume Institute. For more than a decade she has championed the work of Harold Koda and Andrew Bolton and her devotion has been both strengthening and inspiring.

Thomas P. Campbell,

Thomas P. Campbell
Director, The Metropolitan Museum of Art

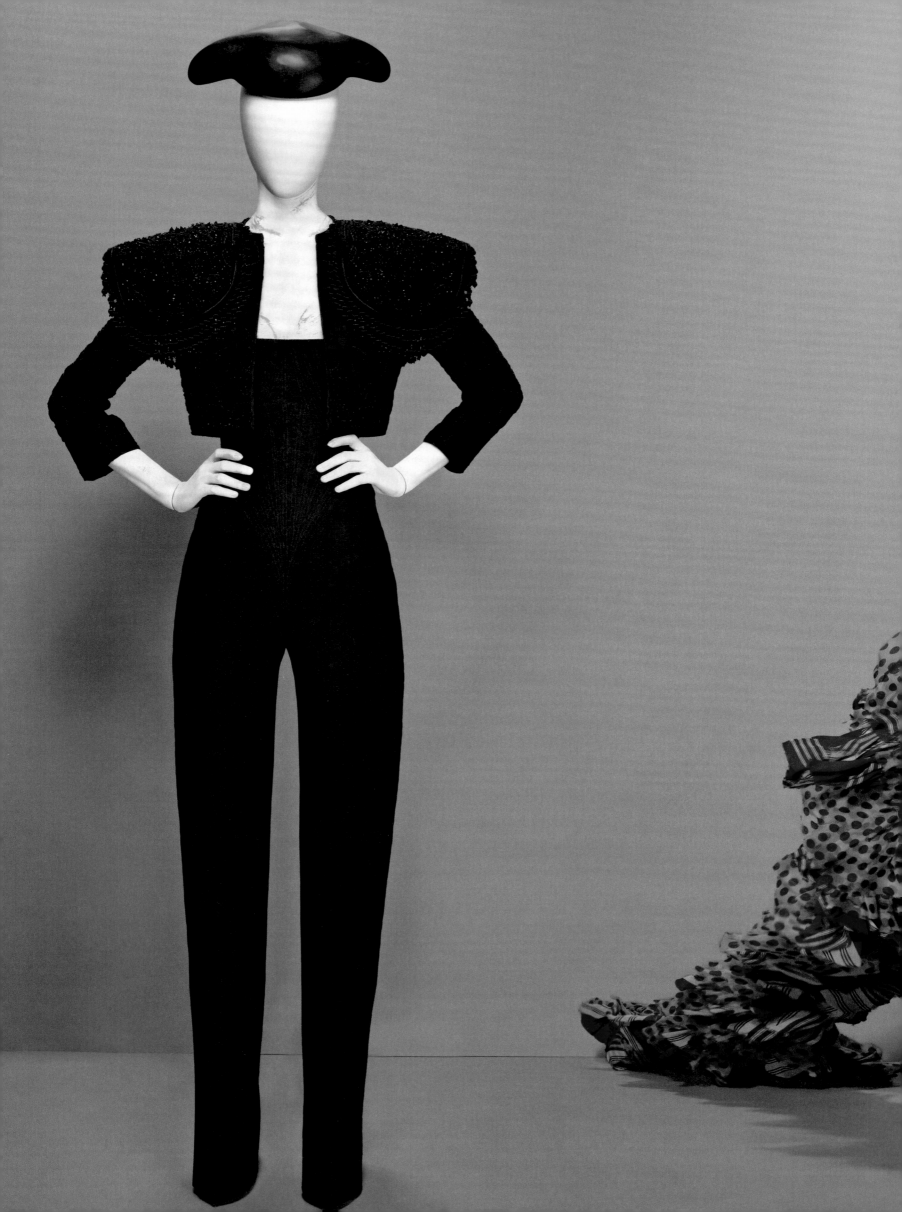

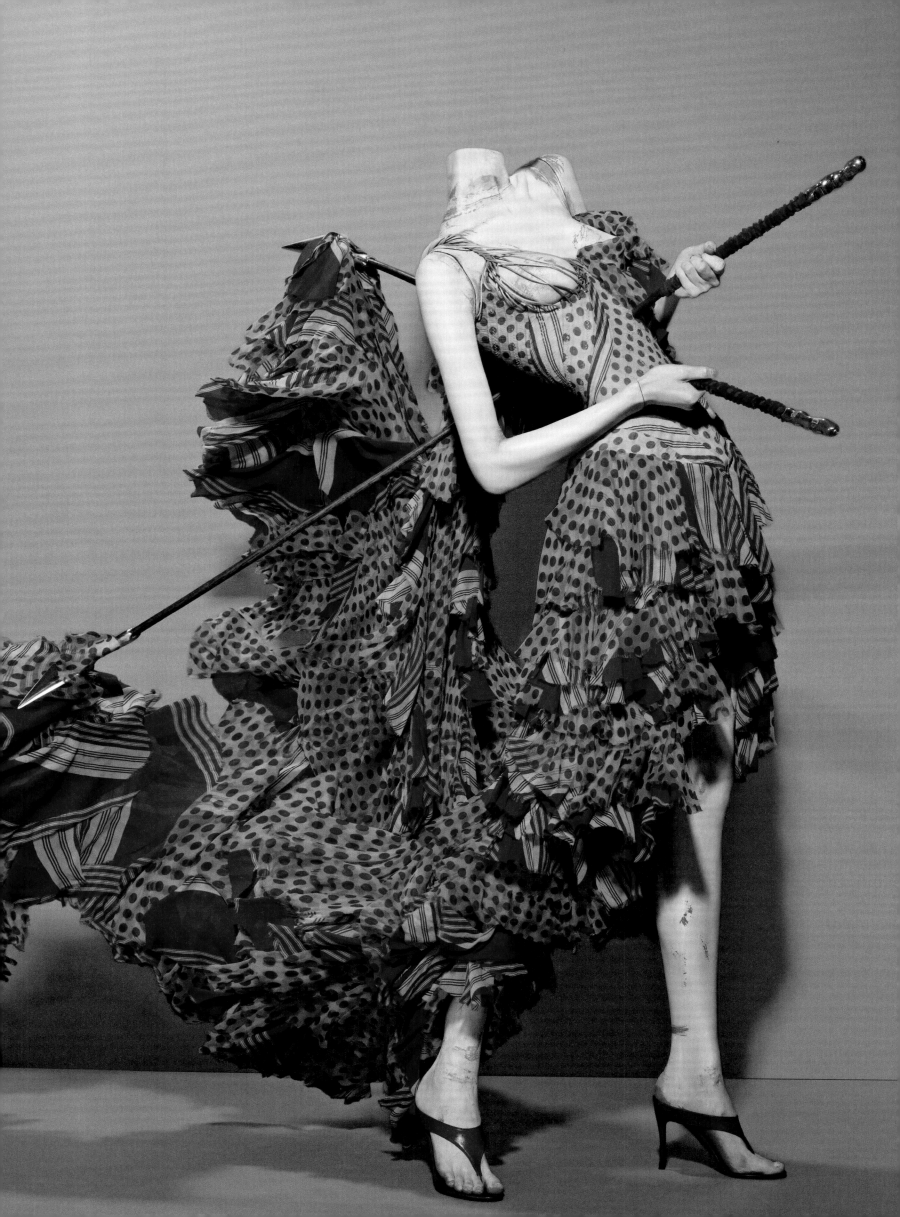

Tattooed on Alexander McQueen's upper right arm were the words "Love looks not with the eyes, but with the mind," a quotation from Shakespeare's *A Midsummer Night's Dream*. Spoken by the lovesick Helena, who has been abandoned by her beloved Demetrius because he loves the more beautiful Hermia, the soliloquy considers the erratic and irrational nature of love. In her contemplations, Helena believes that love has the power to transform something ugly into something beautiful because love is propelled by subjective perceptions of the individual, not by objective assessments of appearance. This belief was not only shared by McQueen but also critical to his creativity. The themes of love and beauty were central to his vision of fashion, which reflected upon the politics of appearance by revealing both the prejudices and the limitations of our aesthetic judgments.

For McQueen, love was the most exalted of human emotions. Once asked in an interview what makes his heart miss a beat, the designer responded without hesitation, "Falling in love."[1] Fashion provided McQueen with a conduit for the conceptual expression of love—both its agonies and its ecstasies. Frequently, this expression was autobiographical. "What you see in the work is the person himself. And my heart is in my work."[2] It was this exposure of the self, this vulnerability, that imbued his fashions with their dignity and humanity, and that instilled in them their intensity and poignancy. However, for McQueen, fashion was not simply a channel for his own emotions. He saw it as a catalyst for the generation and cultivation of a heightened sensitivity to feelings. Commenting on the concept of the runway show, he observed "In fashion . . . the show . . . should make you think, there is no point in doing it if it's not going to create some sort of emotion."[3]

McQueen's runway shows, which suggested avant-garde installation and performance art, provoked powerful, visceral emotions. His friend and mentor Isabella Blow, the stylist whom the designer described as "a cross between a Billingsgate fishwife and Lucrezia Borgia,"[4] believed McQueen to be "the only designer [to make] his audiences react emotionally to a show, be it happy, sad, repelled, or disgusted."[5] McQueen himself once remarked, "I don't want to do a cocktail party, I'd rather people left my shows and vomited. I prefer extreme reactions."[6] The emotional responses to McQueen's presentations were a consequence of their dramatic scenarios, which often hinged on subjects that tapped into our cultural anxieties and uncertainties. McQueen viewed his collections as journalistic, commenting, "I'm making points about my time, about the times we live in. My work is a social document about the world today."[7] Writing about the intense visual content of McQueen's collections, the journalist Suzy Menkes observed, "Distasteful images? But a reflection of our nasty world. And a powerful fashion designer always ingests the ether of modern times."[8]

Through his runway presentations, McQueen validated powerful emotions as compelling sources of aesthetic experience. In equating emotion with aesthetics, he advanced a tradition that emerged in the last decades of the eighteenth century through the Romantic movement. Romanticism associated unfettered emotionalism with the appreciation of beauty. It placed particular emphasis on awe and wonder, fear and terror, emotions closely aligned with the concept of the Sublime. As an experience, the Sublime was both destabilizing and transformative, involving instances that exceeded our capacities for self-control and rational comprehension. These moments of mute encounter describe the experience of McQueen's runway presentations. Over and over again, his shows took his audience to the limits of reason, eliciting an uneasy pleasure that merged wonder and terror, incredulity and revulsion. For McQueen, the Sublime was the strongest of passions, as it contained the potential for exaltation and transcendence beyond the quotidian.

The concept of the Sublime underlies the premise of the exhibition *Alexander McQueen: Savage Beauty*, which explores McQueen's profound engagement with Romanticism. For McQueen, the Sublime provided a connection between Romanticism and Postmodernism, principally expressed through the spectacle of his runway presentations and their aspirations to a heightened, unrestrained emotionalism. Beyond the Sublime, however, McQueen engaged deeply with other ideological and philosophical abstractions of the Romantic movement, which are revealed in the dominant themes of his collections, and which, in turn, provide the themes of this exhibition and publication. The thematic sections are built around fashions selected from a variety of McQueen's collections—from his MA graduation collection in 1992 to his posthumous collection in 2010—as well as featured collections that both illustrate and encapsulate each of the prevailing themes. What comes to light is a vision of fashion that aimed to reconstitute the Romantic past into the Postmodern present.

Central to this vision is the concept of individualism, which emerged out of the writings of Jean-Jacques Rousseau. Epitomized in art by Eugène Delacroix, in music by Ludwig van Beethoven, and in literature by Lord Byron, it asserted the creativity of the individual artist. Like Byron, Beethoven, and Delacroix, McQueen is an exemplar of the Romantic individual, the hero-artist who staunchly followed the dictates of his inspiration. As a designer, he doggedly promoted freedom of thought and expression and championed the authority of the imagination. "What I am trying to bring to [fashion] is a sort of originality,"[9] he once commented. McQueen expressed this originality most fundamentally through the technical virtuosity of his fashions. The section titled "The Romantic Mind" explores McQueen's ingenuity by focusing on his methods of cutting and construction, which were both innovative and revolutionary. This technical brilliance was apparent as early as his graduation collection from the Fashion Design MA course at Central Saint Martins College of Art and Design in London. Titled *Jack the Ripper Stalks His Victims* (1992), it introduced iconic designs such as the three-point "origami" frockcoat. In his first collection after graduating, titled *Taxi Driver* (autumn/winter 1993–94), McQueen launched his "bumsters," pants that sat so low on the hips they revealed the buttocks. Indeed, McQueen was such an assured designer that his forms and silhouettes were established from his earliest collections and remained relatively consistent throughout his career. Referring to his early training on Savile Row in London, McQueen has said, "Everything I do is based on tailoring."[10] "The Romantic Mind," which is organized taxonomically as a series of "studies" (coats, pants, skirts, and jackets), reveals an approach to fashion that combines the precision and traditions of tailoring and patternmaking with the spontaneity and improvisations of draping and dressmaking, an approach that became more refined after his tenure as creative director of Givenchy in Paris. It is this approach, at once rigorous and impulsive, disciplined and unconstrained, that underlies McQueen's singularity and inimitability.

As it was for artists and writers of the Romantic movement, one of the defining features of McQueen's collections was their historicism. While McQueen's historical references were far-reaching, he was inspired particularly by the nineteenth century, drawing especially on the Victorian Gothic. "There's something . . . kind of Edgar Allan Poe, kind of deep and kind of melancholic about [my] collections,"[11] McQueen commented. As revealed in the section "Romantic Gothic," the "shadowy fancies" that Poe writes about in *The Fall of the House of Usher* (1839) are vividly present in the majority of McQueen's collections, most notably *Dante* (autumn/winter 1996–97) and *Supercalifragilisticexpialidocious* (autumn/winter 2002–3). Like the Victorian Gothic, which combines elements of horror and romance, McQueen's collections often reflected paradoxical relationships such as life and death, lightness and darkness. Indeed, the emotional intensity of his runway presentations was frequently the consequence of the interplay between such dialectical oppositions. In the featured collection of "Romantic Gothic," McQueen's posthumous collection for autumn/winter 2010–11 (unofficially titled *Angels and Demons*)—which was inspired by old master paintings—the contrasting forces of good and evil and heaven and hell are the principal dichotomies. The relationship between victim and aggressor was especially apparent within McQueen's collections, particularly in his accessories. He once remarked, "I especially like the accessory for its sadomasochistic aspect."[12] This position is strikingly apparent in "Cabinet of Curiosities," an addendum to "Romantic Gothic" that focuses on atavistic, fetishistic paraphernalia produced by

McQueen in collaboration with a number of accessory designers, including the milliners Dai Rees and Philip Treacy and the jewelers Shaun Leane, Erik Halley, and Sarah Harmarnee. The featured collection is *No. 13* (spring/summer 1999), which was inspired by the Arts and Crafts movement and which focused on the contrasting opposites of man and machine, craft and technology.

Typically, McQueen's collections were fashioned around elaborate narratives that were profoundly autobiographical, often reflecting upon his ancestral history, specifically his Scottish heritage. When he was asked once what his Scottish roots meant to him, McQueen responded, "Everything."[13] McQueen's patriotic impulses are explored in "Romantic Nationalism," which features *Highland Rape* (autumn/winter 1995–96), the first collection to introduce McQueen tartan. The clothes were shown on semi-naked models staggering down a runway strewn with heather and bracken. "People thought there was real blood and tampon strings hanging," McQueen remarked about the controversy the collection generated. "[But] it was really just a hedonistic collection: wild women in the Highlands."[14] Based on the eighteenth-century Jacobite Risings and the nineteenth-century Highland Clearances, it was, in fact, a powerful and heartfelt declaration of McQueen's Scottish national identity. As it did for Romantic artists and writers, nationalism for McQueen found its natural expression in folkloric narratives. In *Widows of Culloden* (autumn/winter 2006–7), a sequel to *Highland Rape* based on the final battle of the Jacobite Risings and featuring exaggerated silhouettes inspired by the 1880s, McQueen conceived a plaintive narrative inspired by the widows of Scottish Highlanders who "got on a ship and moved to America, and ended up on Plymouth Rock."[15] Although more wistful than *Highland Rape*, its message remained defiantly political: "What the British did there was nothing short of genocide."[16] Despite these heartfelt declarations of his Scottish national identity, McQueen felt intensely connected to England, especially London. "London's where I was brought up. It's where my heart is and where I get inspiration,"[17] he once stated. His deep interest in the history of England was most apparent, perhaps, in *The Girl Who Lived in the Tree* (autumn/winter 2008–9), a dreamy, quixotic fairy tale inspired by an elm tree in the garden of McQueen's country home near Fairlight Cove in East Sussex. Influenced by "The British Empire, Queens of England, The Duke of Wellington," it was, in fact, one of McQueen's most romantically nationalistic collections, albeit tinged with irony and pastiche. Of the collection, McQueen joked, "I thought, I'll do this thing on the Queen, and I'll get the knighthood. I'll become Sir Alexander McQueen."[18]

McQueen's Romantic sensibilities expanded his imaginary horizons not only temporally but also spatially, as reflected in the section "Romantic Exoticism." The lure of the exotic was a central theme of Romanticism, advanced in literature by Lord Byron and Samuel Taylor Coleridge, the latter of whom chose the Asian setting of Xanadu for his poem *Kubla Khan* (1797). For the Romantics, "exotic" settings ranged from Spain to Asia to Africa, places that also sparked McQueen's imagination. Japan was particularly significant to McQueen, both thematically and stylistically. The kimono, especially, was a garment that the designer endlessly reconfigured in his collections. Indeed, McQueen's exoticism was often formalistic. Remarking on the direction of his fashions, he commented, "[My work will be about] taking elements of traditional embroidery, filigree and craftsmanship from countries all over the world. I will explore their crafts, patterns and materials and interpret them in my own way."[19] As with many of his themes, however, McQueen's exoticism often expressed itself in contrasting opposites. This was the case with *It's a Only a Game* (spring/summer 2005), a show staged as a chess game inspired by a scene in the film *Harry Potter and the Sorcerer's Stone* (2001), which pitched the East (Japan) against the West (America). Films often inspired McQueen, as did contemporary art. *VOSS* (spring/summer 2001), which featured a number of exotic garments, was inspired by Joel Peter Witkin's photograph *Sanitarium* (1983), a depiction of an obese woman connected via a breathing tube to a stuffed monkey. On McQueen's runway, the role of the woman was played by the fetish writer Michelle Olley. Typical of McQueen's collections, *VOSS* offered a commentary on the relationship between the beautiful and the grotesque. For McQueen, the body was a site of contravention, where normalcy was questioned and where the spectacle of marginality was embraced and celebrated.

In his collections, McQueen often explored notions of diversity, difference, and distinction, notions that are played out in the section "Romantic Primitivism." Throughout his career, McQueen frequently returned to the theme of primitivism, which drew upon the ideal of the noble savage living in harmony with the natural world. It was the focus of his second collection after graduating, titled *Nihilism* (spring/summer 1994). He said of the collection, "[It] was a reaction to designers romanticizing ethnic dressing, like a Masai-inspired dress made of materials the Masai could never afford."[20] It famously included a latex dress with locusts, McQueen's statement on famine. Many of the pieces were coated with mud, a conceit the designer repeated in *Eshu* (autumn/winter 2000–1), a collection inspired by the well-known deity of Yoruba mythology. The clothes, including a coat of black synthetic hair, came close to fetishizing materials. This was also the case in *It's a Jungle Out There* (autumn/winter 1997–98), which was based on the theme of the Thomson's Gazelle. The collection was a meditation on the dynamics of power, particularly as seen in the relationship between predator and prey. Indeed, McQueen's reflections on primitivism were frequently represented in paradoxical combinations, contrasting modern and primitive, civilized and uncivilized. The storyline of *Irere* (spring/summer 2003), the featured collection in "Romantic Primitivism," involved a shipwreck at sea and was peopled with pirates, conquistadors, and Amazonian Indians. Typically, McQueen's narrative glorified the state of nature and tipped the moral balance in favor of the "natural man" or "nature's gentleman" unfettered by the artificial constructs of civilization.

Nature was the greatest, or at least the most enduring, influence upon McQueen. "Everything I do is connected to nature in one way or another,"[21] he explained. Nature was also a central theme, if not the central theme, of Romanticism. The artists J. M. W. Turner and John Constable and the writers Samuel Taylor Coleridge and William Wordsworth often presented nature itself as a work of art. McQueen both shared and promoted this view, as revealed in the fashions in the section "Romantic Naturalism," which take their forms and raw materials from the natural world. For McQueen, however, as it was for the Romantics, nature was also a locus for ideas and concepts. This is most clearly reflected in *Plato's Atlantis* (spring/summer 2010), the featured collection in "Romantic Naturalism." Inspired by Charles Darwin's *On the Origin of Species* (1859), it presented a narrative that centered not on the evolution of humankind but on its devolution, predicting a time when "the ice cap would melt . . . the waters would rise and . . . life on earth would have to evolve in order to live beneath the sea once more or perish."[22] The collection was streamed live over the Internet on Nick Knight's SHOWstudo.com, in an attempt to "[make] fashion into an interactive dialogue between creator and consumer."[23] As Alexander Fury, fashion director of SHOWstudio.com, remarked, "Before our very eyes . . . garments became image rather than object, pixellated and broadcast worldwide within seconds."[24] For the Romantics, nature was the primary vehicle for the Sublime—starry skies, stormy seas, turbulent waterfalls, vertiginous mountains. In *Plato's Atlantis*, the sublime experience of nature was paralleled by and supplanted with that of technology—the extreme space-time compressions produced by the Internet. It was a powerful evocation of the Sublime and its coincident expression of the Romantic and the Postmodern. At the same time, it was a potent vision of the future of fashion that reflected McQueen's sweeping imagination. He once remarked, "I'm overly romantic."[25] But it was precisely his romantic yearnings that propelled his creativity and advanced fashion in directions both unimagined and unprecedented.

"My collections have always been autobiographical,

a lot to do with my own sexuality and coming

to terms with the person I am—it was like

exorcising my ghosts in the collections.

They were to do with my childhood, the way

I think about life and the way I was brought up

to think about life."

Alexander McQueen—both the man and the artist—has been the subject of much mythologizing. For his is the story of a young man who rose to fame provoking extreme reactions, not only among the public and press but also within the supposedly shockproof fashion industry. Here was a working-class boy who spent his early career intent on subverting the intricate artifice and anachronistic hierarchy that the fashion world guards so jealously. Even at the end of his life, and height of his fame, McQueen remained magnificently antiestablishment at heart. Against all the odds, and always unflinchingly plainspoken, he found his way into an apprenticeship on Savile Row and then graduated with distinction from the world's most famous fashion course, the MA at Central Saint Martins College of Art and Design. After only eight seasons showing his own label, to ever more sensational effect, he was catapulted to international recognition when he succeeded John Galliano as head designer at Givenchy, the polite Parisian couture house best known for dressing Audrey Hepburn. From there, he went into partnership with the Gucci Group, a move that enabled his fashion house to develop into a globally recognized brand.

In less than a decade, McQueen had traveled from the insalubrious thoroughfares of London's East End—throughout his life, the authenticity of that environment continued to appeal to him—to the grand boulevards of Paris and, finally, to an elegant apartment in Mayfair. He quipped that he wanted to be "close to the Queen" when he received his knighthood. By then he had been voted four times Designer of the Year by the British Fashion Council (1996, 1997, 2001, 2003) and once International Designer of the Year by the Council of Fashion Designers of America (2003).

The folklore that sprang up in his wake, then, was far from surprising. More remarkable still, though, is the manner in which Alexander McQueen CBE (Commander of the Order of the British Empire) rose above any fairy-tale connotations, the sheer determination with which he defied, flouted, and fought endlessly against the unyielding British class system and relentless stereotyping. Unfairness always outraged him, whether directed toward himself or others. And as a human being, he was far more complex, elusive, and indeed magical than any reductive media incarnation.

Lee Alexander McQueen was born on March 17, 1969, in Lewisham, South London. When he was less than a year old the McQueen family moved farther east, from Burley Road in Stepney to a terrace on Biggerstaff Road in Stratford. He was the youngest of six children, having three sisters and two brothers. His father, Ronald, drove a black cab. His mother, Joyce, stayed at home with her children until Lee was sixteen, after which she taught evening classes in genealogy and social history. She traced her own family heritage back 250 years to the French Huguenots, who had fled religious persecution to settle in Whitechapel and Spitalfields. The designer never ceased to be interested in his own ancestry, almost to the point of obsession.

McQueen attended Carpenters Primary School and then Rokeby, the local all-boys comprehensive. From the start, his interests were rather different from those of his classmates. A member of the Young Ornithologists Club of Great Britain, after school he would climb onto the rooftop of an apartment building near his home to watch the kestrels flying overhead. He took classes in synchronized swimming, but, far from the most attentive of students, he was more likely to be found swimming beneath the surface, oblivious to his hapless instructor. He made the school team nonetheless—his proficiency in the water would later surprise his friends—but once miscalculated a back somersault dive, landing on the concrete around the pool and shattering his front teeth. It was not until much later that he had them fixed properly. McQueen loved gospel singing, too, and went to church with his young, black friends to listen to the local choir.

From an early age, the designer knew that he would, in his own words, "be something in fashion." A sheet of paper stamped with *Calvin Klein* was plastered to his bedroom wall. "I was literally three years old when I started drawing," he said. "I did it all my life, through primary school, secondary school, all my life. I always, always wanted to be a designer. I read books on fashion from

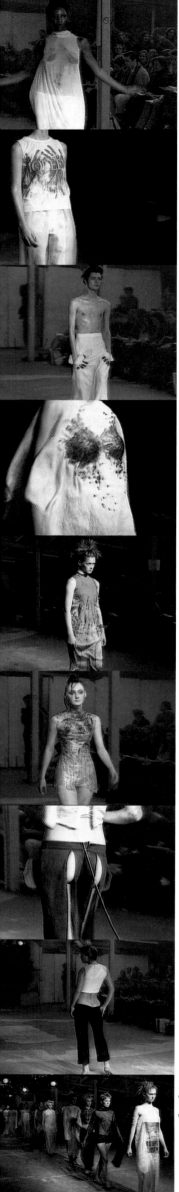

the age of twelve. I followed designers' careers. I knew Giorgio Armani was a window-dresser, Emanuel Ungaro was a tailor."[1] Although this mind-set was presumably somewhat at odds with the brute maleness of his school environment, McQueen always claimed that his classmates simply ignored him. "That was fine. I was doing it for myself. But I always knew I would be something in fashion. I didn't know how big, but I always knew I'd be something."[2]

He left school in 1985, at the age of sixteen, with only one academic qualification—in art—to his name. That same year, his mother saw a television news feature bemoaning the lack of young apprentices on London's Savile Row and urged her son to apply for a job. He soon found himself working under Cornelius ("Con") O'Callaghan, among the most respected and demanding coat makers in the business, at Anderson & Sheppard, tailors by appointment to the British royal family.

At that time, the firm's policy was to take on apprentices who had not had any formal fashion education in the belief that they would be easier to train. McQueen stayed for two years. He was generally quiet, according to those who worked with him, and in the beginning, highly focused, endlessly asking questions of the master tailors. He learned to make a *forward*—the term for a jacket before its sleeves, back lining, top collar, buttonholes, and finishing stitches have been completed—a year earlier than is usually expected. After a while, however, his attendance became erratic, and he told family and friends that he was bored. Famously, he later informed journalists that during his time at Anderson & Sheppard he had scrawled obscenities into the lining of a jacket destined for the Prince of Wales. Responding to these claims, the company called back any pieces that he had worked on for that client but nothing was ever found. In the early 1990s, while struggling to establish himself, McQueen was certainly not averse to any controversy. In fact, he fueled it, although much of it came back to haunt him. In particular, the designer was furious each time this story was repeated, which, given the heat of the subject matter concerned, was indefatigably.

"Despite his seeming lack of guile, his what-you-see-is-what-you-get stance, McQueen is a deft and subtle media player," wrote the journalist Alix Sharkey in the *Guardian* in 1996. "He knows how easy it is, speaking his mind, to send shudders of delight and horror through the kissy-kissy world of fashion—where bitching about others is always done behind their backs. . . . Beyond this is a need to put others' sincerity to the test. Despite all the mouth and swagger, you can tell McQueen wants to be liked but his insecurity leads him to adopt this spiky, provocative attitude. It's a classic emotional defence mechanism: rather than waiting for someone to disappoint, he provokes them into a hostile reaction, which confirms his worst suspicions and justifies his own behaviour."[3]

"Yes, there has been this big thing about the East End yob made good," McQueen said of his media image in the early days. "But the press started that, not me. It's the Pygmalion syndrome. It's not true. . . . At the end of the day you're a good designer or not and it doesn't matter where you come from. . . . I don't think you can become a good designer, or a great designer, or whatever. To me, you just are one. To know about colour, proportion, shape, cut, balance, is part of a gene. My sister is an amazing artist. My brother is an amazing artist. Amazing. Much better than I am. The difference is, they thought they had no chance but to do a manual job. That really upsets me."[4]

In 1988 the designer moved a few doors down "the Row" to Gieves & Hawkes, where he worked on military tailoring. He stayed for a little more than a year—leaving on his twentieth birthday in 1989—and then took a post at the theatrical costumers Angels, cutting clothes for major London shows, including most memorably, he said, *Les Misérables*.

It is worth noting the careful deliberation behind McQueen's every early career move. Having mastered the intricacies of cut that are integral to British bespoke men's tailoring, which would later inform his own work, he then focused on historical costume, particularly the women's nineteenth-century line that would also become a signature of his designs. Before long, he changed course again, this time to work for Koji Tatsuno, a London-based, Japanese designer with great respect for tradition and craftsmanship, particularly in menswear, but also at the forefront of the avant-garde and backed at the time by Yohji Yamamoto. The British clothing industry was suffering from the ravages of a recession. When Tatsuno, one of many casualties from that period, went bankrupt, McQueen moved to Romeo Gigli, then among the most feted of fashion's big names.

"There was nothing going on in London," he explained, "and the biggest thing at that time was Romeo Gigli. He was everywhere. I thought this is the only person I want to work for. My sister was a travel agent. I got a flight, a one-way ticket to Milan. I was twenty years old. I walked into Romeo Gigli with the worst portfolio you've ever seen, full of costume design. They said they had nothing for me and that they'd call me if anything came up. Anyway, I was walking down the street afterwards and this girl came screaming up to me like a madwoman: 'Stop, stop, stop, Romeo wants to see you. He wants to see you tomorrow. Come back.'"[5] The following morning McQueen was hired.

His time at Gigli, which lasted less than twelve months, was "brilliant," he said. "I was like a nutty little raver, used to go to work in my denim patchwork flares and happy, happy smiley T-shirt. It freaked a lot of people out, all these dressy fashion students and PR people, but Romeo seemed to like that."[6] Most importantly, the experience taught him the power of the press. "He [Gigli] had all this attention and I wanted to know why. It had very little to do with the clothes and more to do with him as a person. And that's fundamentally true of anybody. Any interest in the clothes is secondary to interest in a designer. You need to know that you're a good designer as well, though. . . . If you can't design, what's the point of generating all that hype in the first place?"[7]

Back in London, McQueen, with by then quite impressive credentials, went to see Bobby Hillson, founder of the postgraduate fashion course at Central Saint Martins and teacher of Rifat Ozbek and John Galliano, among others. "He came in [hoping] for a job teaching pattern cutting," she said later. "We didn't have one. I thought he was very interesting and clearly had terrific talent. . . . To have left school at sixteen, studied on Savile Row, gone to Italy alone and found a job with Gigli—that was incredible. He was also technically brilliant, even though he'd never actually studied design. And still only twenty-one or twenty-two."[8]

According to Louise Wilson, McQueen's tutor and now the course director, there was not very much to differentiate McQueen from the other students in his year. "He was like any other student," Wilson recalls. "I remember he loved Callaghan, which seems funny when you think back to it now. He was very into cutting and had an affinity with fabric. He knew, from his time in Italy, that certain fabrics worked with certain shapes. He wasn't a great paper person but always worked in 3-D. He liked being in the studio when nobody else was there. He was always interested, inquisitive really, about something that had been beaded in India, say, or asking questions in the print room. He used the college as it should be used, getting the most out of it."[9]

McQueen graduated from Central Saint Martins in 1992, basing his degree collection on Jack the Ripper. Wilson remembers that his marketing report focused not on banalities such as projected sales figures or the look of any future retail outlet, but instead traced his genealogy back to the infamous Victorian serial killer. In attendance at his year's final group show, which took place in a small theater at Kensington Olympia, was Isabella Blow, then a freelance stylist, who arrived so late that she was forced to find a place on the stairs. Although McQueen's collection was not shown as the finale, Blow immediately identified it as something special. The designer laughed when describing "this nutty lady" who "wouldn't stop badgering me,"[10] calling his mother at home. Famously, she bought every piece. Although wellborn, Blow was not rich. She paid McQueen in weekly installments and established herself as his unofficial public-relations representative, stylist, and muse. For a short time McQueen lived in her house on Elizabeth Street in southwest London. The two would become great friends.

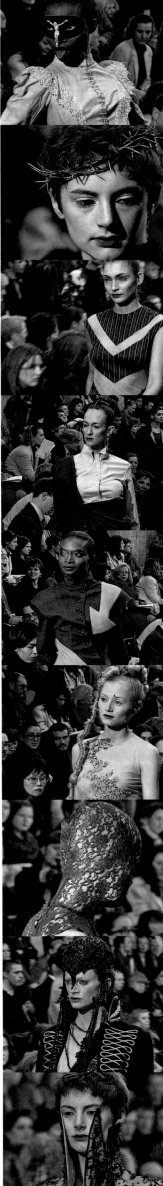

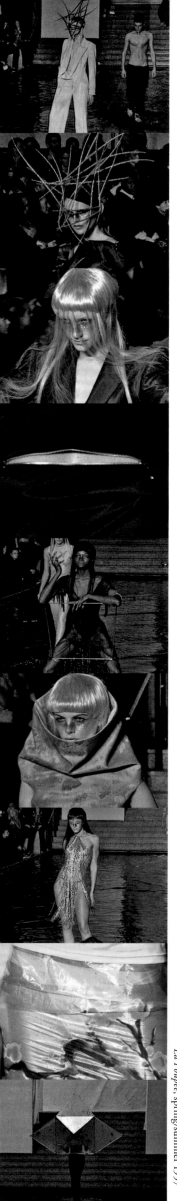

Very little remains of McQueen's early collections. His first after graduating, *Taxi Driver* (autumn/winter 1993–94), was shown on a single clothes rail at the Ritz Hotel. Those who saw it remember black crow feathers, intricate jet beading, and the sharp, corseted tailoring that would always be integral to his work. The infamous "bumster" trouser—cut outrageously low on the hip, McQueen argued, to elongate the line of the torso—was also introduced here, although it received more widespread attention in *Nihilism* (spring/summer 1994), *Banshee* (autumn/winter 1994–95), and *The Birds* (spring/summer 1995). It was not until his fifth show, *Highland Rape* (autumn/winter 1995–96), that the attention surrounding McQueen reached fever pitch.

With its torn and far-from-fine lace—bought for next to nothing from low-priced fabric suppliers—ravaged tartans, and blatant exposure of the female form, this collection caused a scandal. The liberal press, in particular, was quick to label McQueen as the latest in a long line of male homosexual designers who exploit women while pandering to their own fantasies. In fact, the show, which referenced the massacre of the Scottish Highlands at the hands of the British, was a comment on the designer's heritage, personal history, and psychology—as most of his work would be. McQueen later explained:

> We're not talking about models' personal feelings here, we're talking about mine. It's all about the way I'm feeling about my life. Scotland for me is a harsh, cold and bitter place. It was even worse when my great, great grandfather used to live there. I have no respect for what the English did there, they wiped whole families out. The reason I'm patriotic about Scotland is because I think it's been dealt a really hard hand. It's marketed the world over as, you know, fucking haggis, fucking bagpipes. But no one ever puts anything back into it. I hate it when people romanticise Scotland. There's nothing romantic about its history.[11]

Looking back, he may have concluded correctly that *Highland Rape* attracted attention for the wrong reasons. Ever a champion of the underdog, on this occasion he extended such sentiments to embrace an entire country. However, there is no disputing the fact that this show made Alexander McQueen's name.

By the mid-1990s Great Britain was enjoying an unparalleled creative surge. Britpop was in the ascendant—Oasis's "Some Might Say" was the best-selling single of 1995. Brit Art was making waves both at home and abroad—Damien Hirst, famed for his dissection and preservation in formaldehyde of cows, sheep, and, of course, sharks, was awarded the Turner Prize that same year. McQueen spearheaded a similarly iconoclastic movement in fashion. In this designer's case, the ephemeral business of passing trends and straightforward runway presentation were irrelevant. Instead, he had his eye on a broader cultural picture. Most important to him was the desire to provoke an emotional response in his audience that went way beyond the creation of pretty clothes.

McQueen's seventh collection—*Dante* (autumn/winter 1996–97)—was staged in a church in Spitalfields. Models stalked the aisles while a skeleton occupied pride of place in the front row alongside the most respected members of the fashion press. It was later reported erroneously that the location was deconsecrated. In a letter to the *Guardian*, the churchwarden at the time, Fay Cattini, wrote: "It [Christ Church, Spitalfields] is not, and never was, deconsecrated. Your reporter assumed (always a dangerous thing to do) that no consecrated church would allow a fashion show to be held in it. . . . McQueen's rep (a very nice lady) had assured us that nothing would be done in the church that was unsuitable, i.e.: the dresses would be modest! Anyway, what's done is done."[12]

The "nice lady" in question was Trino Verkade, who went to work for McQueen not long before the *Highland Rape* show. "I'd met him earlier but at that point he employed me full-time as his PR [representative]," she says. "But, as it was just me and Lee, I did everything. I remember I dressed the set for the *Highland Rape* show. There was no show producer back then. Professionally he was very demanding. He never wanted anyone to say 'no' to him. He always wanted us at least to try. We all learned that from Lee."[13]

And try she did, on this occasion and many more, eventually succeeding and thus achieving the apparently impossible. Because in the *Dante* collection's constricting corsetry, razor-sharp tailoring, vampish pale lilac silks and black lace, and fabrics printed with war photography by Don McCullin (used without securing McCullin's permission), McQueen's models looked anything but demure. This, then, was a very early example of the conviction with which he would fight for what he wanted. It is small wonder, given his sheer audacity, that the fledgling fashion designer was drawing an international audience to London that was unprecedented.

Despite the growing visibility of his collections, very few portraits of McQueen were in circulation during this period, which only added to his enigmatic persona. In fact, the reason for his reluctance to be photographed was pragmatic. Although critically acclaimed, he was living and working in a small basement in Hoxton Square and receiving social-security benefits from the government. He did not want his picture to appear in the press, he went on to explain, for fear that he would be recognized and have his claim revoked. "I was signing on at the time," says Verkade, "and so was Lee. Neither of us was making any money. In fact, there were times when I actually had to pay for bits and pieces myself."[14] This also explains why as a designer he used his middle name, Alexander, as opposed to his first name, Lee, by which he was known personally.

Nonetheless, by 1996 McQueen had come to the attention of Bernard Arnault, CEO of the French luxury-goods conglomerate LVMH (Louis Vuitton Moët Hennessy), who in October of that year appointed him chief designer at Givenchy. McQueen succeeded John Galliano, who, after a year at the smaller house, had been moved to Dior. The appointment was certainly controversial, but while McQueen's less-than-genteel roots may have proved useful as a crass marketing strategy, at least some commentators identified the fact that here was a phenomenal young talent who might have the ability to haul the then-floundering fashion house into the twenty-first century.

"He is certainly one of the strongest designers to emerge in the last four years," the fashion historian Katell Le Bourhis (who knew McQueen through Isabella Blow) said the day that his appointment was officially announced. "He is a very powerful and original force and one with enormous creative potential."[15] She, among forward-thinking observers, understood that teaming McQueen's raw and often dark design sensibility with the skills of the *petites mains* who staffed the Givenchy ateliers might make for explosive, even visionary, results.

In 1994 McQueen had met the stylist Katy England. By the time he arrived at Givenchy, she was creative director of McQueen's label. She also worked alongside him at Givenchy. "We grew up together," she later said. "I was very happy working at McQueen and thought we'd progress quite slowly and carefully. Suddenly the Givenchy thing came up and I just couldn't see how we'd be able to do it. I remember Lee and I going over to Paris on our own to do that first show and there was no one to help us, there was no organisation. We just had to do the best we could. I don't regret it at all. To do four shows a year for them as well as working on the McQueen show was a really great learning experience, design-wise, fittings-wise. And, of course, working with the ateliers was a privilege."[16]

The reviews of McQueen's spring/summer 1997 haute couture debut at Givenchy were mixed. The following morning, reflecting on the experience in unusually self-deprecating form, he said:

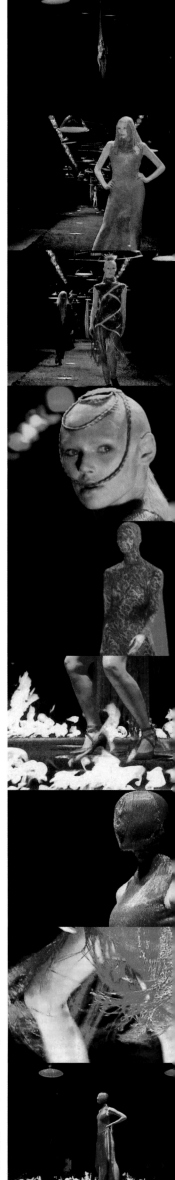

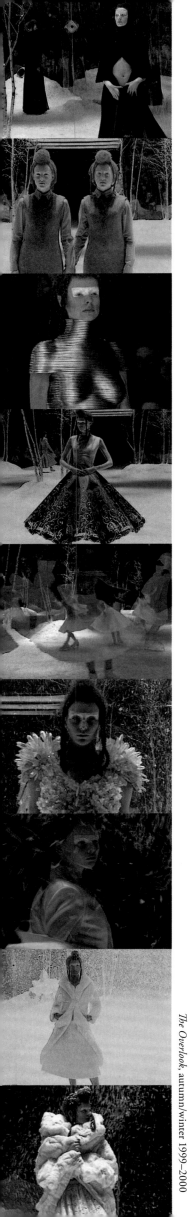

I've got four appointments today. I'm really nervous because I can only be myself, and couture's not for the average person on the street. It's about paying twenty thousand pounds and upwards for a dress. It's for the select few. I mean, you never see these people. You never get invited to their dinner parties. I just work for them. I've never worked in a couture salon before but I tried not to get too carried away with it. . . . Structure and finesse is what couture is all about. I don't want to embroider everything in sight or play around with metres and metres of tulle. That has no relevance.[17]

Over the next four and a half years McQueen designed two haute couture and two ready-to-wear collections annually for Givenchy. In the case of the former, in particular, he created pieces of exquisite beauty. However, the designer made no secret of the fact that, while he had only the greatest respect for the studio, he was less than enamored by the corporate arm of the business. His heart, everyone knew, was in his own label. With the Givenchy salary behind it, his company grew quickly, operating from new offices on Amwell Street. And his shows, increasingly, had more in common with art installations than anything more obviously consumer-driven by nature. McQueen sent his models out onto a raised Plexiglas catwalk filled with ink-stained water and showered with golden rain (*Untitled*, spring/summer 1998). *Joan* (autumn/winter 1998–99) featured a lava runway exploding into flames. *The Overlook* (autumn/winter 1999–2000) was dominated by a larger-than-life snowstorm inside which models appeared in ice skates, opulent jacquards, and furs. Working with a loyal, close-knit team the designer seemed not only fulfilled but also at his creative best.

Watching his staff backstage, often overwhelmed by the emotional force of his presentations, McQueen said that he was not quite sure what all the fuss was about. Only one show ever made him cry—*No. 13* (spring/summer 1999), during which models revolved on turntables like music-box dolls, clad in skirts made of balsa wood and dresses entirely embroidered with crystals. The finale featured former ballerina Shalom Harlow dancing while her white gown was spray-painted yellow and black by robots shipped in from an Italian car factory. Amid the spectacle it could have been easy to miss Paralympics champion Aimee Mullins, who as an infant had lost her legs from the knees down, wearing hand-carved wooden prostheses designed for her by McQueen. (On more than one occasion in the months that followed, fashion editors attempted to call them in for shoots, believing they were a particularly unusual pair of boots.) Leading up to the show McQueen had been a guest editor of the September 1998 issue of *Dazed & Confused* magazine, putting Mullins on the cover and conceiving and art directing a shoot (styled by Katy England and photographed by Nick Knight) that featured Mullins and seven other men and women with physical disabilities.

"I suppose the idea is to show that beauty comes from within," McQueen said of the motivation behind this project—and his words seem all the more resonant coming as they did from the mouth of a fashion designer.

You look at all the mainstream magazines and it's all about the beautiful people, all of the time. I wouldn't swap these people I've been working with for a supermodel. They've got so much dignity and there's not a lot of dignity in high fashion. I think they're all really beautiful. I just wanted them to be treated like everyone else. . . . I assume people will say I'm doing it for shock value. That's what they always say and it's so easy, they'll have found the easiest possible way of looking at it. I know I'm provocative. You don't have to like it but you do have to acknowledge it.[18]

In December 2000, McQueen sold a 51 percent share of his business to the Gucci Group, which is owned by PPR (originally called Pinault Printemps Redoute). Although the actual sum involved was never disclosed, it was thought to be in excess of 20 million dollars. The designer celebrated the deal not with a high-profile party or even dinner. Instead, he went to Brighton with a close friend and took his dogs for a nighttime stroll on the beach.

Anyone expecting McQueen's Paris debut under his own name to be a quietly respectful, transitional affair was sorely mistaken. While the venue was not quite the rundown warehouse space familiar to his London audience, a smoke-screen opener and pornographic sound track caused at least some attendees to threaten mutiny. *The Dance of the Twisted Bull* (spring/summer 2002) was shocking, McQueen's detractors argued, because it took place only a matter of days after the terrorist attack of September 11, 2001. Characteristically, McQueen remained unapologetic. "I know other designers changed course with their collections," he said, "but I didn't. I don't believe you should succumb to things like that. Let's face it, when people look back to September 11 in fifty years' time, they're not going to wonder what sort of fashion people were designing. There's no link between the two things as far as I can see. Fashion should never be politically correct, otherwise it wouldn't be revolutionary. I just did what I always do."[19]

And true to himself, he continued in that vein. With a comparatively solid infrastructure underpinning it, Alexander McQueen the label expanded into menswear, accessories, eyewear, and fragrance, and flagship stores opened in New York, London, Milan, Las Vegas, and Los Angeles. The company headquarters relocated to a five-story building on Clerkenwell Road, all polished aluminum and glass. But while the designer was always aware of the commercial side to his business, his attention remained focused primarily on his women's collections and, inevitably, their presentation. Both became increasingly sophisticated. McQueen had indeed learned a huge amount while working at Givenchy and understood more than ever the potential of pioneering cut and fabric development. By this time the refinement of his output almost belied the unharnessed energy that drove it.

Whereas today very few designers are responsible for executing their own patterns, McQueen could cut a garment, single handedly, in minutes, while crouching on his studio floor. His team— led by Sarah Burton, who had been working quietly in the background since 1996, before which she, too, was a student at Central Saint Martins—formed an intimate circle around him, passing fabric, scissors, chalk, and so forth. The process appeared not unlike an elaborately choreographed dance. Throughout, McQueen, for once, stayed silent. Slicing fabric with extreme dexterity and an intensity of concentration, he then pinned it onto Polina Kasina, his fit model of many years, in an equally deft manner. If a piece turned out to be more complicated, the designer moved around Kasina for hours if necessary, studying and finessing every detail with his own hands.

In 2008 he collaborated with the prima ballerina Sylvie Guillem on the costumes for *Eonnagata*, an improvisational performance created with playwright and stage director Robert Lepage and choreographer Russell Maliphant. It was inspired by the life of the Chevalier d'Éon, the French diplomat and spy who lived the first half of his life as a man and the second as a woman. Of working with McQueen, Guillem later remarked:

> In fittings Alexander was serious but at the same time we laughed, we laughed a lot.
> There was one moment, though, that was particularly extraordinary. Alexander was doing
> a costume for Russell, and it was supposed to suggest someone quite dark, quite negative—
> a bad character. Russell was wearing it, and Alexander said: "It's not sinister enough."
> He said: "Give me some fabric, give me scissors," and right in front of our eyes, he cut
> another costume. It took about three minutes. It was just so fast—and so completely
> right. Afterwards he turned to me and said: "So, what do you think?" I didn't know
> what to say. "It's great. Genius."[20]

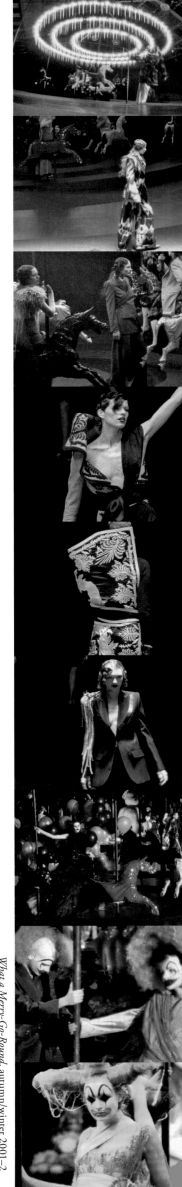

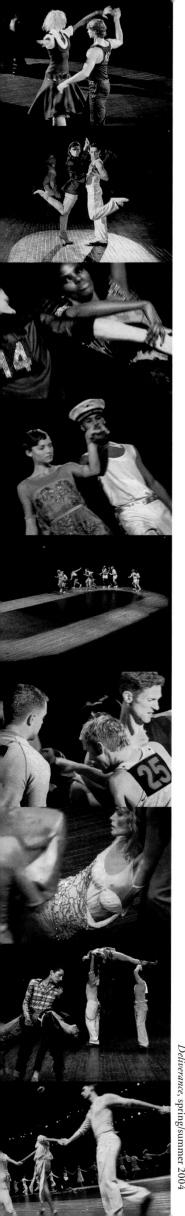

Ultimately, the greatest insight into McQueen was always to be found in his shows. The primary purpose of a runway presentation is to launch a particular collection. It also functions as an extremely effective marketing tool to broadcast the values of a house more broadly. McQueen was aware of this, of course. More importantly, though, it was here that he strove to realize the most pure and vivid expression of his ideas.

"They [the shows] meant so much more to him than what they represented on paper," says Janet Fischgrund, who met McQueen in 1993 and helped him unofficially until she became his PR director in 1997. "Really, he was way over somewhere no one else was. Of course, he had to take the basics into account, but the platform the shows gave him as an artist was enormous. Almost everything else became irrelevant to the message at any given time. Even if he knew that what he wanted made no financial sense, he would do it. For Lee, it was all about the shows. I'm not sure people realize quite how passionate he was about that. The ideas were what were important to him, the clothes were his canvas in a way."[21]

"He could never design a collection without knowing what the show was," confirms Sam Gainsbury, who produced all of McQueen's presentations from *The Hunger* (spring/summer 1996) onward. In the first instance, she remembers, McQueen provided her with a mere six hundred pounds from start to finish, although over time her budgets rose to hundreds of thousands. Well financed or not, it was an intensely difficult, if hugely rewarding, process. "Sometimes we'd be on idea fifteen, and we'd always go away and research it. Even if we knew it wasn't quite right, we'd never say so. You were biding your time, in a way. And then he'd hit on the one, the right one, and he'd nailed it, and we'd all be so happy. After that it was plain sailing. Two days before the show, he'd be over it and onto the next one. A week later he'd say to me: 'You're going to love this,' and we'd start up again."[22] McQueen himself said:

> I need inspiration. I need something to fuel my imagination and the shows are what spur me on, make me excited about what I'm doing. When you start getting into the mindset where this is a business and you've got to bring in money, when you're designing with a buyer in mind, the collection doesn't work. The danger is that you lose the creativity that drives you. . . . I want people to see that this is what fashion is about. This is what we're here for. This is why we're unique. And we are unique. There isn't anyone else doing anything like I do. It's taken me fifteen years to come up with that concept as a designer, to become fully aware that what I'm doing is personal to me. I don't think I always do it for the people in the audience. I do it for the people who see the pictures in the press afterwards, in newspapers and in magazines. I design the shows as stills and I think that if you look at those stills they tell the whole story.[23]

And what stories they were. For example, when McQueen collaborated with the dancer and choreographer Michael Clark on *Deliverance* (spring/summer 2004)—which was based on the 1969 Sydney Pollack movie *They Shoot Horses, Don't They?*—he spoke of broken hopes and dreams, of man's futile quest for capital gains at the expense of dignity, and of the flawed and ultimately alienating belief that fame, money, or class leads to a better life.

"The film the show was based on was about putting all the social classes together under one roof," he said. "We're all born the same and die the same. These people were all fighting for one thing: to survive." McQueen expressed this view most poetically through two sequined dresses:

> The one at the beginning was really bright metallic silver. The dancer at the end of the show wore exactly the same dress but the sequins were tarnished. More people can

understand the dress if it's tarnished and distressed. If you walked out in the first dress you'd be setting yourself apart from everyone but if you wore the second one people would be able to accept you. I find that untouchable Hollywood glamour alienating. It has no relevance to the way I live my life. Remember where you came from. The second dress is beautiful in a different and more authentic way.[24]

Widows of Culloden (autumn/winter 2006–7) revisited the themes of *Highland Rape*. "I needed to do something that was close to my heart," McQueen remarked. "I wanted to start from the crux and the crux is my heritage. I know a lot about Scotland—my mother is a genealogist—and I know my family tree, my dynasty." The show was also a testament to the value of his clothing as empowering and life enhancing, as the most breathtaking armor. As McQueen explained, "Fundamentally, the collection is luxurious, romantic but melancholic and austere at the same time. It was gentle but you could still feel the bite of the cold, the nip of the ice on the end of your nose. It's clear, crisp, completely understandable. With bustles and nipped in waists, I was also interested in the idea that there are no constraints on the silhouette. I wanted to exaggerate a woman's form, almost along the lines of a classical statue." For him, these clothes epitomized the beauty of couture, as well as its exceptionality.

> I think that couture has complete relevance today. Designer fashion shouldn't be throwaway. I remember when I first started out, I used to walk past what was then Valentino in Bond Street, and just look in amazement at the way the clothes were finished. I was working in Savile Row at the time, it was about 1985, and it was miraculous, so inspiring. I think that during the nineties, care and attention to detail got lost somehow. This collection is about going back to that level of refinement. Every piece is unique and has emotional content. I want to create pieces that can be handed down, like an heirloom. I want people to get joy out of clothes again.[25]

Over the years, McQueen became less open to the outside world, both personally and professionally. In many ways, this was a result of circumstance. He wanted people to respect and believe in him because of who he was, not what he had become. Whereas other designers dutifully remain backstage after a show, meeting and greeting editors with the requisite pleasantries and explanations of their work, McQueen had a car waiting and disappeared within seconds. When he did agree to attend an awards ceremony, an opening, or a party, it was not uncommon for him to cancel at the last minute and stay home instead. There, he spent time with a handful of people he had known since the early days. They ate dinner from a suitably salacious Allen Jones table, surrounded by a burgeoning fine-art collection that also included works by the Chapman Brothers, Sam Taylor-Wood, Joel Peter Witkin, and Francis Bacon.

Although, in terms of material wealth, the designer's life had changed immeasurably, neither status nor protocol was of interest to him. Instead, he was concerned with communicating on a more direct level. "He wasn't at ease in very many social situations," Fischgrund says. "But the way he connected to people was very important to him. You could have been the best fashion photographer in the world, but unless he connected with you he wasn't interested. Lee had no inhibitions about what was appropriate or inappropriate. If you're middle class you're brought up to be careful about what you say, but that didn't matter to him at all. He'd say the most outrageous things, and because of who he was, and how powerful he'd become, people had to listen to him."[26]

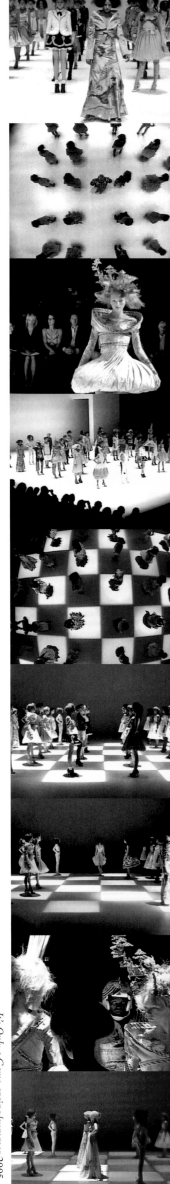

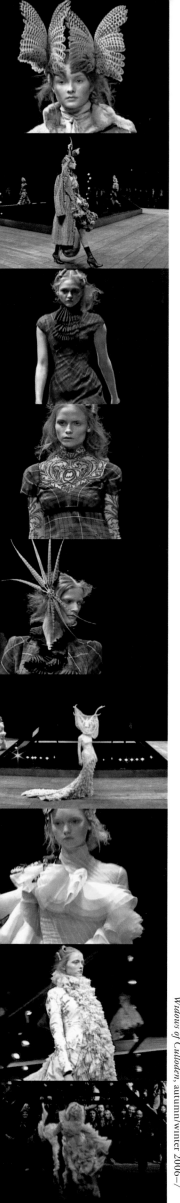

For all his bravado, there were times when the designer's fragility appeared obvious. Certainly, both friends and family were aware that the acutely sensitive side of his nature made life difficult for McQueen. England commented,

> Lee is quite a closed shop. He's a private person and there are only very few people he's prepared to listen to and trust. Yes, he does isolate himself, he does cut himself off. It's a huge pressure when you're constantly having to meet new people, go for dinners, be interviewed, have your photograph taken. You're putting yourself on the line, you're having to expose your personal details and I don't think he wants to do that any more. Of course, there is a dark side. But there is also a truly romantic side. Lee's such a romantic character and he has these dreams. It's all about him looking for love, isn't it? It's him looking for love and his idea of love and romance, well, it's way above and beyond reality. I don't know how you ever find that.[27]

Verkade confirms that McQueen was increasingly withdrawn. "I think Lee definitely became more introverted and, in the end, he could only handle being around very few people. On a creative level, though, nothing ever really changed. Right from the start, he always needed to see how far he could push things, how far he could push himself and everyone who worked with him. He always used to look at us and say: 'What bit don't you understand?' He said it all the time. It made us feel so stupid, but somehow you always felt proud being stupid next to him."[28]

For his part, the designer often looked back nostalgically to a time when he had less responsibility. His success was a double-edged sword, freeing him in many ways but tying him down in others. On the one hand, any investment allowed his wildest imaginings to be realized; on the other, it exerted pressure for his business to succeed. When asked whether he had envisaged his career turning out the way it had, he said: "Not really. When I think back, I was quite happy just doing the performance, happy working as a performance artist. I always looked forward to doing the show with no ties. At the beginning, I never even used to sell the collection. I did that on purpose. It was all about making a statement and the communication of that statement was—and still is—very important to me."[29]

On May 7, 2007, following a long struggle with physical and mental illness, Isabella Blow committed suicide. McQueen, alone among her cohorts, refused to comment on her passing in the press, but the impact it had on him was clearly significant. He dealt with it the only way he knew how, by dedicating a show, *La Dame Bleue* (spring/summer 2008), to her. This he was prepared to talk about, remembering Blow tenderly.

> Isabella flew. The collection is exuberant and excessive. It's about her way of thinking and that way of thinking brought light into fashion. Even when she was down she was up with what she wore. I had the best times with Isabella. I remember going to Mauritius with her and I'd come back from scuba diving and it would be 100 degrees and she'd be standing on the beach head-to-toe in McQueen with a Philip Treacy hat on. Or we'd be sitting round the pool and she'd still be head-to-toe in McQueen with a Philip Treacy hat on. I've thought a lot about why she would wear things like that and she wore them because they made her feel like a diva. She was a diva in what she wore. She pulled it off. I never blinked at what she wore. It just seemed normal. So this was a collection about Isabella and about wearing clothes that transform you.[30]

McQueen lived only long enough to complete four more collections. They were among the most brilliant, if not the most brilliant, of his career, representing the convergence of his considerable experience and remarkable thought processes.

The Girl Who Lived in the Tree (autumn/winter 2008–9) boasted as its centerpiece a tree clad in silk tulle, which, McQueen said, was based on a majestic elm in the garden of his country house near Fairlight Cove in East Sussex, a much-loved refuge. Few could have missed the autobiographical content of this story, in which a princess descended from tangled branches to pick up discarded clothing and recycle it into principally black, patchwork gothic confections. When the princess met her prince, her wardrobe exploded into color and more opulent materials: crimson velvet, ermine, silver, and old gold. Her jewels were inspired by those of the Raj. *NATURAL DIS-TINCTION UN-NATURAL SELECTION* (spring/summer 2009) was a commentary on humankind's lack of consideration for the environment. The collection began an exploration of engineered prints derived from the natural world that would continue to fascinate the designer.

The Horn of Plenty (autumn/winter 2009–10), a scathing satire of the fashion industry, was described by the designer as "a sackable offense."[31] Its unflinching critique of the seemingly impossible and unpalatable ideals promoted by the world in which he worked was as difficult to watch as it was bleakly beautiful.

McQueen's final collection, *Plato's Atlantis* (spring/summer 2010), was, he said, "Darwin's theory of evolution in reverse." Here was an underwater dystopia populated by hybridized humans: "We came from water and now, with the help of stem cell technology, we must go back to survive."[32] If the concept was among his most ambitious, its execution was even more so. Futuristic robots tracked not only the progression of models, dressed in increasingly otherworldly and challenging designs, but also the reactions of the captivated audience. "I've always loved nature," McQueen said, "and it's just a bit of fun really,"[33] typically undercutting the need to search for more profound meaning in this, the last grand statement he was to make.

On February 2, 2010, Joyce McQueen died. Alexander McQueen took his own life just over a week later, on February 11. He was forty years old.

The coupling of McQueen's respect for history—and especially the history of fine art and craftsmanship—with his passionate desire to push fashion into the future may well have reached its zenith in the collection he was working on at the time of his death. Completed by Sarah Burton and the designer's team, it was nothing if not a testament to their extraordinary devotion to their mentor.

McQueen's autumn/winter 2010–11 collection sprang directly from the work of some of his favorite old masters—Hieronymus Bosch, Hugo van der Goes, and Jean Fouquet among them—as well as the woodcarvings of Grinling Gibbons and the grand, golden flourishes of Byzantium. Out of respect for the late designer, it was presented not on the runway but in an elegant eighteenth-century Parisian *hôtel particulier* owned by François Pinault, in showings limited to groups of no more than ten people at one time.

In a formidable demonstration of technical expertise, entire paintings (as well as details of them) were captured digitally, and woven into jacquards or embroidered and engineered to fit individual garments. Fabrics included *fil coupé* satin organza, a material first introduced by McQueen in *Plato's Atlantis*. Here, too, were delicate embroideries, rendered by hand in fragile, metal thread and gemstones, derived from altar glories. A final outfit, covered entirely with gilded feathers, recalled McQueen's fascination with winged creatures, which stretched back to his youth.

In our dreams, flight represents release and freedom. It also evokes angels, at once mischievous, manipulative and dangerous; noble, just, and true. To all who knew him, Alexander McQueen was a more down-to-earth creature than that. But his imagination—dark and light, deeply troubled and profoundly optimistic—soared to brave and beautiful heights.

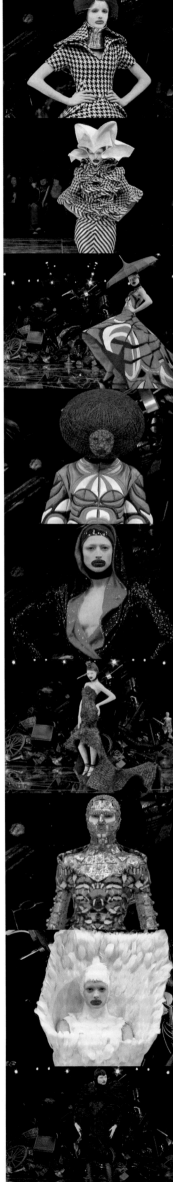

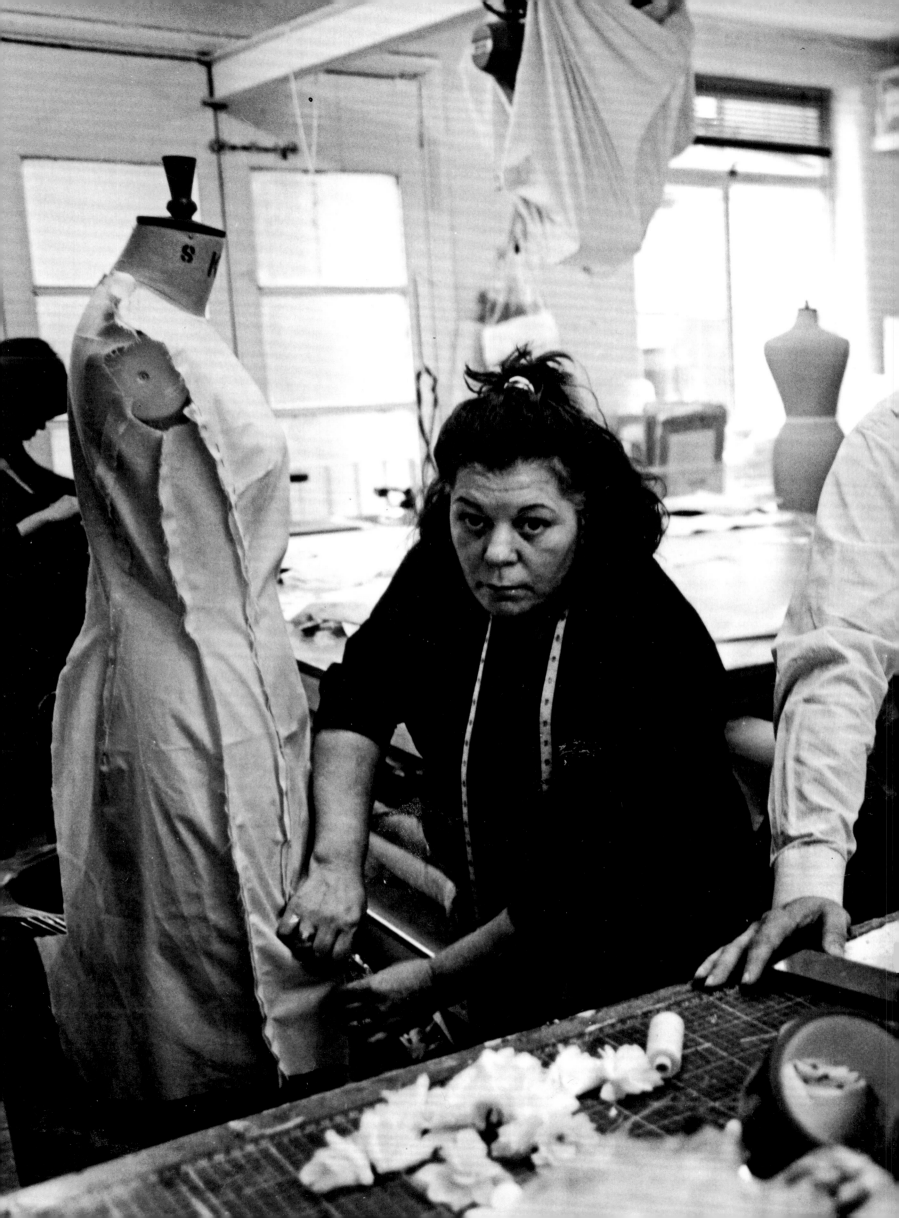

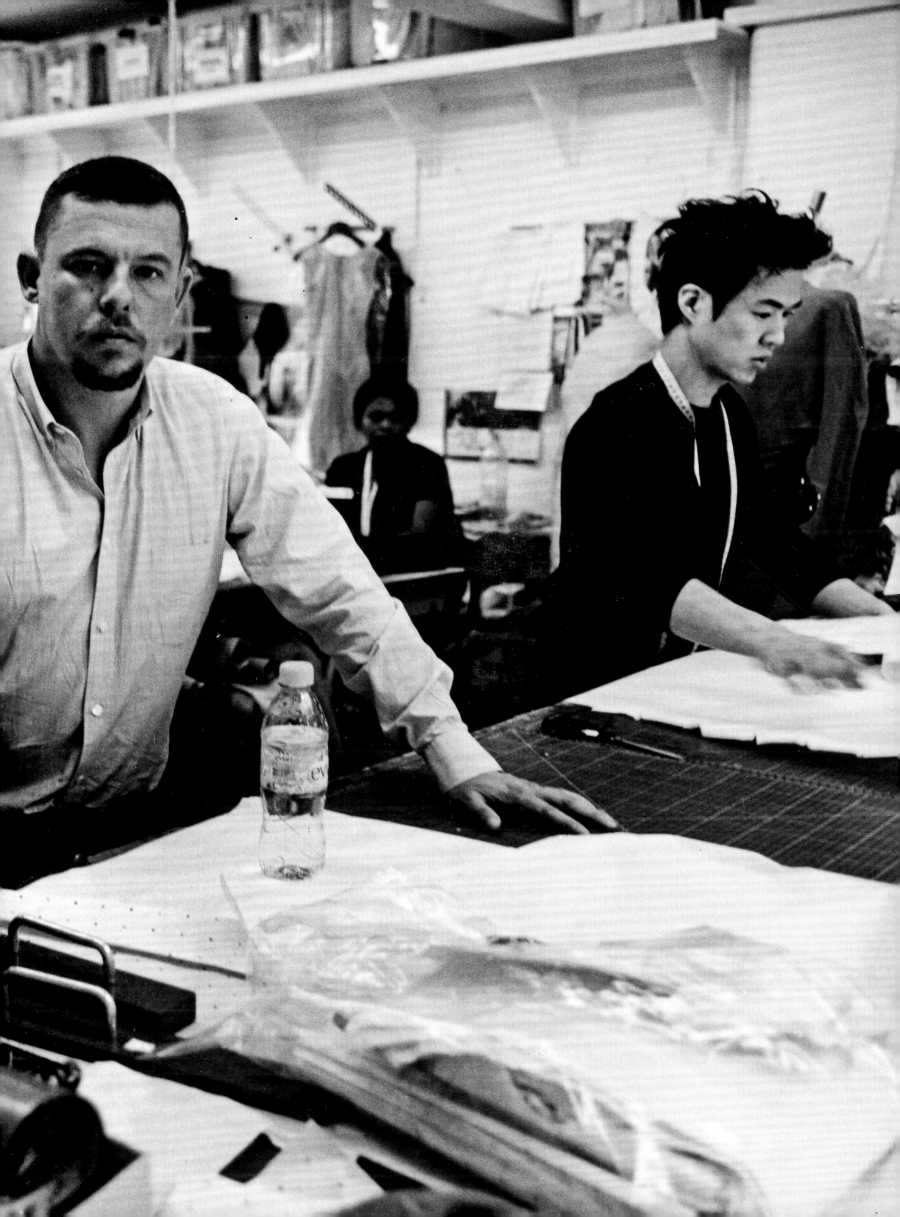

"You've got to know the rules to break them.
That's what I'm here for, to demolish the rules
but to keep the tradition."

"I spent a long time learning how to construct
clothes, which is important to do before you
can deconstruct them."

"I want to be the purveyor of a certain silhouette
or a way of cutting, so that when I'm dead and
gone people will know that the twenty-first
century was started by Alexander McQueen."

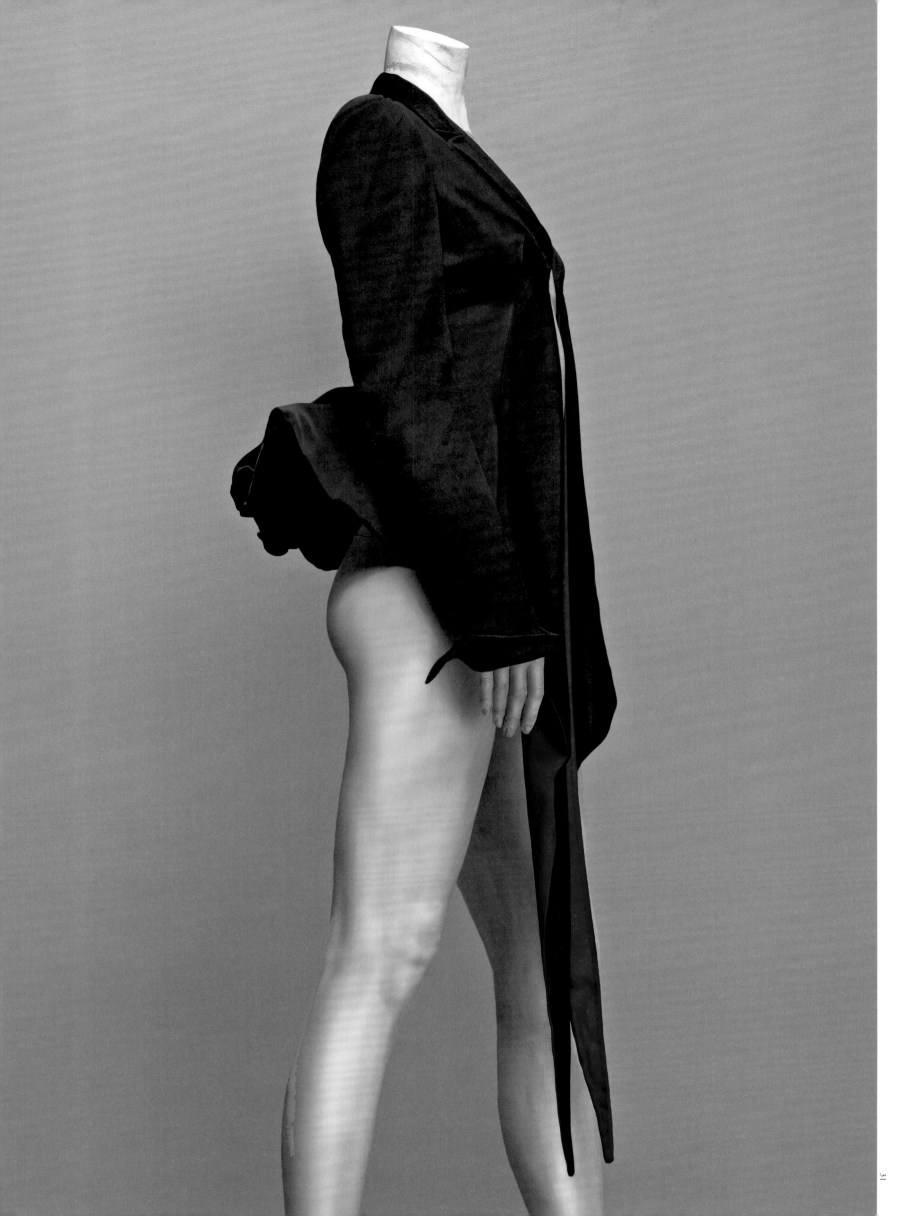

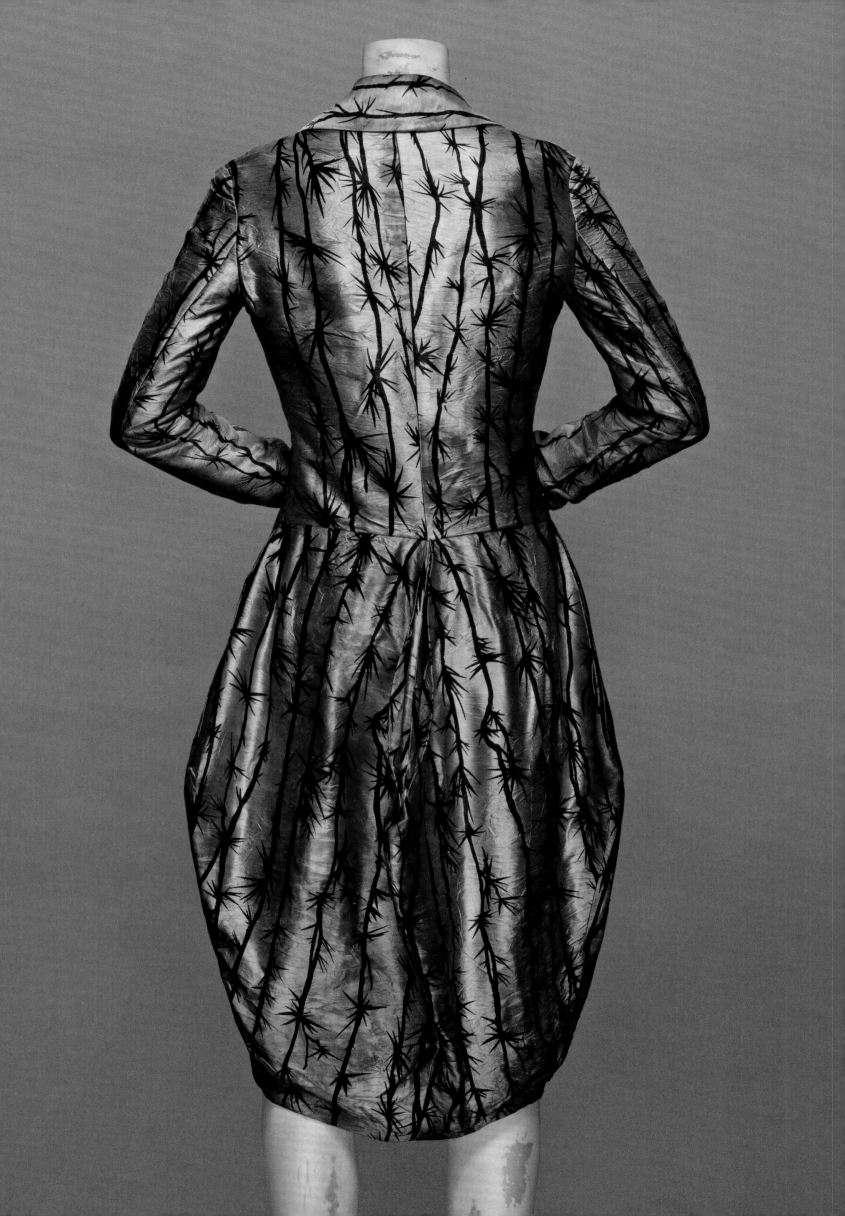

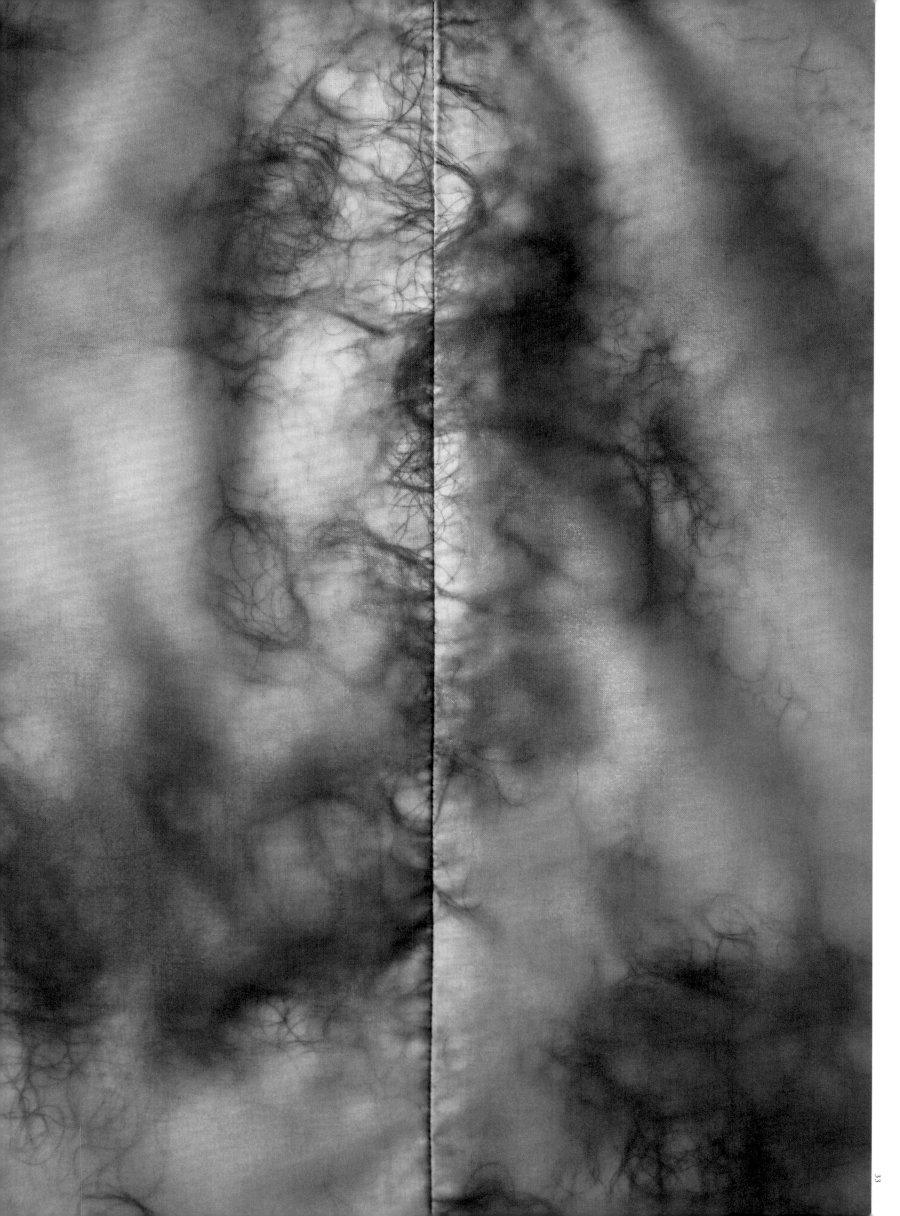

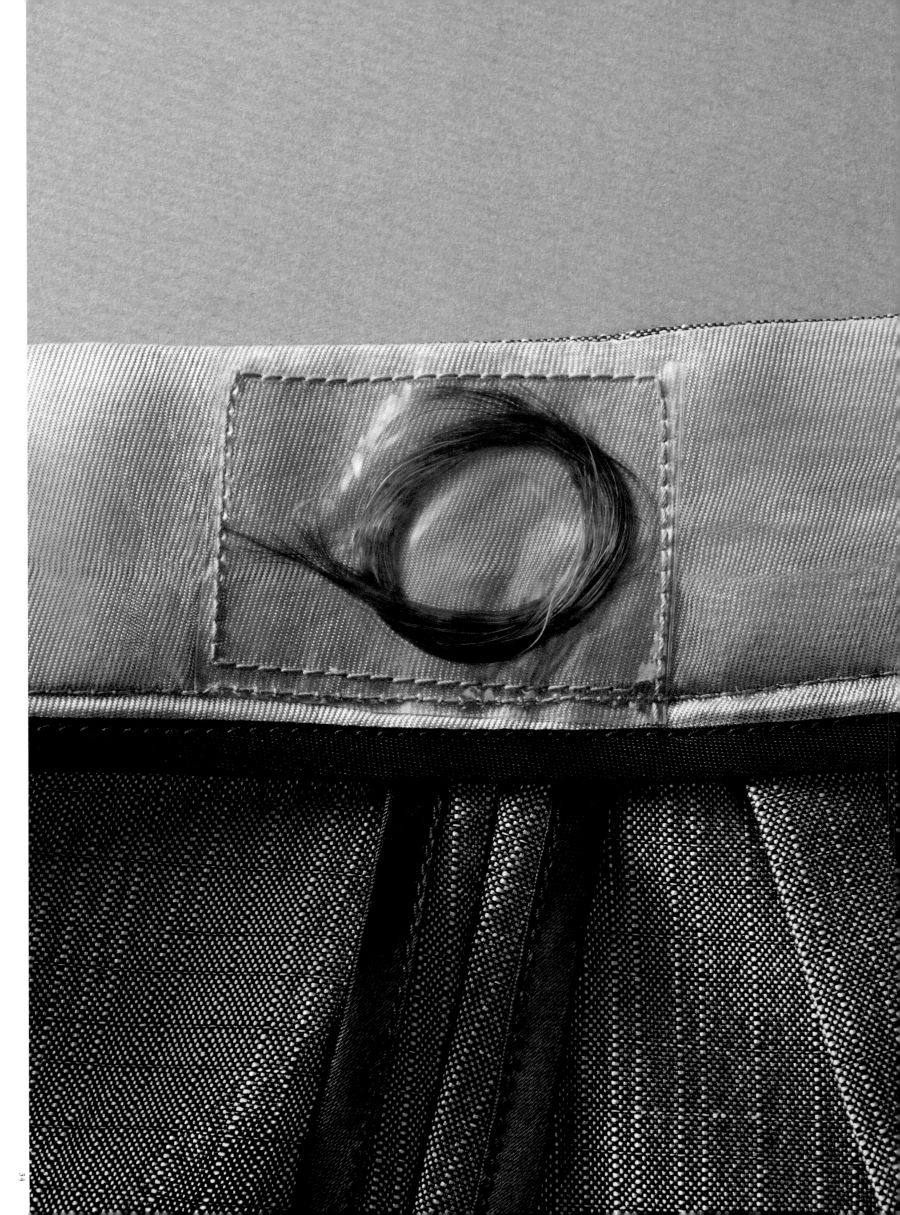

"The inspiration behind the hair came from Victorian times when prostitutes would sell theirs for kits of hair locks, which were bought by people to give to their lovers. I used it as my signature label with locks of hair in Perspex. In the early collections, it was my own hair."

"[I design from the side,] that way I get the worst angle of the body. You've got all the lumps and bumps, the S-bend of the back, the bum. That way I get a cut and proportion and silhouette that works all the way round the body."

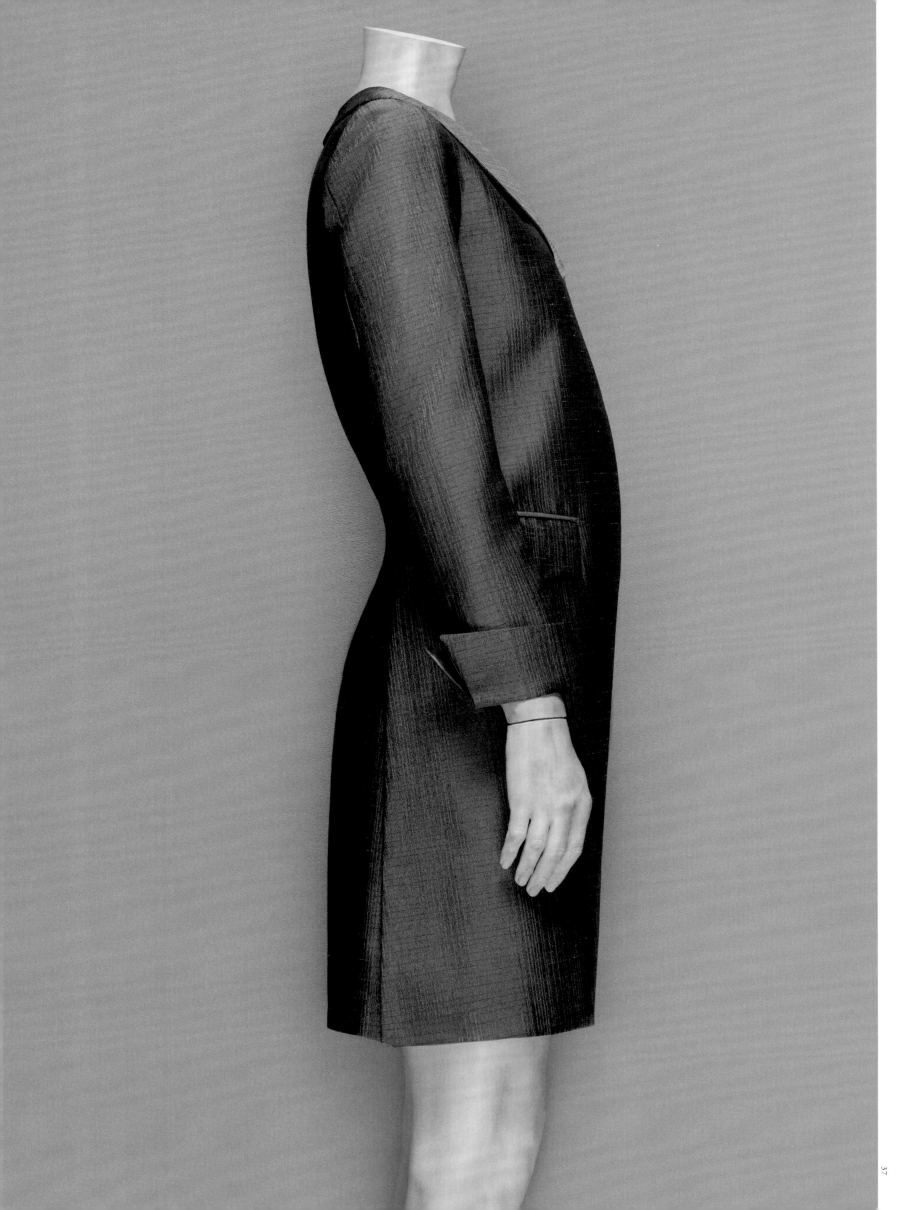

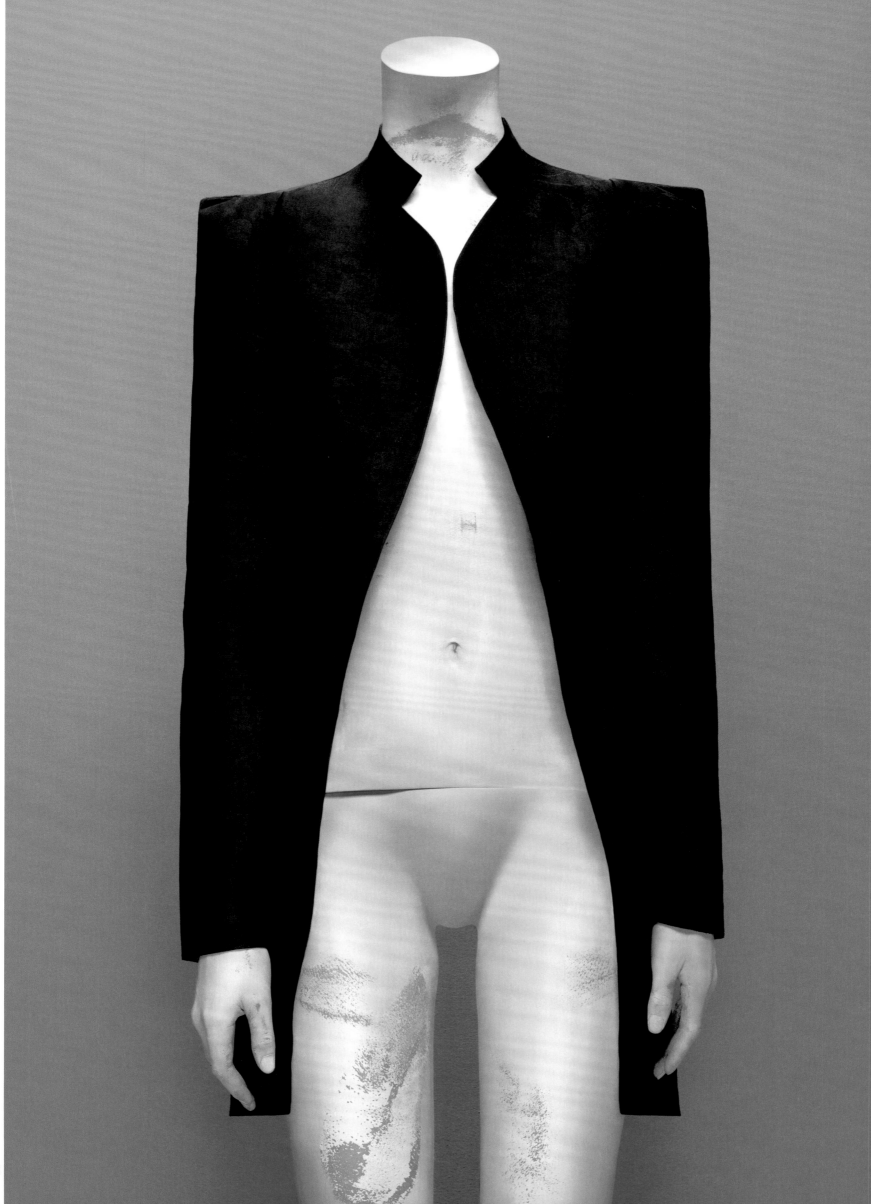

"My designing is done mainly during fittings.
  I change the cut."

"[Through cutting, I try] to draw attention to
  our unrelenting desire for perfection. The body
  parts that I focus on change depending on the
  inspirations and references for the collection
  and what silhouettes they demand."

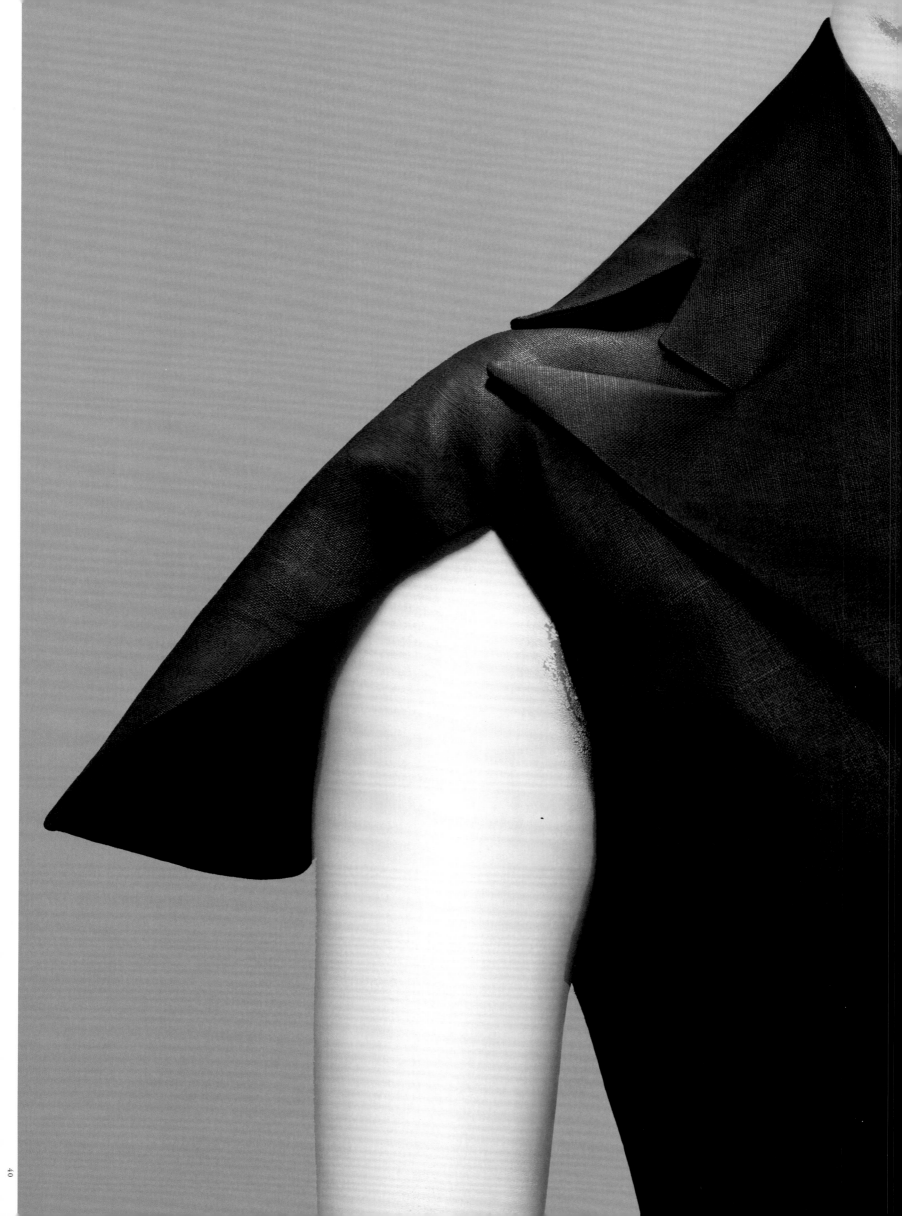

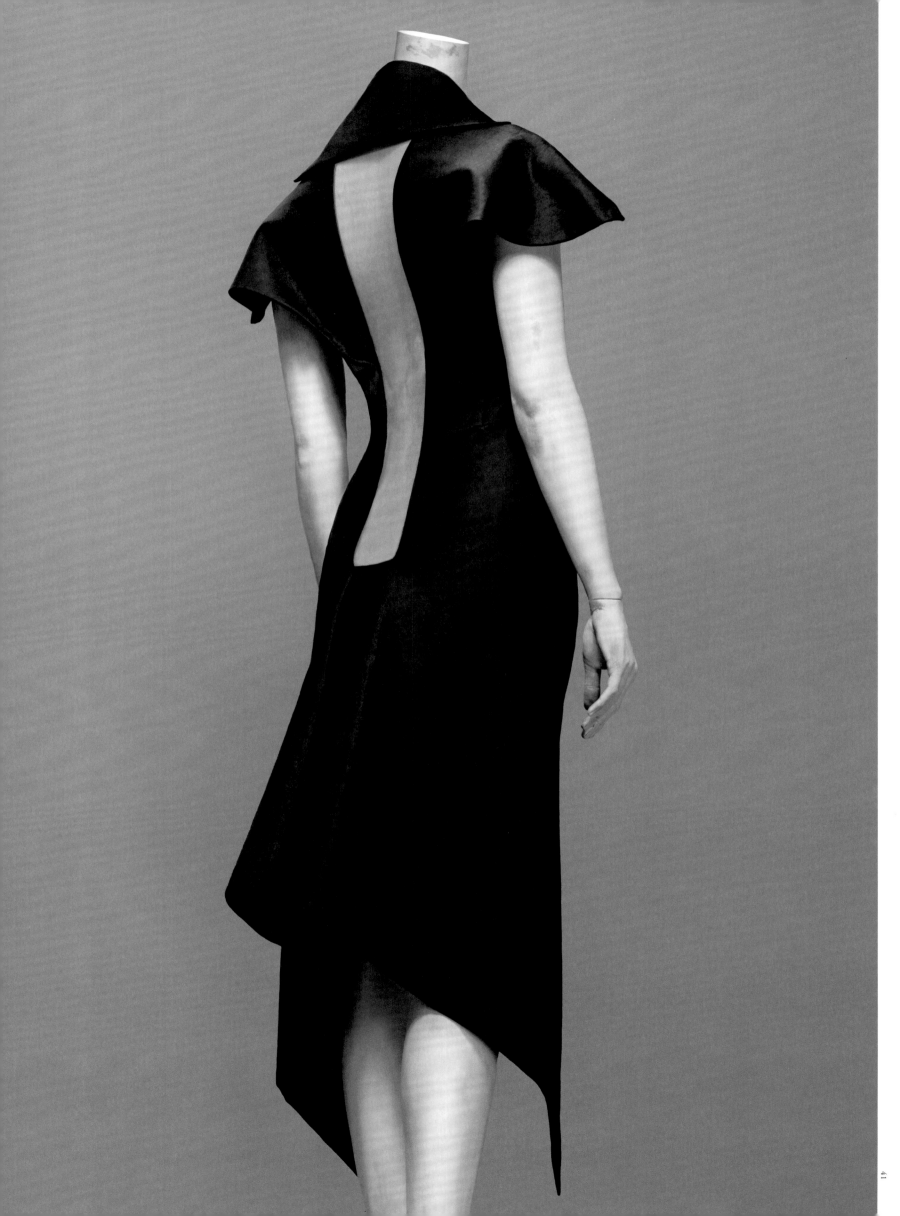

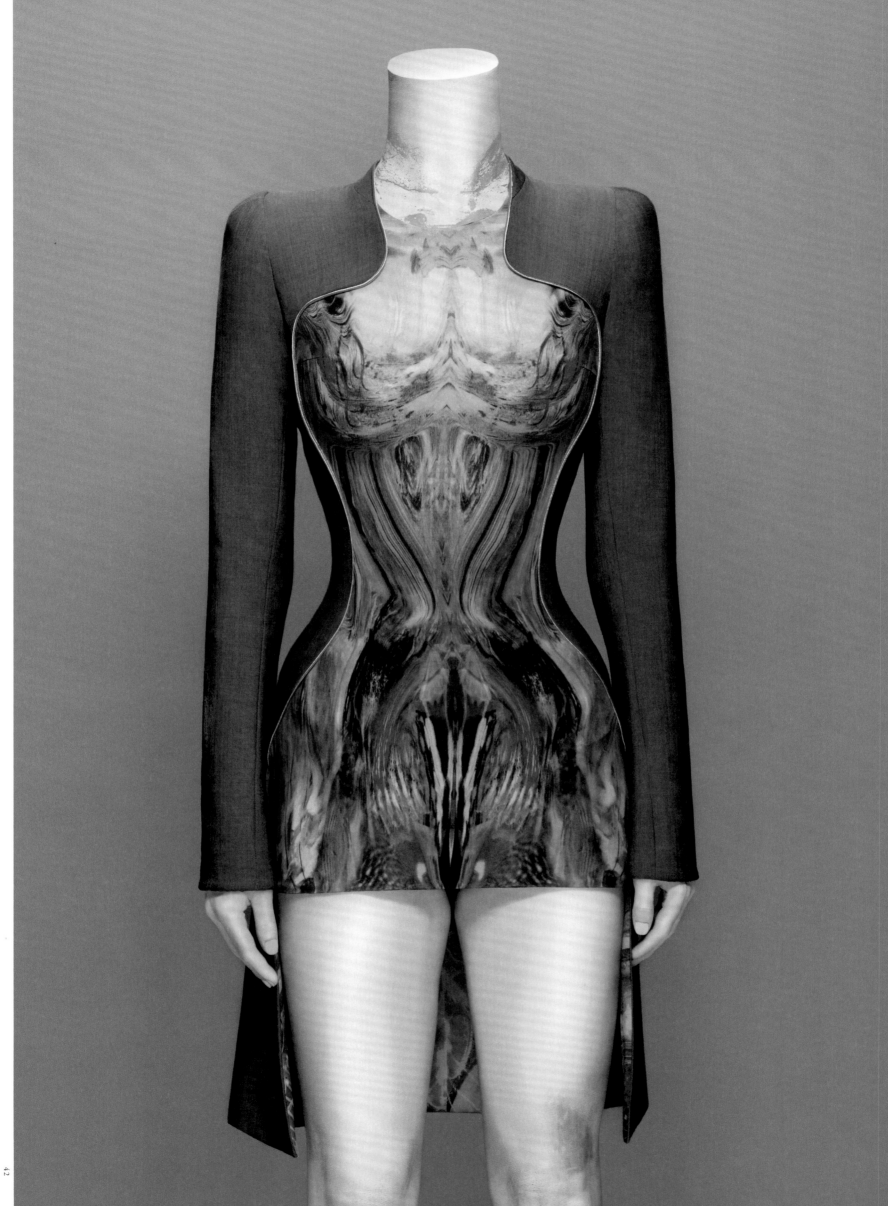

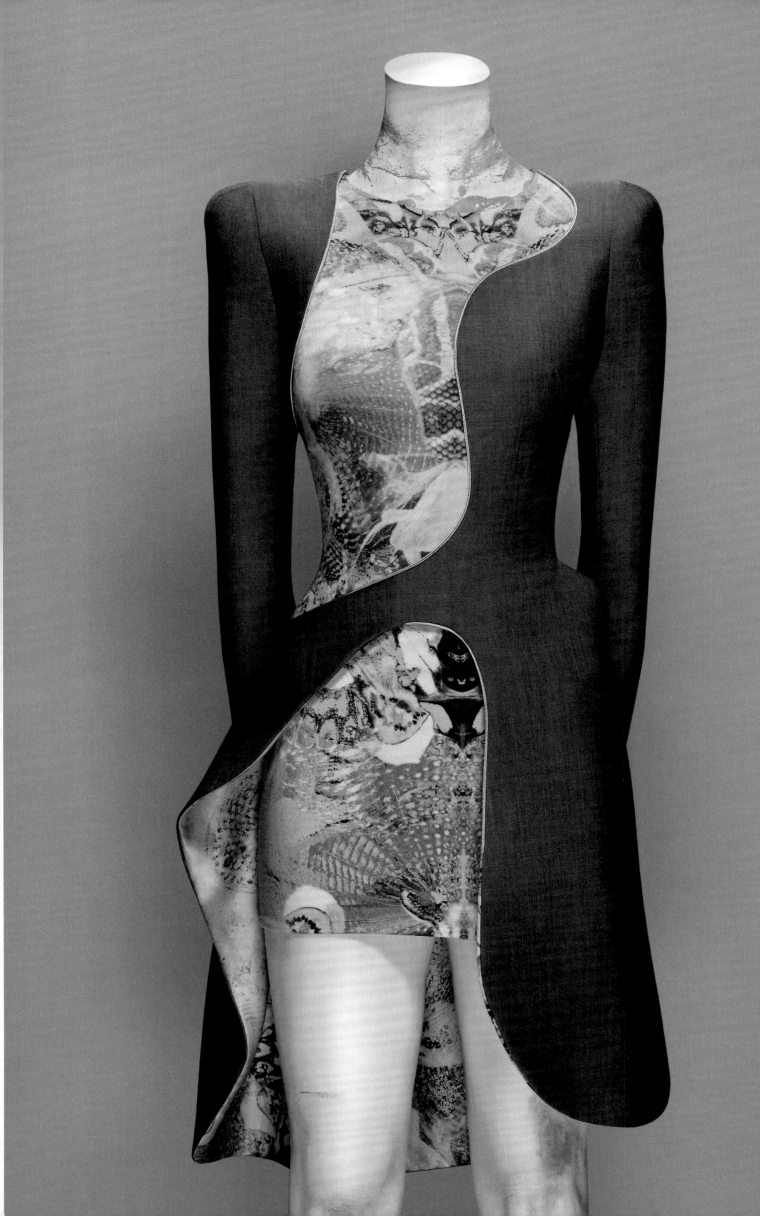

"I like to think of myself as a plastic surgeon with a knife."

"With me, metamorphosis is a bit like plastic surgery, but less drastic. I try to have the same effect with my clothes. But ultimately I do this to transform mentalities more than the body. I try and modify fashion like a scientist by offering what is relevant to today and what will continue to be so tomorrow."

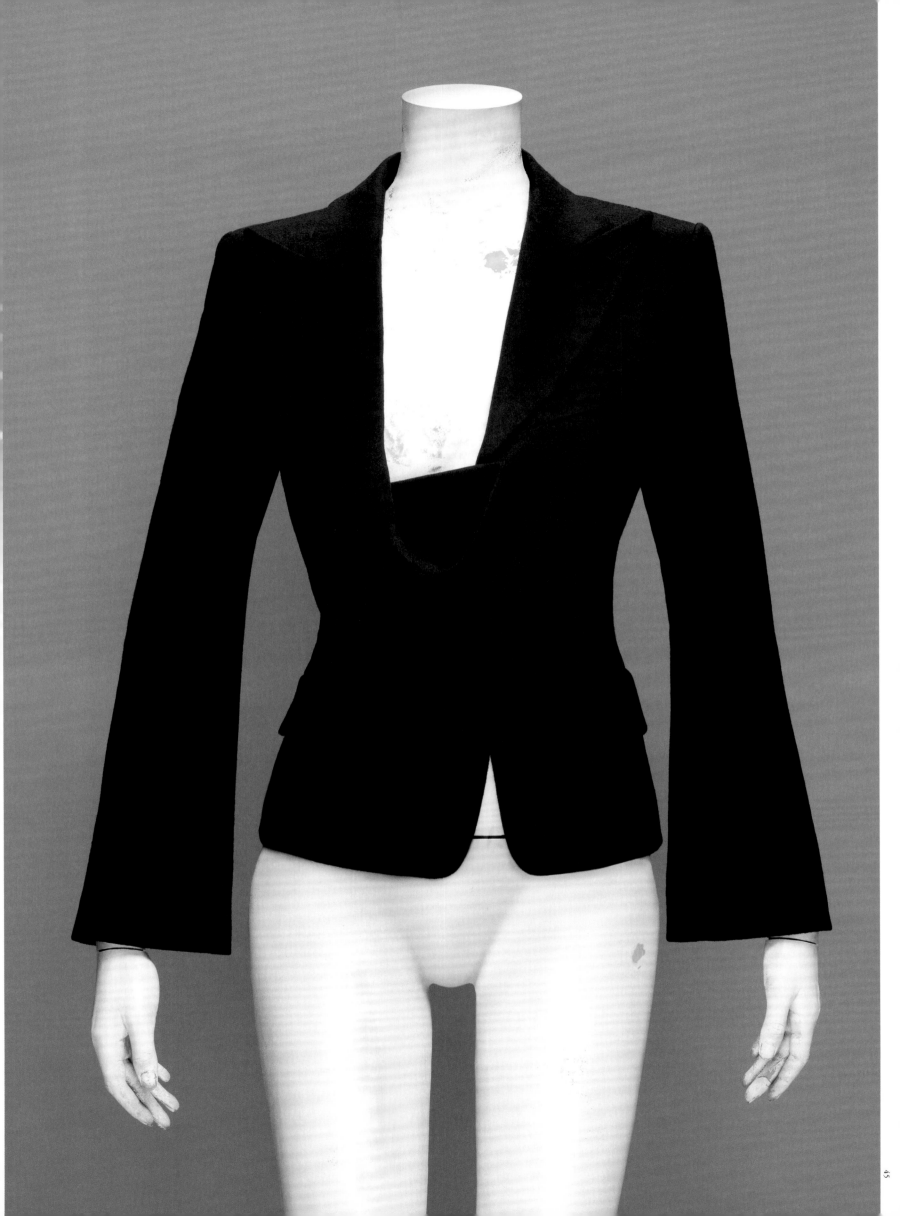

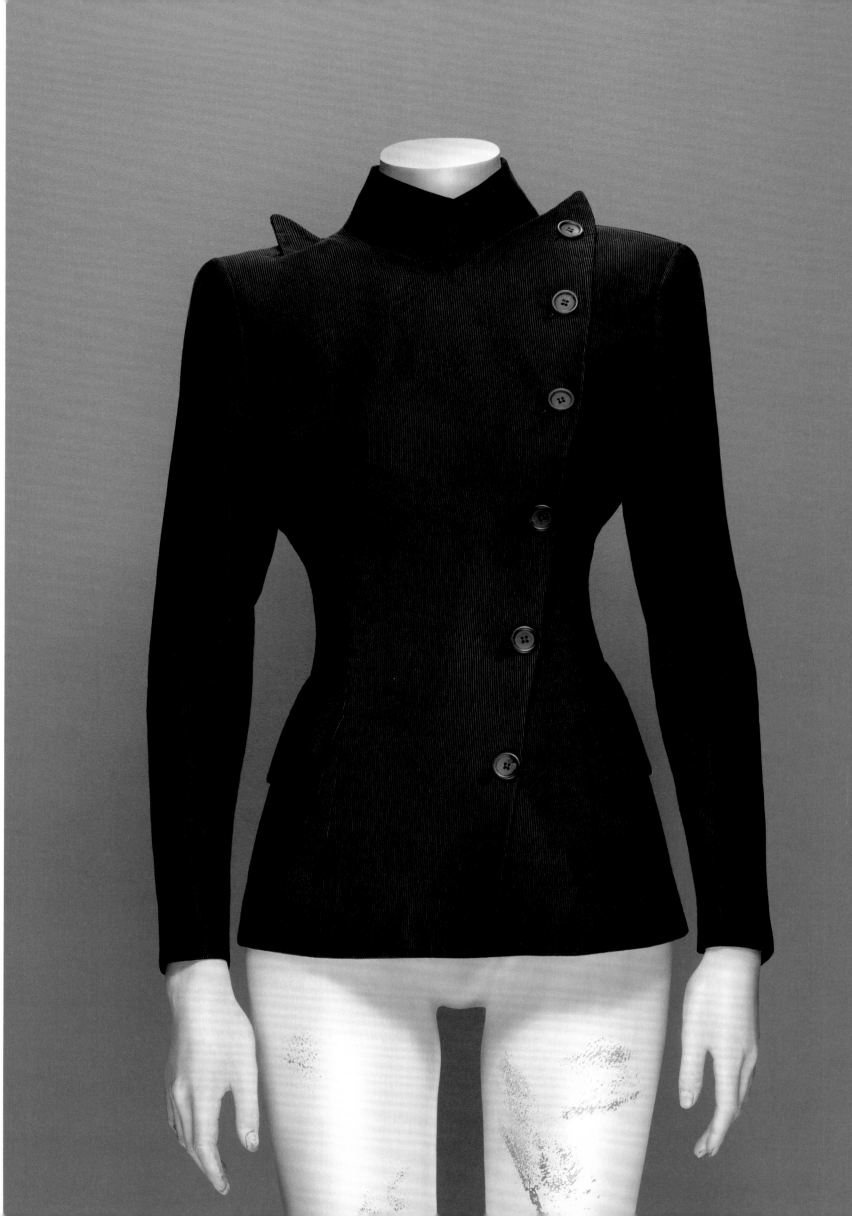

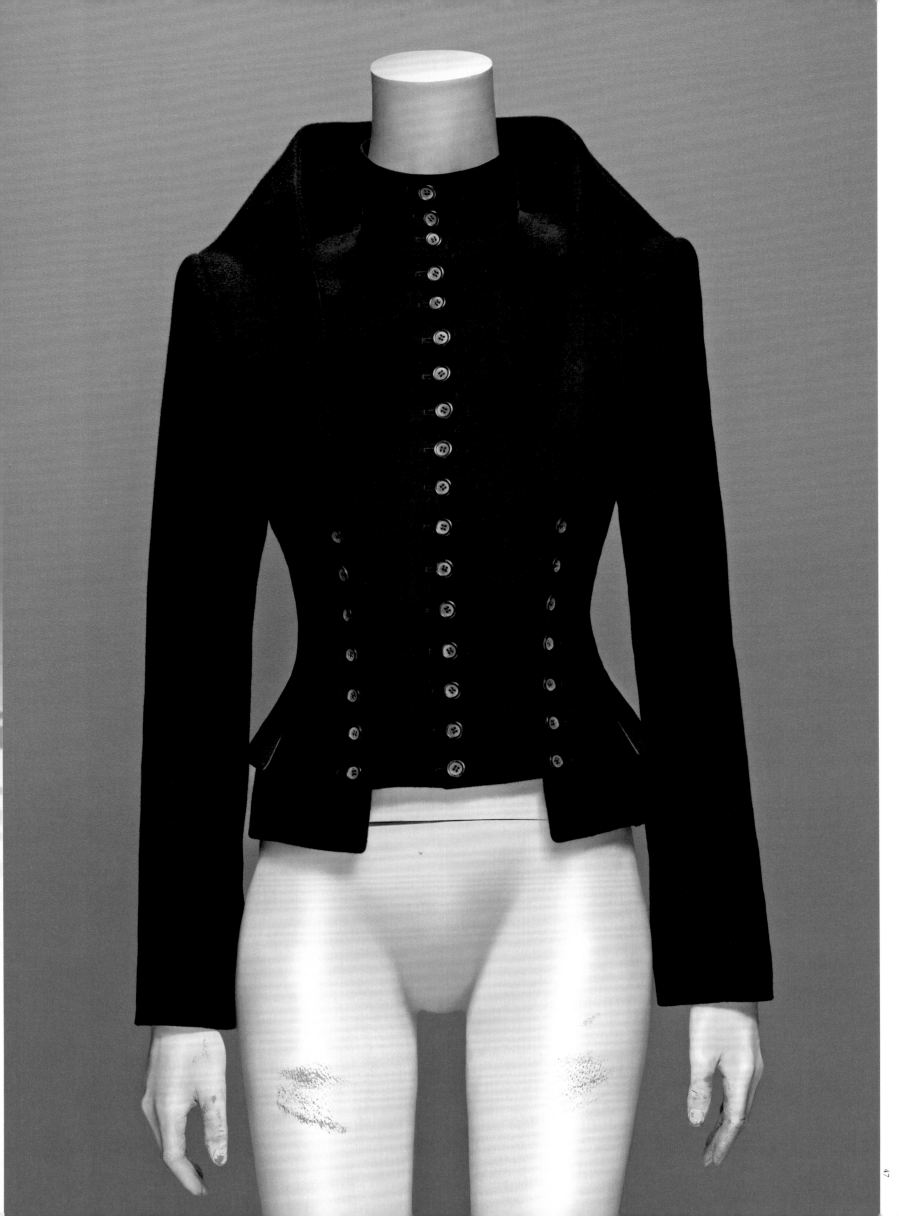

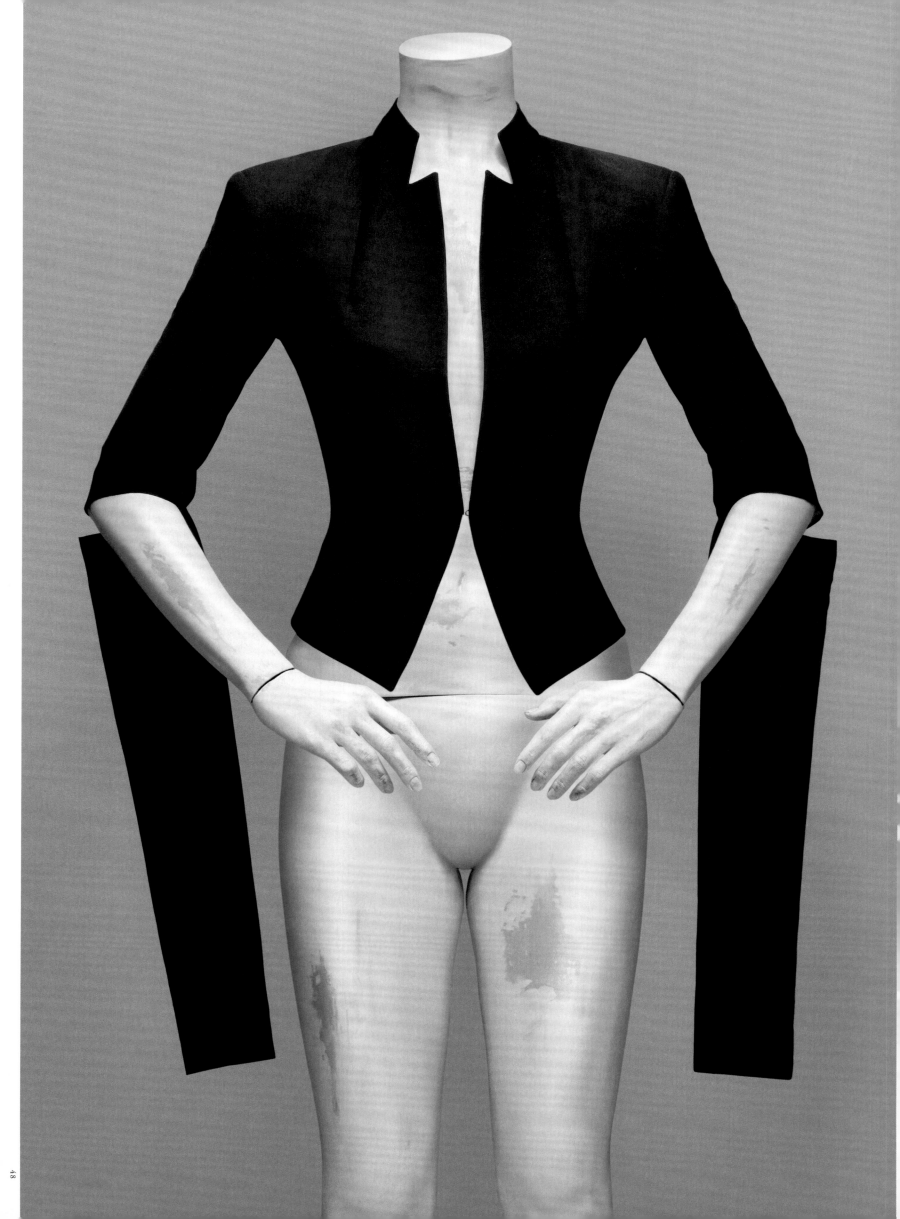

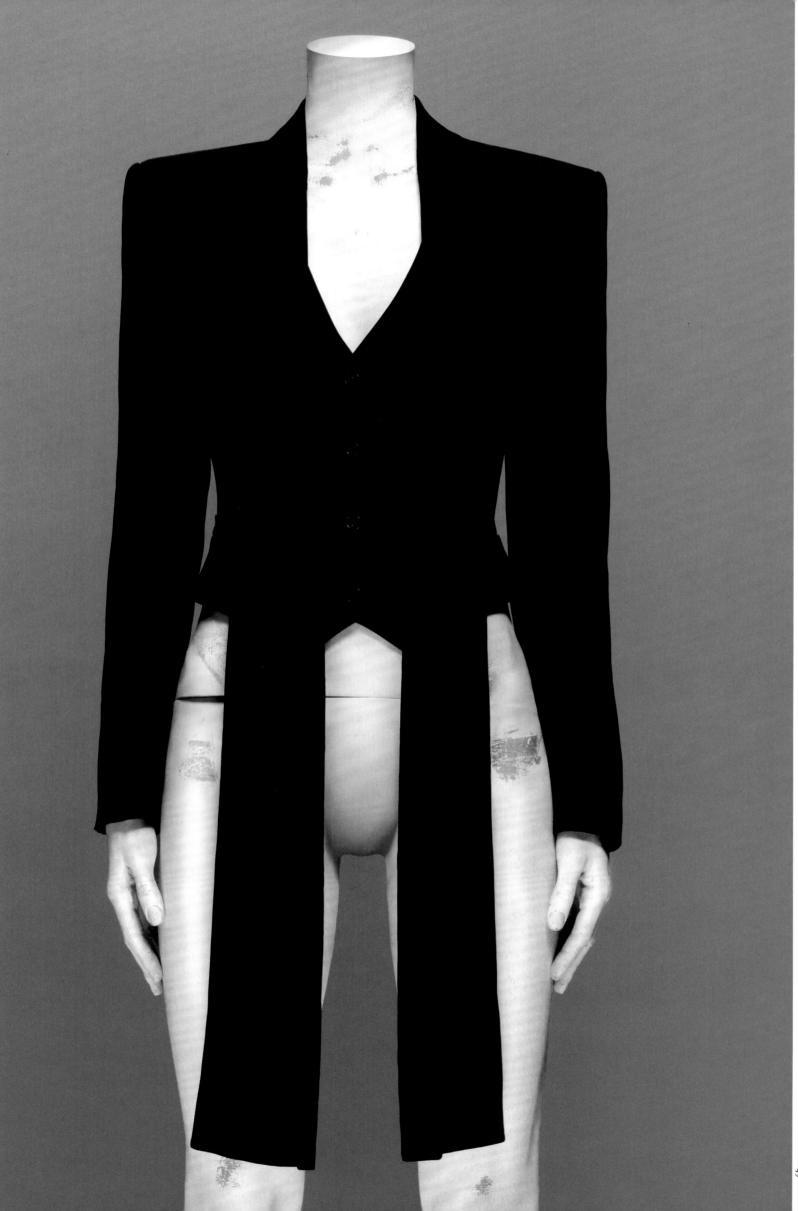

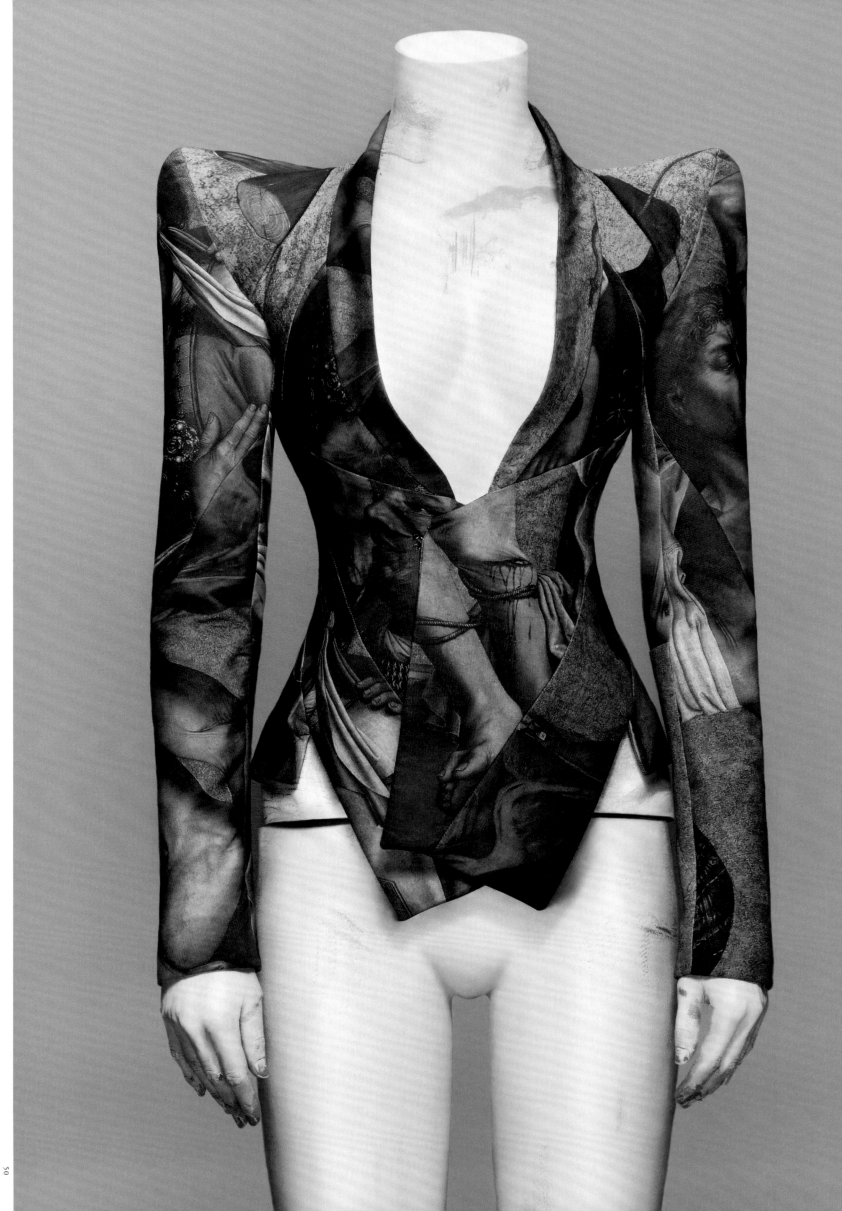

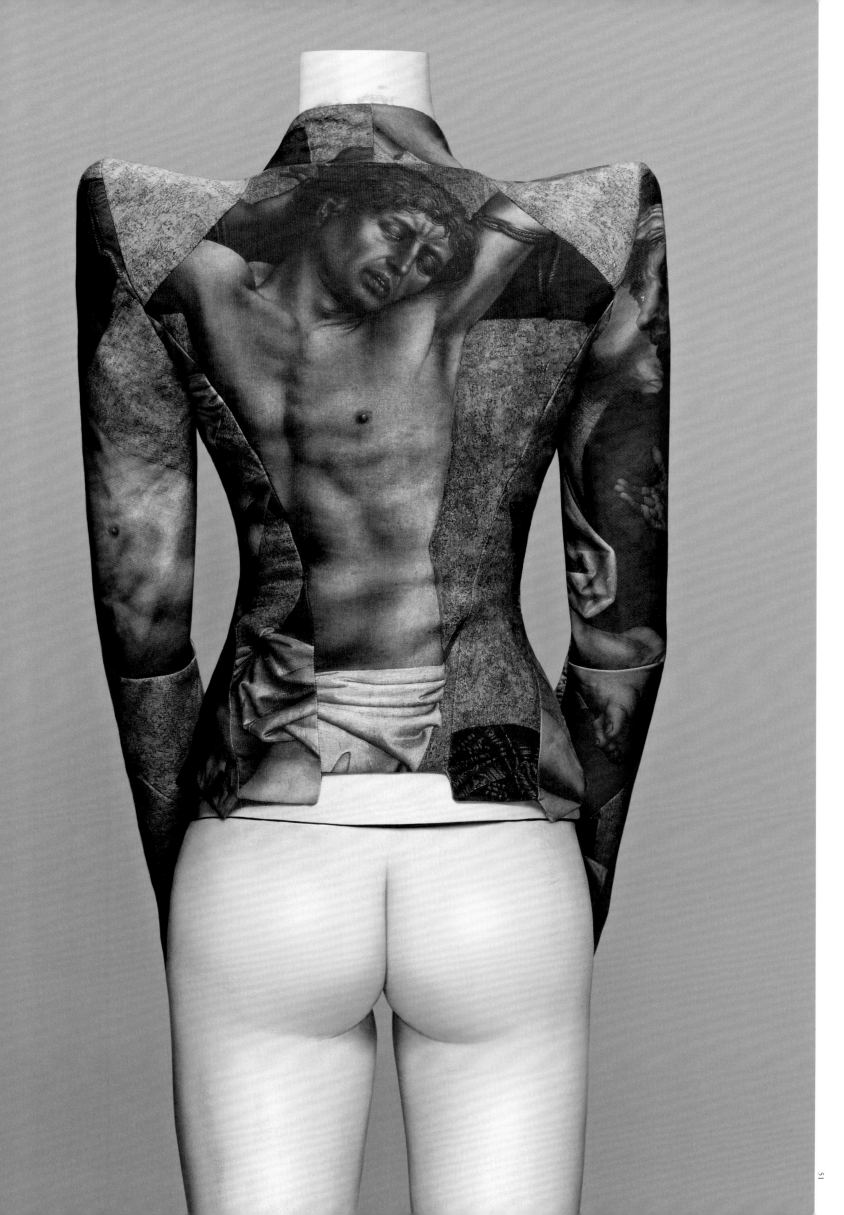

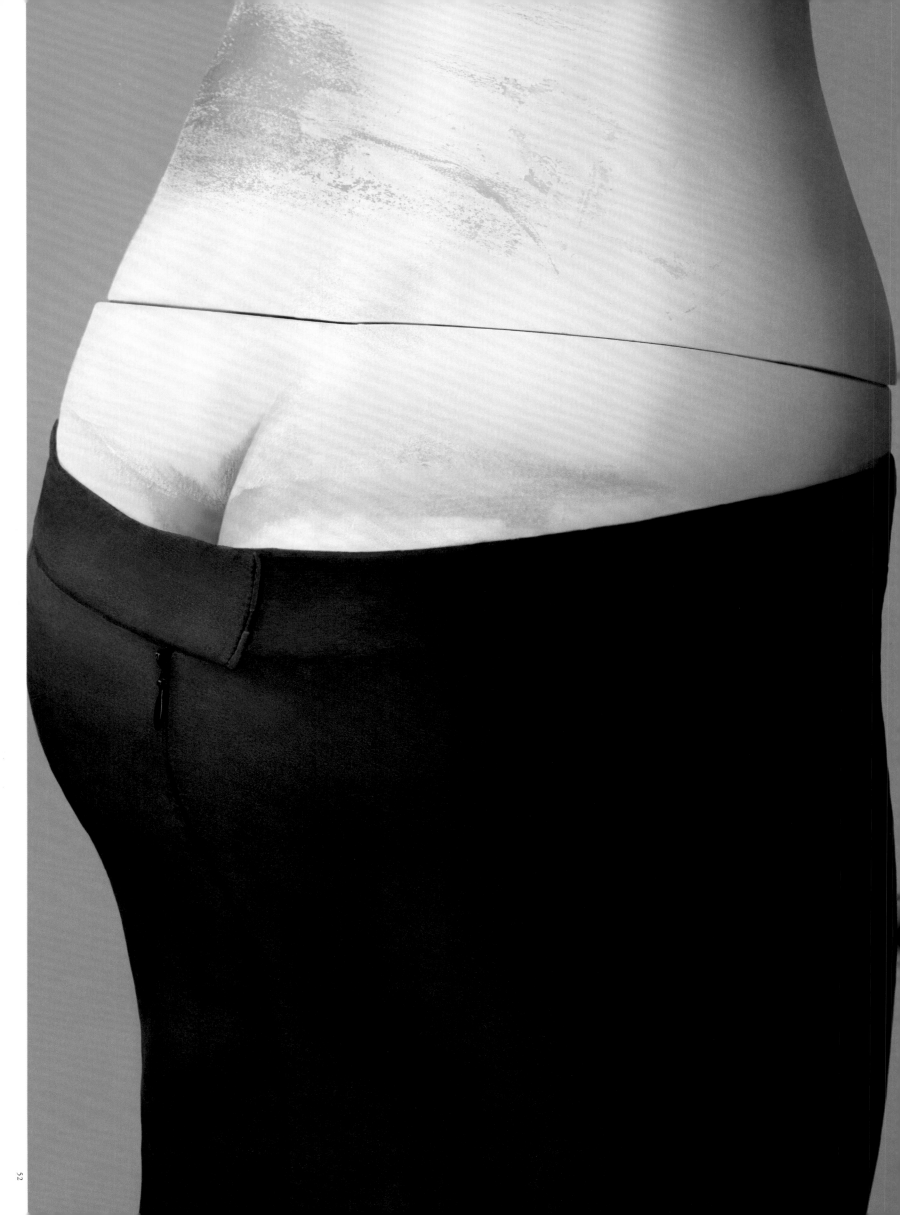

"[With 'bumsters,'] I wanted to elongate the body, not just show the bum. To me, that part of the body—not so much the buttocks, but the bottom of the spine—that's the most erotic part of anyone's body, man or woman."

"It was an art thing, to change the way women looked, just by cut, to make a longer torso. But I was taking it to an extreme. The girls looked quite menacing, because there was so much top and so little bottom, because of the length of the legs."

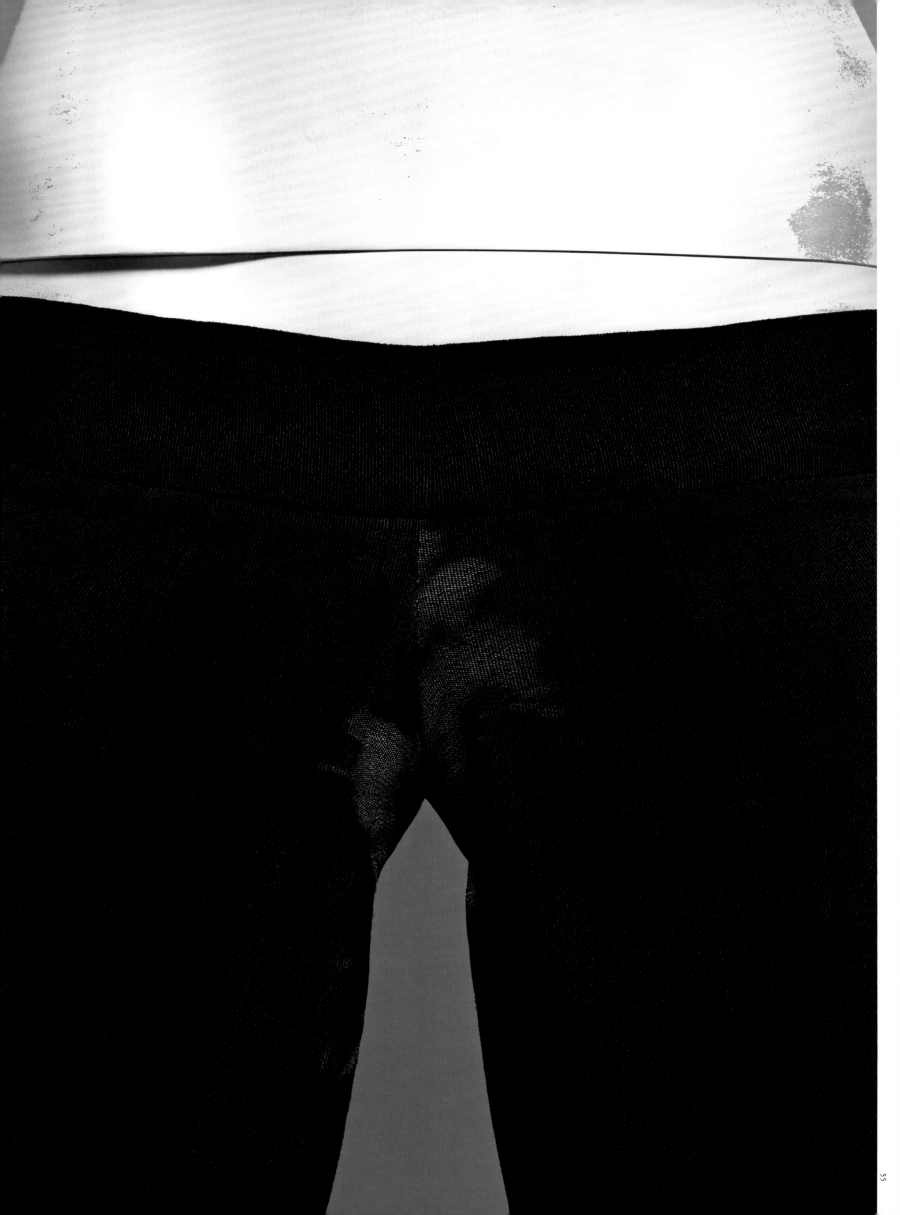

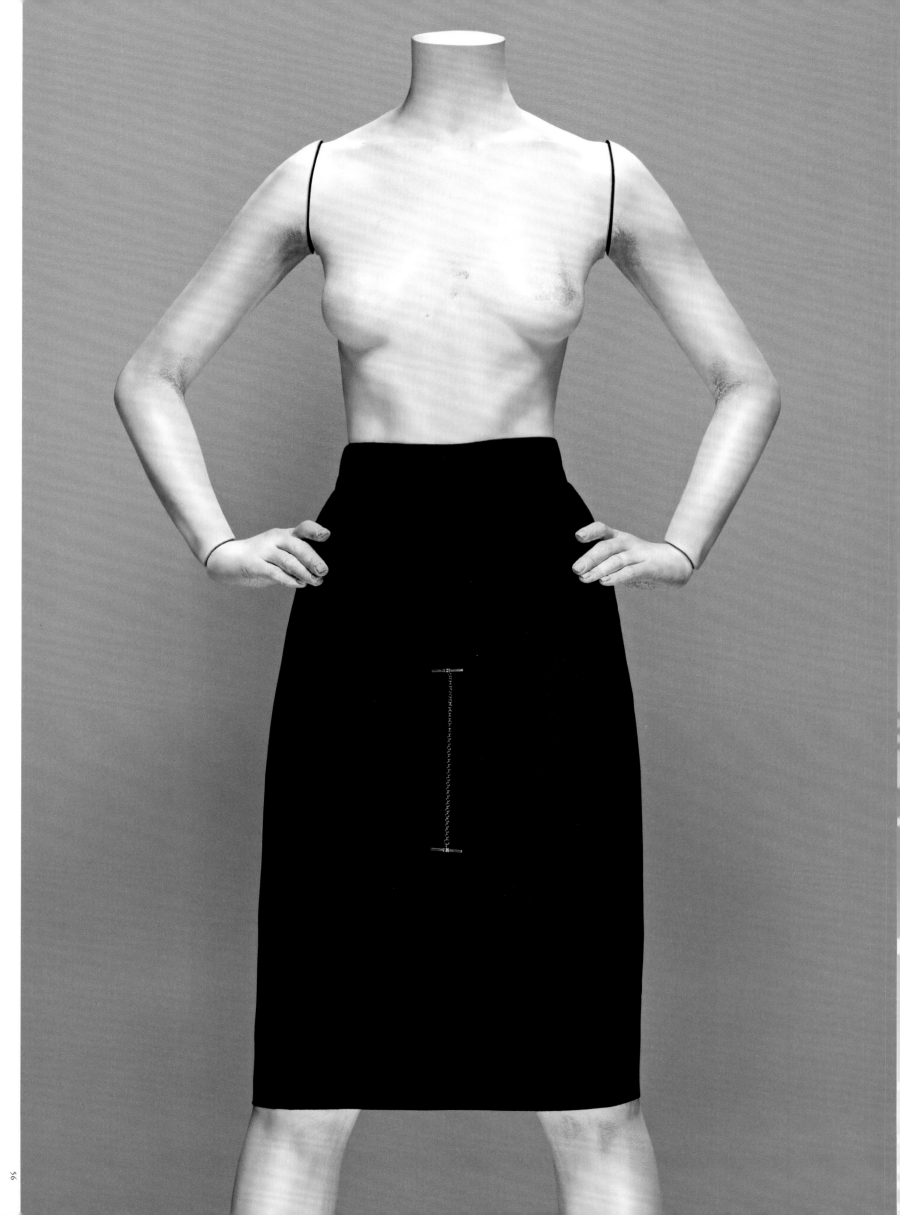

"Someone wrote that [the watch chains] were

tampons. . . . That's not even perverse; it's just gross."

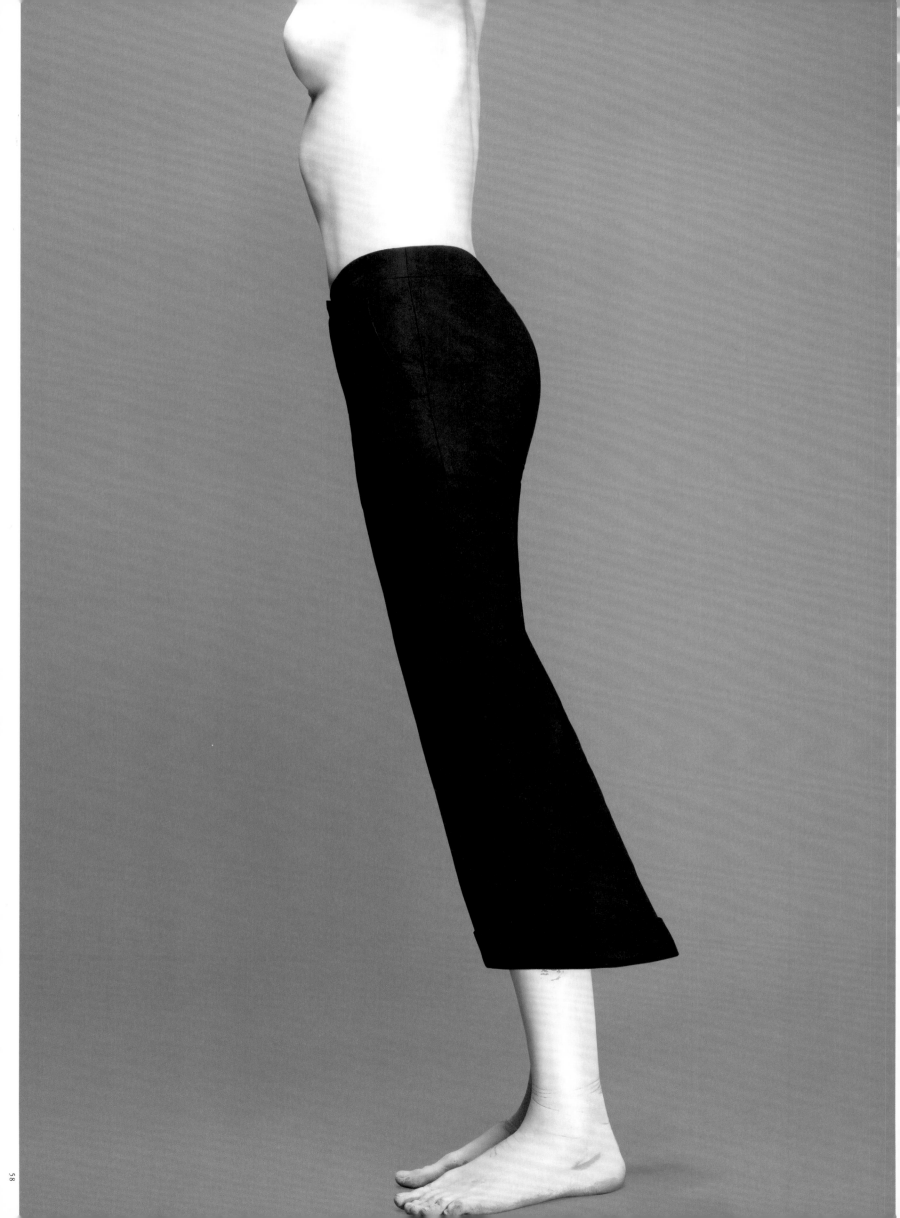

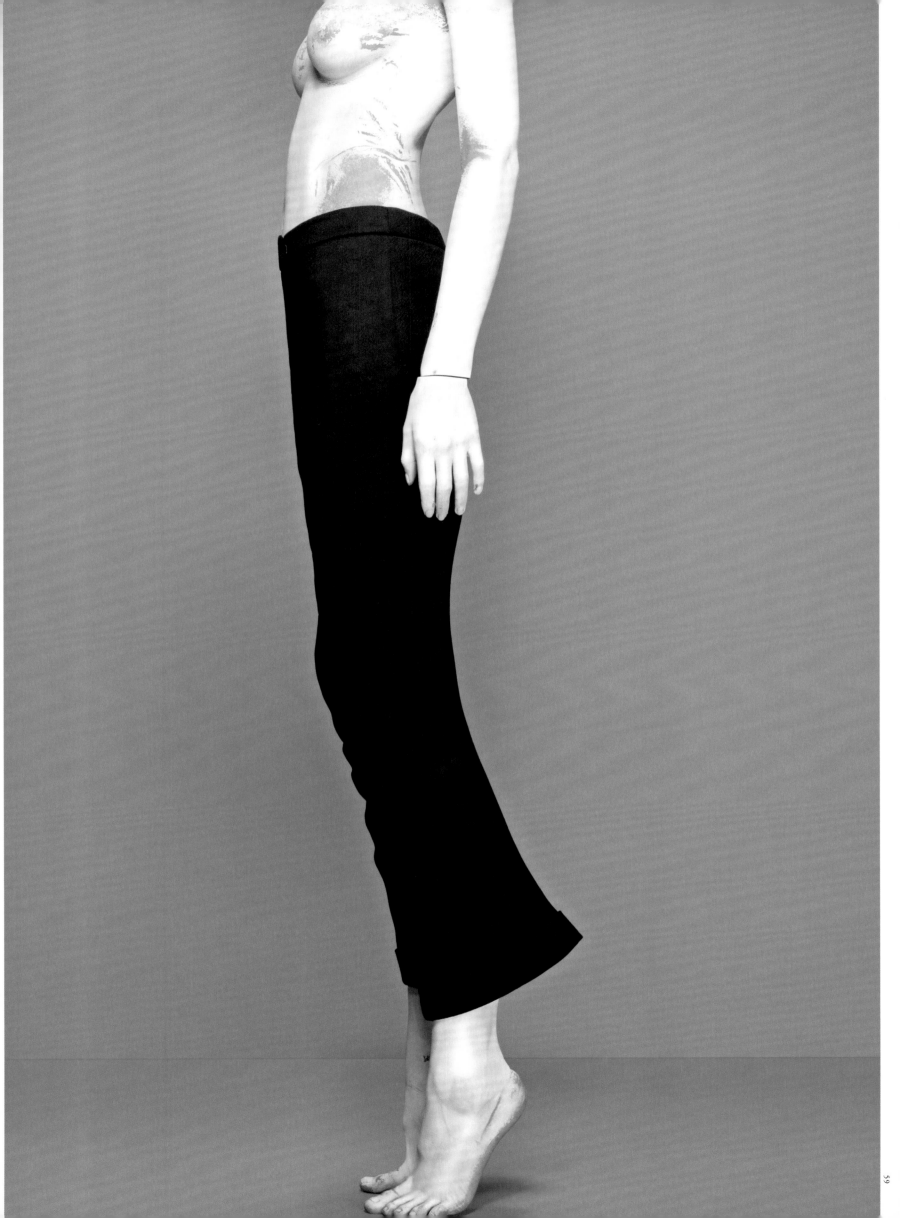

"I want to empower women. I want people to be

afraid of the women I dress."

"When you see a woman wearing McQueen,

there's a certain hardness to the clothes that makes

her look powerful. It kind of fends people off."

"It's almost like putting armor on a woman. It's a

very psychological way of dressing."

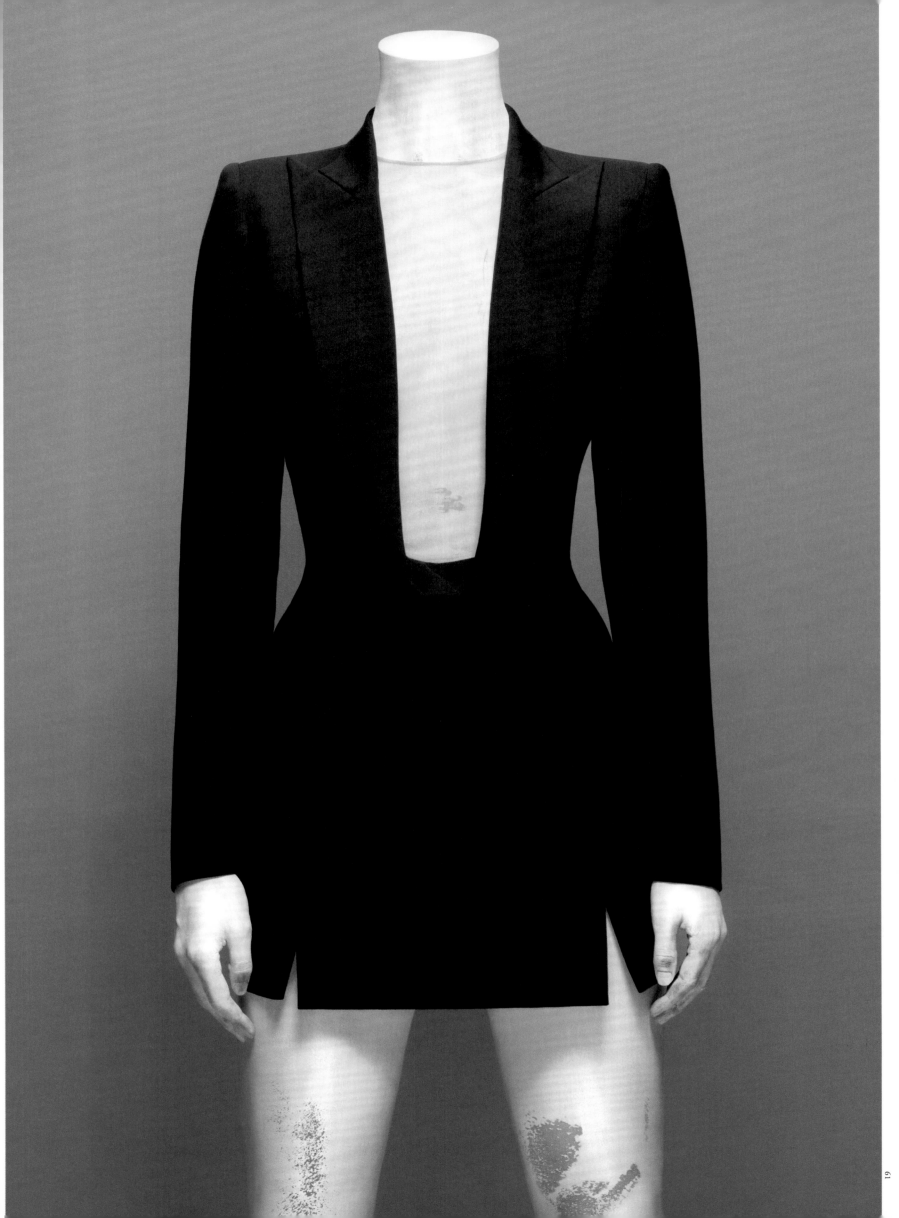

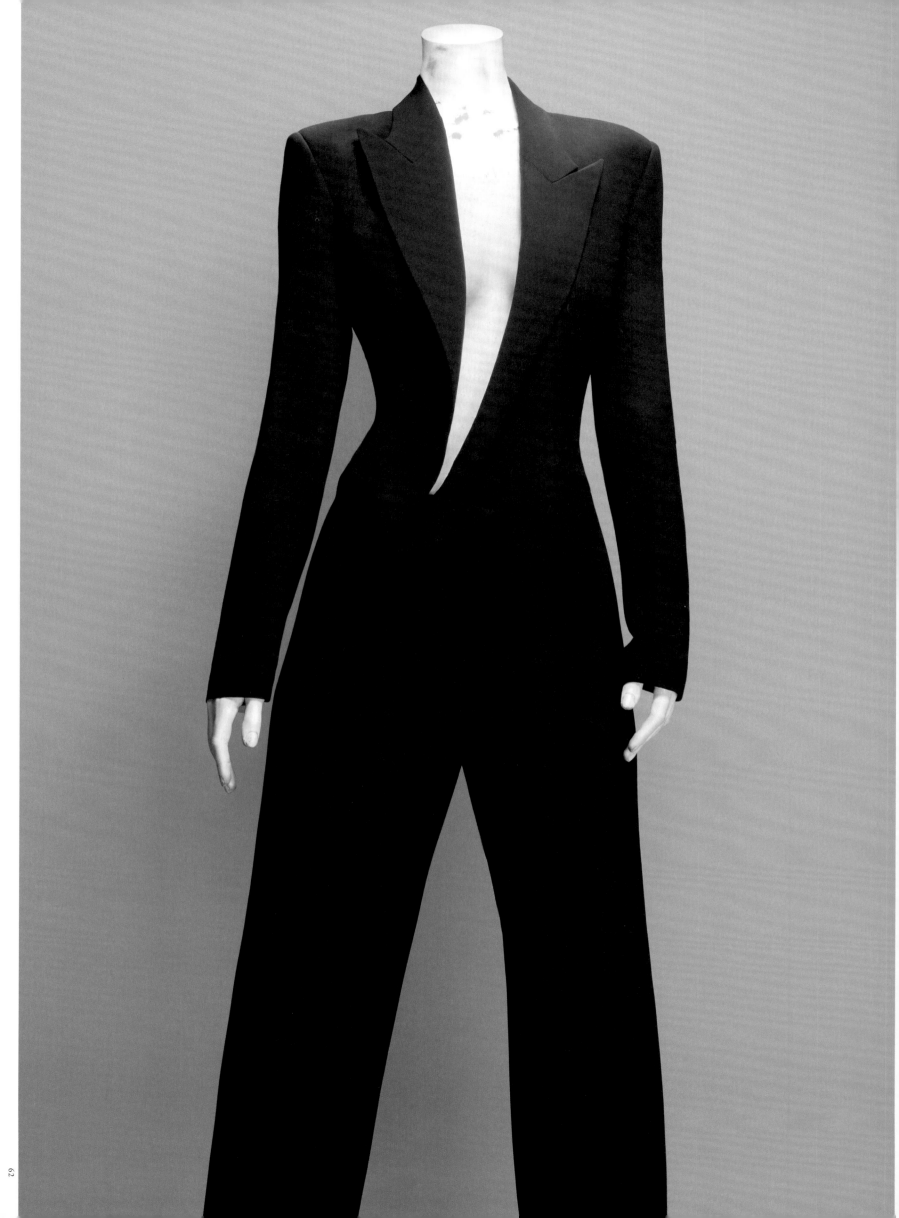

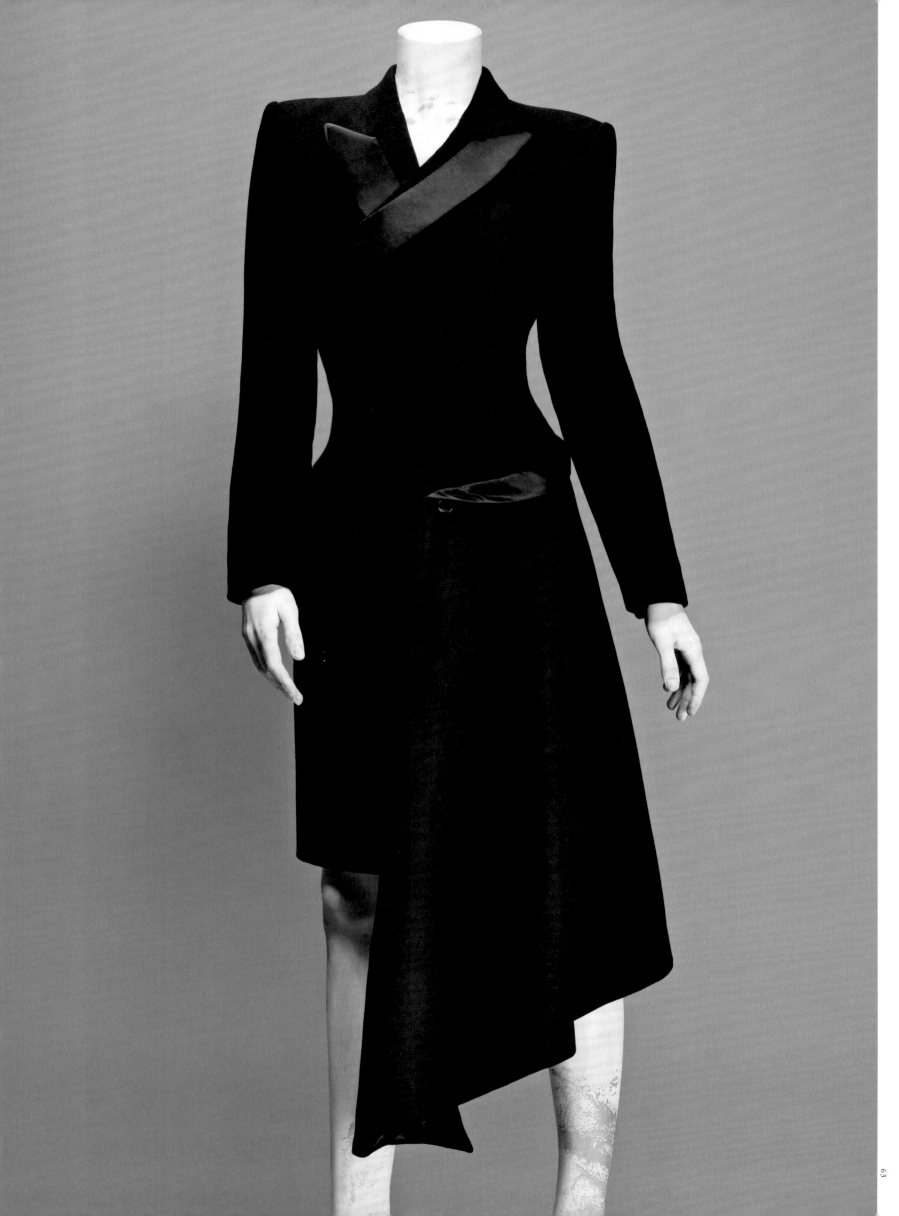

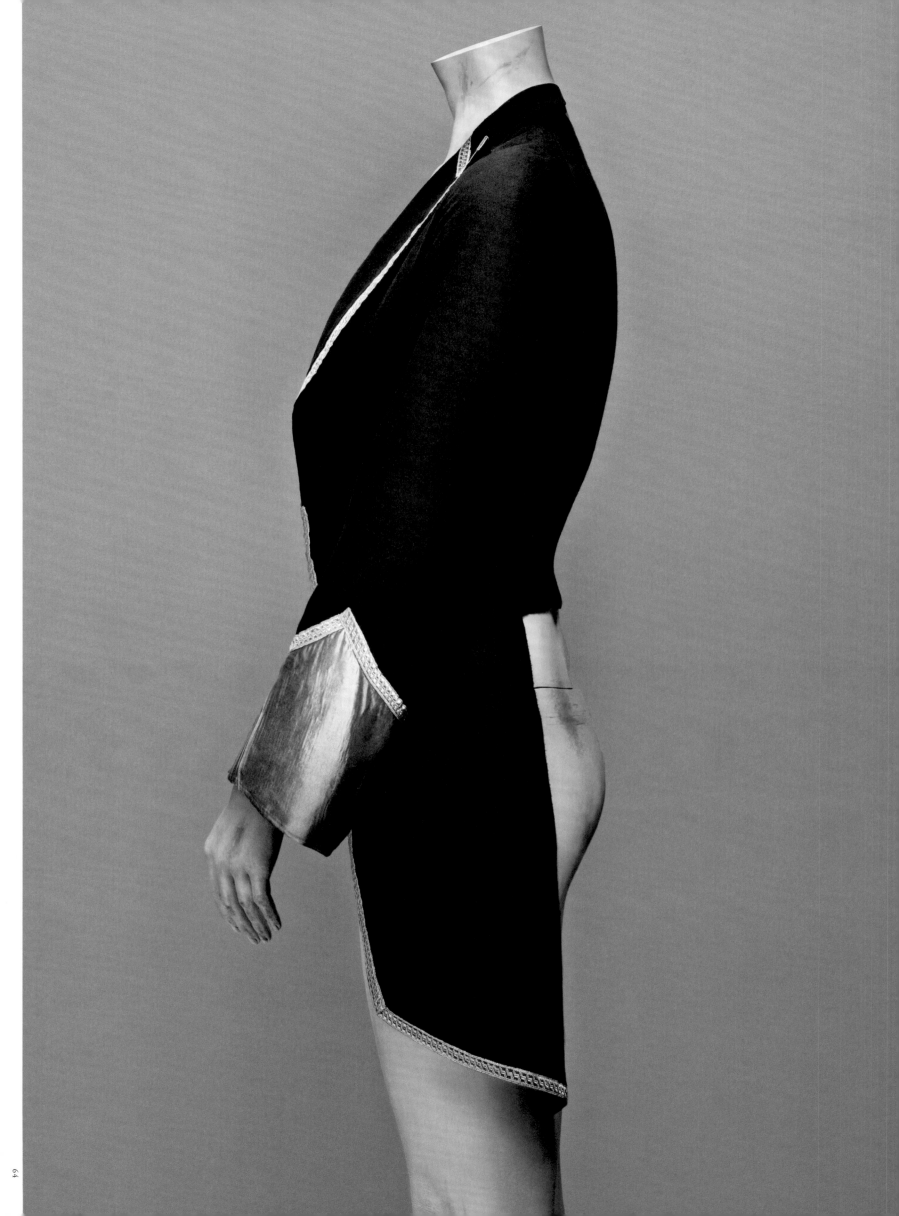

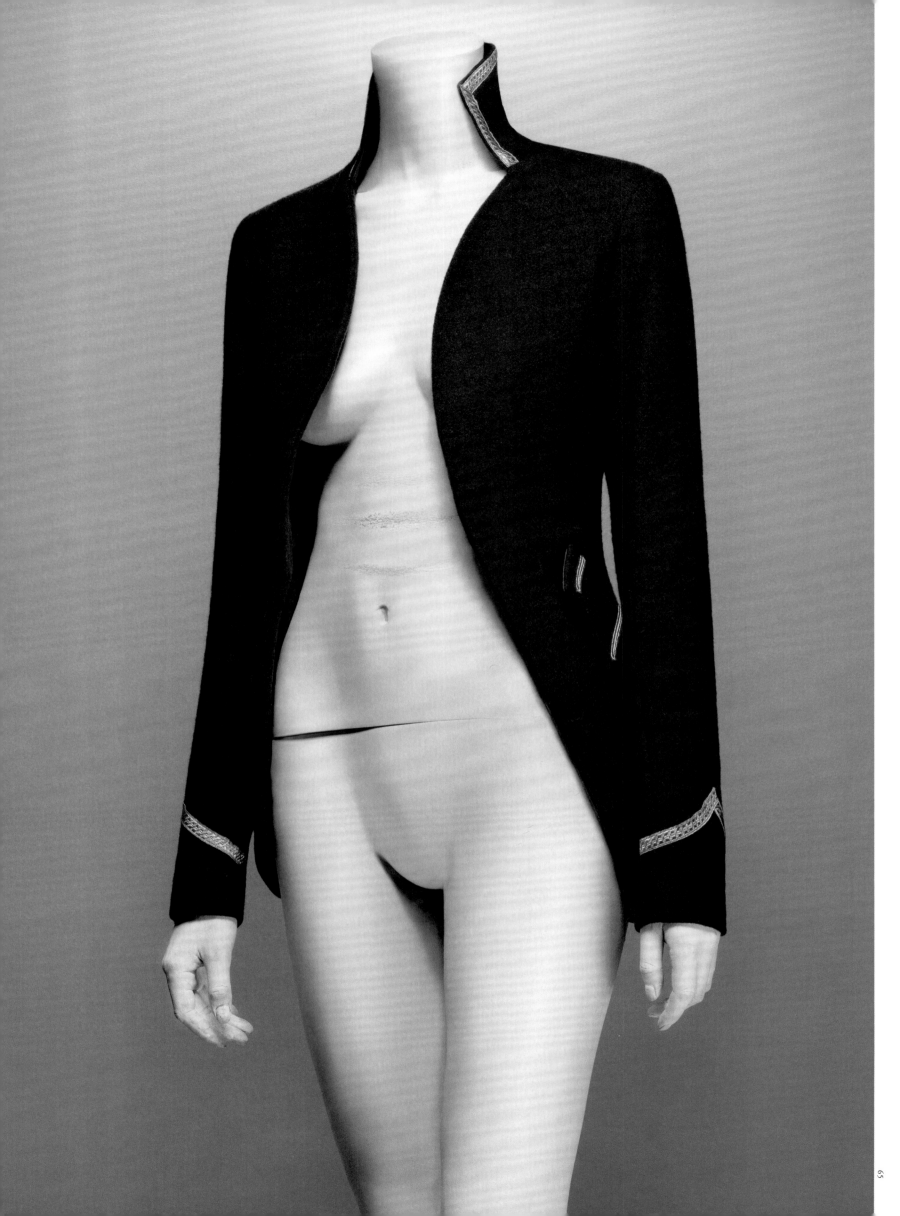

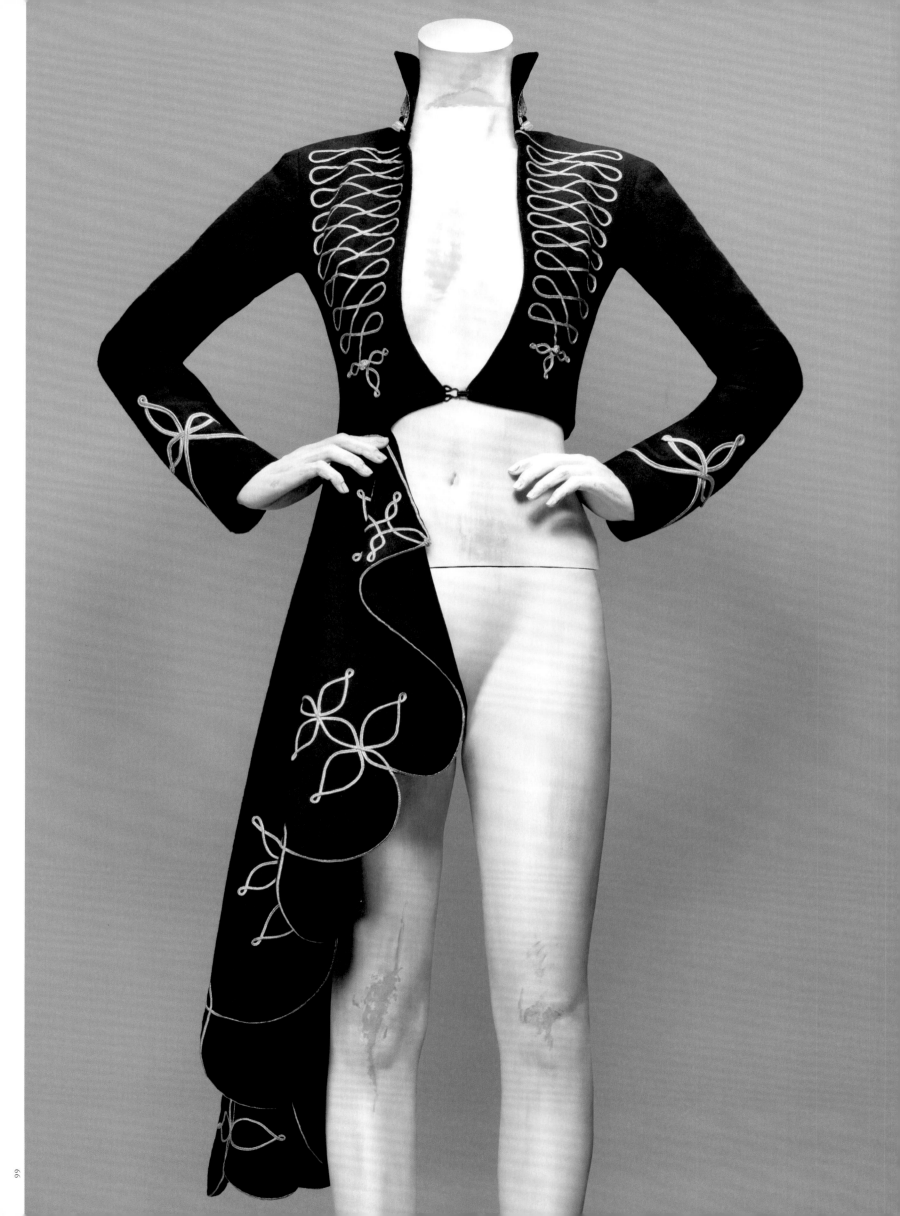

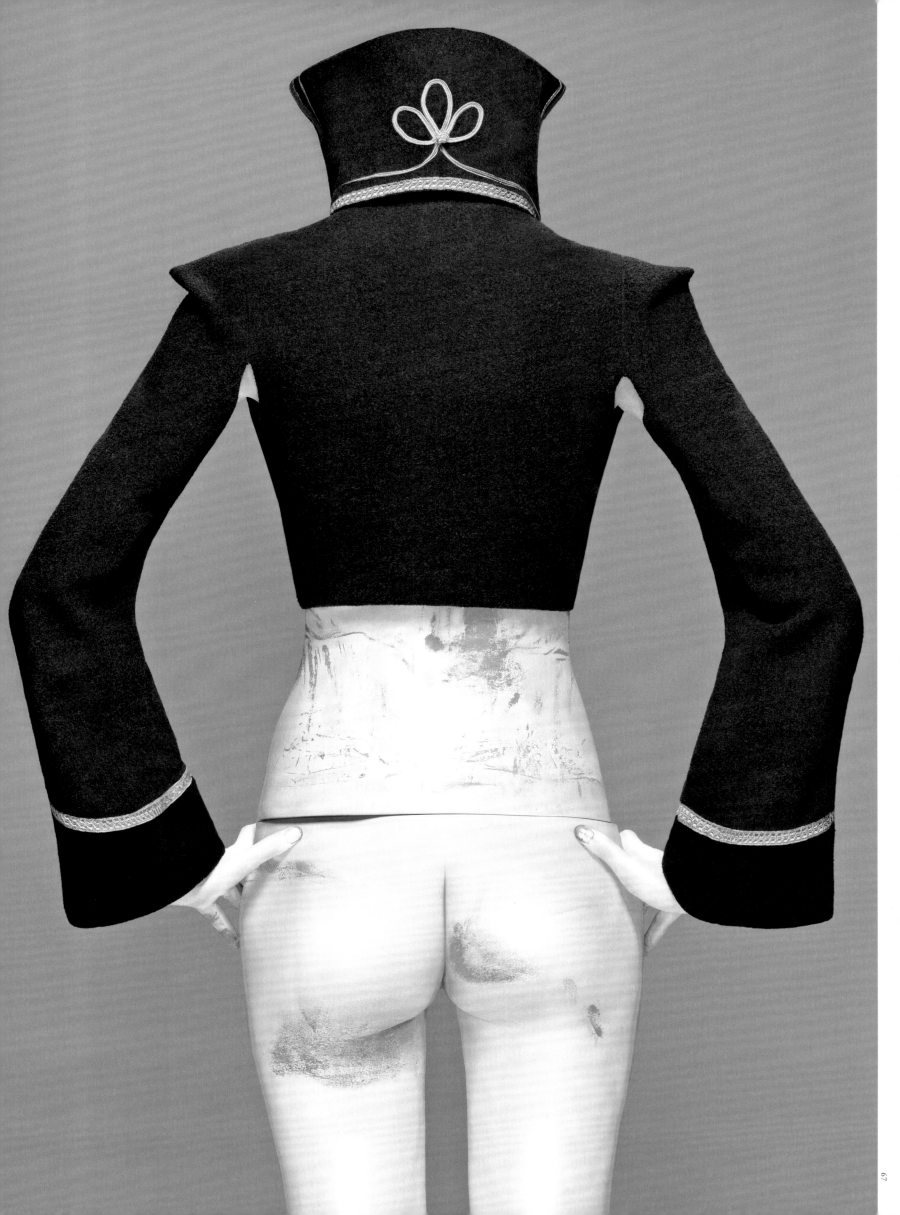

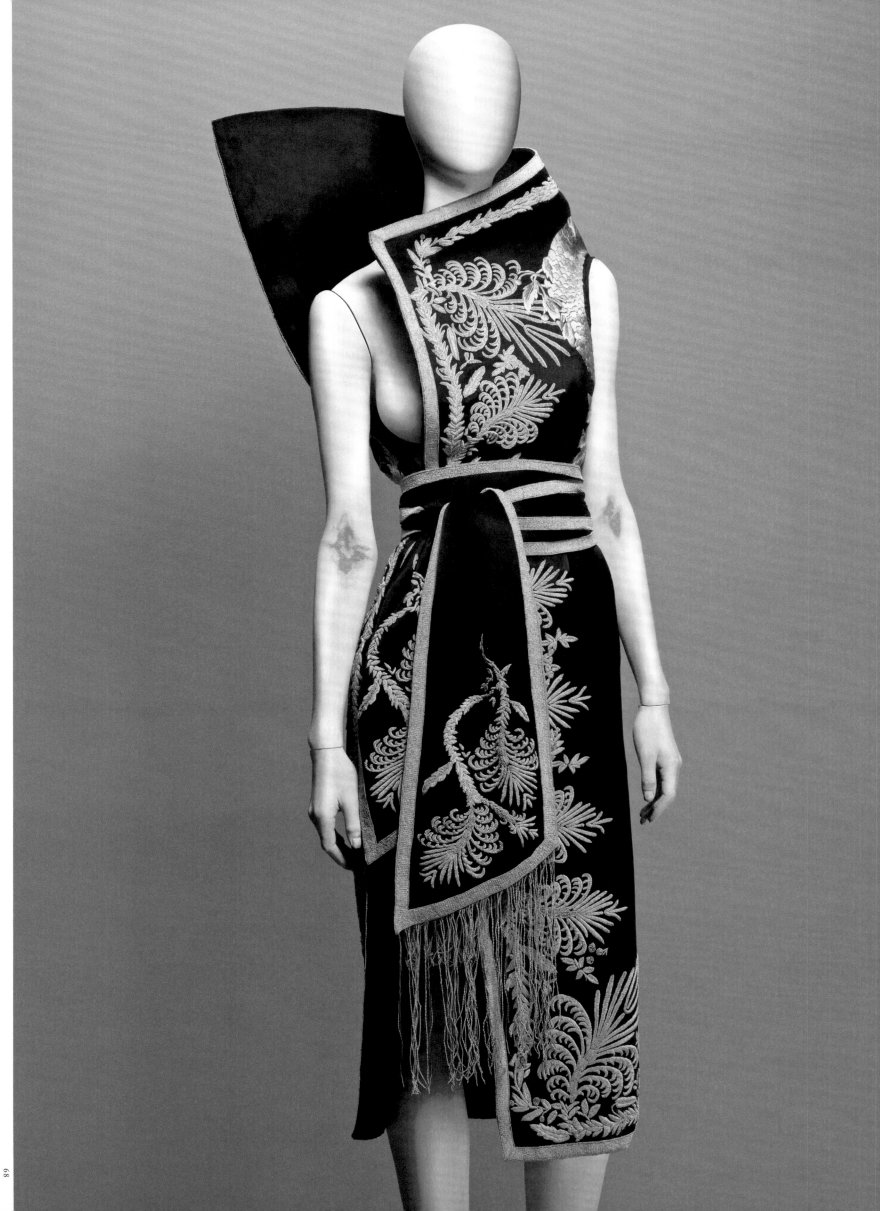

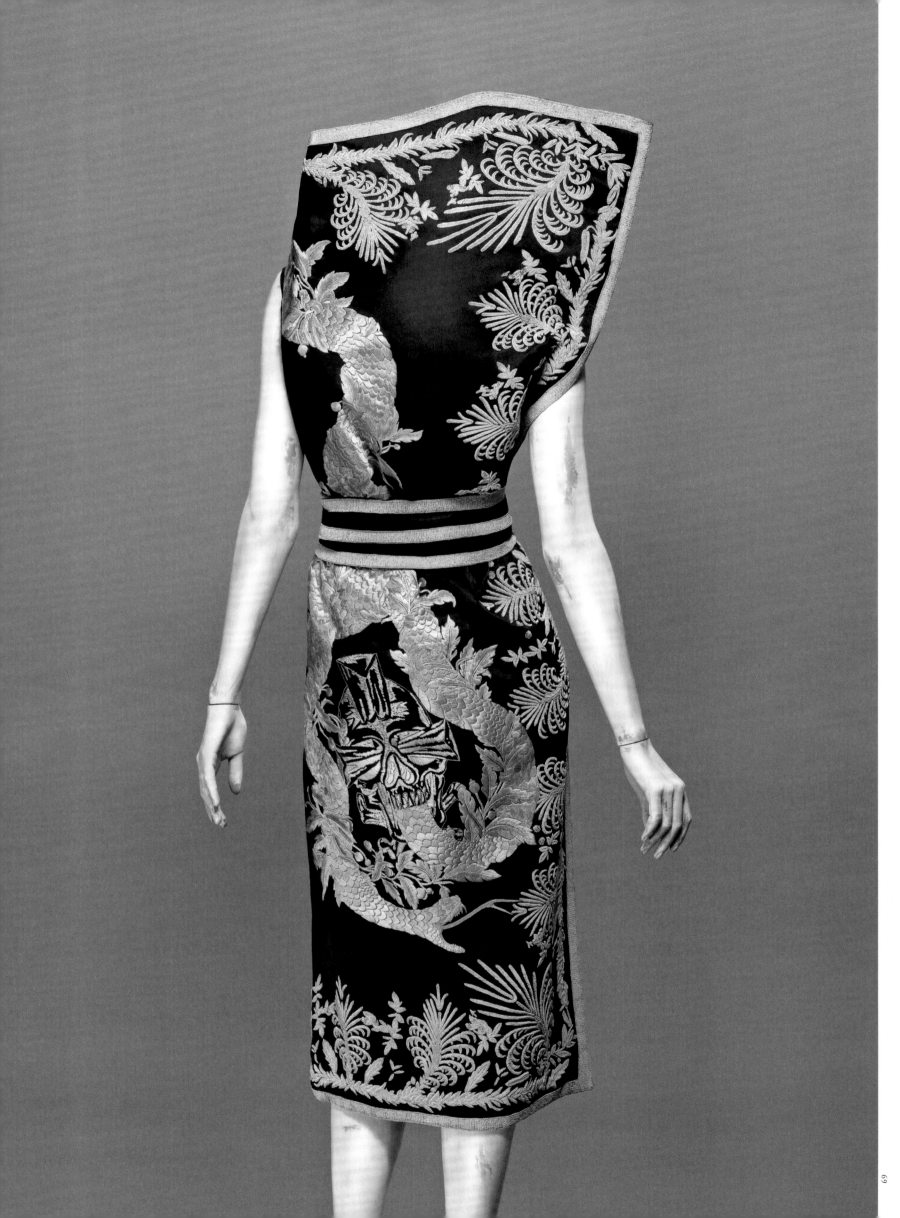

"People find my things sometimes aggressive.

But I don't see it as aggressive. I see it as romantic,

dealing with a dark side of personality."

"I oscillate between life and death, happiness and

sadness, good and evil."

"I'm about what goes through people's minds, the

stuff that people don't want to admit or face up to.

The shows are about what's buried in people's psyches."

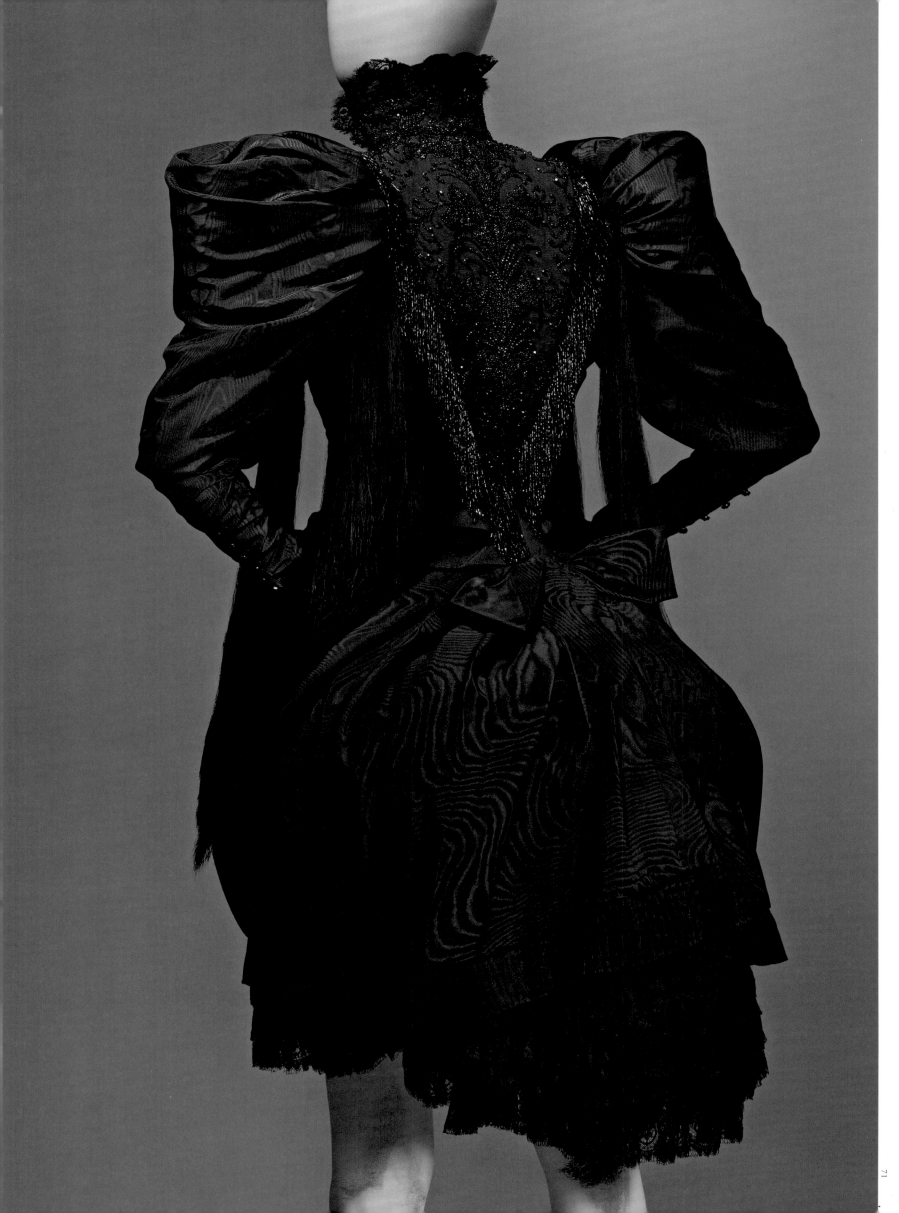

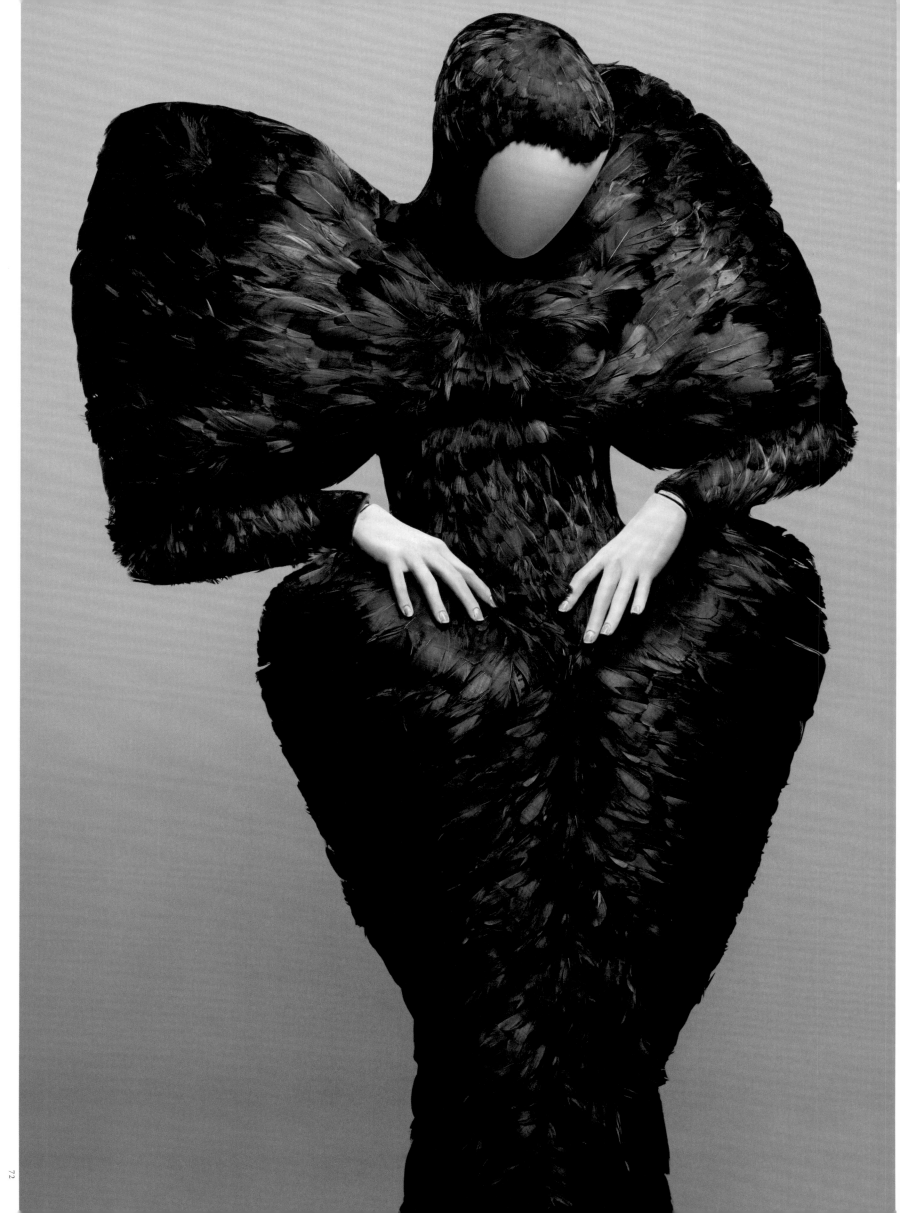

"It is important to look at death because it is a part of life. It is a sad thing, melancholic but romantic at the same time. It is the end of a cycle— everything has to end. The cycle of life is positive because it gives room for new things."

"There's blood beneath every layer of skin."

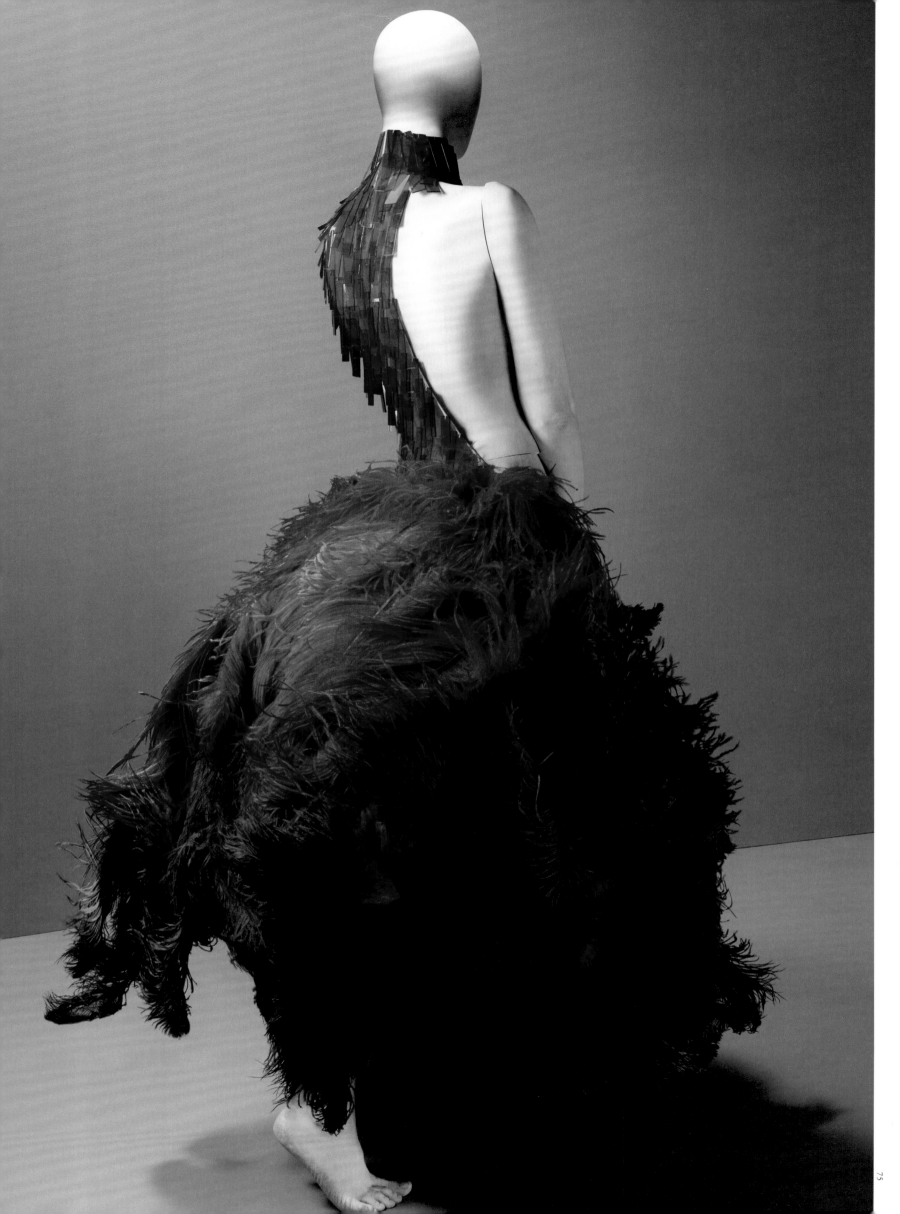

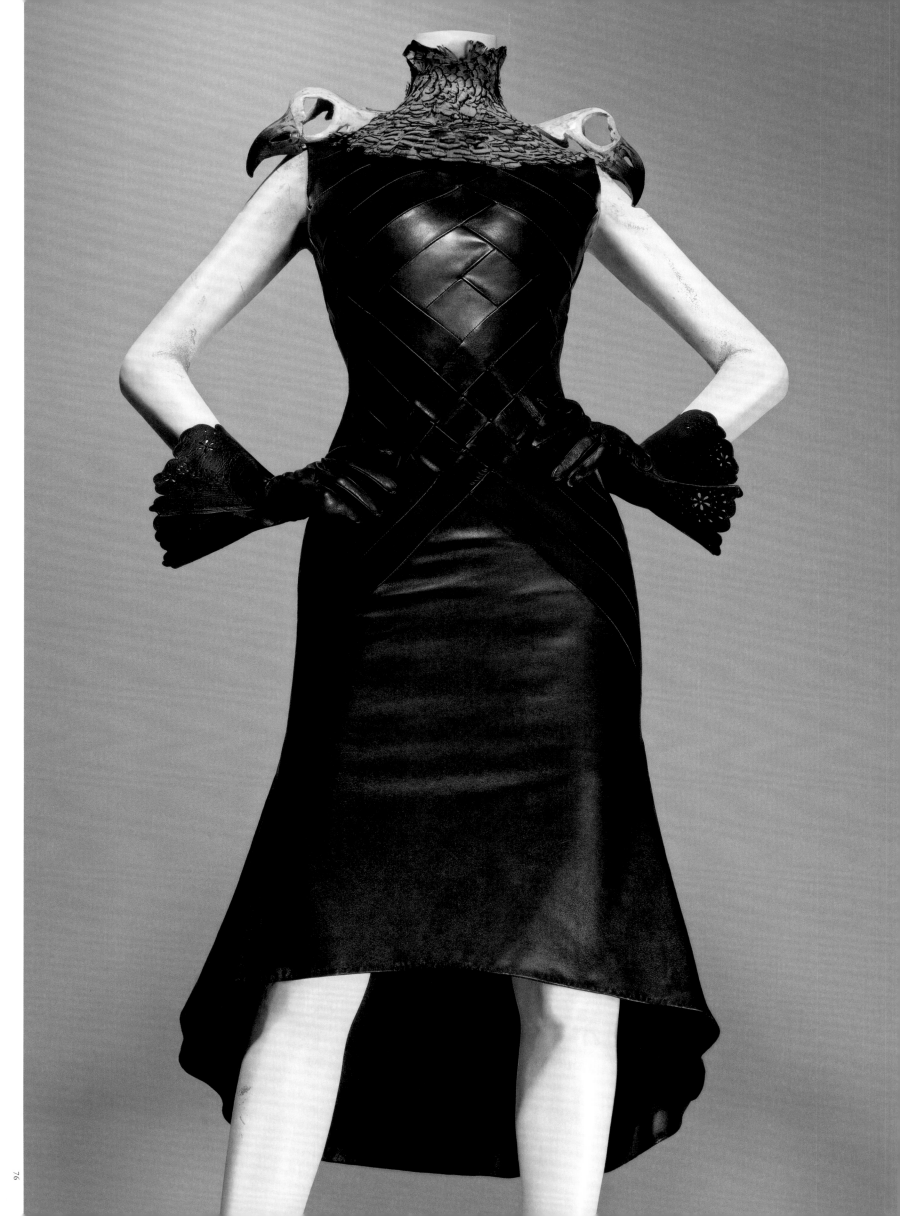

"[In this collection,] my idea was this mad

scientist who cut all these women up and mixed

them all back together."

"I don't think like the average person on the street.

I think quite perversely sometimes."

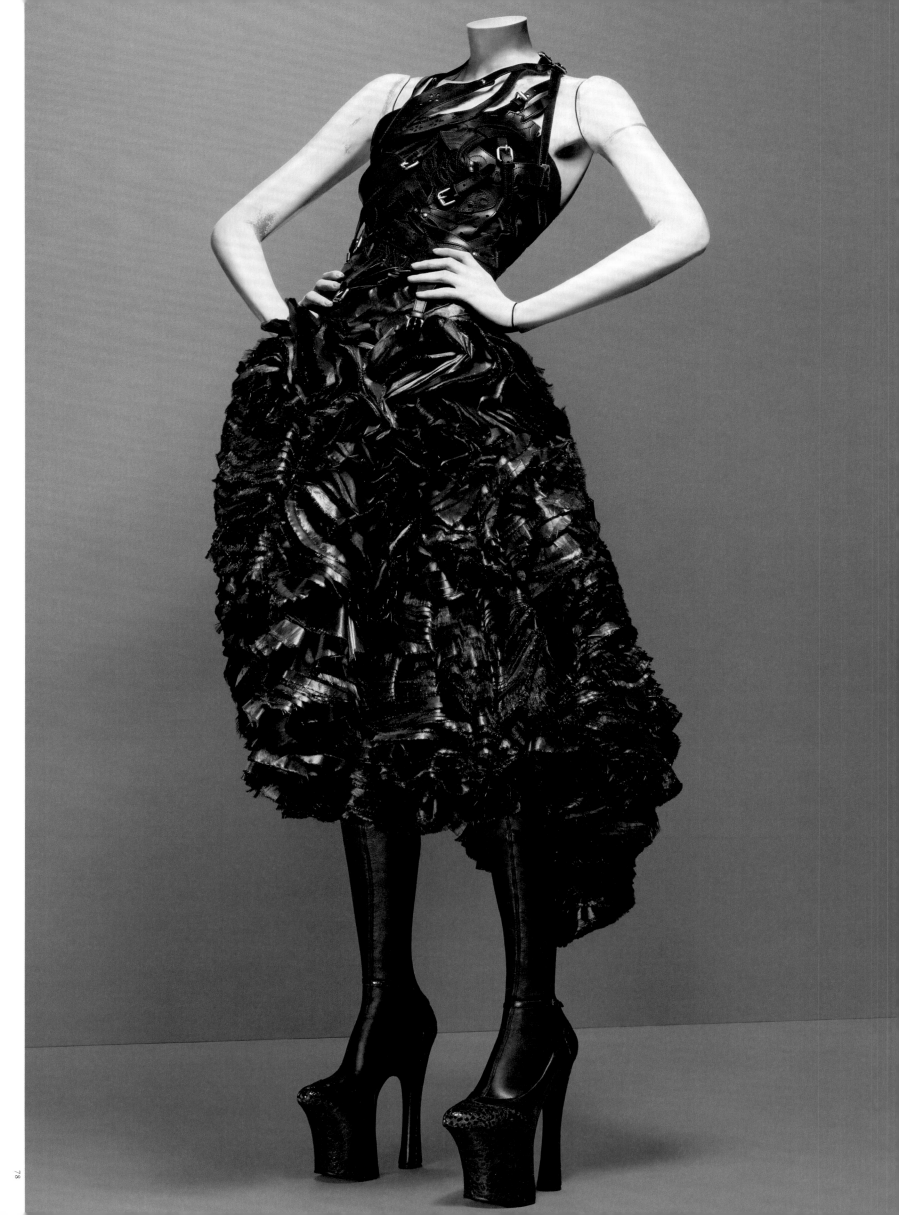

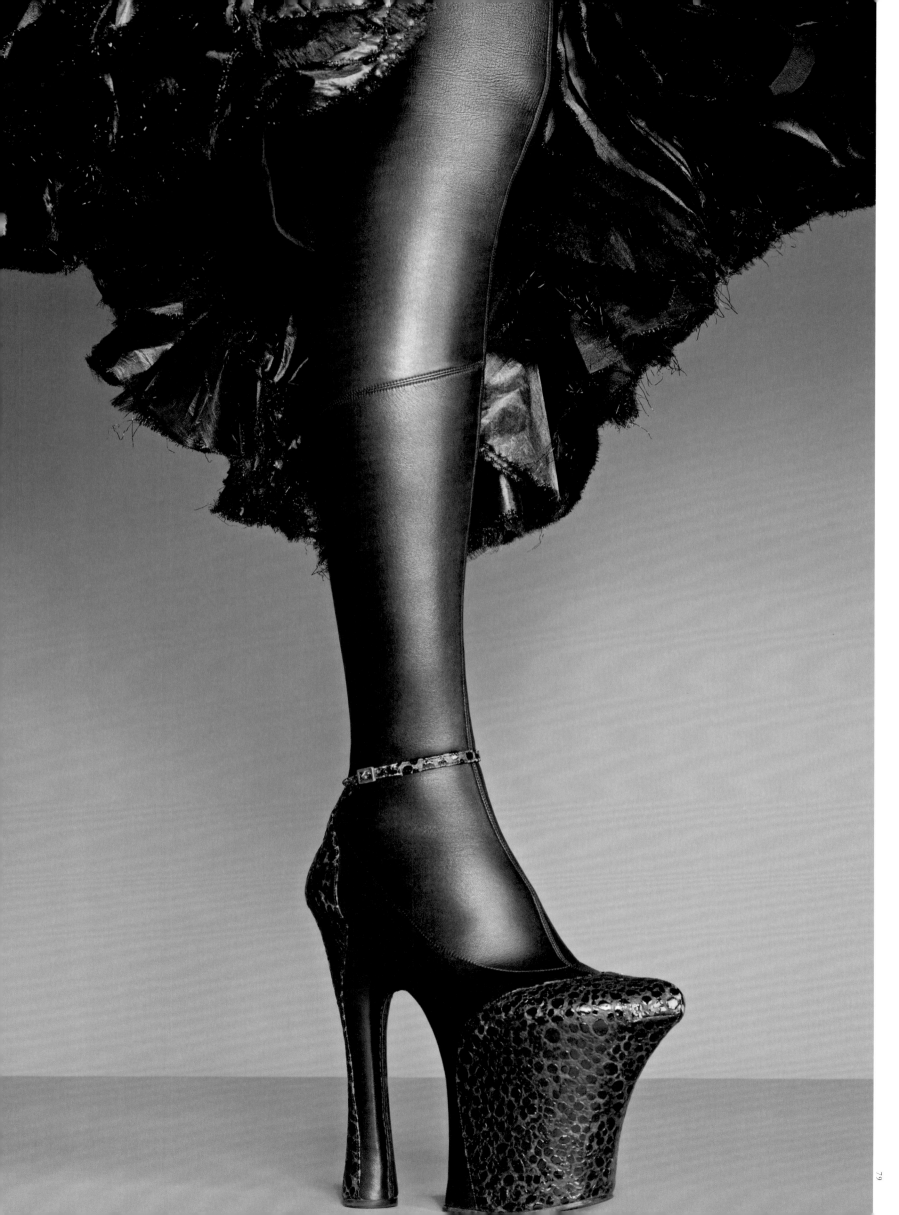

"I think there has to be an underlying sexuality. There has to be a perverseness to the clothes. There is a hidden agenda in the fragility of romance. It's like the *Story of O*. I'm not big on women looking naïve. There has to be a sinister aspect, whether it's melancholy or sadomasochist. I think everyone has a deep sexuality, and sometimes it's good to use a little of it—and sometimes a lot of it—like a masquerade."

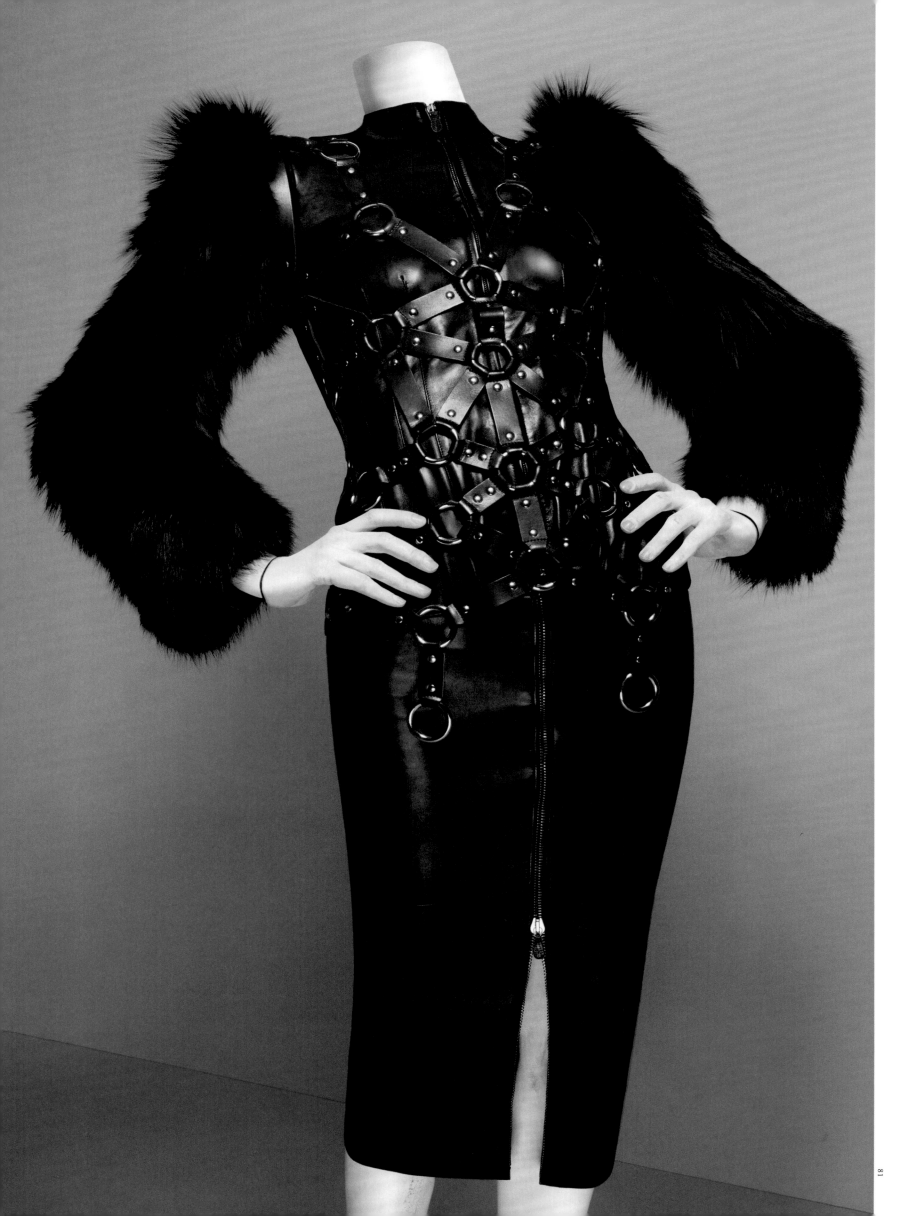

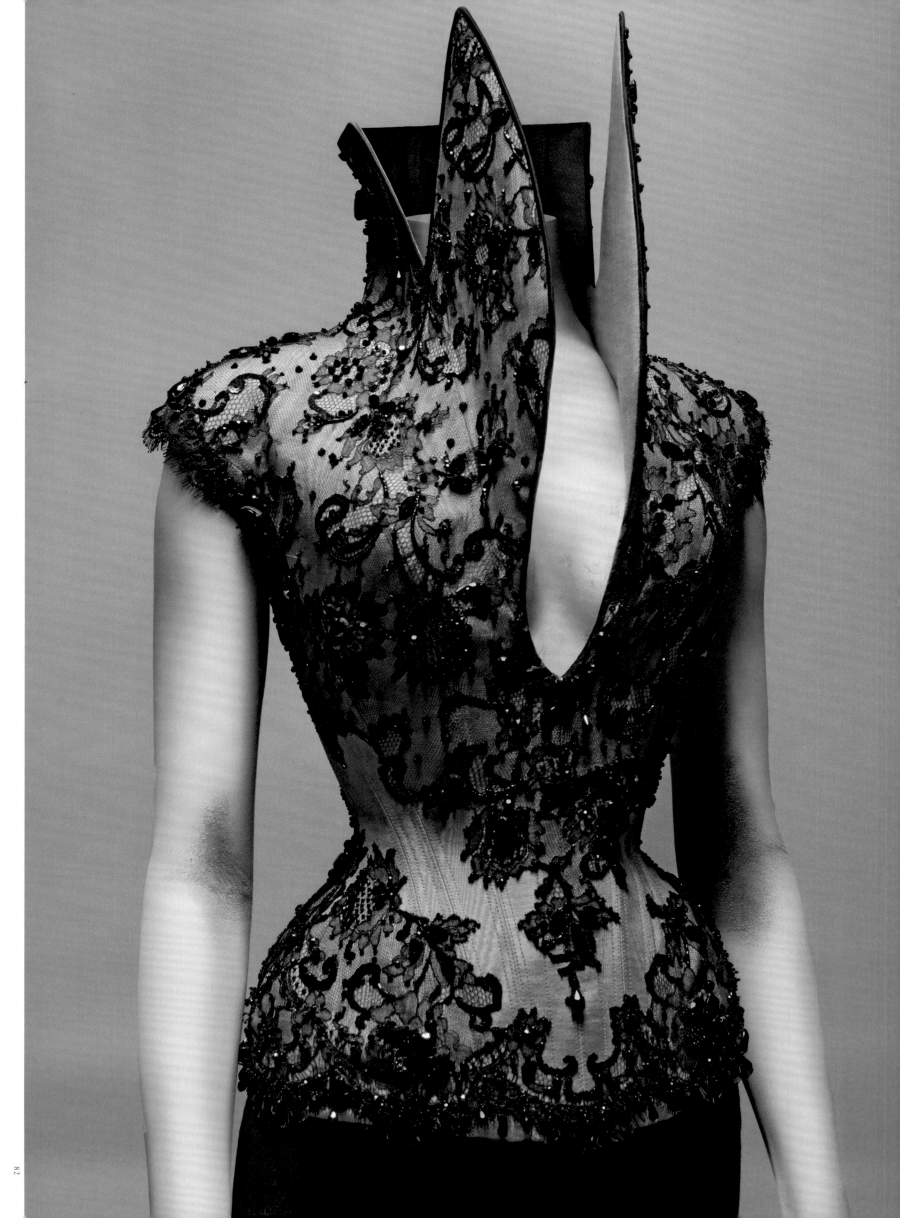

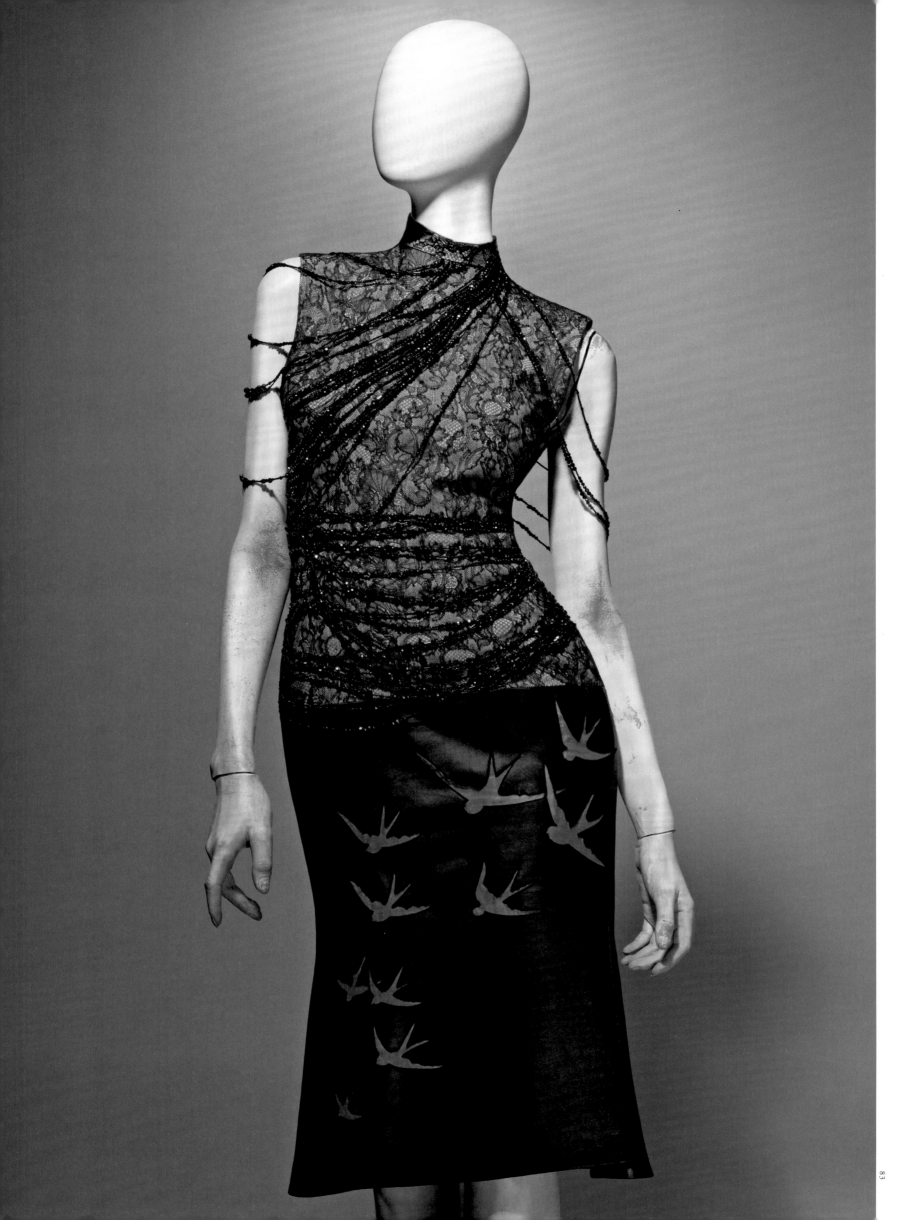

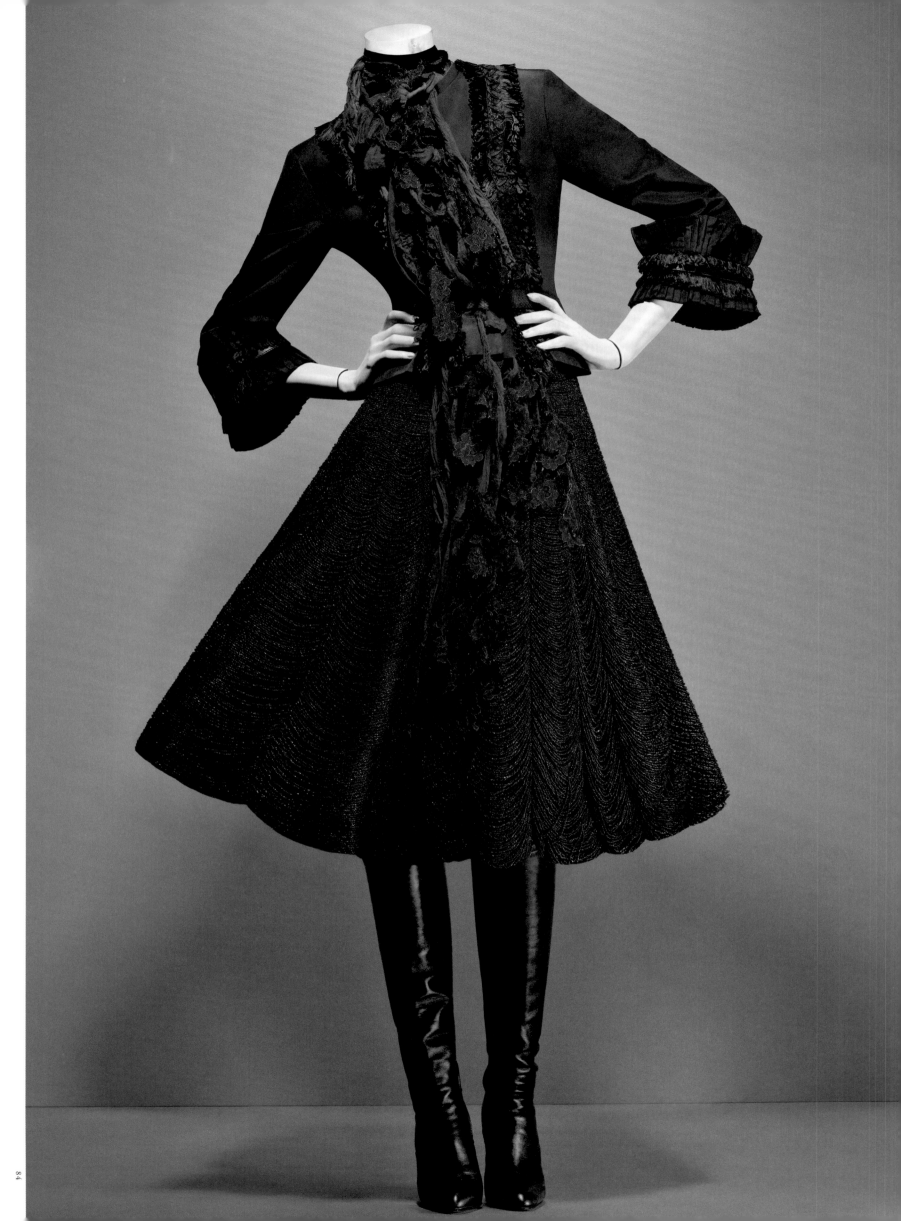

"This collection was inspired by Tim Burton. It started off dark and then got more romantic as it went along."

"Life to me is a bit of a [Brothers] Grimm fairy tale."

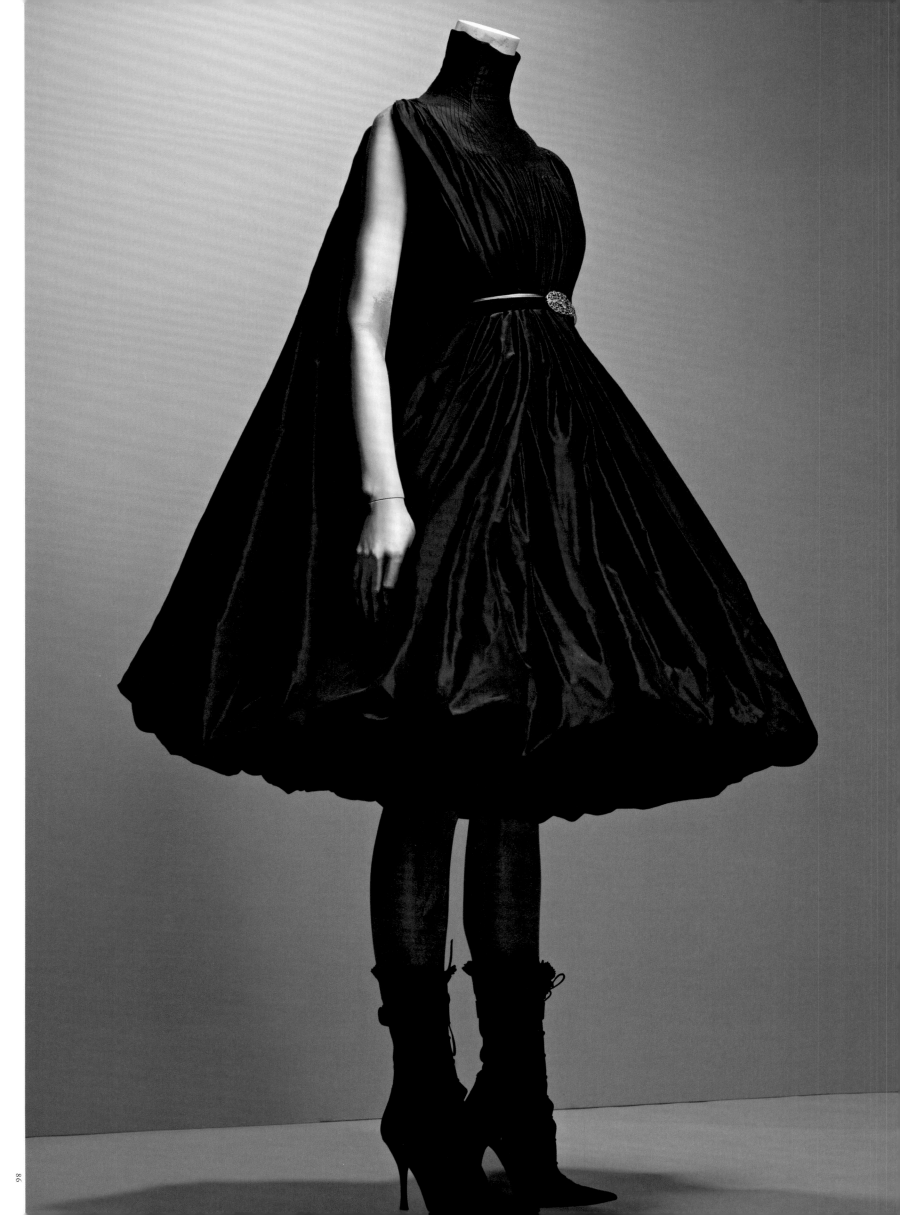

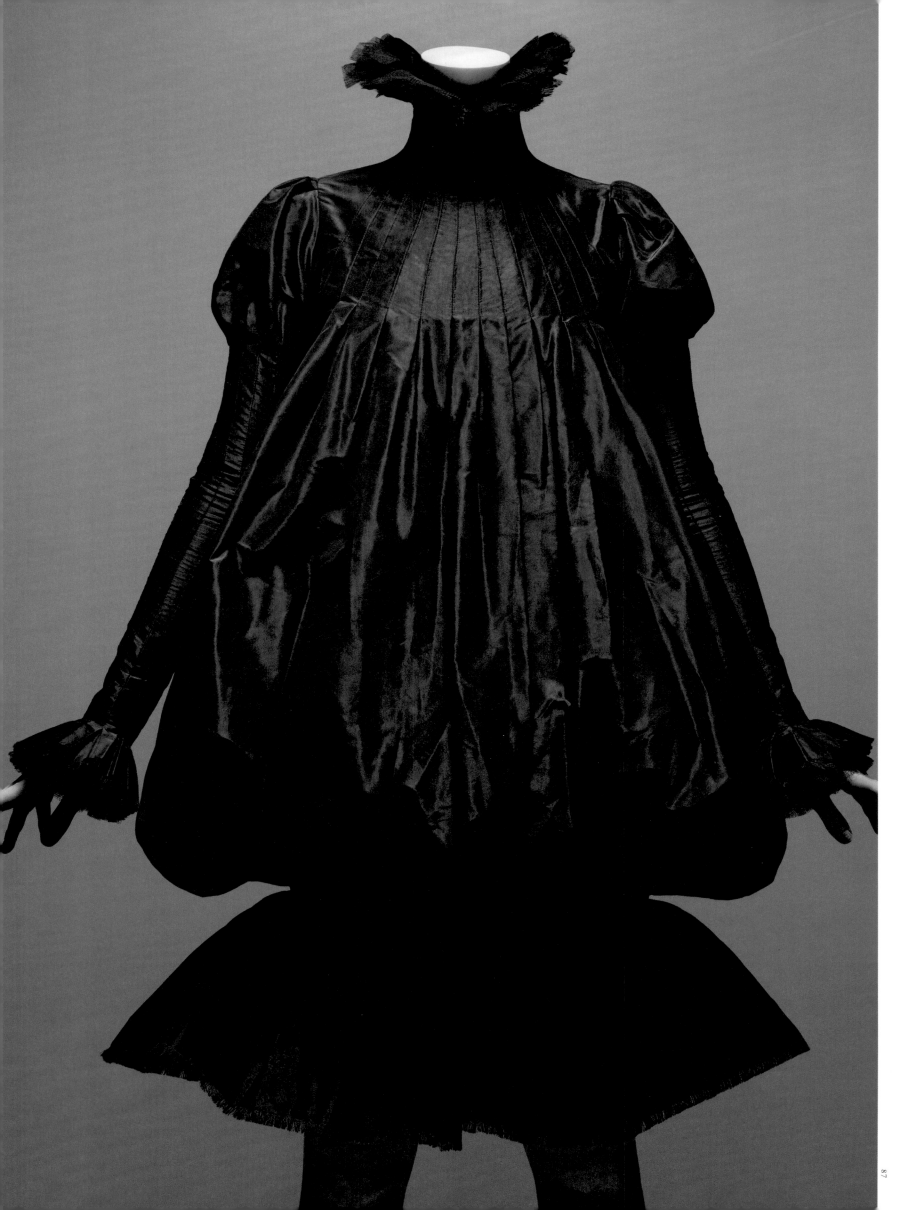

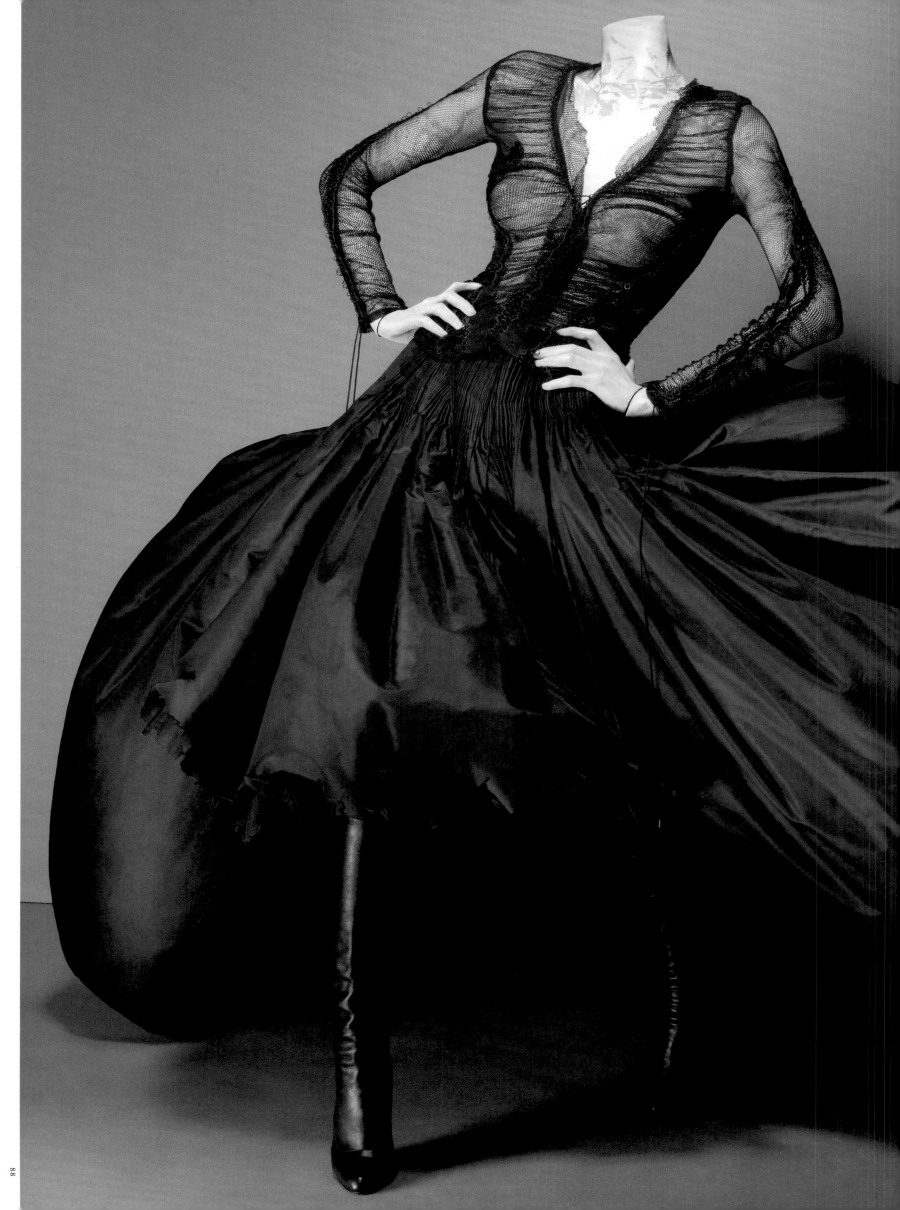

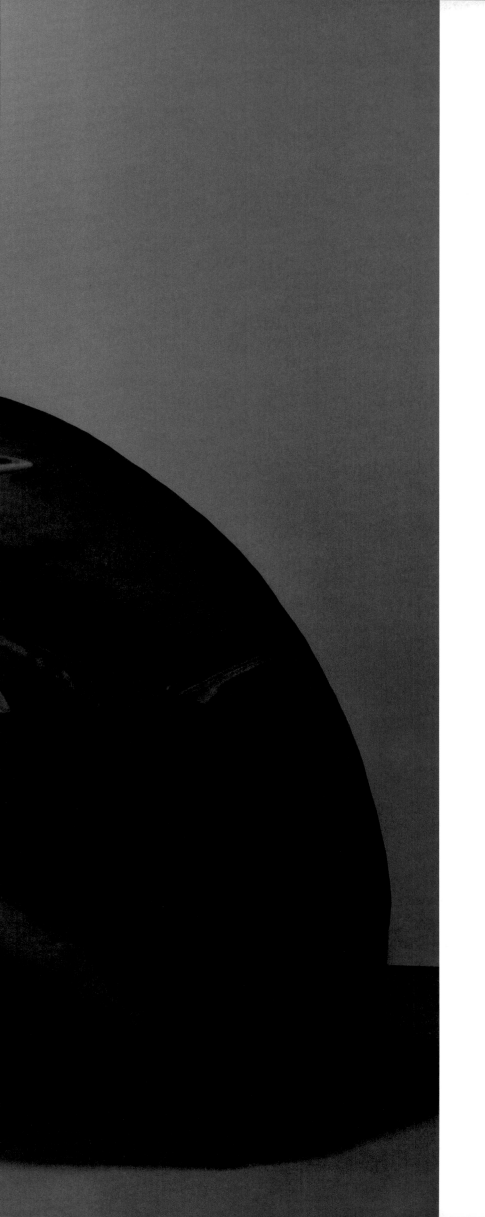

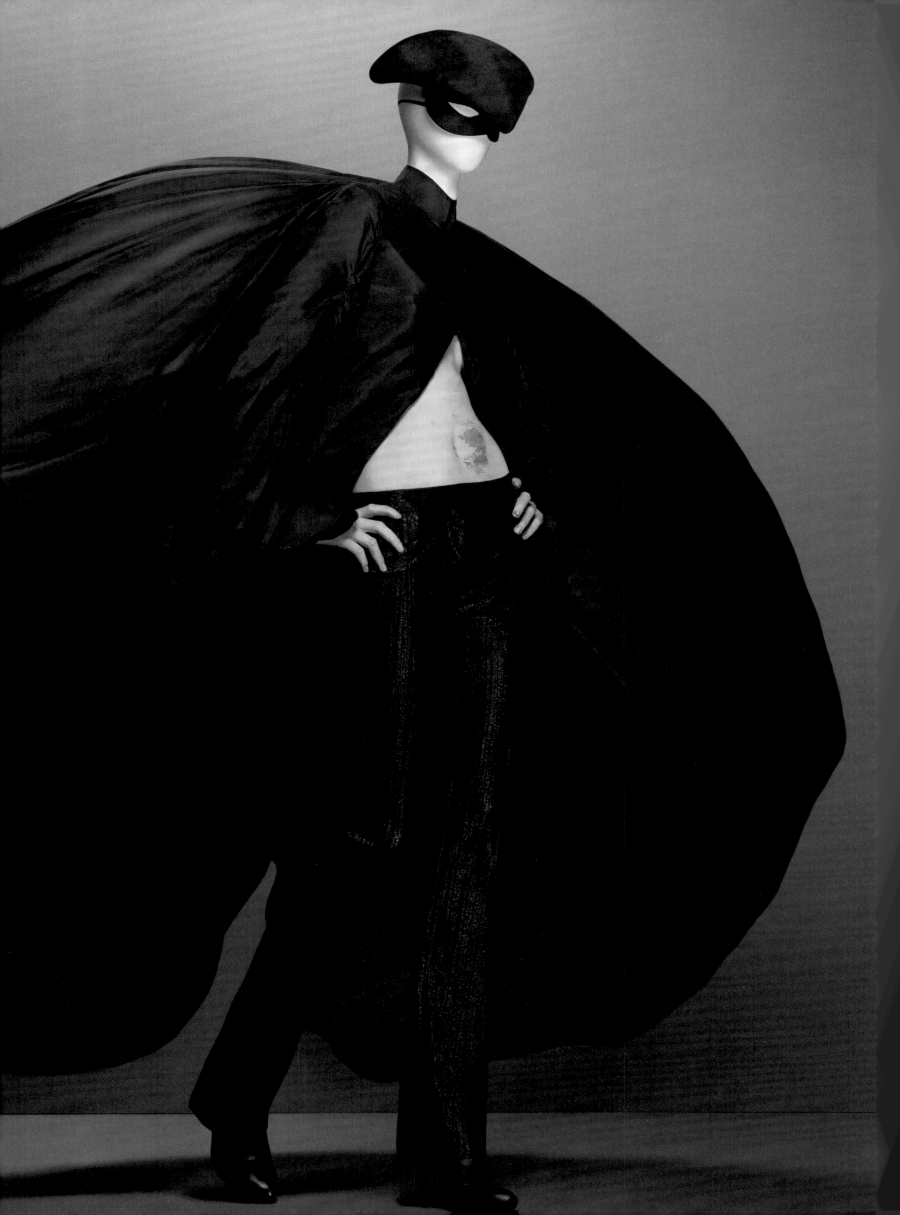

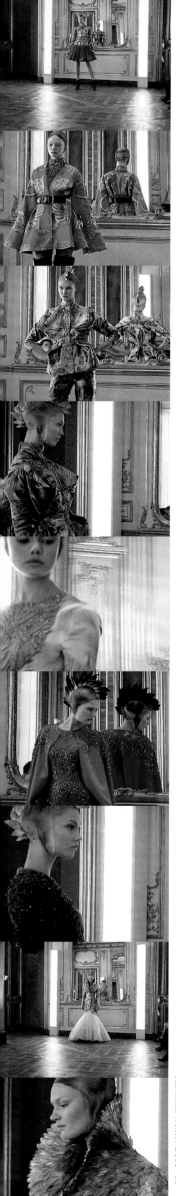

"I relate more to that cold, austere asceticism of the Flemish masters, and I also love the macabre thing you see in Tudor and Jacobean portraiture."

"For me, what I do is an artistic expression which is channeled through me. Fashion is just the medium."

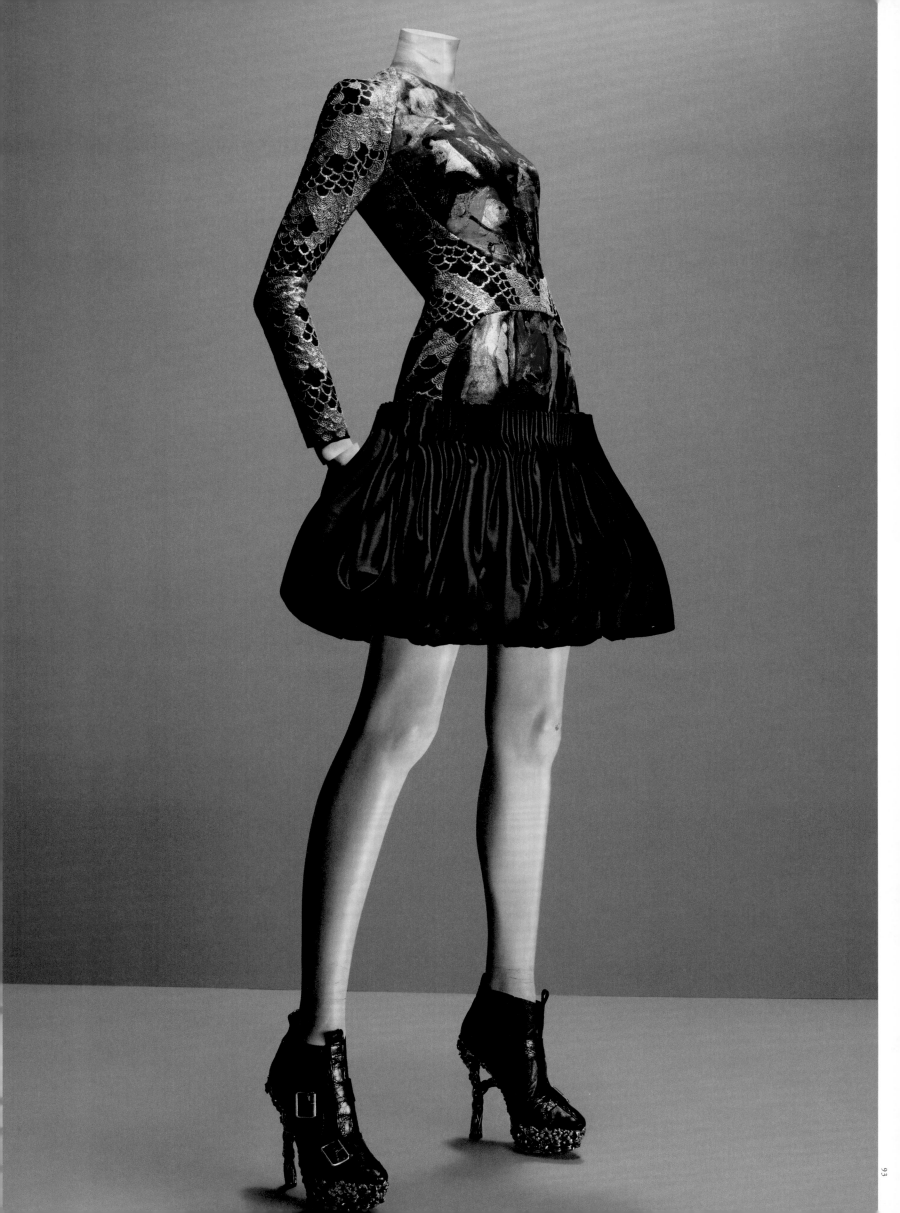

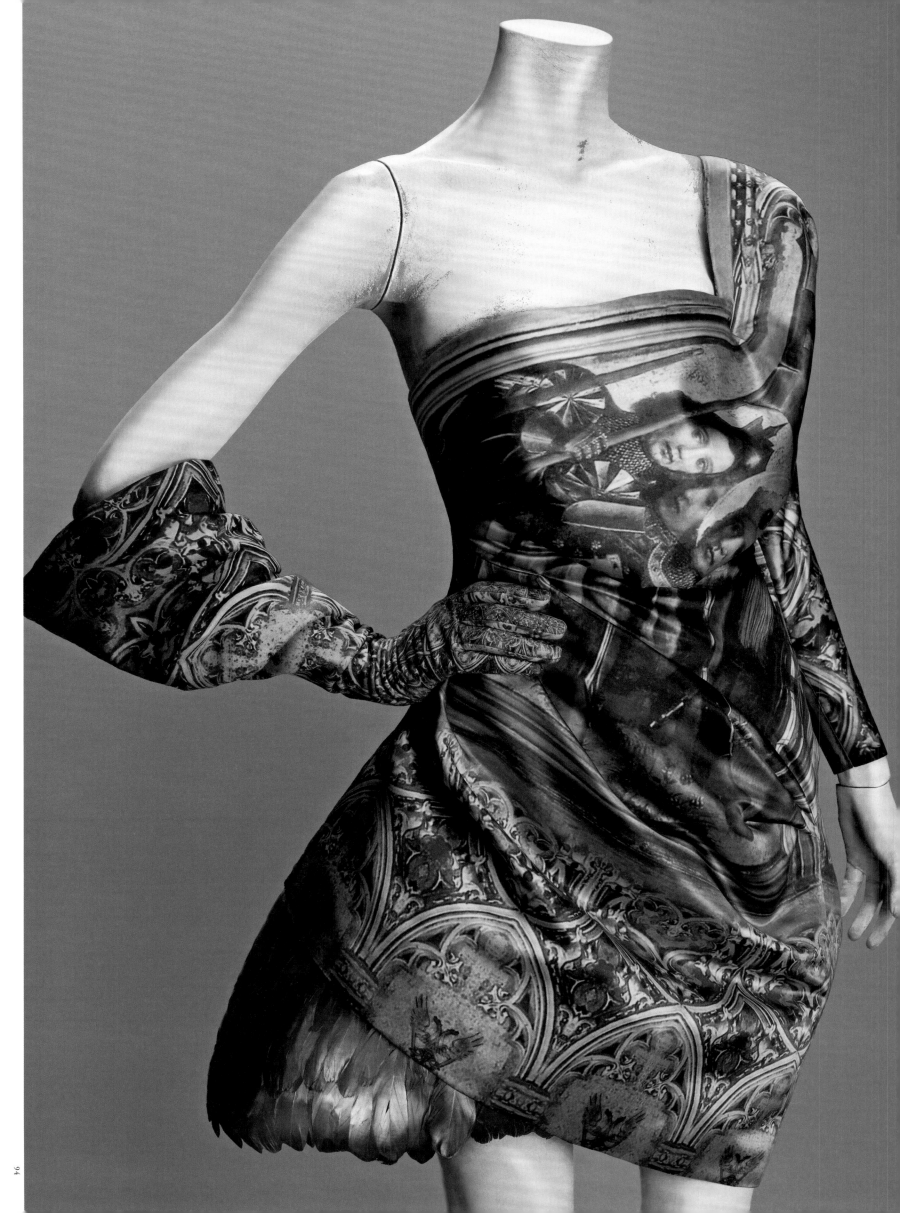

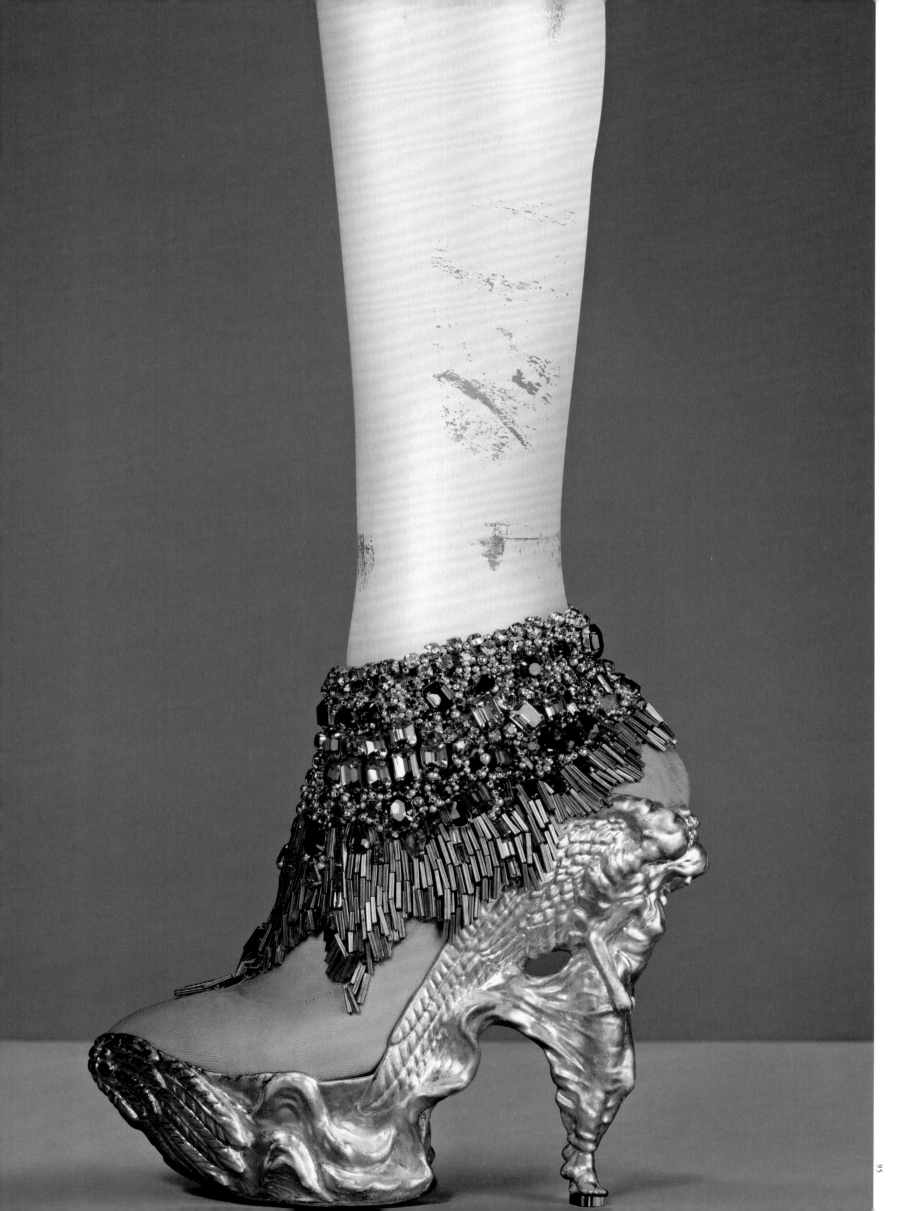

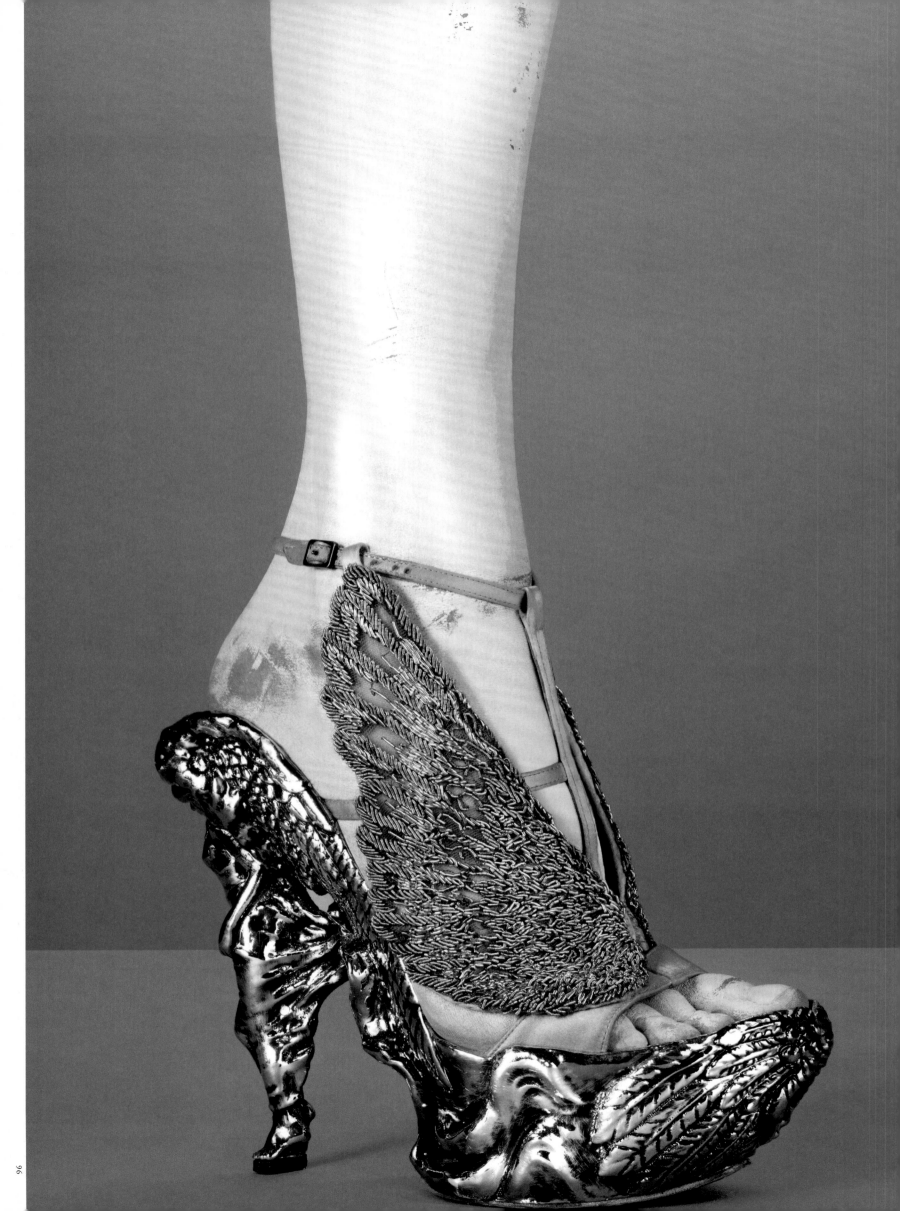

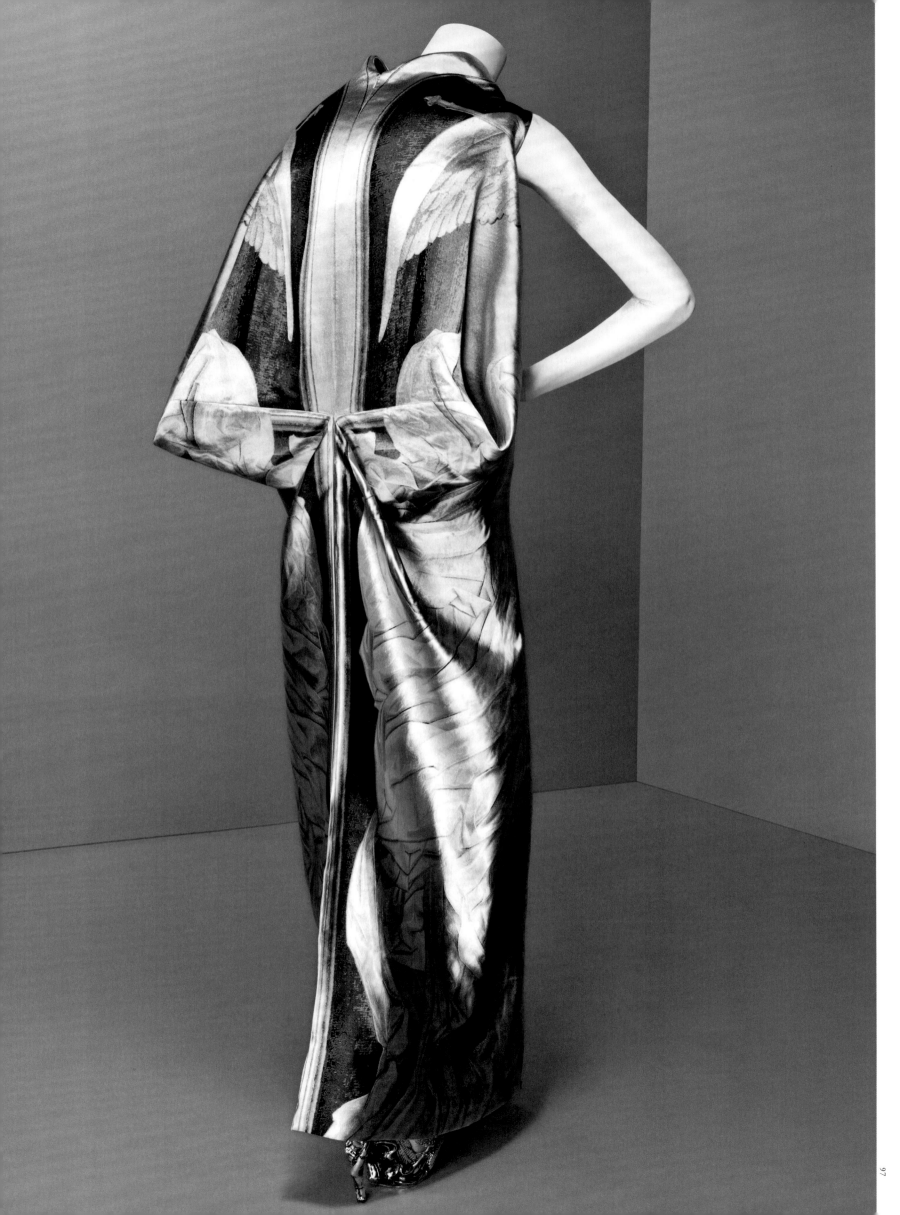

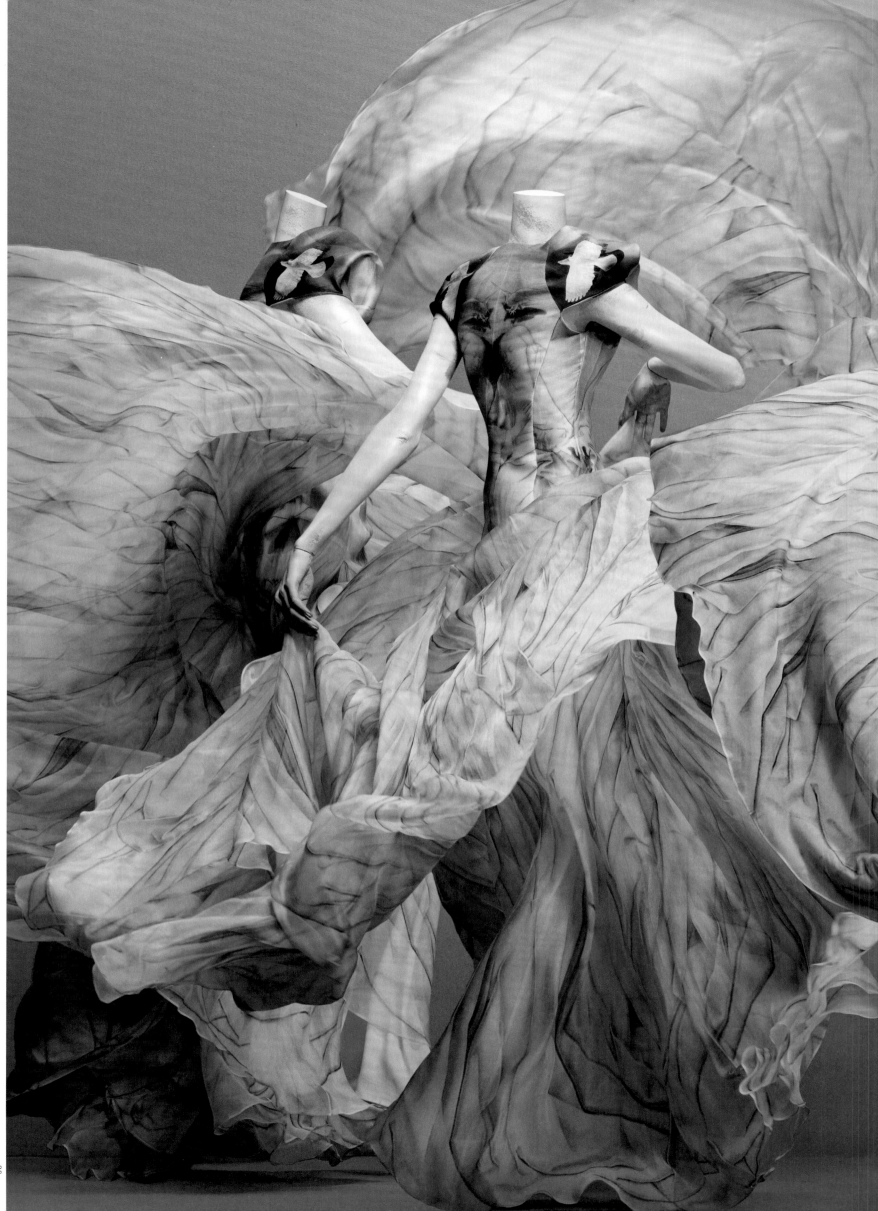

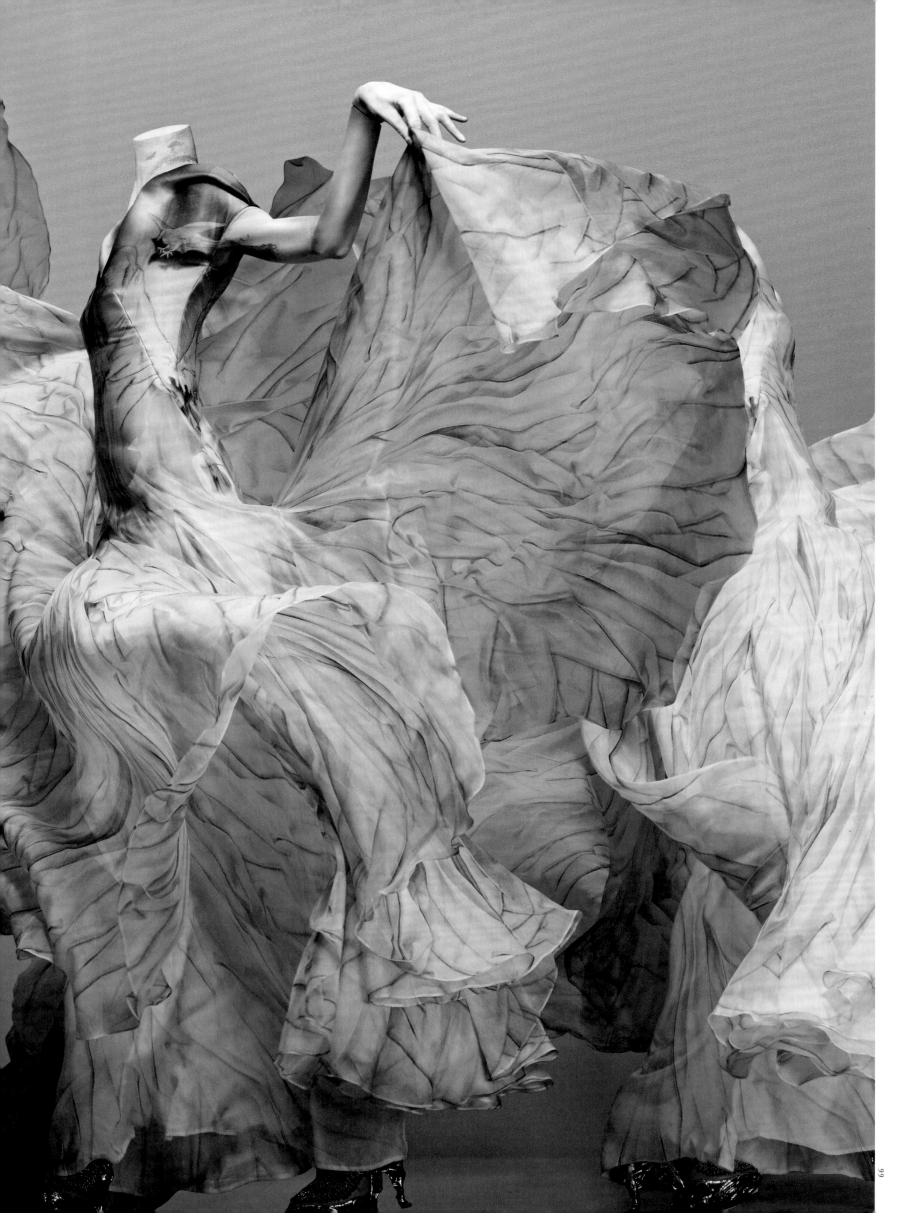

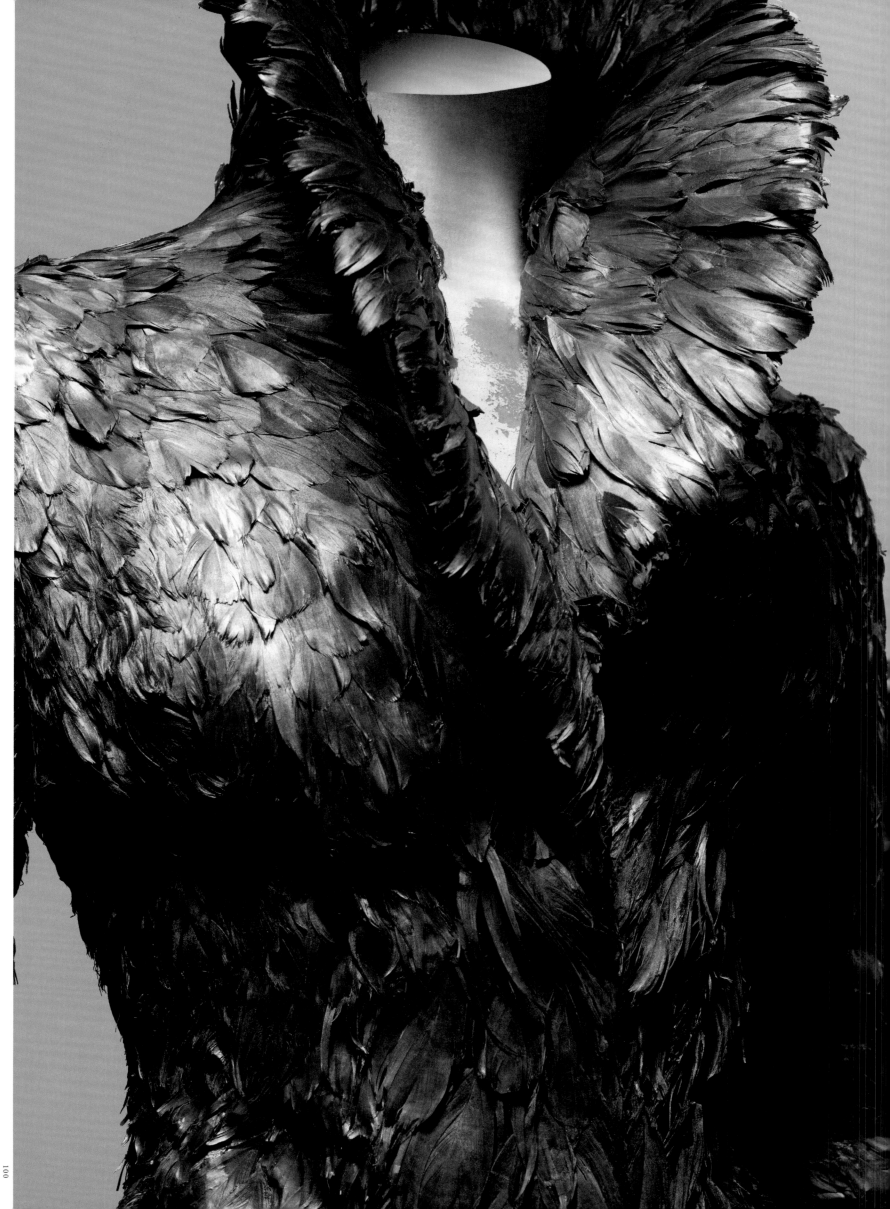

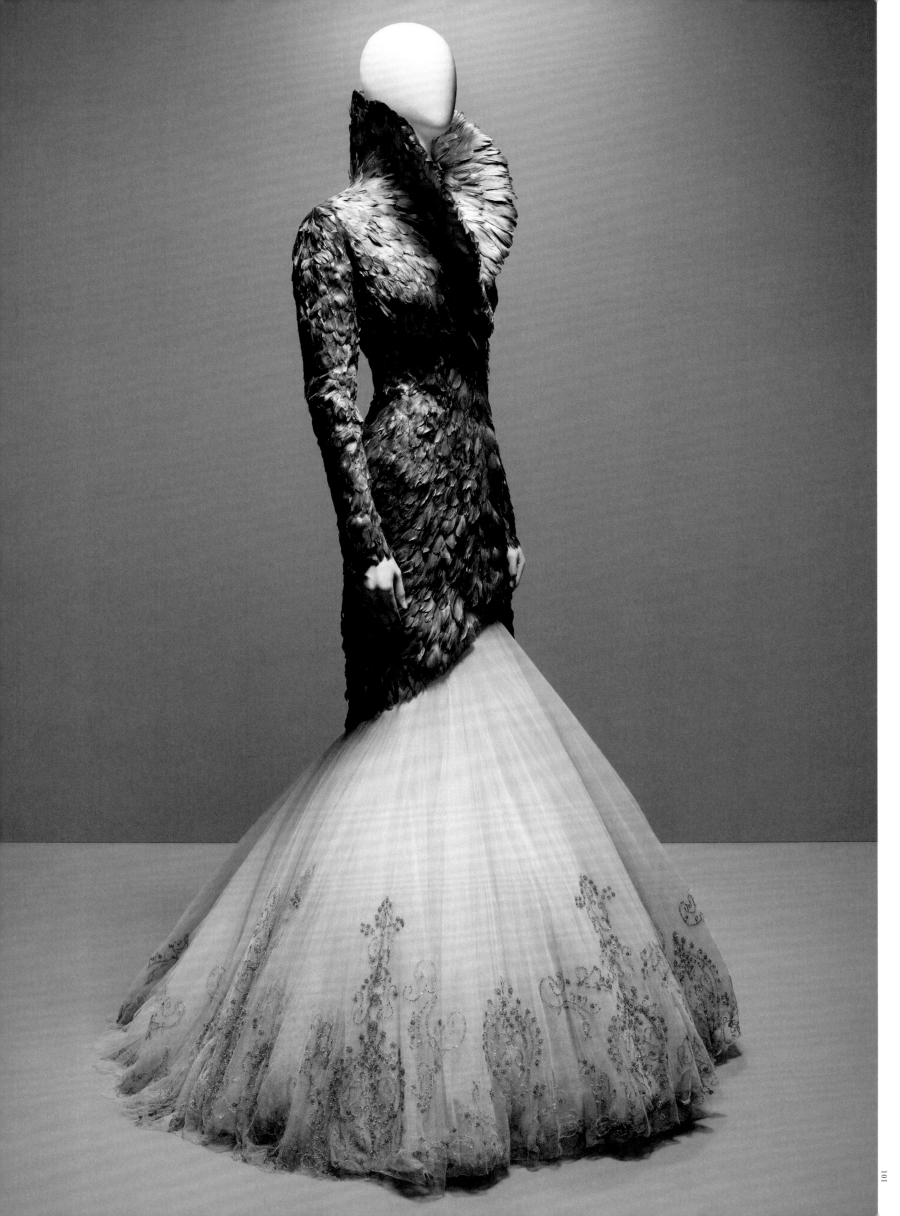

"Scotland for me is a harsh, cold and bitter place. It was even worse when my great, great grandfather used to live there. . . . The reason I'm patriotic about Scotland is because I think it's been dealt a really hard hand. It's marketed the world over as . . . haggis . . . bagpipes. But no one ever puts anything back into it."

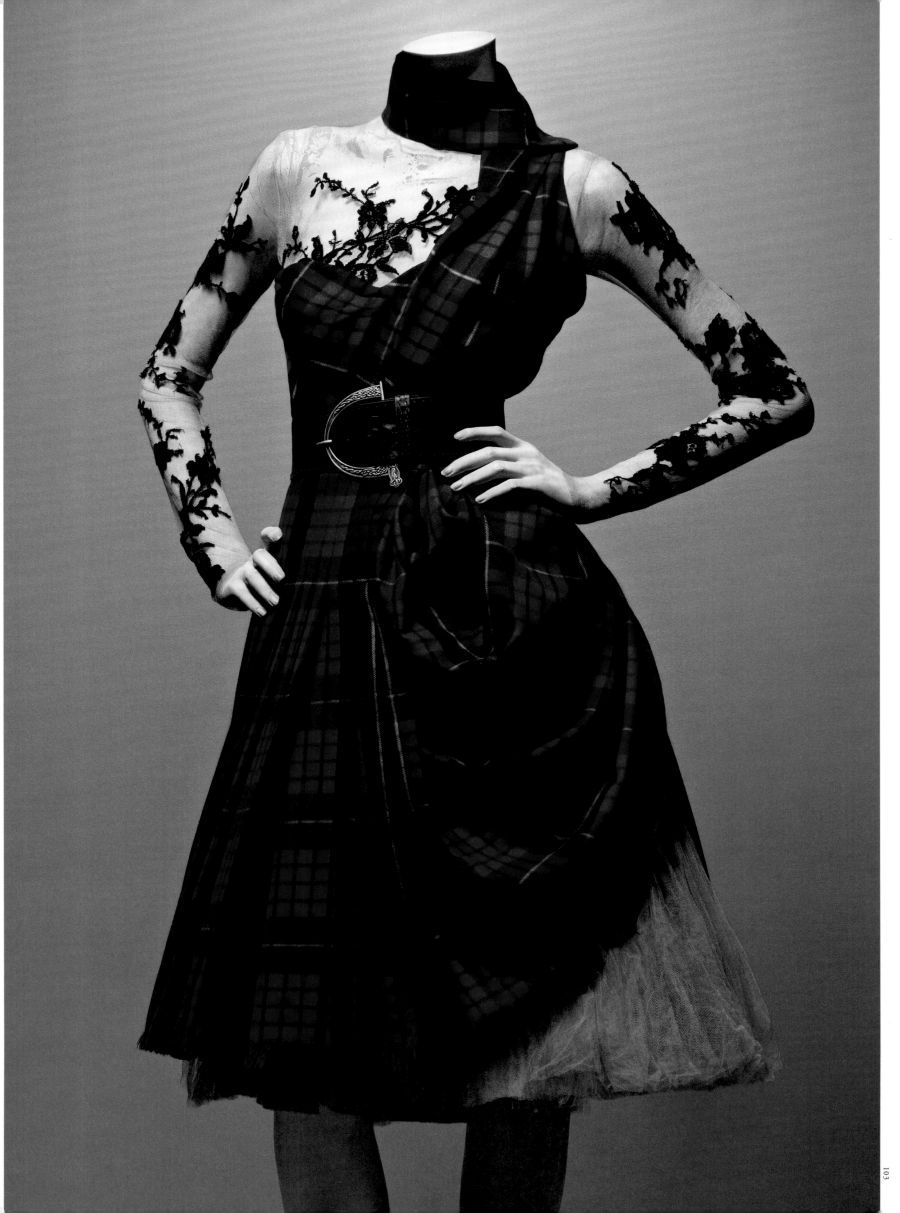

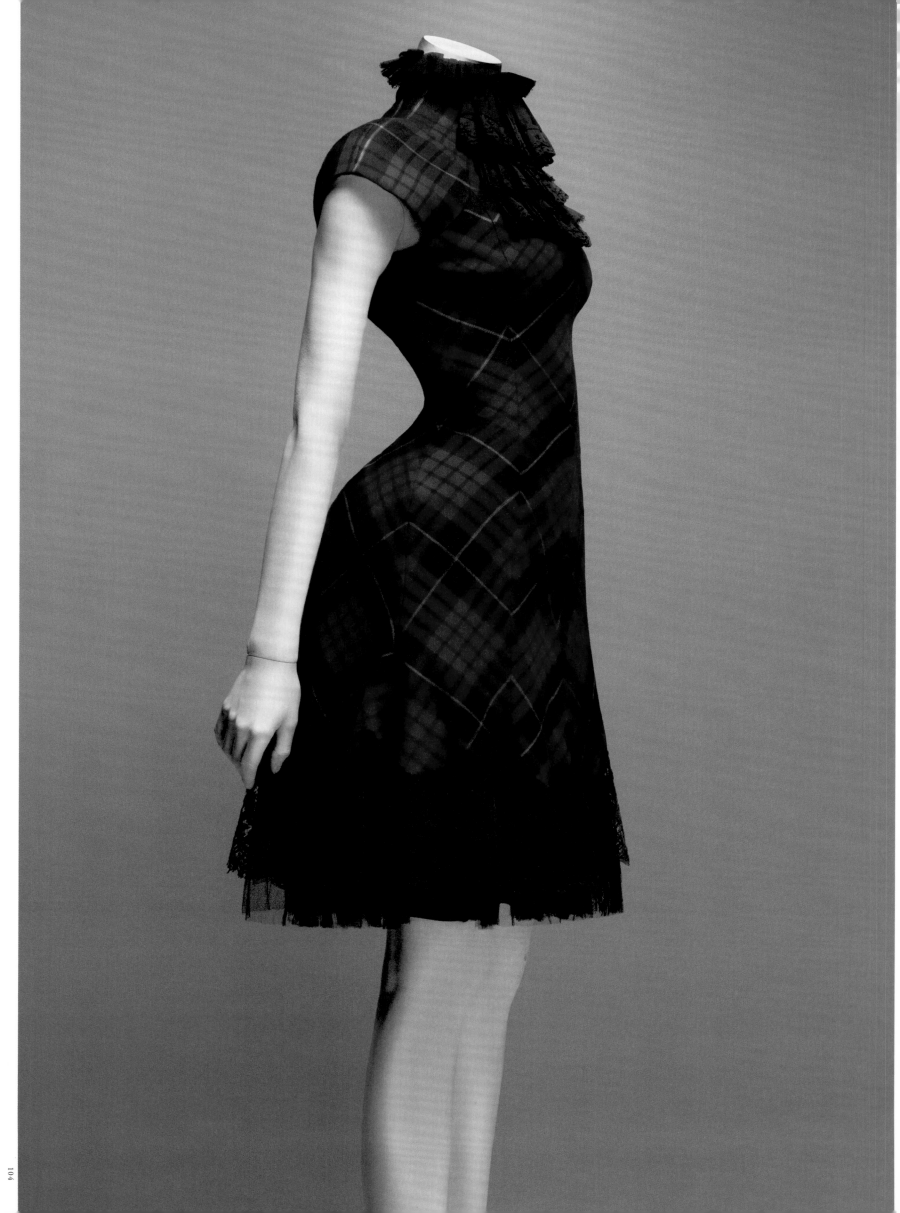

"[This] collection is . . . romantic but melancholic and austere at the same time. It was gentle but you could still feel the bite of the cold, the nip of the ice on the end of your nose. . . . With bustles and nipped waists, I was interested in the idea that there are no constraints on the silhouette. I wanted to exaggerate a woman's form, almost along the lines of a classical statue."

"During the nineties, care and attention to detail got lost somehow. This collection is about going back to [a] level of refinement. Every piece is unique and has emotional content. I want to create pieces that can be handed down, like an heirloom."

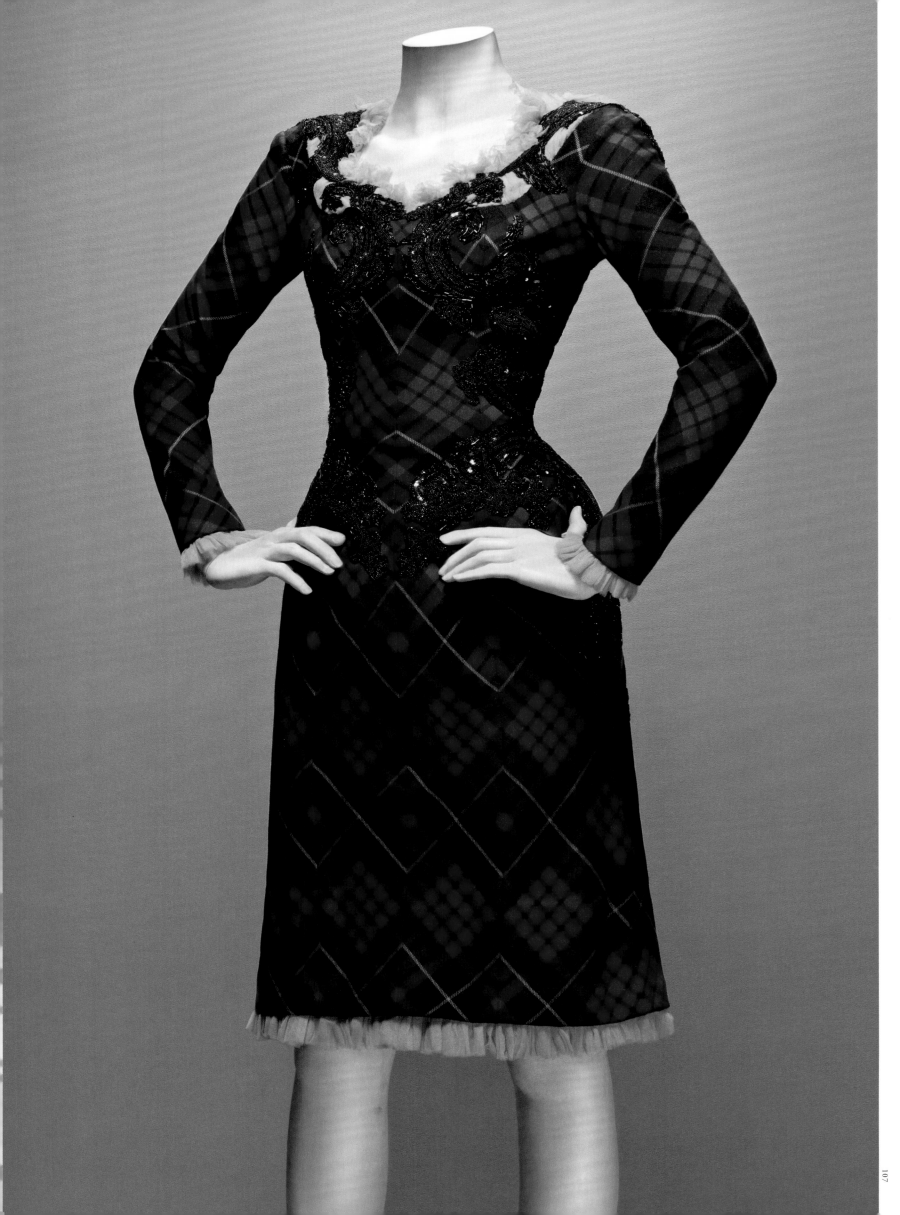

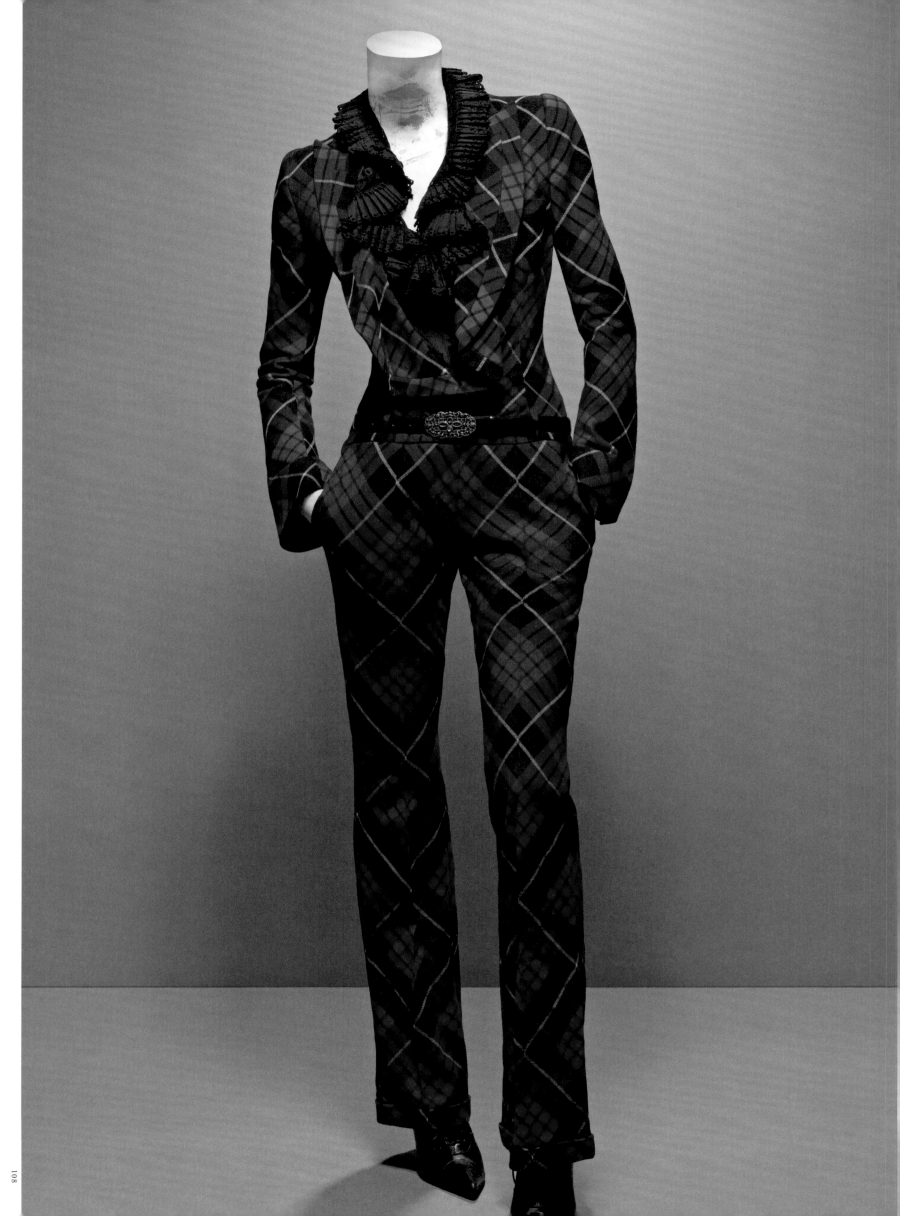

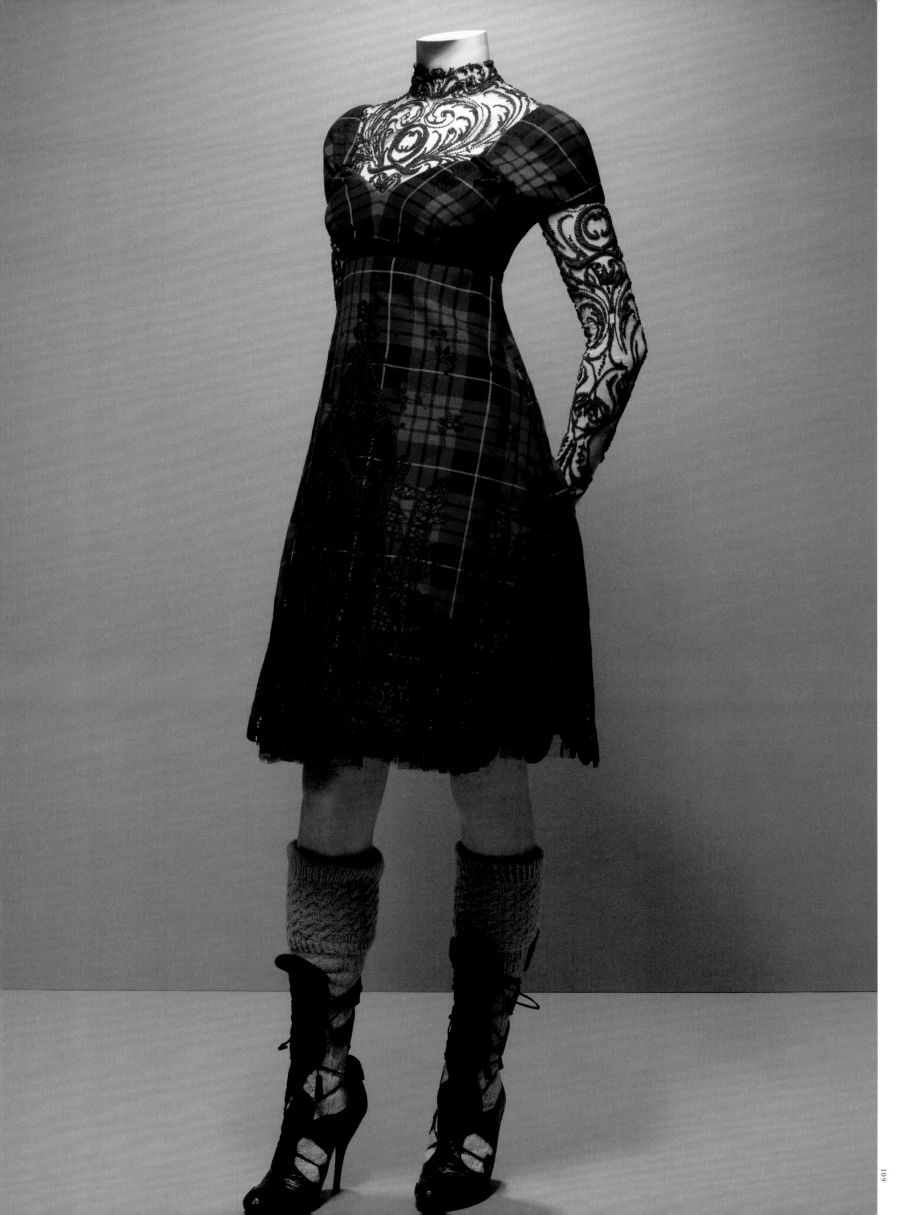

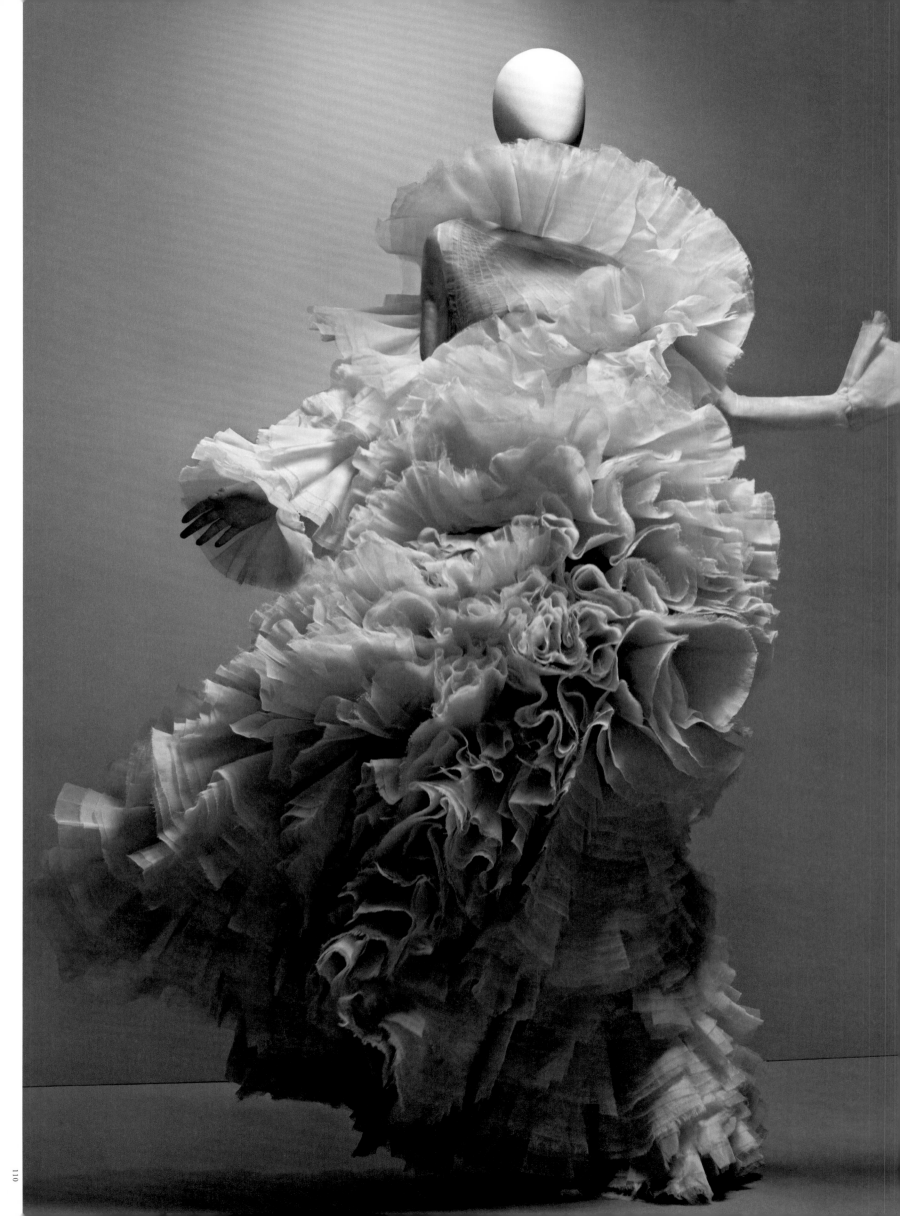

"I'm an avid follower of the news, and sometimes

you just can't take any more war, any more disasters,

and you want to remind yourself there's beauty in

the world. [With this collection] I wanted to show a

more poetic side to my work. It was all about . . .

a feeling of sadness, but in a cinematic kind of way.

I find beauty in melancholy."

"Britain always led the way in every field possible in the world from art to pop music. Even from the days of Henry VIII. It's a nation where people come and gloat at what we have as a valuable heritage, be it some good, some bad, but there's no place like it on earth."

"As a place for inspiration it's the best in the world. . . . You're inspired by the anarchy in the country."

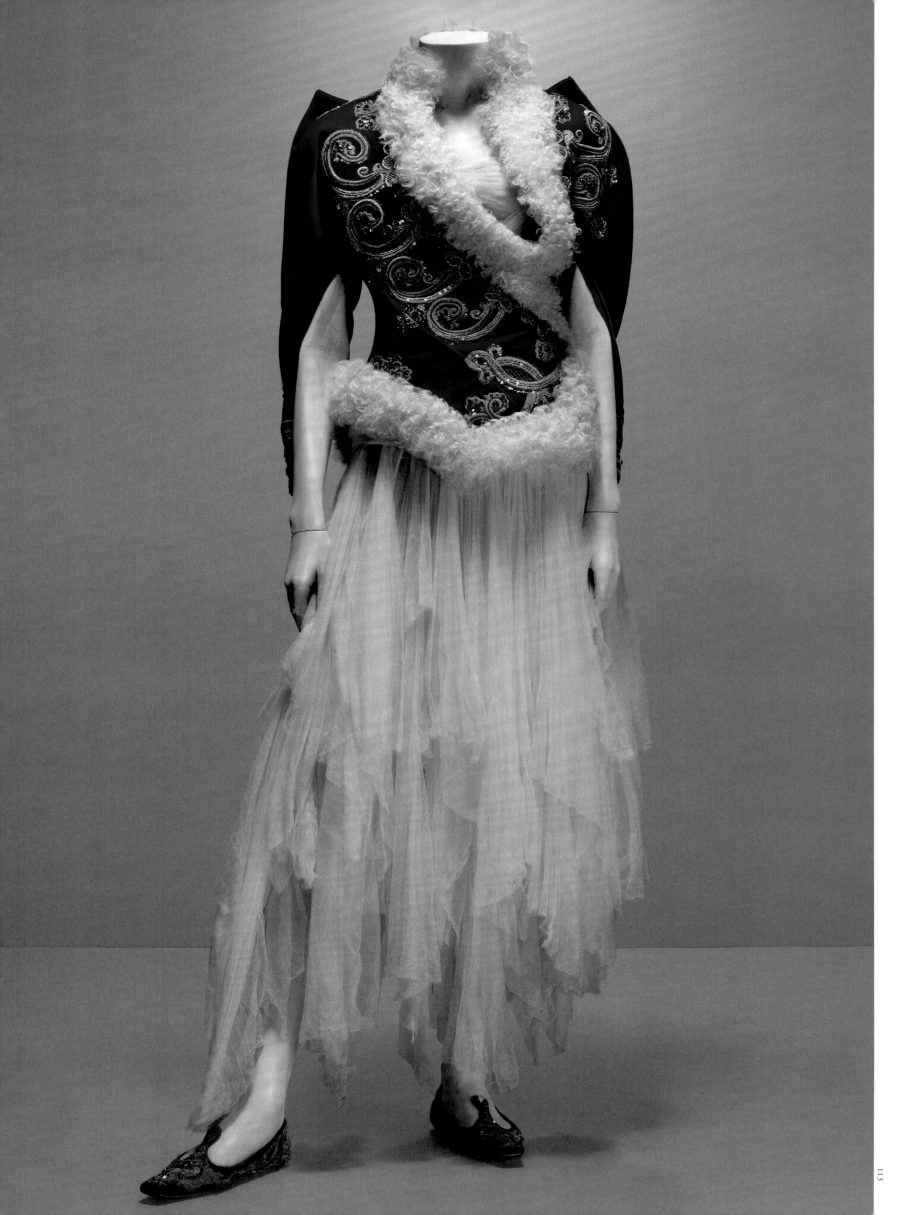

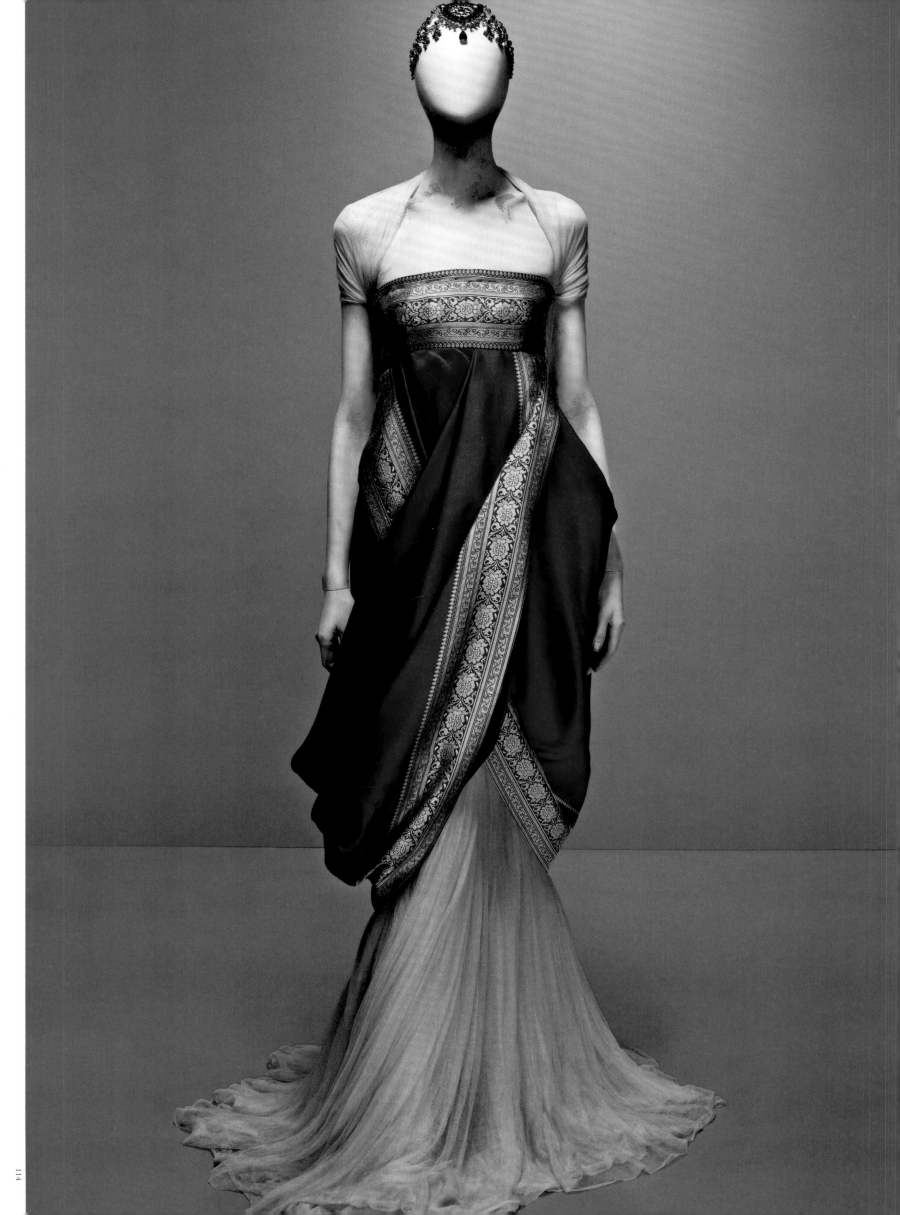

"When I design, I try to sell an image of a woman that I have in [my] mind, a concept that changes dramatically each season."

"[In this collection] she was a feral creature living in the tree. When she decided to descend to earth, she was transformed into a princess."

"I don't really get inspired [by specific women]. . . . It's more in the minds of the women in the past, like Catherine the Great, or Marie Antoinette. People who were doomed. Joan of Arc or Colette. Iconic women."

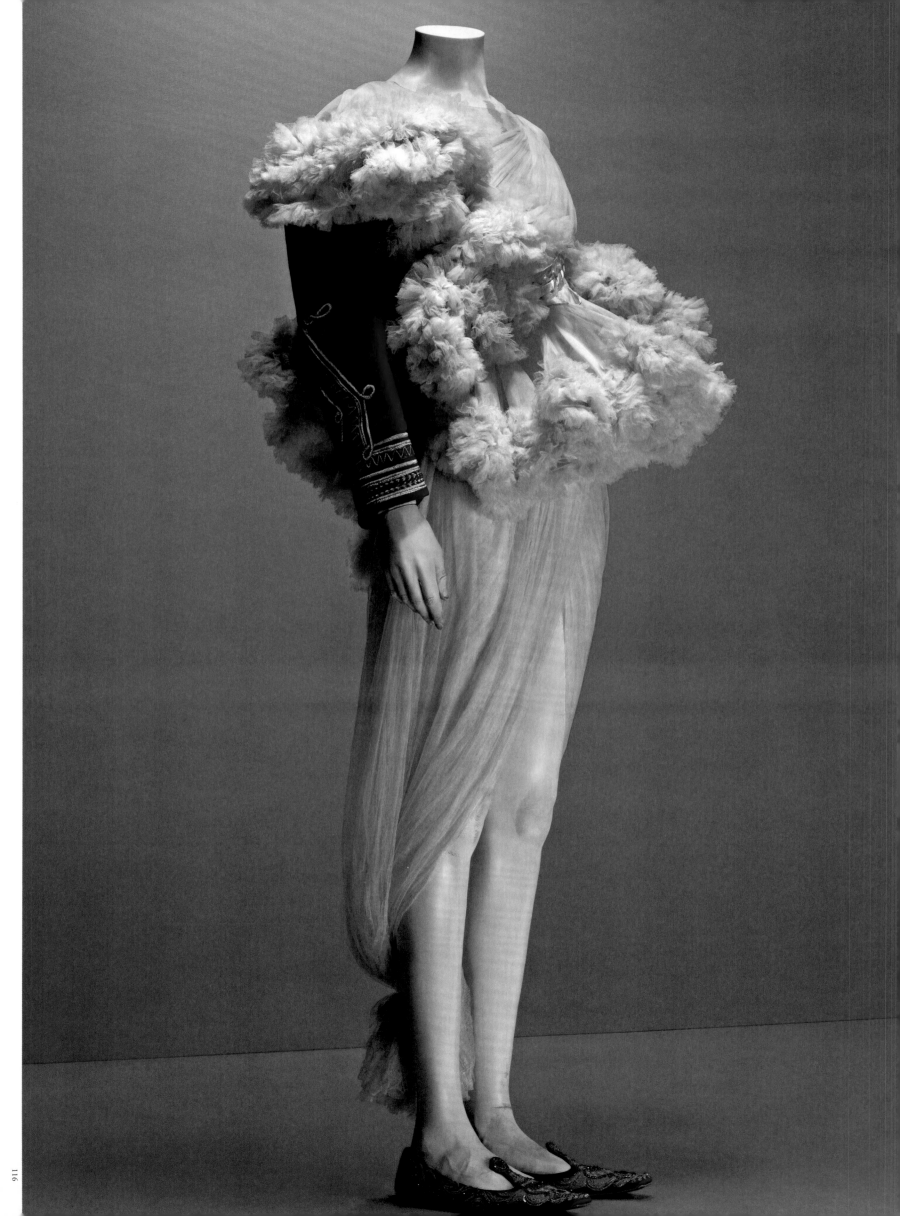

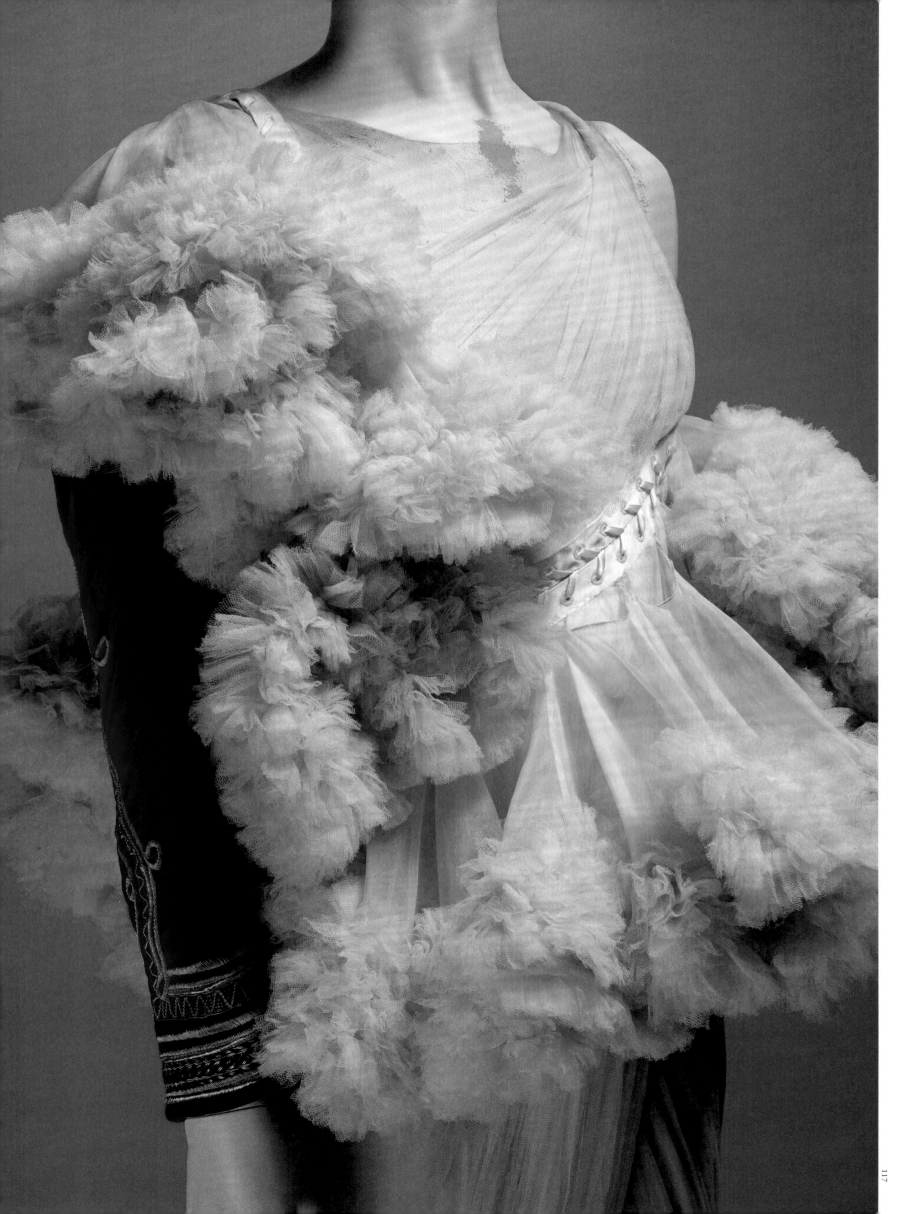

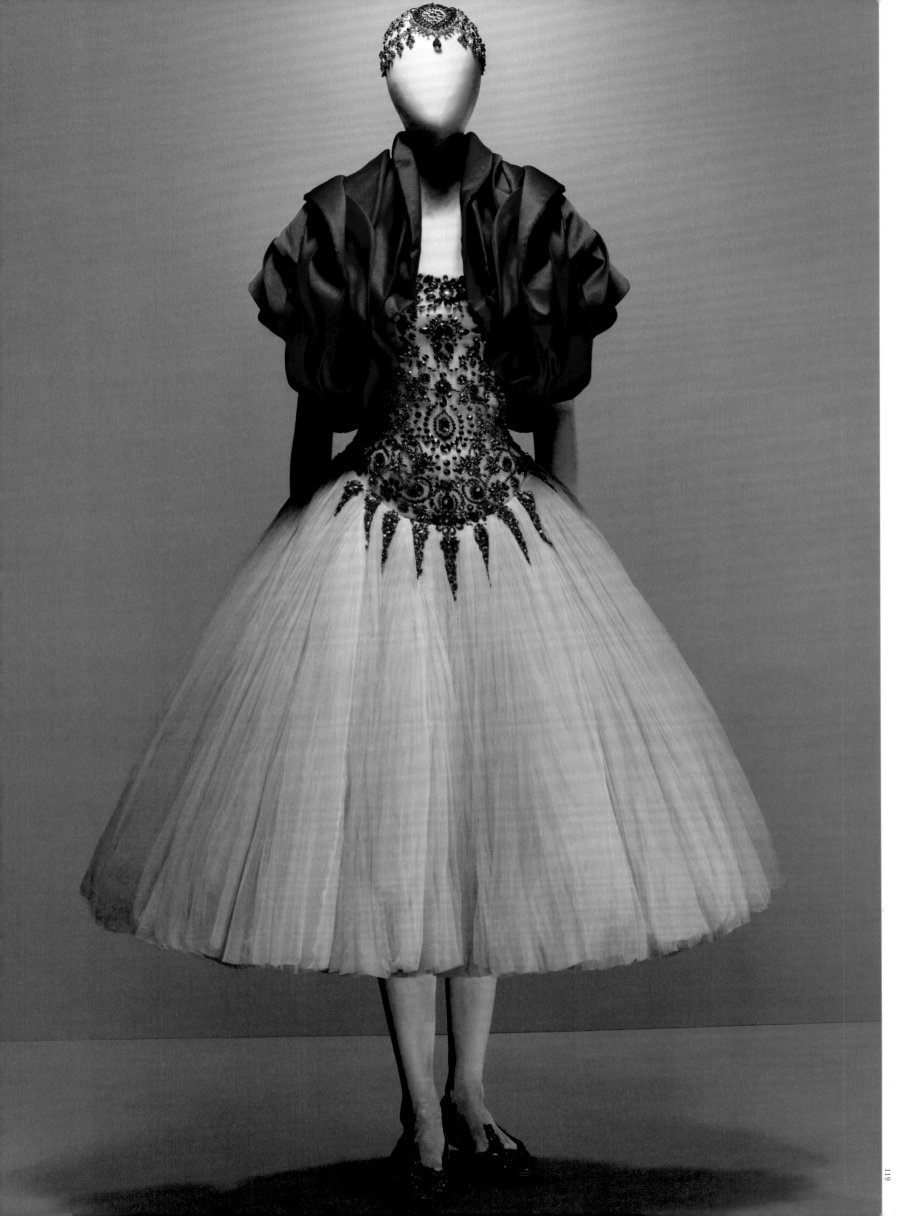

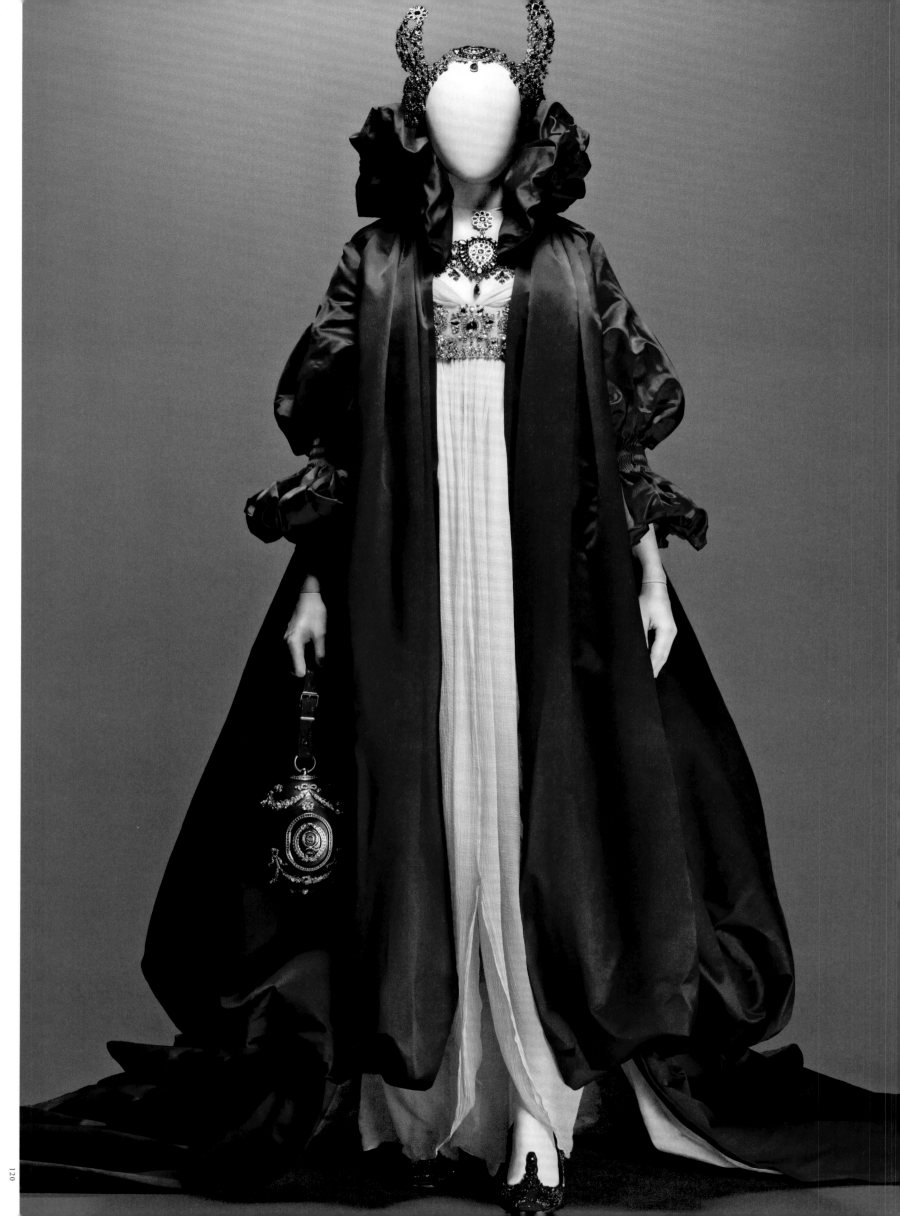

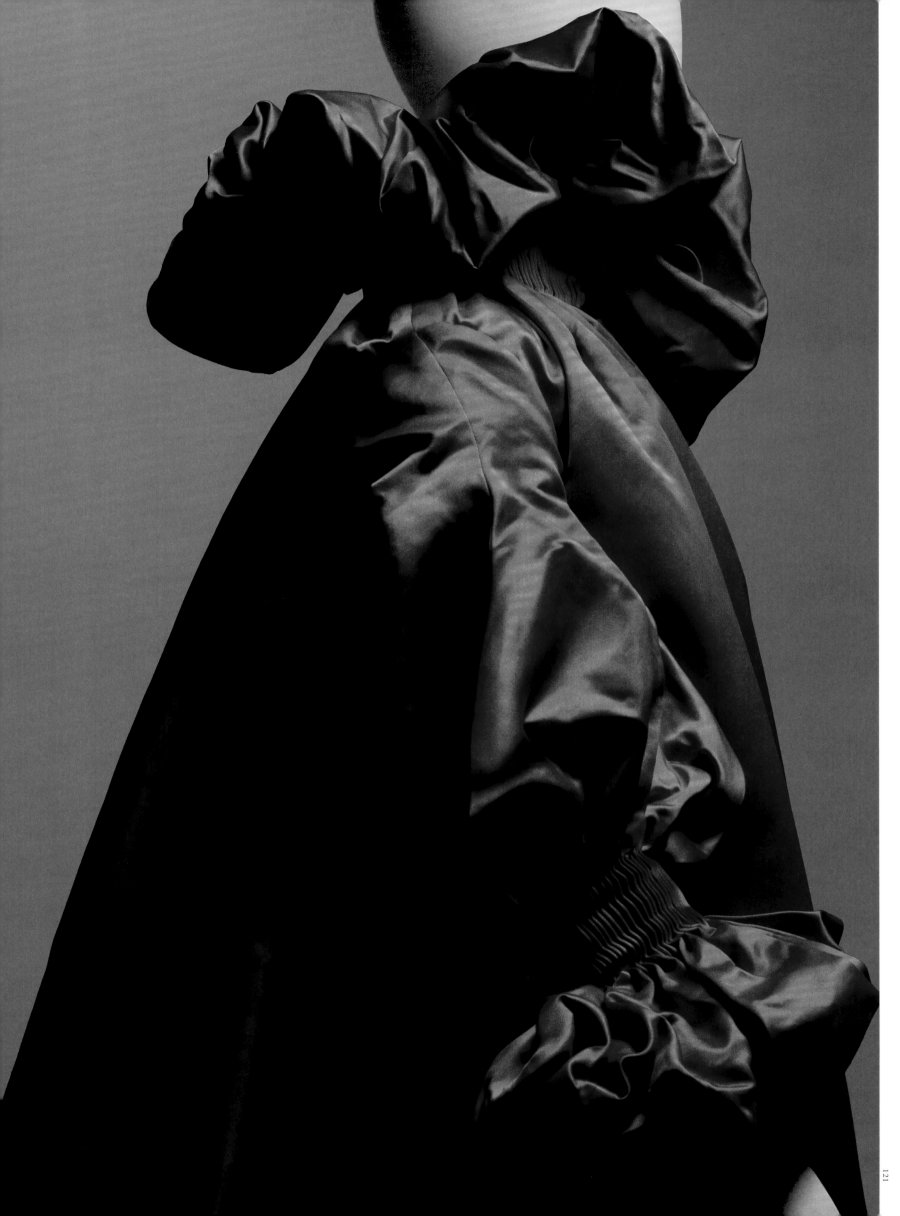

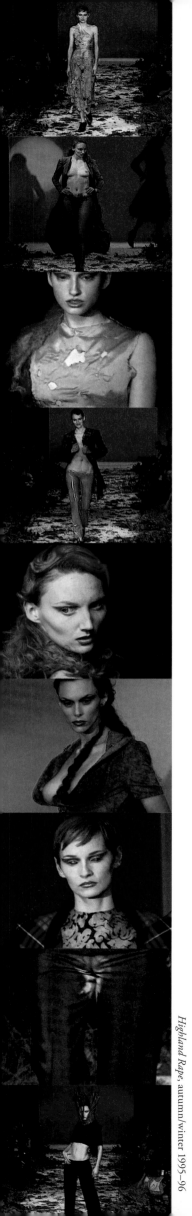

"[This collection] was a shout against English designers . . . doing flamboyant Scottish clothes. My father's family originates from the Isle of Skye, and I'd studied the history of the Scottish upheavals and the Clearances. People were so unintelligent they thought this was about women being raped—yet *Highland Rape* was about England's rape of Scotland."

Highland Rape, autumn/winter 1995–96

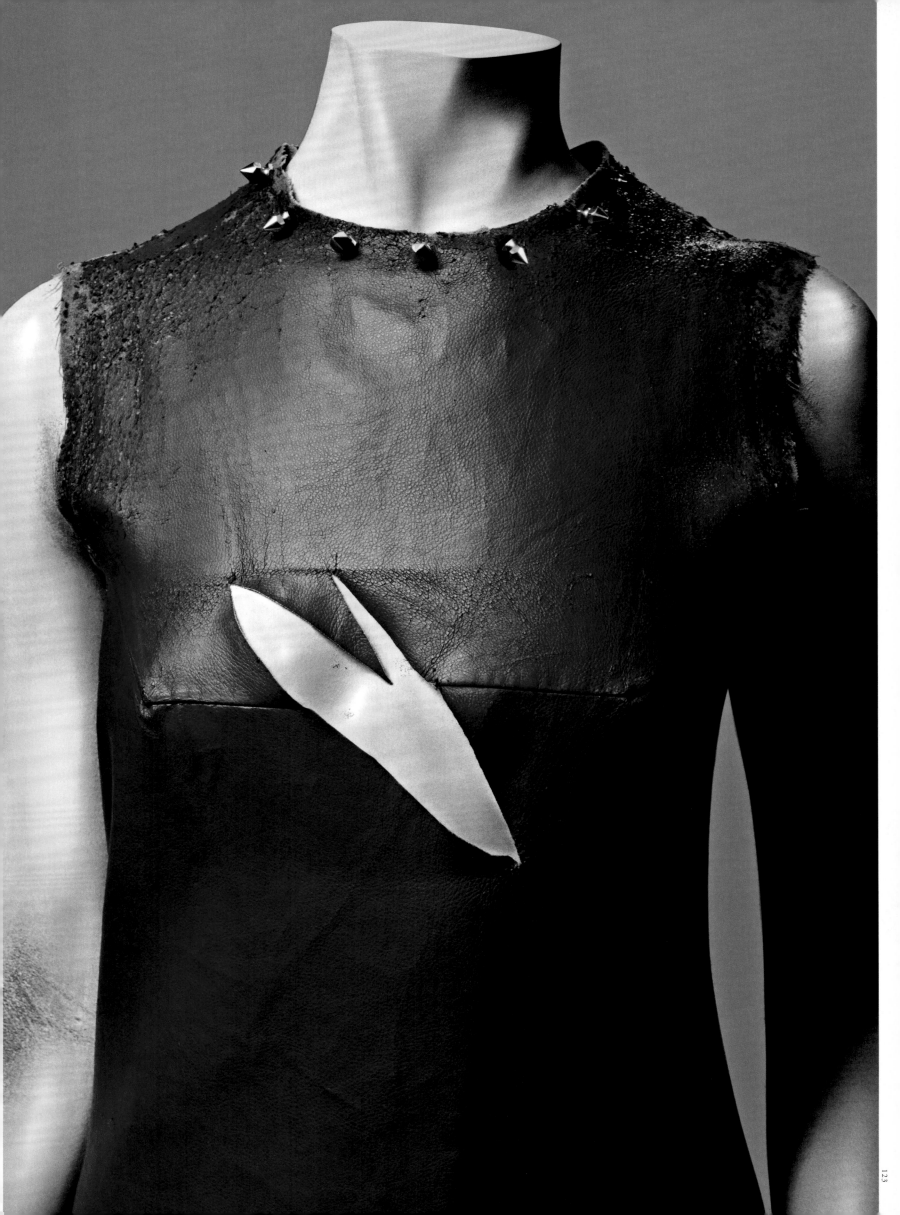

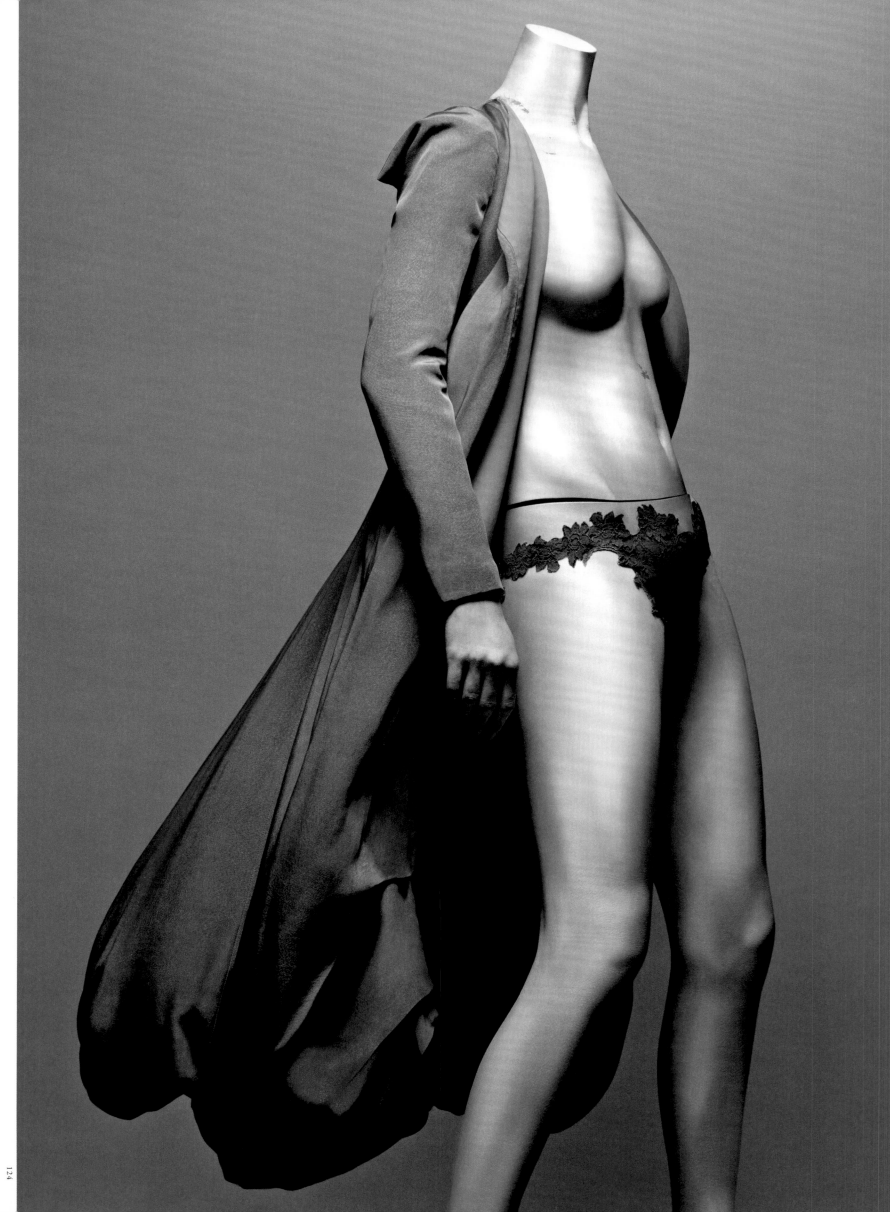

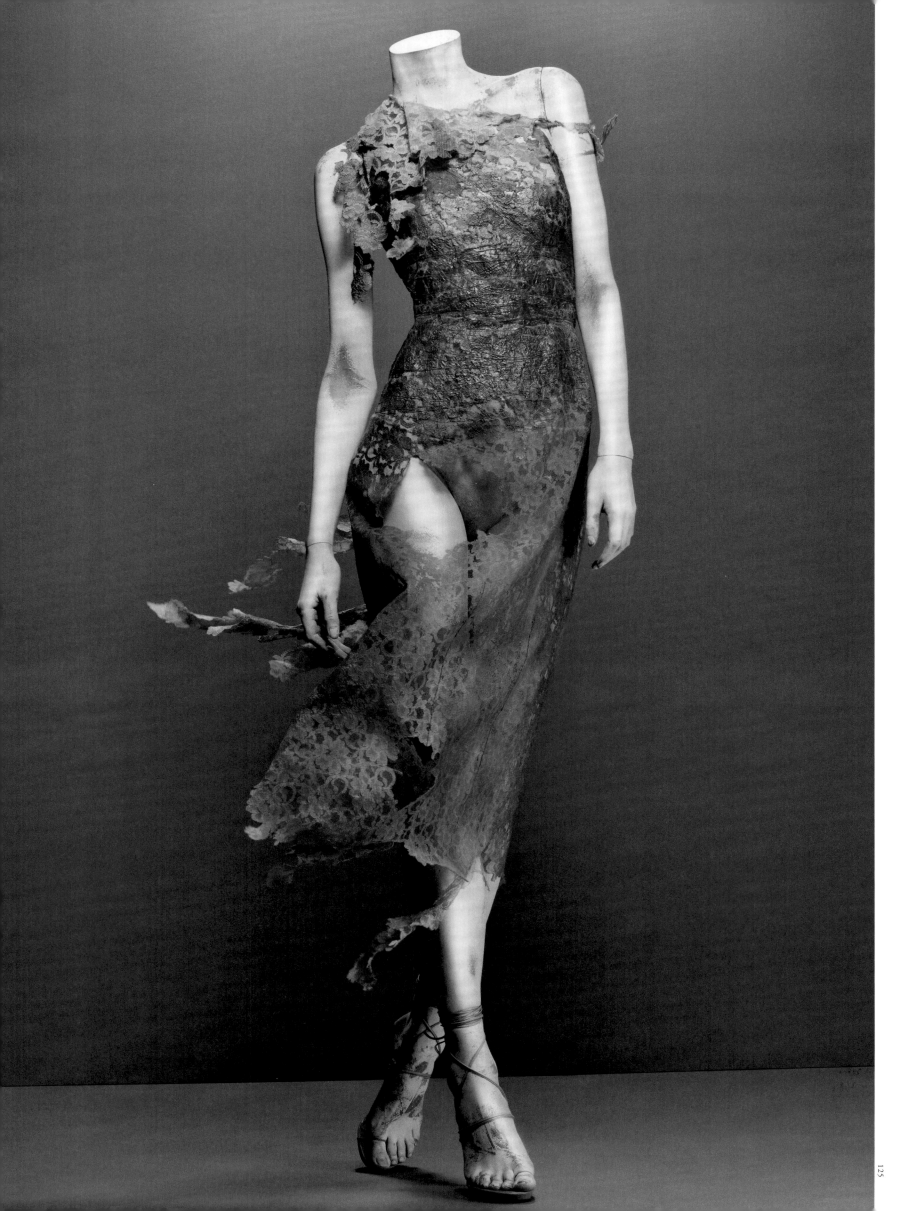

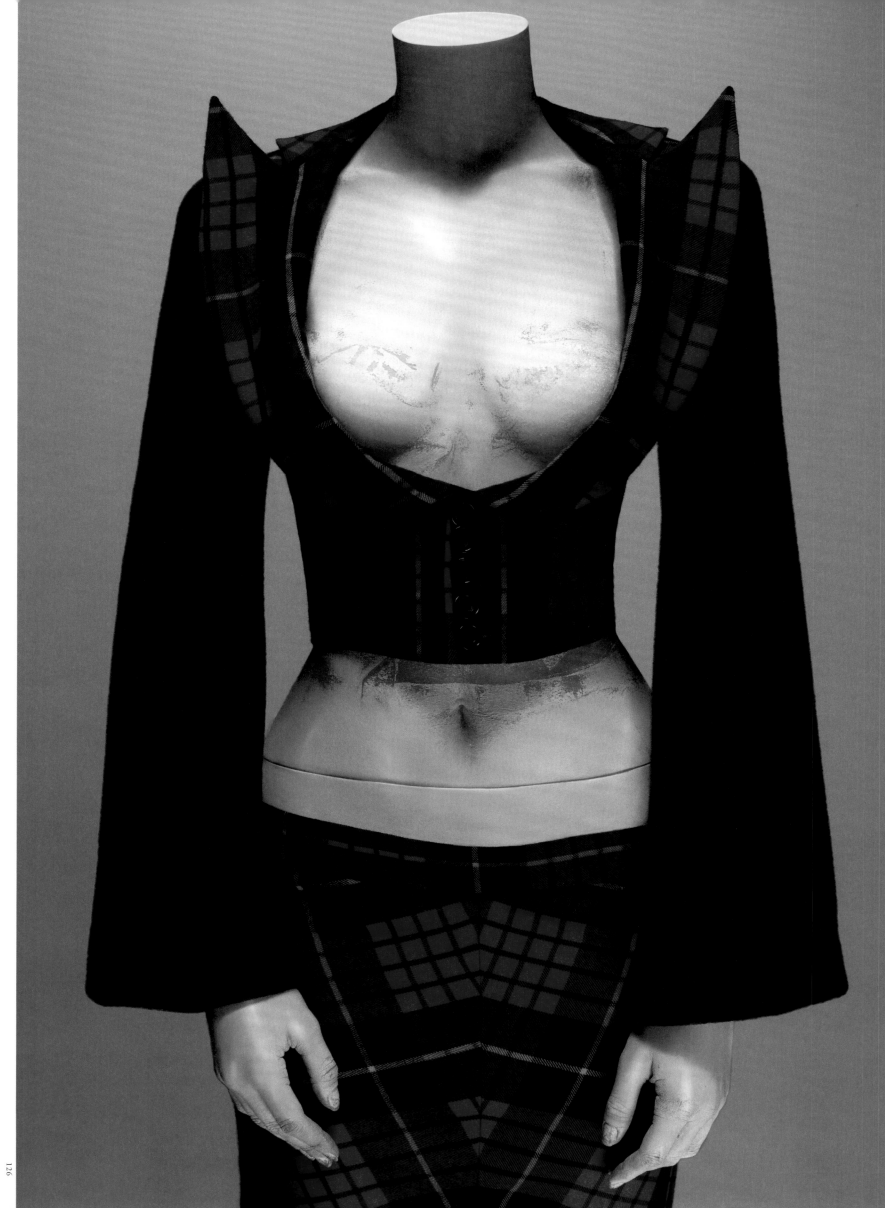

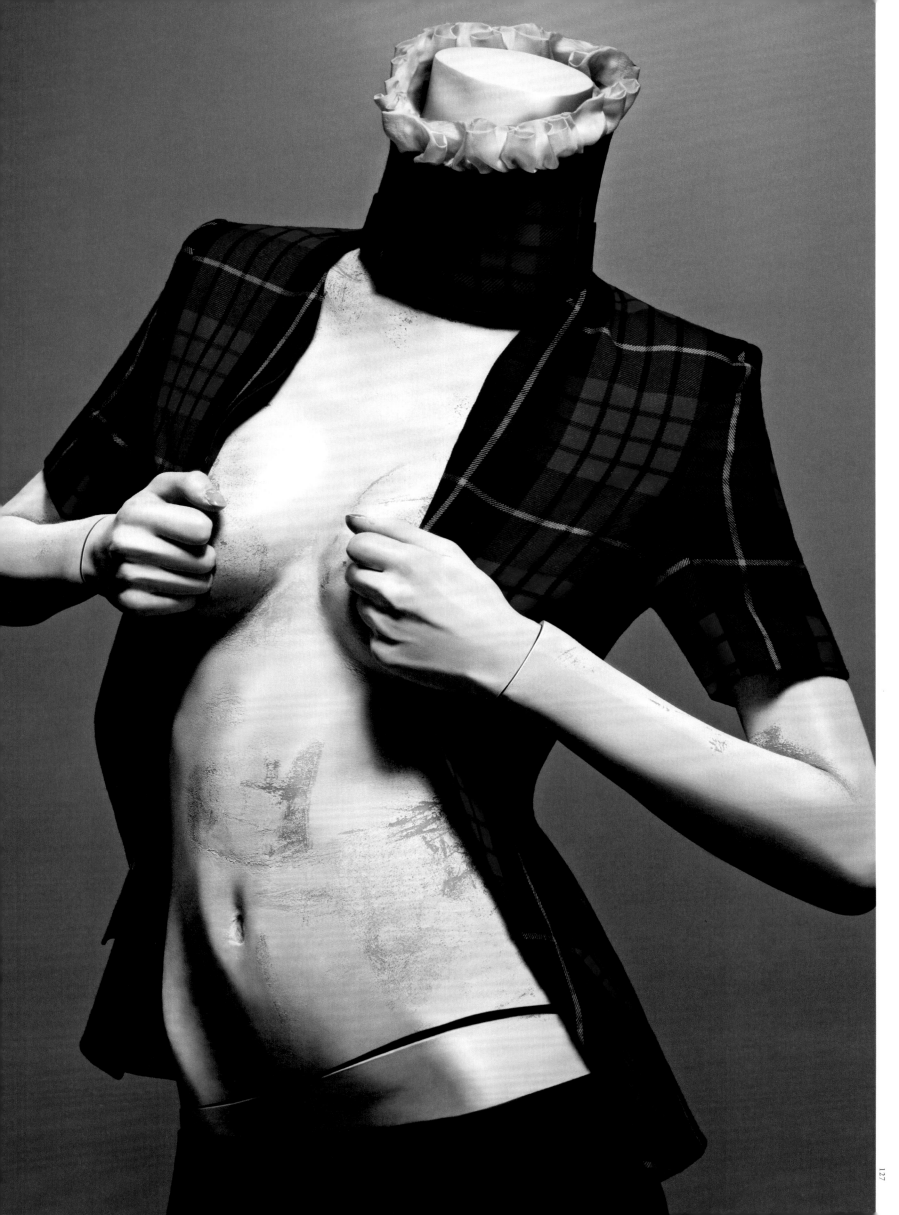

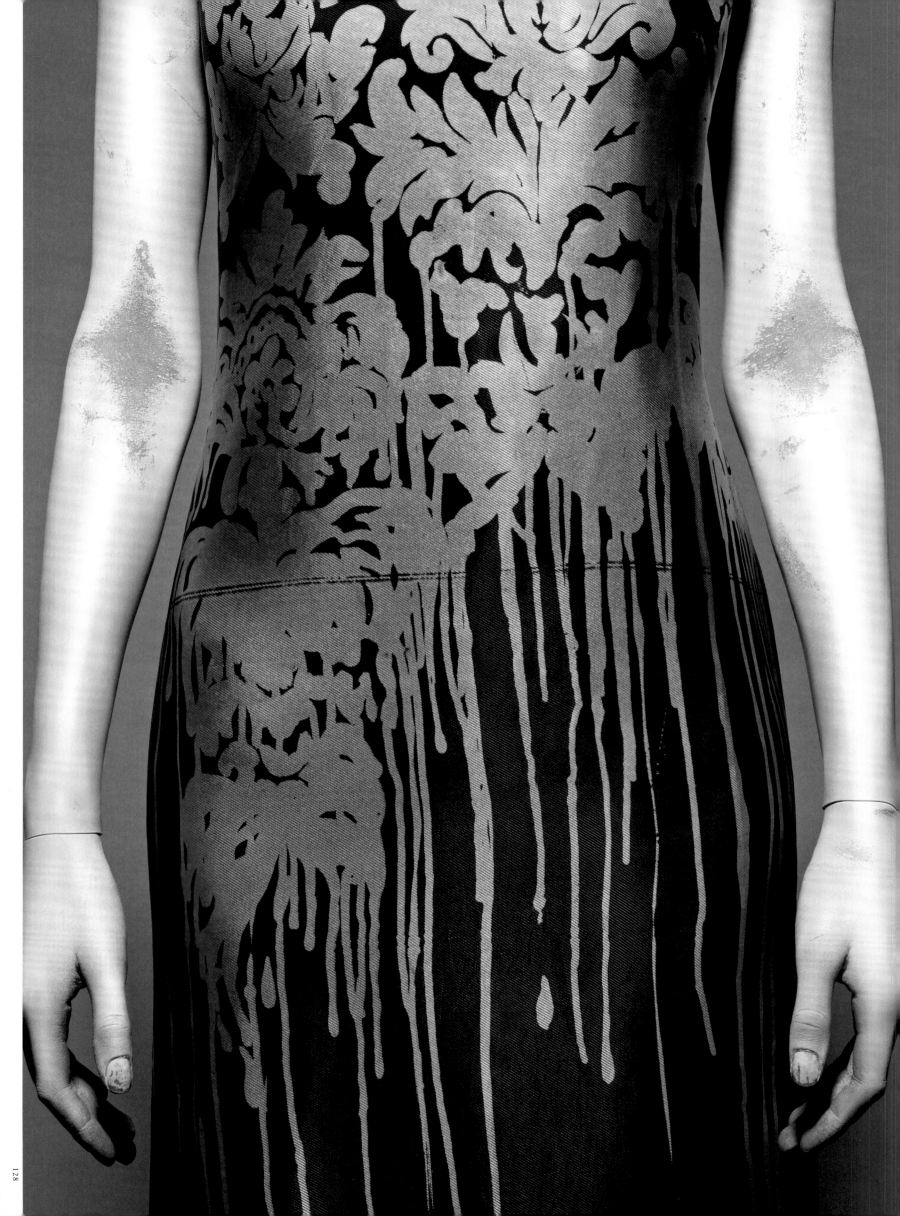

"Most of [this collection] was built on remnants from fabric shops. I think I made most everything myself."

"I want to be honest about the world that we live in, and sometimes my political persuasions come through in my work. Fashion can be really racist, looking at the clothes of other cultures as costumes. . . . That's mundane and it's old hat. Let's break down some barriers."

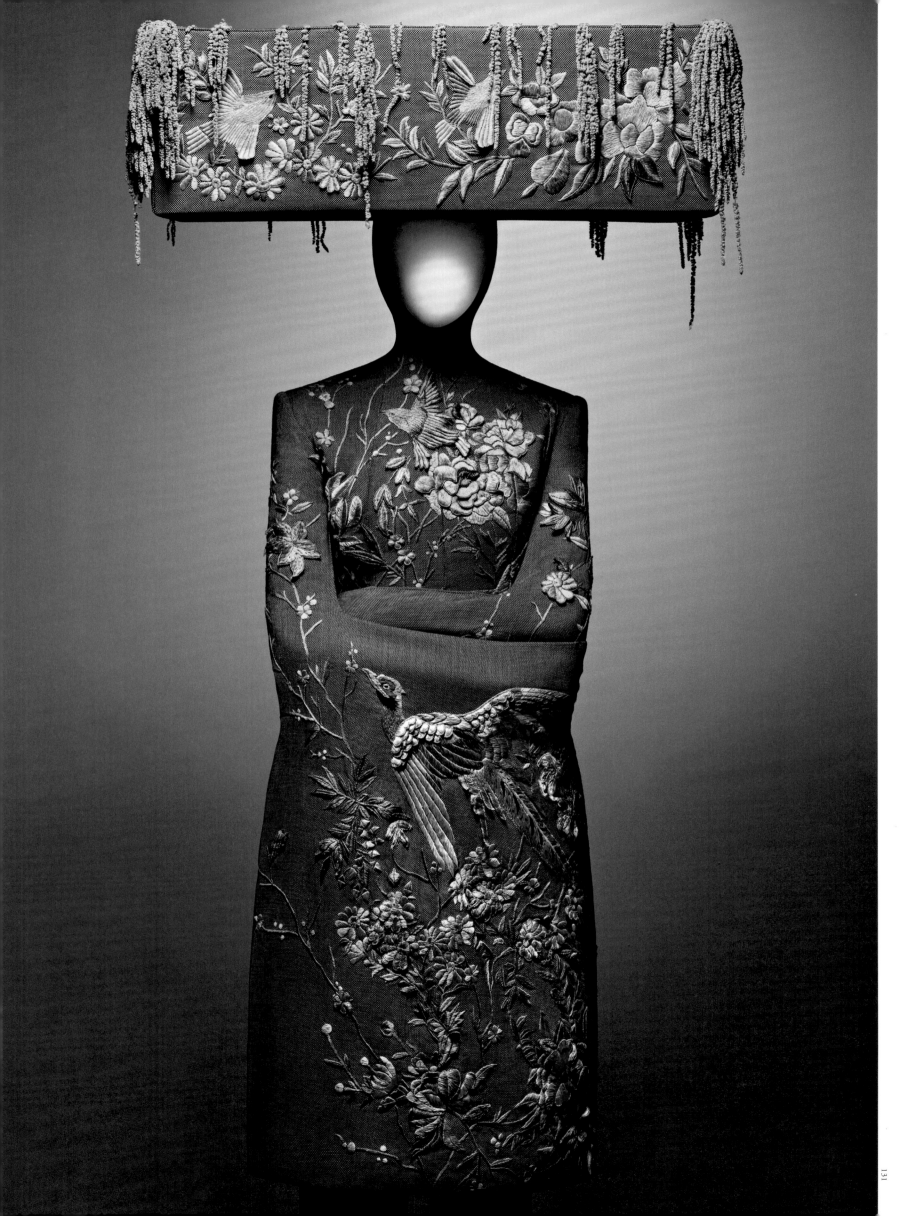

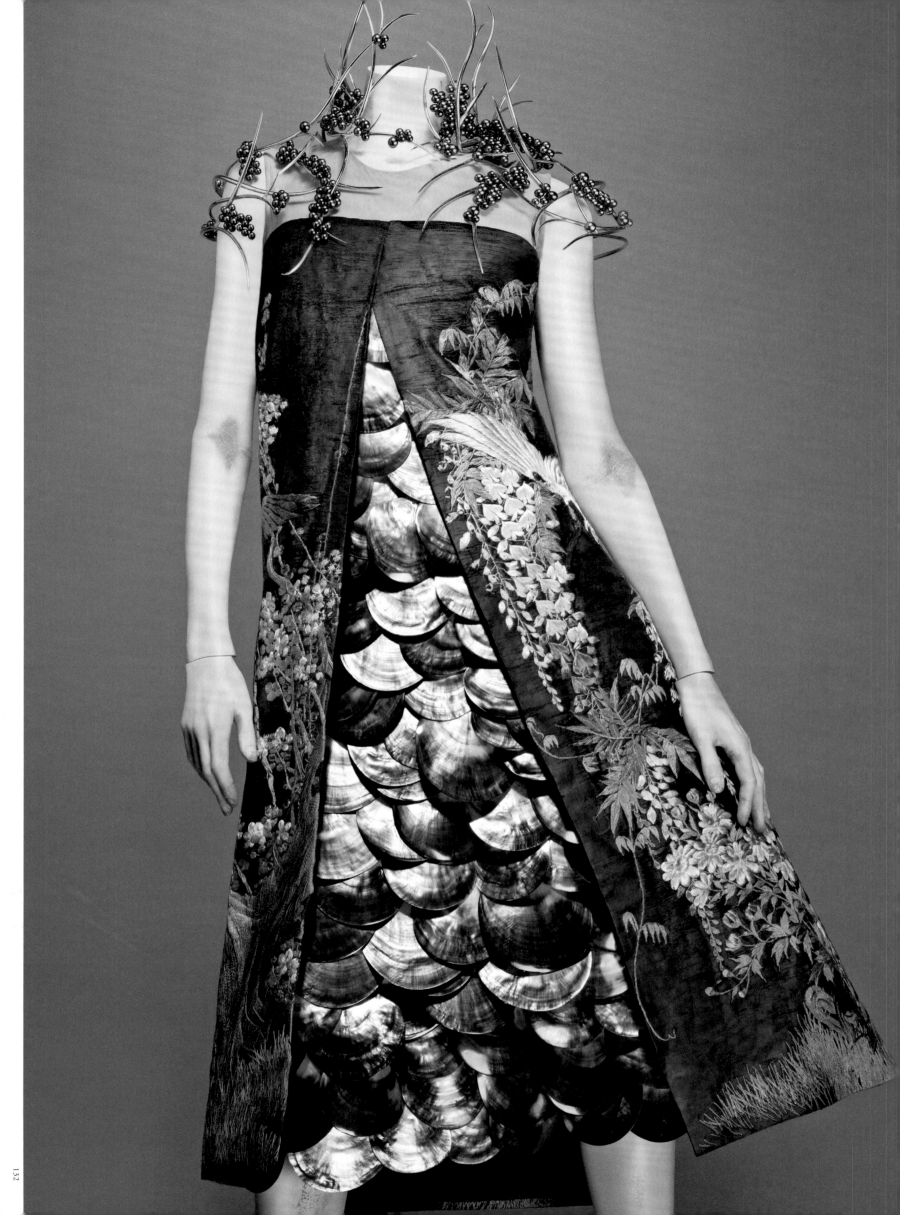

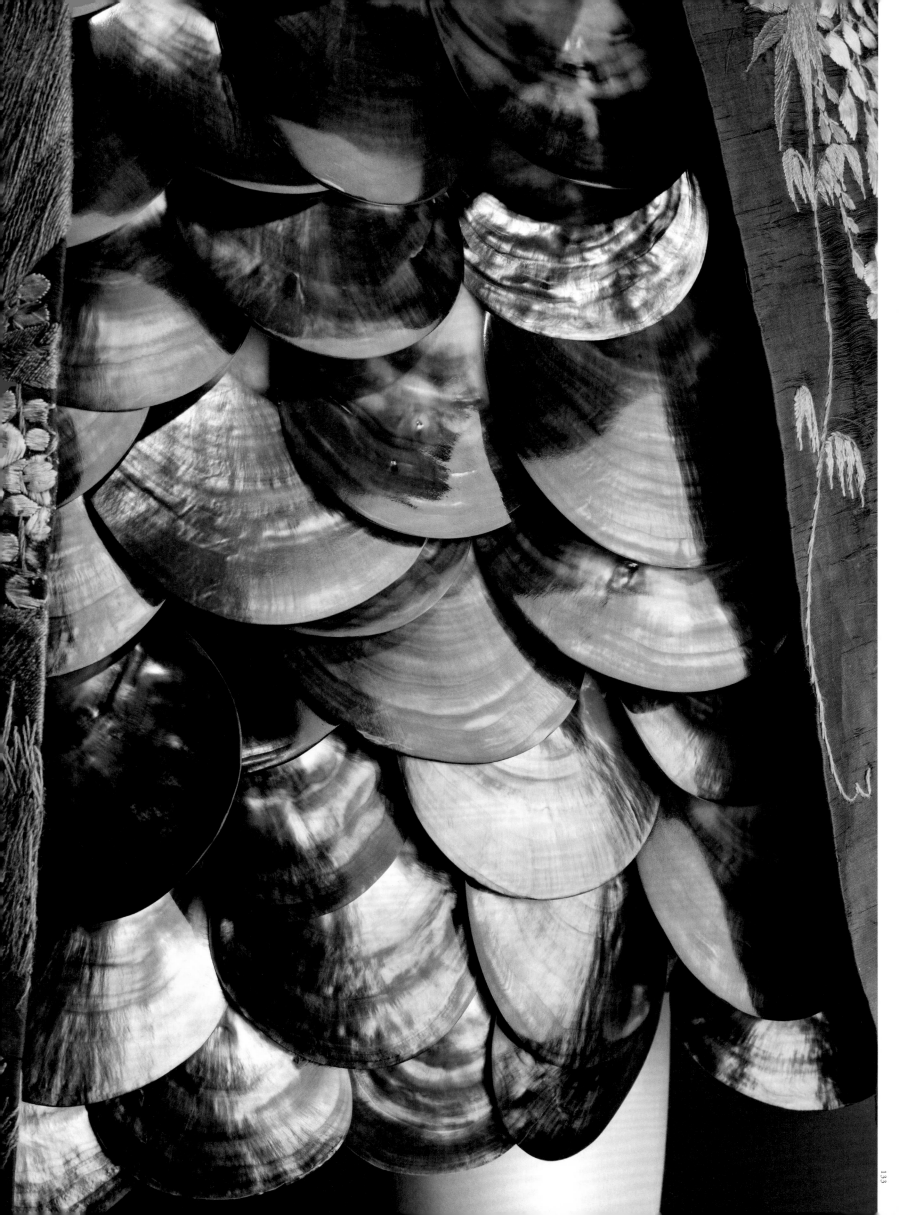

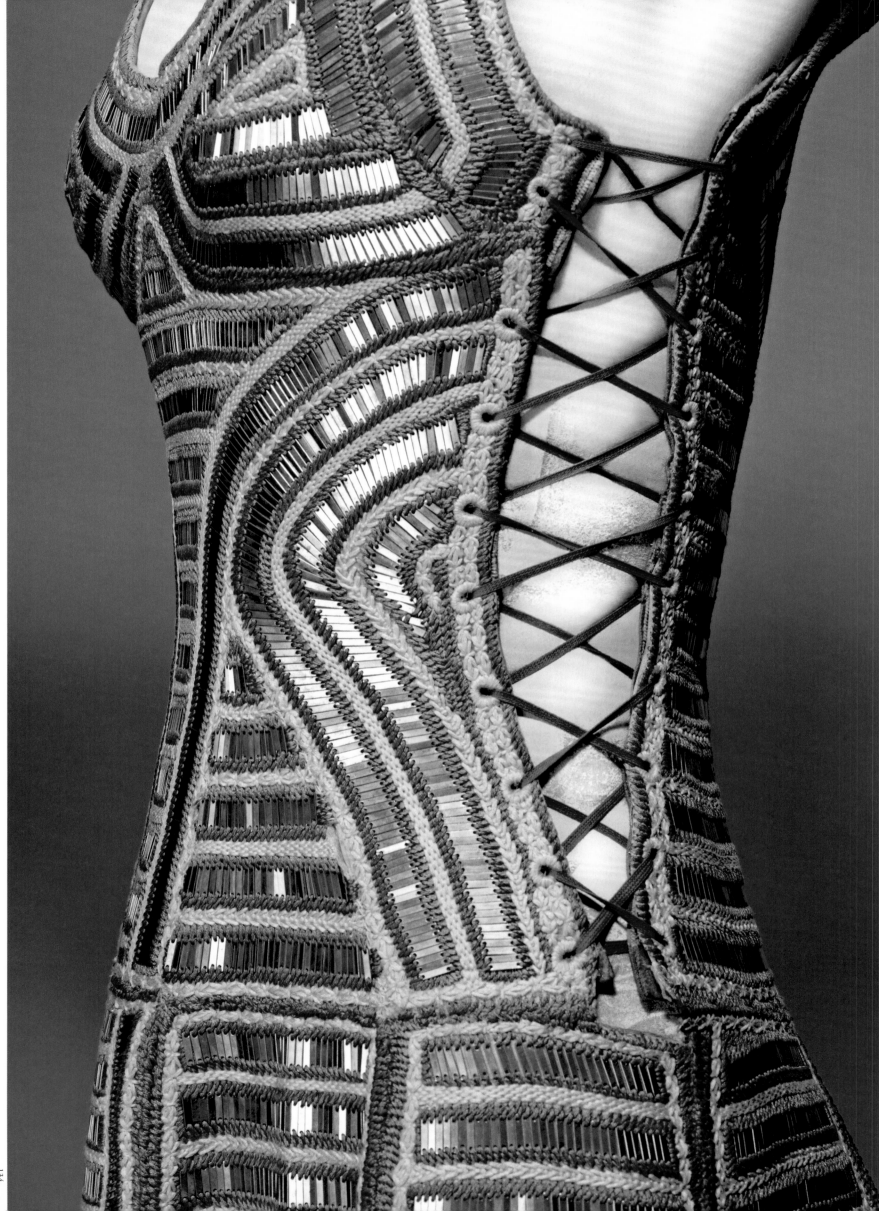

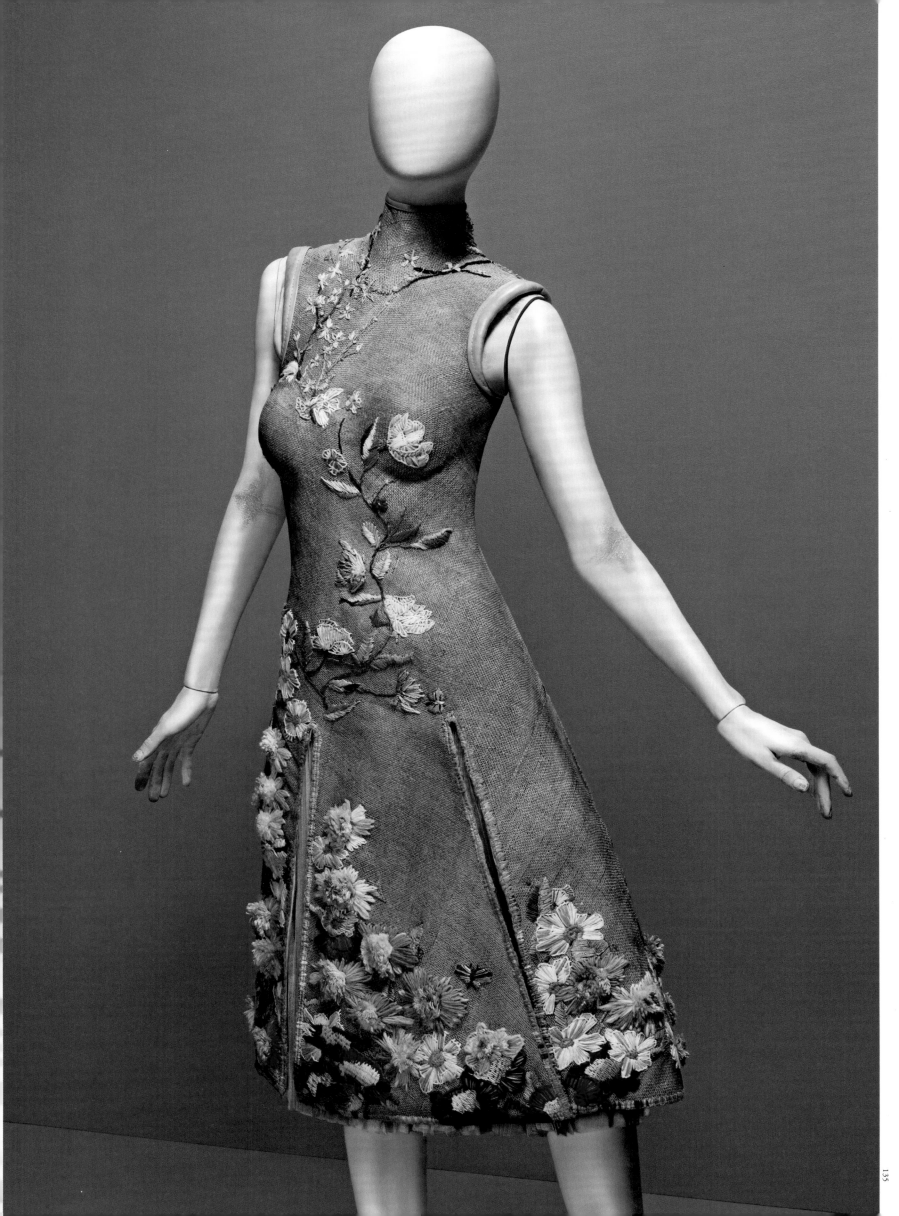

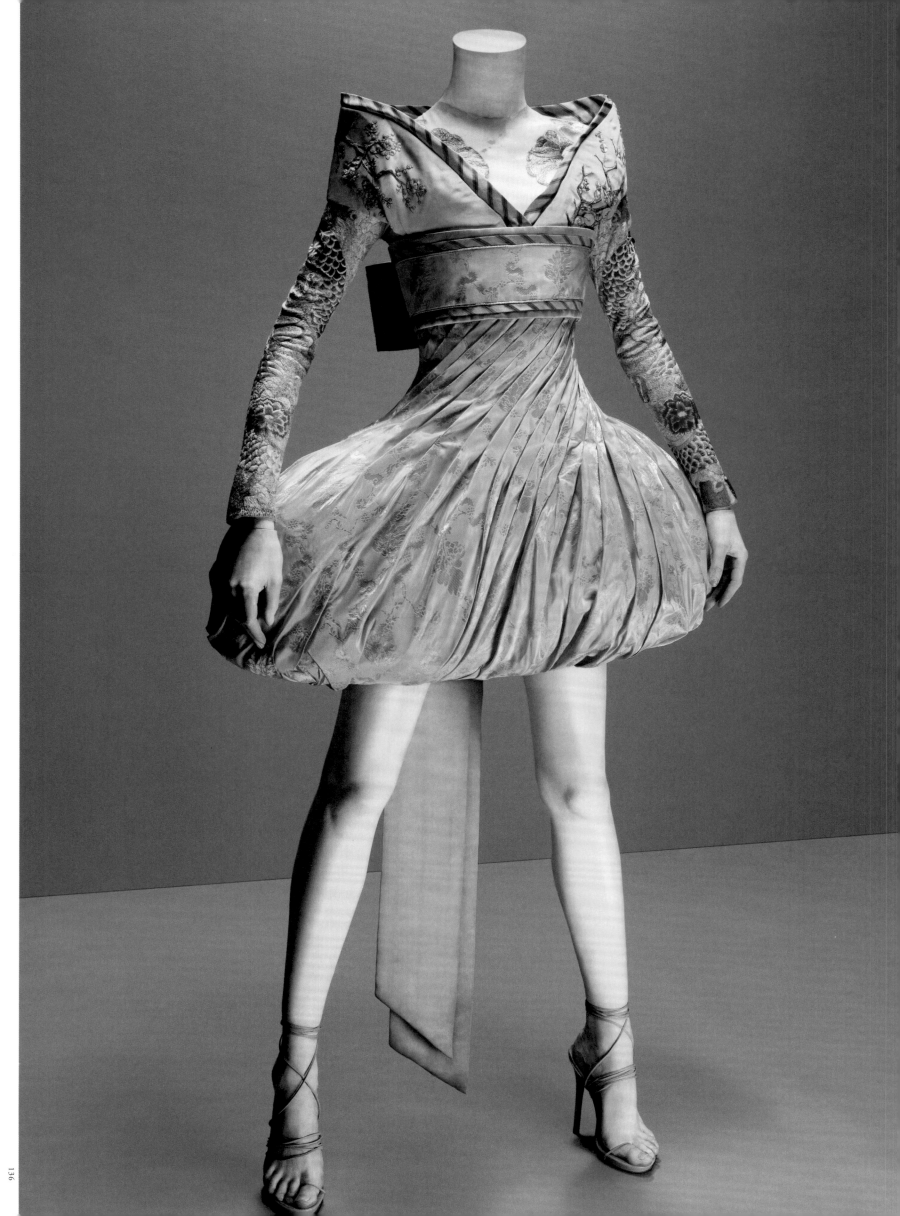

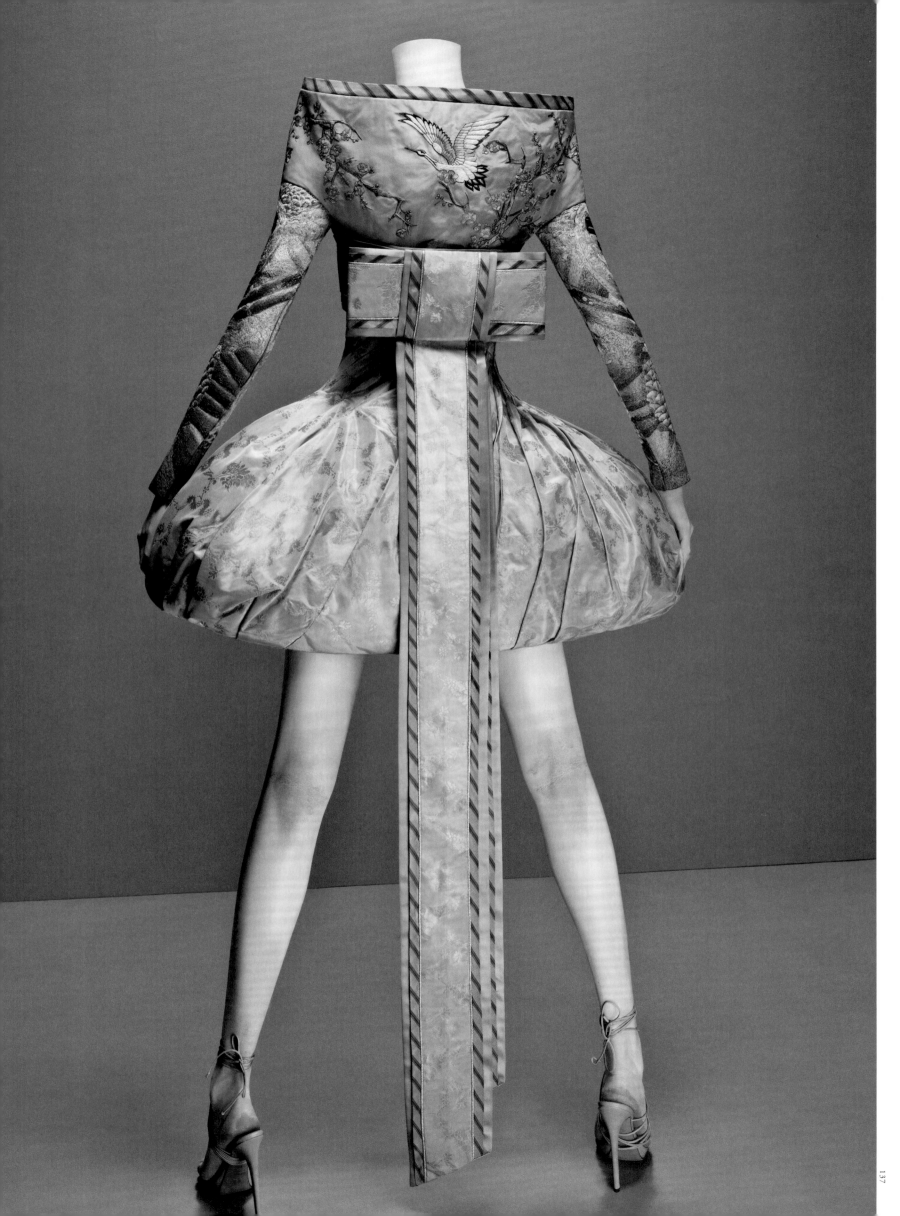

"[In this collection] the idea of the chess game meant that we looked at six different types of women, women on opposing sides. We had the Americans facing the Japanese and the redheads facing the tanned Latinos."

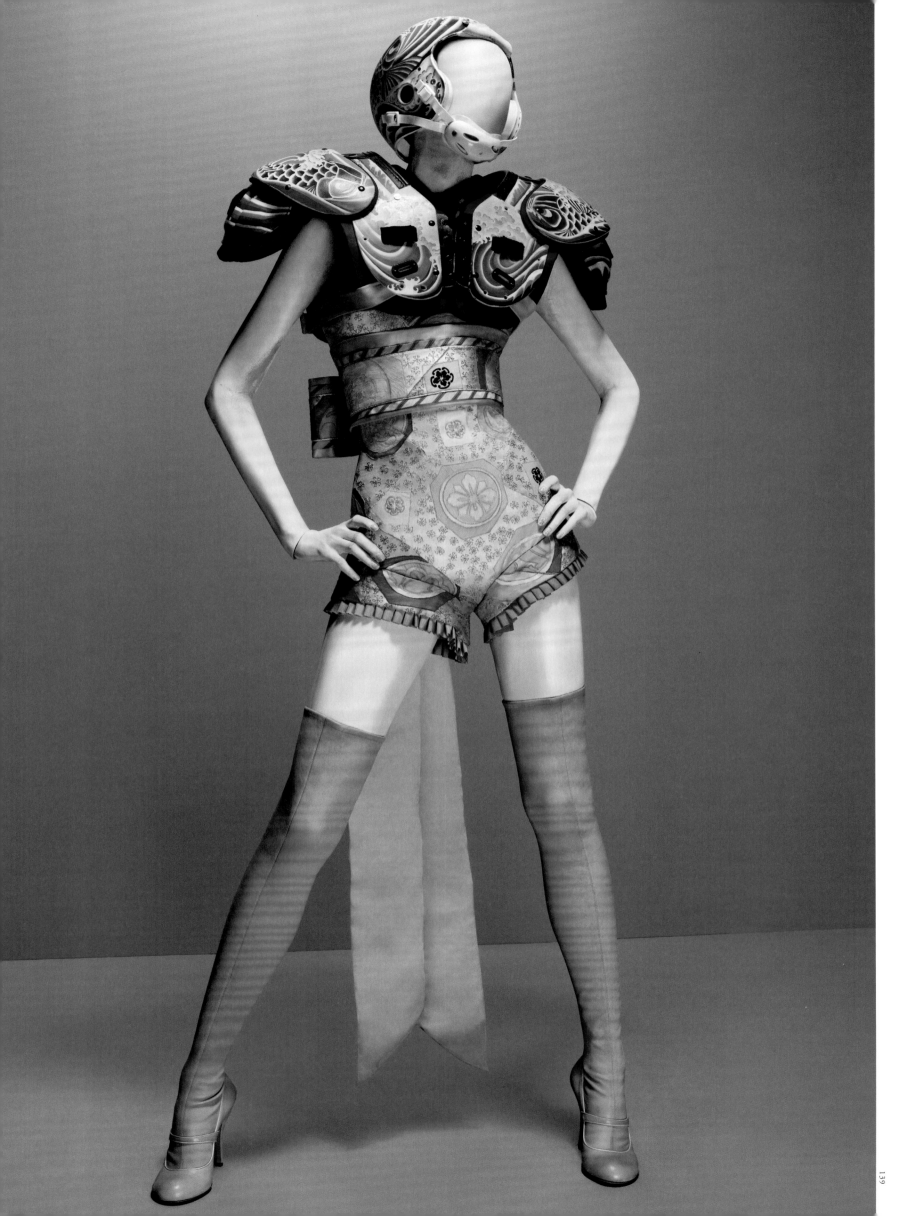

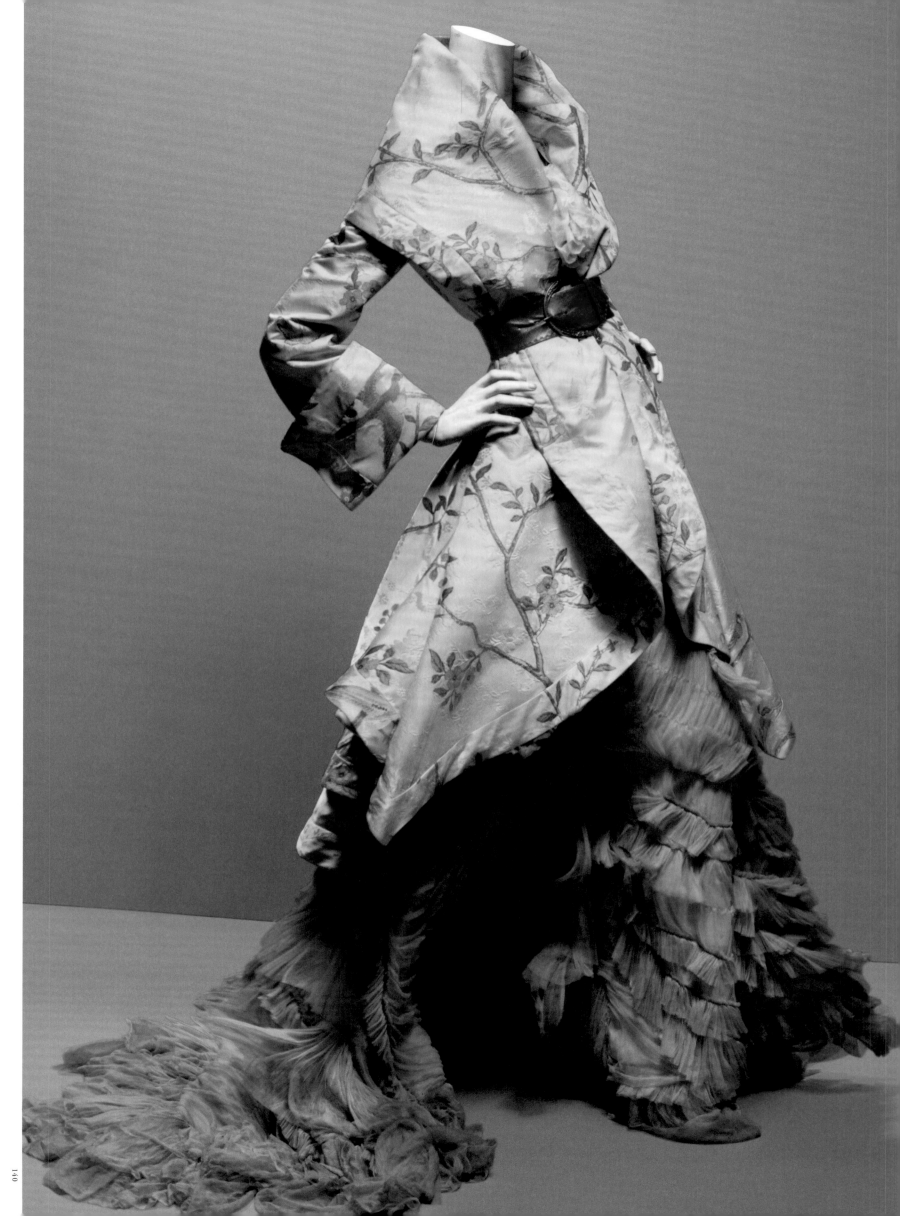

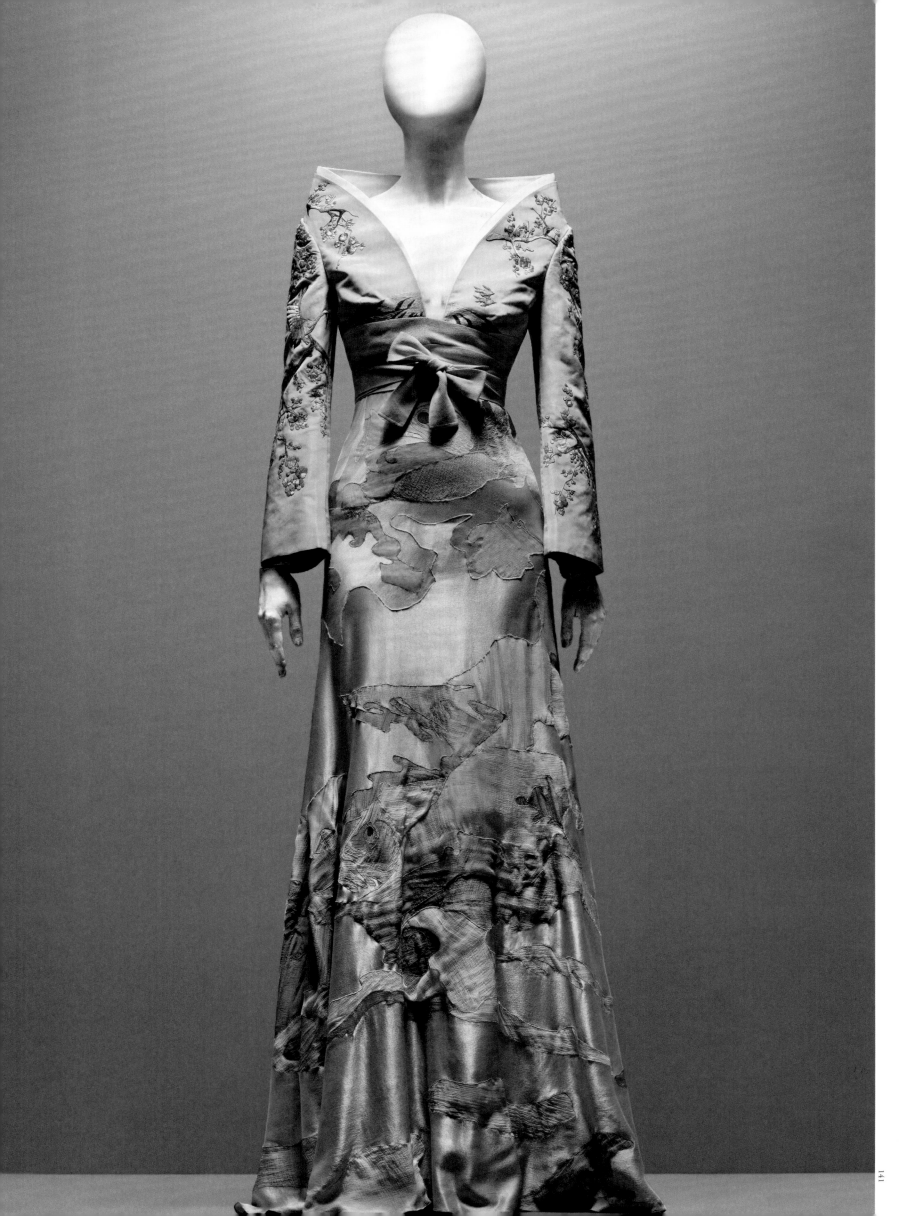

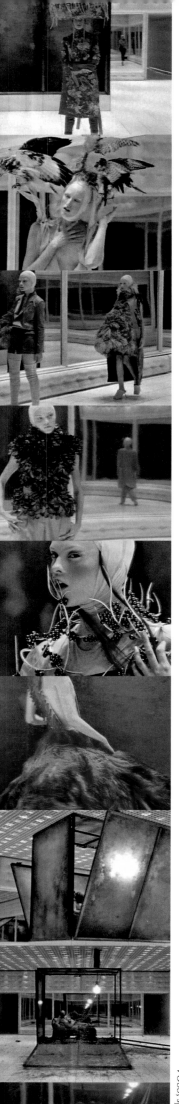

VOSS, spring/summer 2001

"[In this collection] the idea was to turn people's faces on themselves. I wanted to turn it around and make them think, am I actually as good as what I'm looking at?"

"The show was staged inside a huge two-way mirrored box, whereby the audience was reflected in the glass before the show began and then the models could not see out once the show started."

"These beautiful models were walking around in the room, and then suddenly this woman who wouldn't be considered beautiful was revealed. It was about trying to trap something that wasn't conventionally beautiful to show that beauty comes from within."

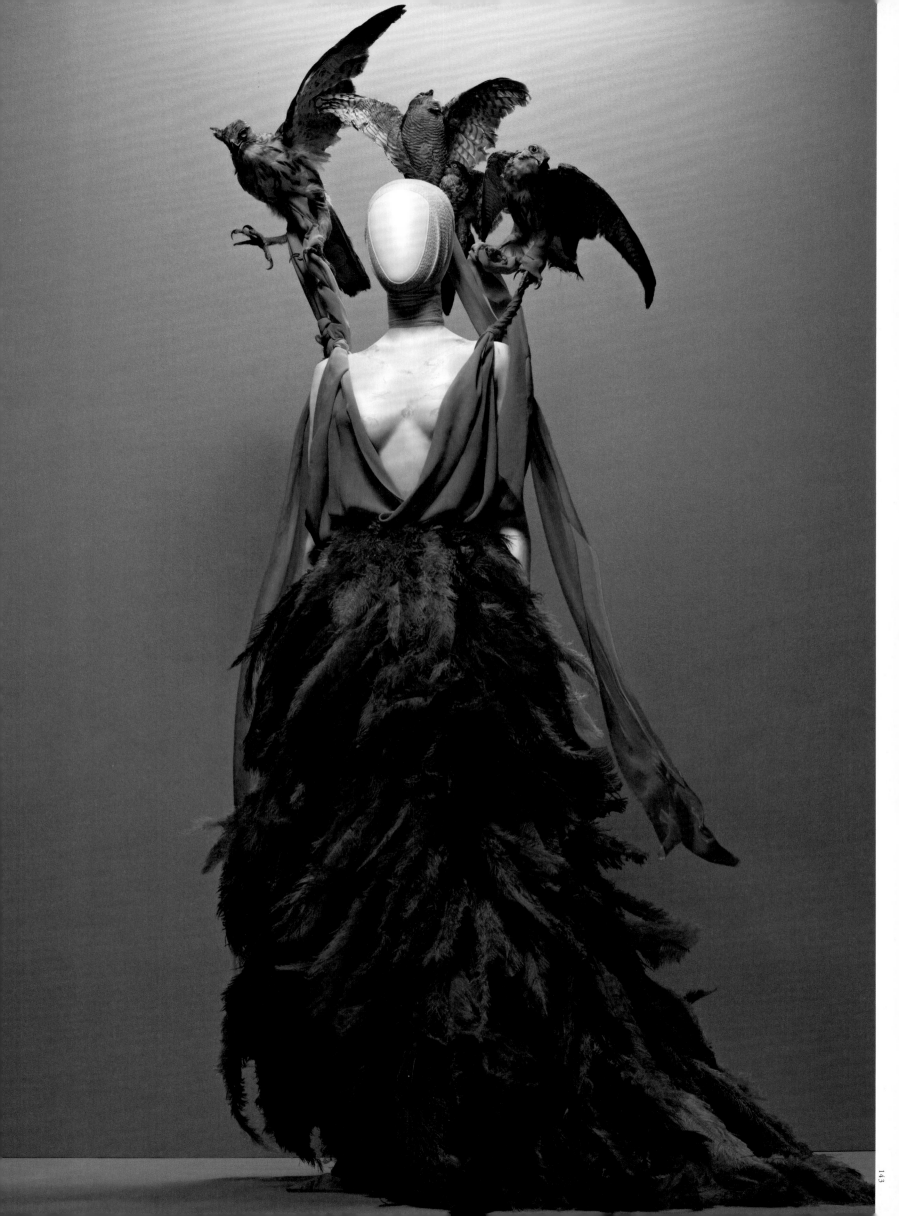

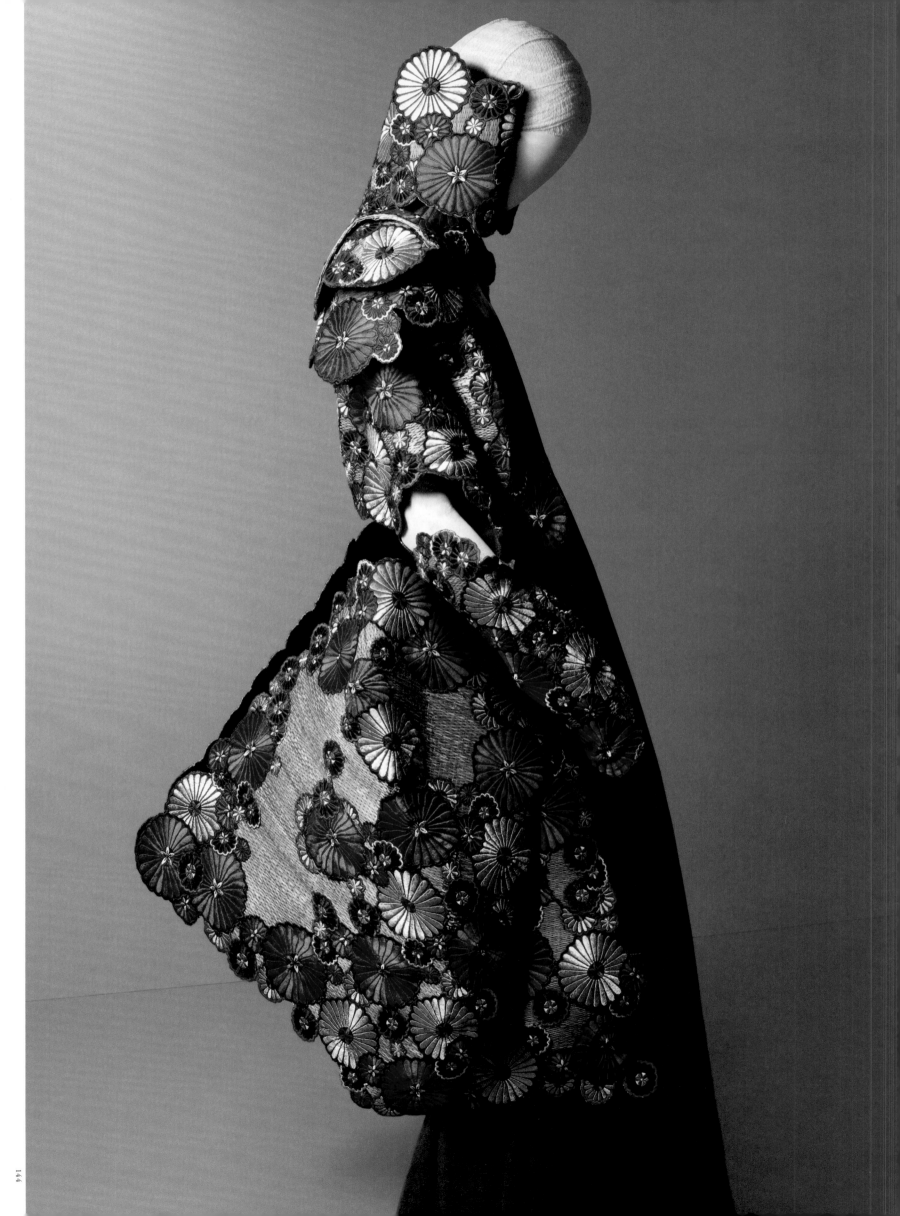

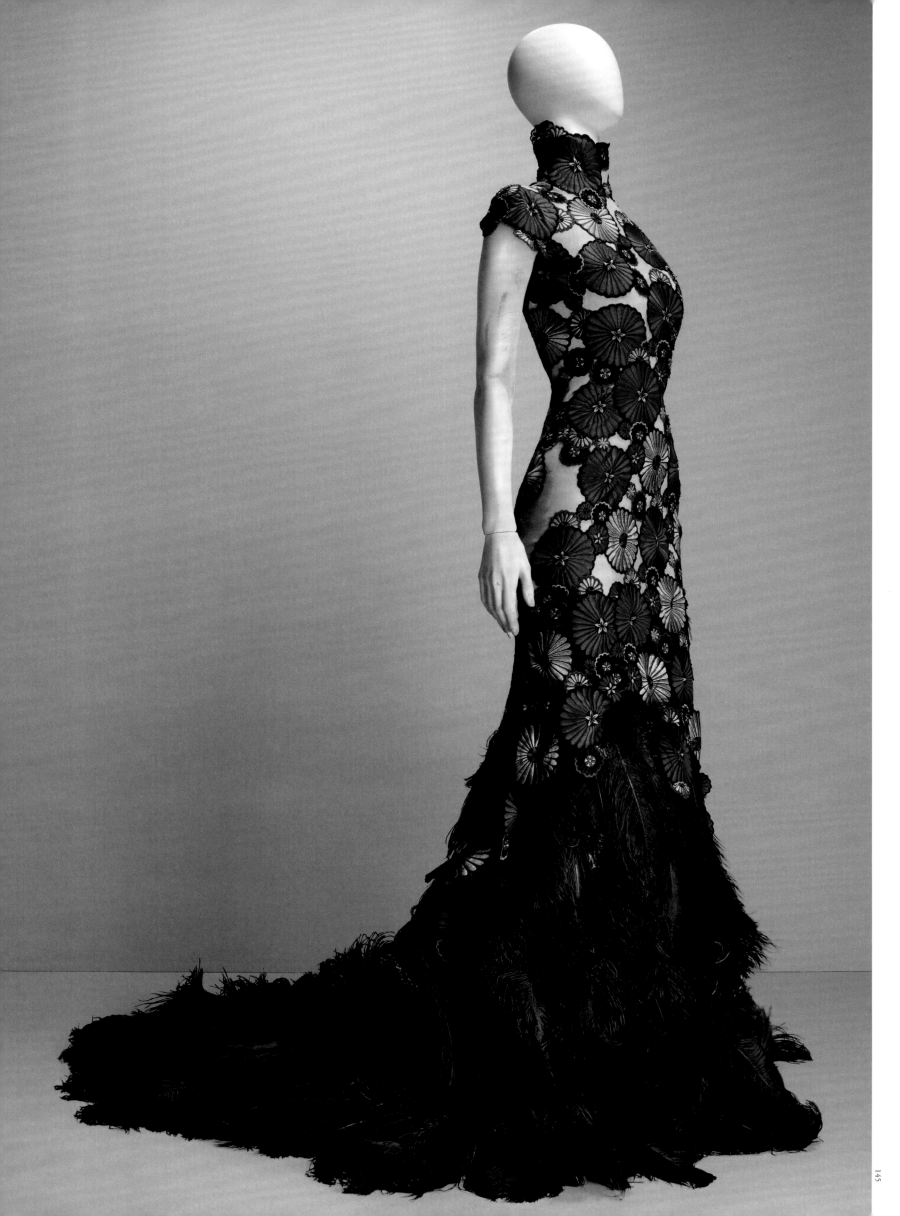

"My friend George and I were walking on the beach in Norfolk and there were thousands of [razor-clam] shells. They were so beautiful, I thought I had to do something with them. So, we decided to make [a dress] out of them. . . . The shells had outlived their usefulness on the beach, so we put them to another use on a dress. Then Erin [O'Conner] came out and trashed the dress, so their usefulness was over once again. Kind of like fashion, really."

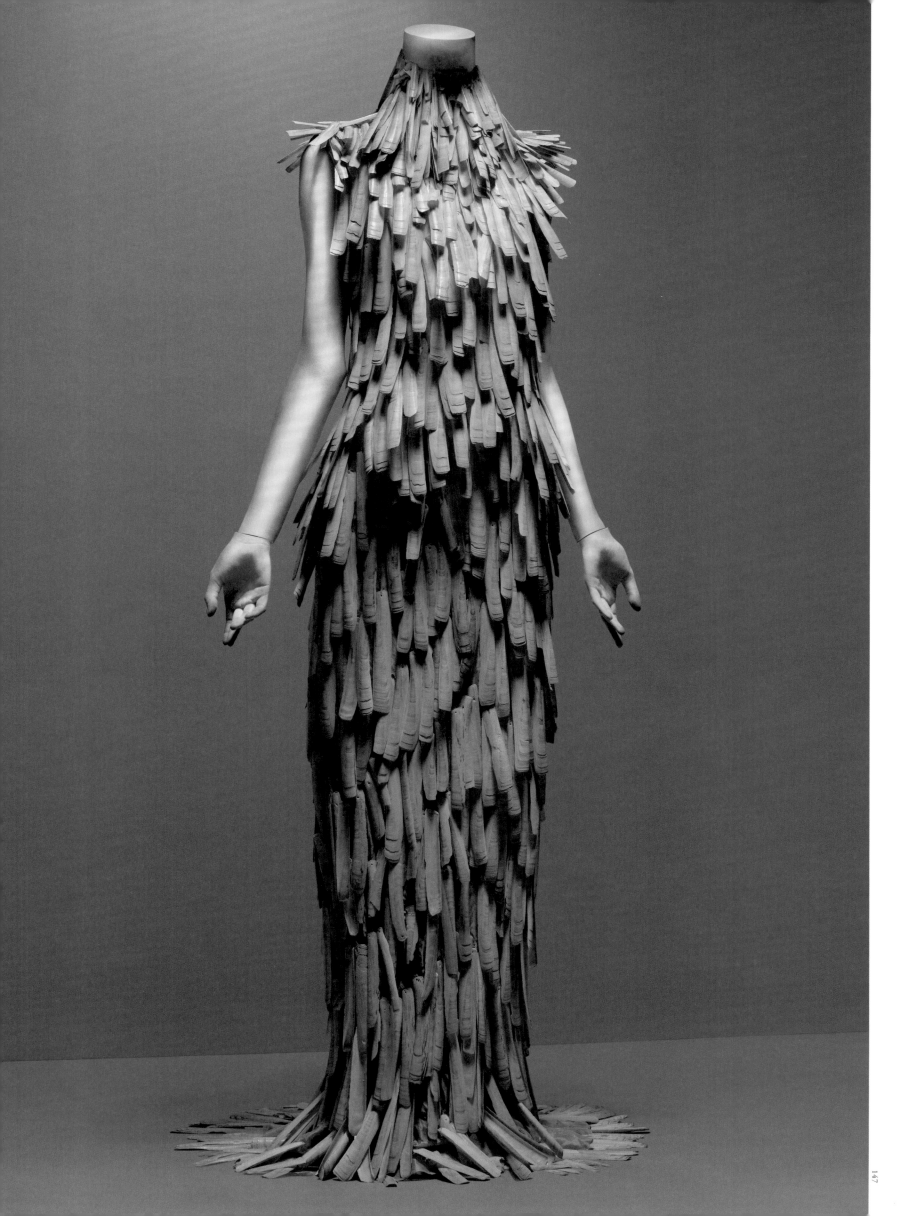

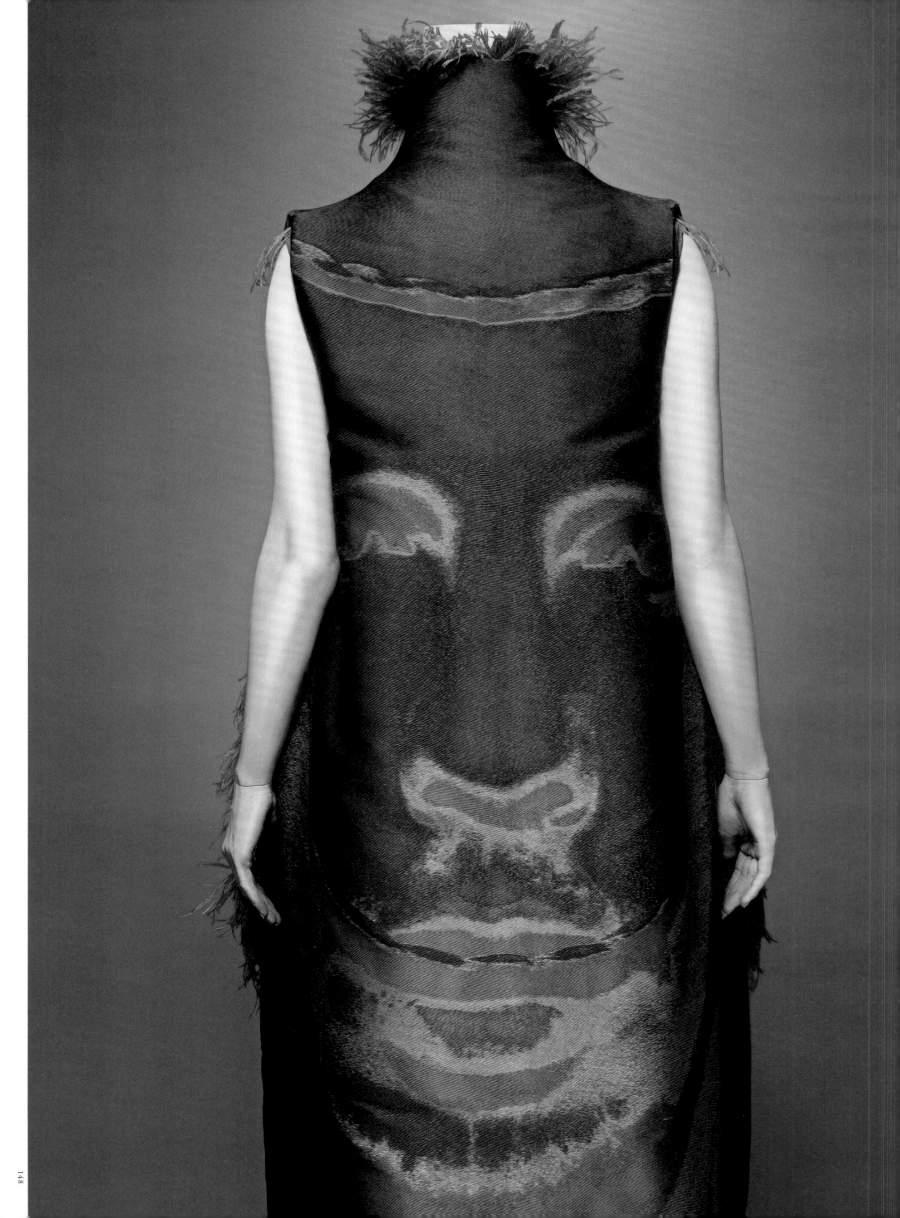

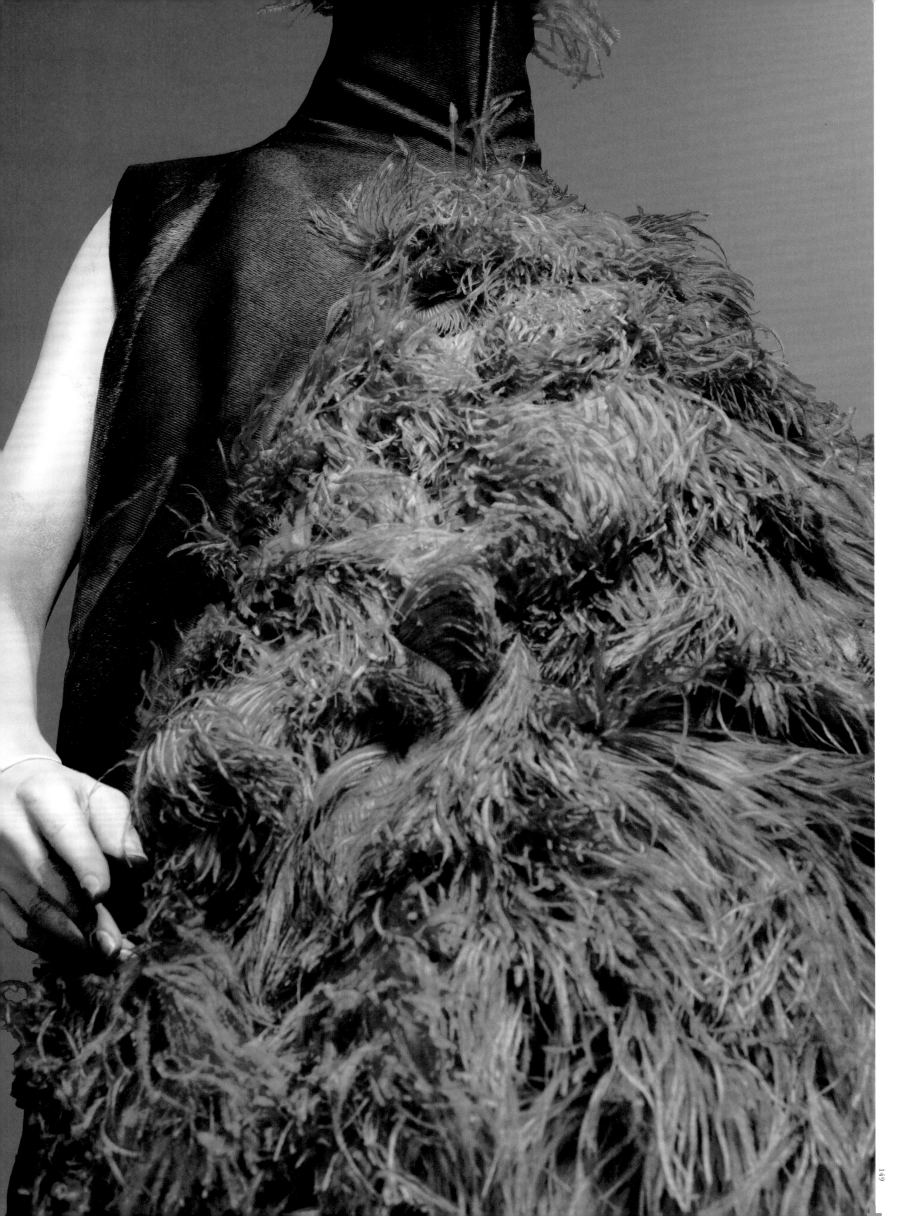

"[I try to] push the silhouette. To change the

silhouette is to change the thinking of how we

look. What I do is look at ancient African tribes,

and the way they dress. The rituals of how

they dress. . . . There's a lot of tribalism in

the collections."

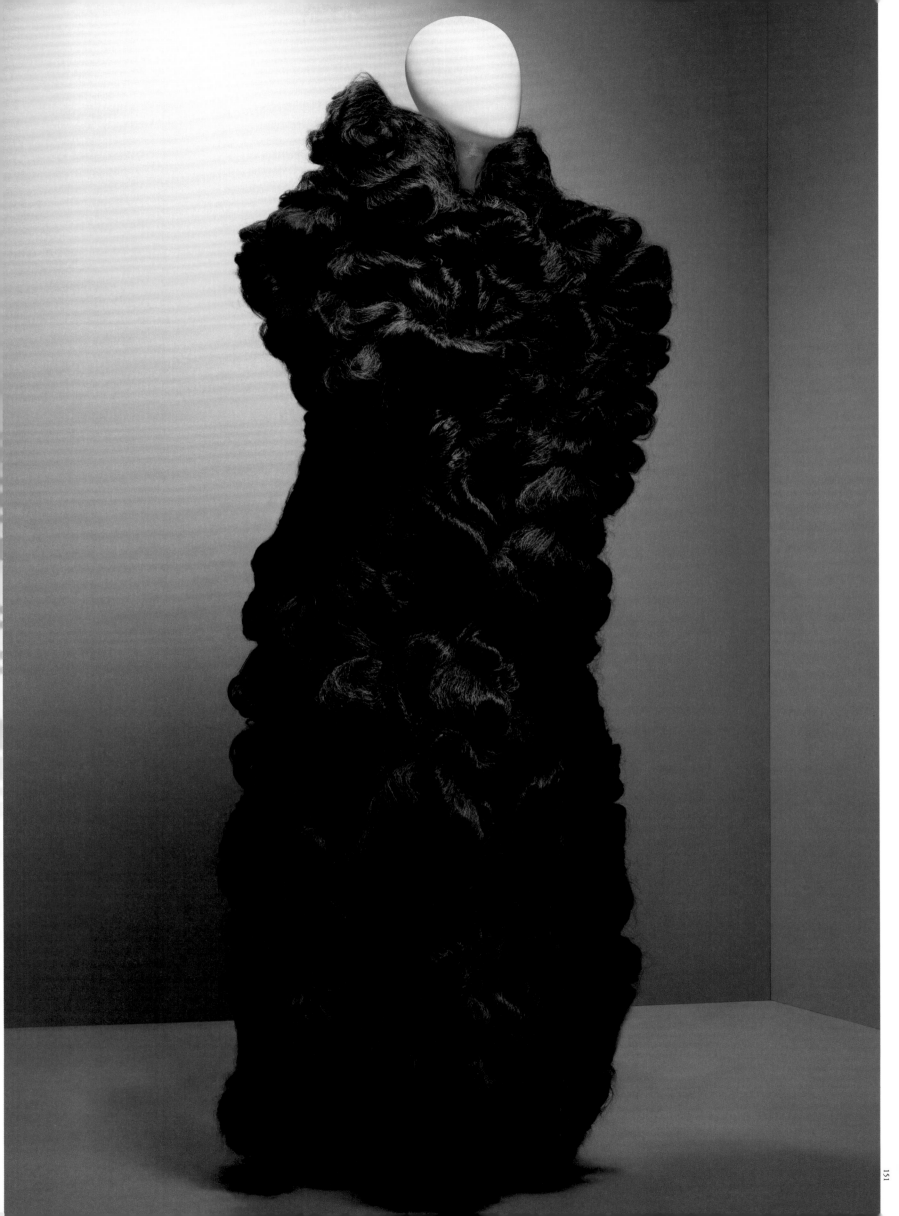

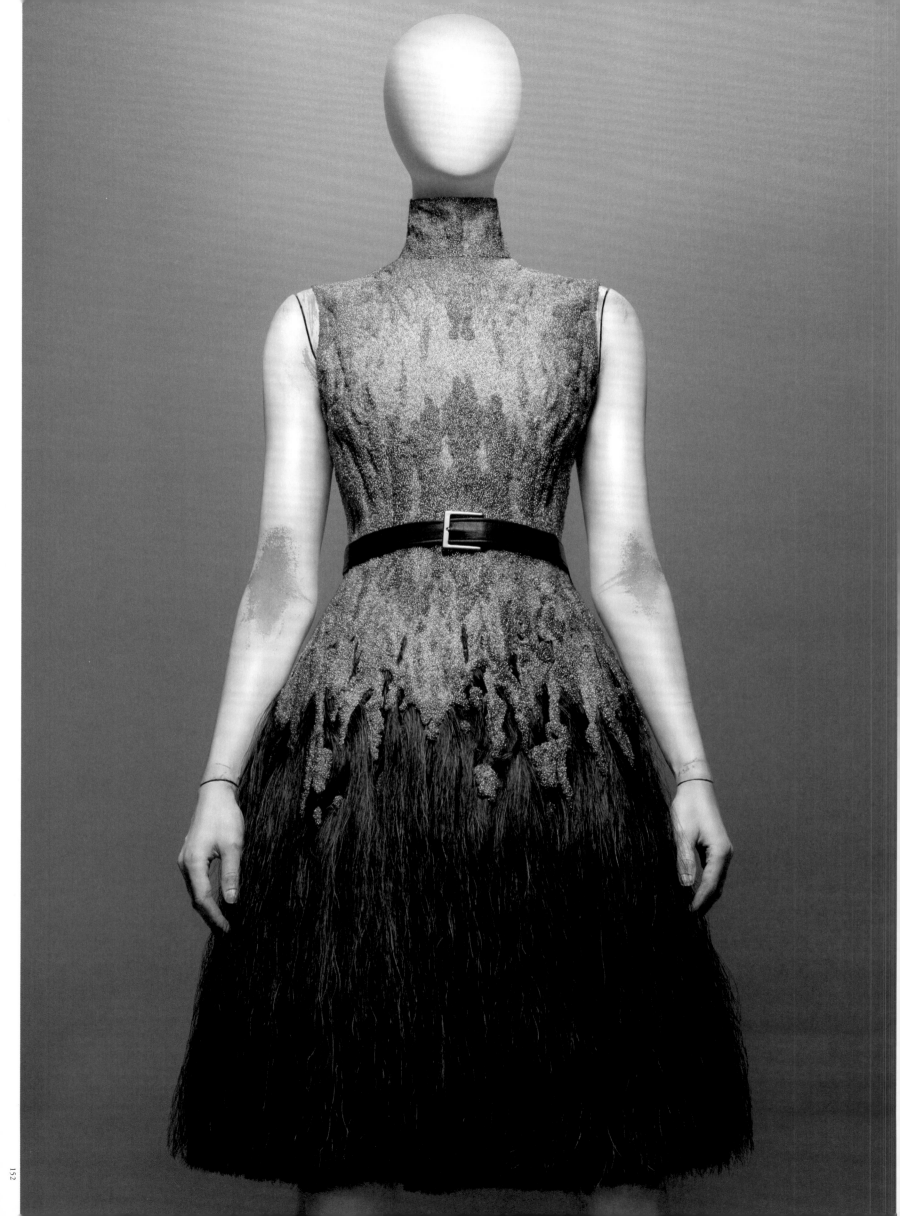

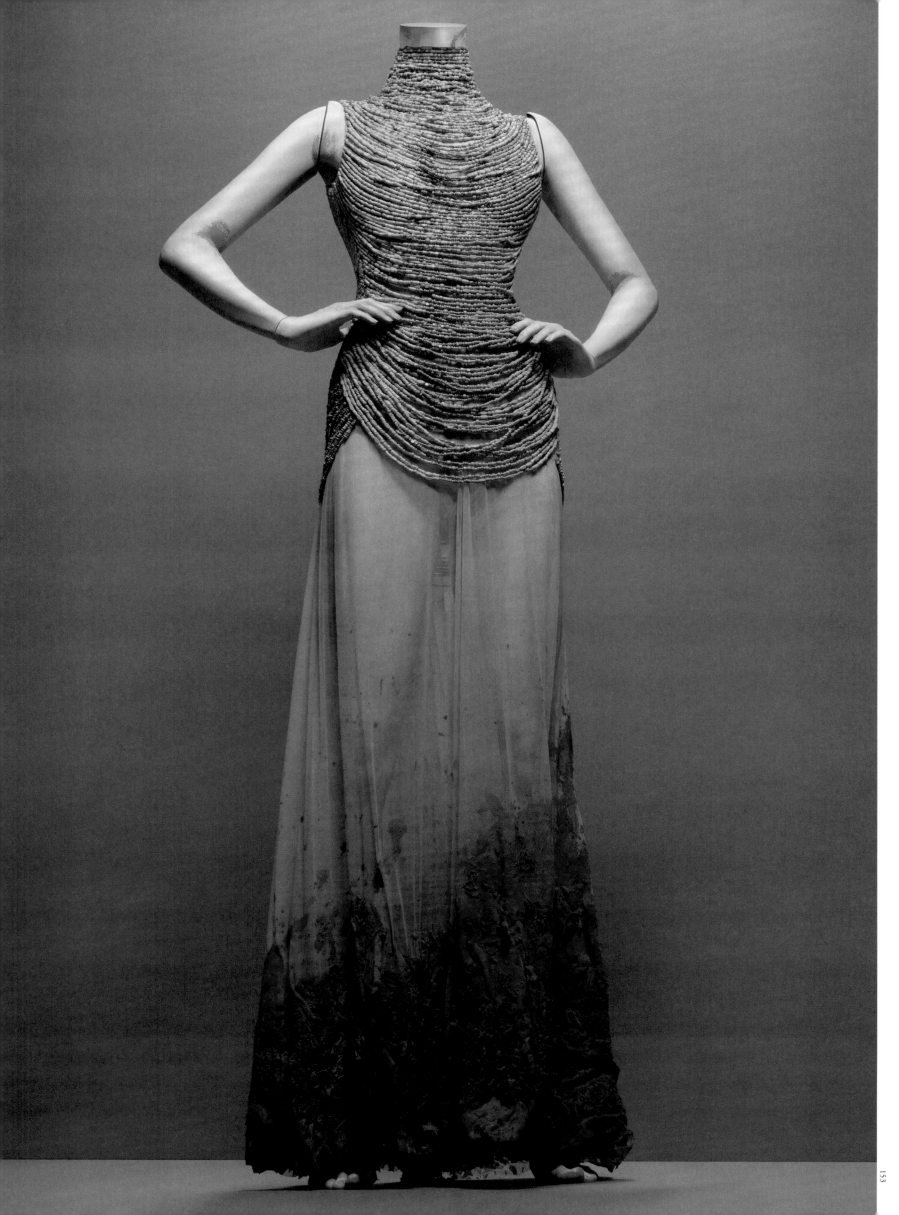

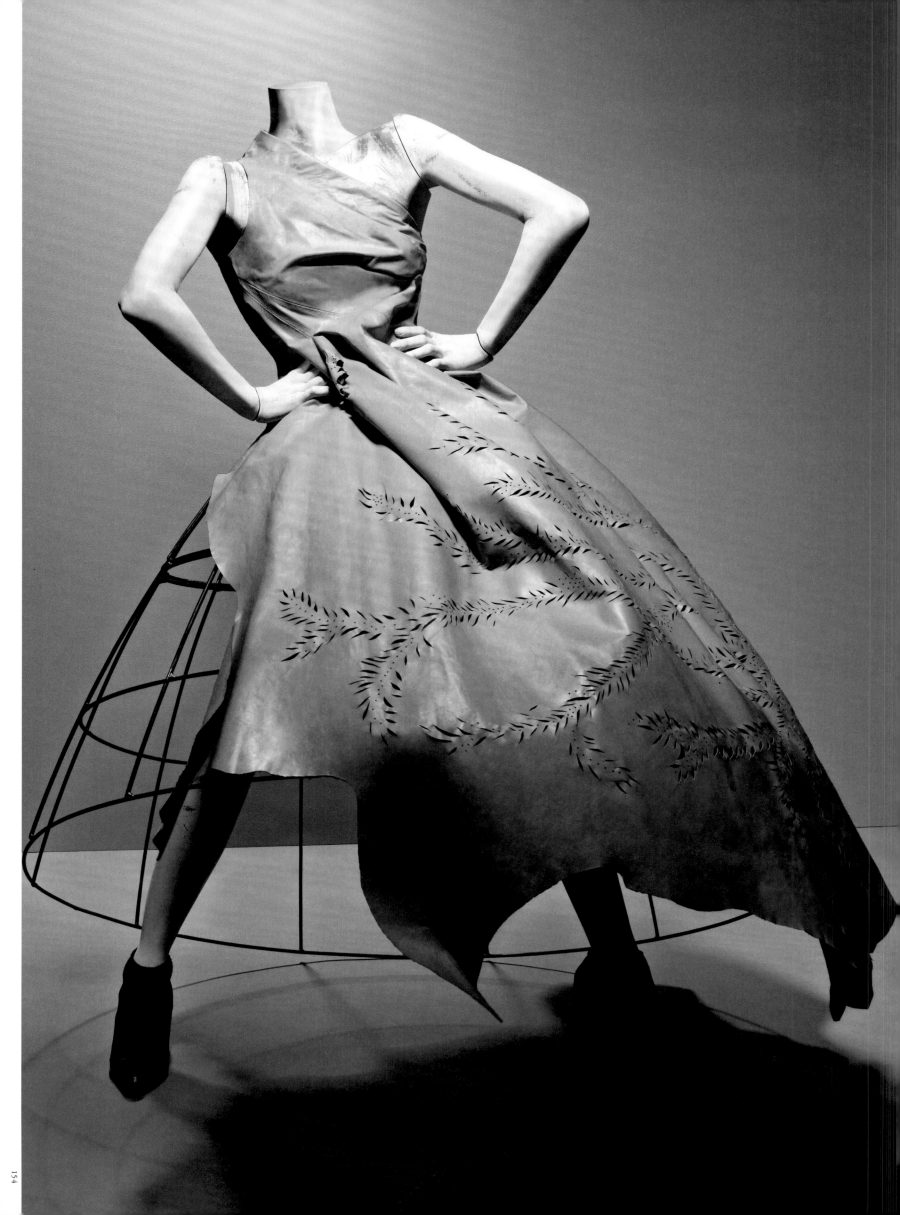

"I like things to be modern and still have a bit
   of tradition."

"I believe in history."

"Animals . . . fascinate me because you can find a
force, an energy, a fear that also exists in sex."

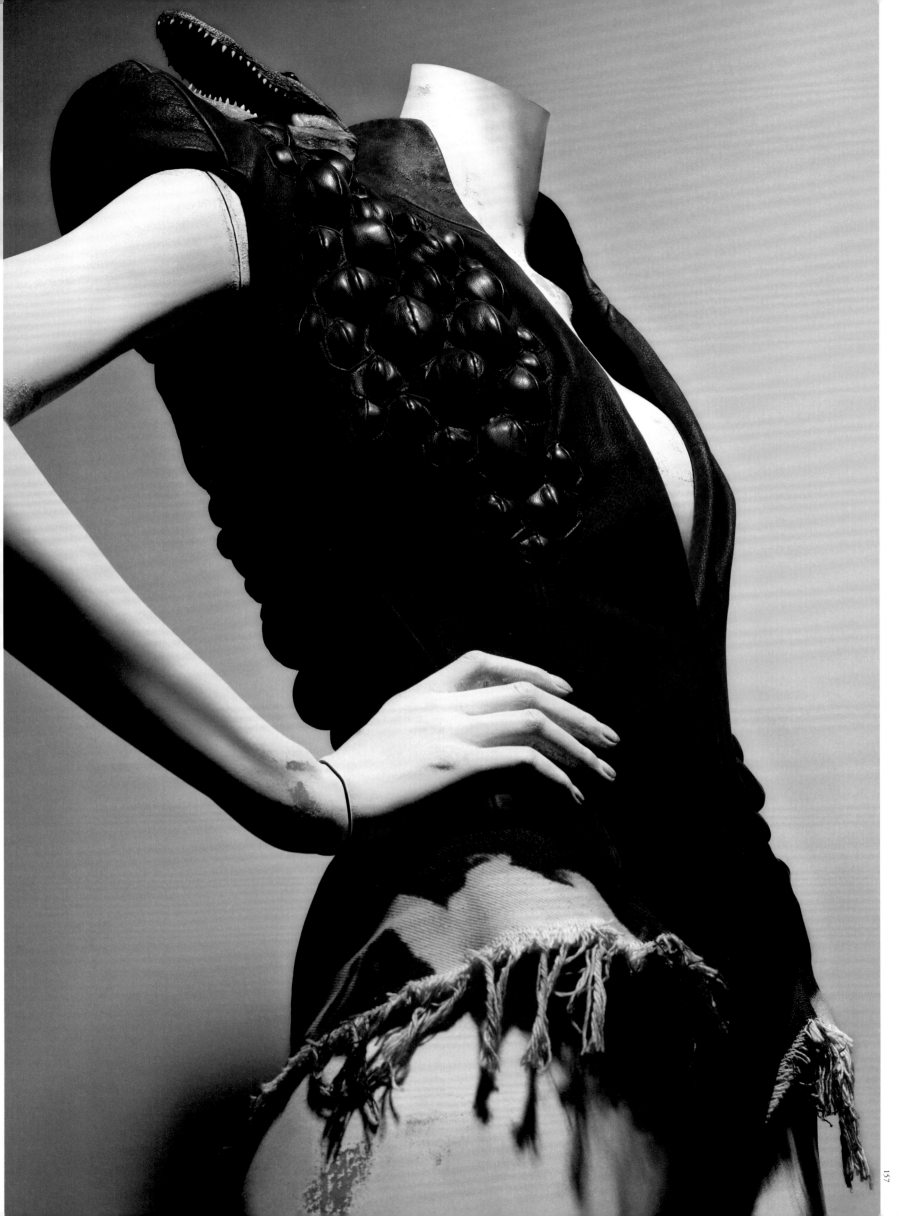

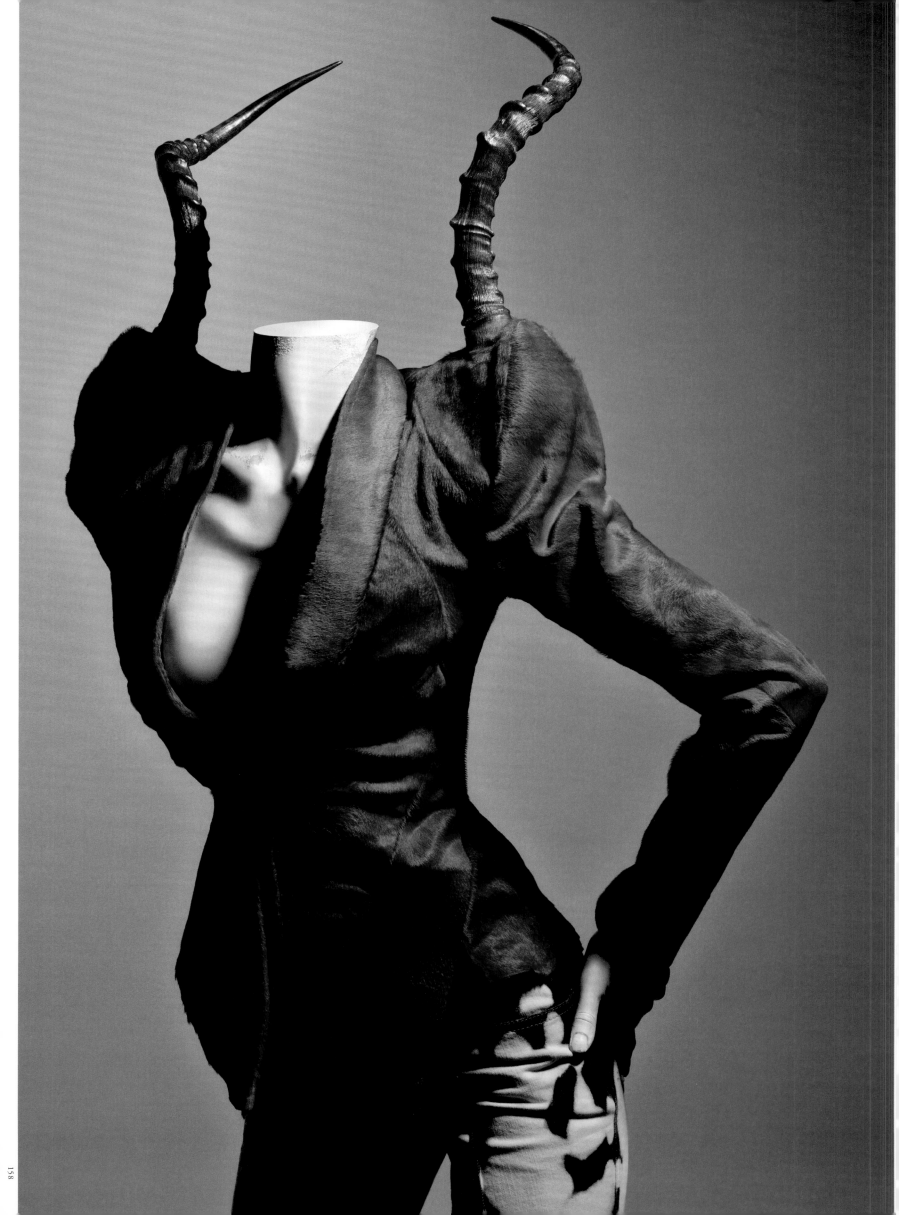

"The whole show feeling was about the Thomson's gazelle. It's a poor little critter—the markings are lovely, it's got these dark eyes, the white and black with the tan markings on the side, the horns—but it is the food chain of Africa. As soon as it's born it's dead, I mean you're lucky if it lasts a few months, and that's how I see human life, in the same way. You know, we can all be discarded quite easily. . . . You're there, you're gone, it's a jungle out there!"

"[We used] a lot of real skins. Animal skins, but they [were] all by-products. None [were] killed for their fur, they have all been killed for their meat. The title of the show [was] . . . a play on animal and man. They are both gross and very much the same."

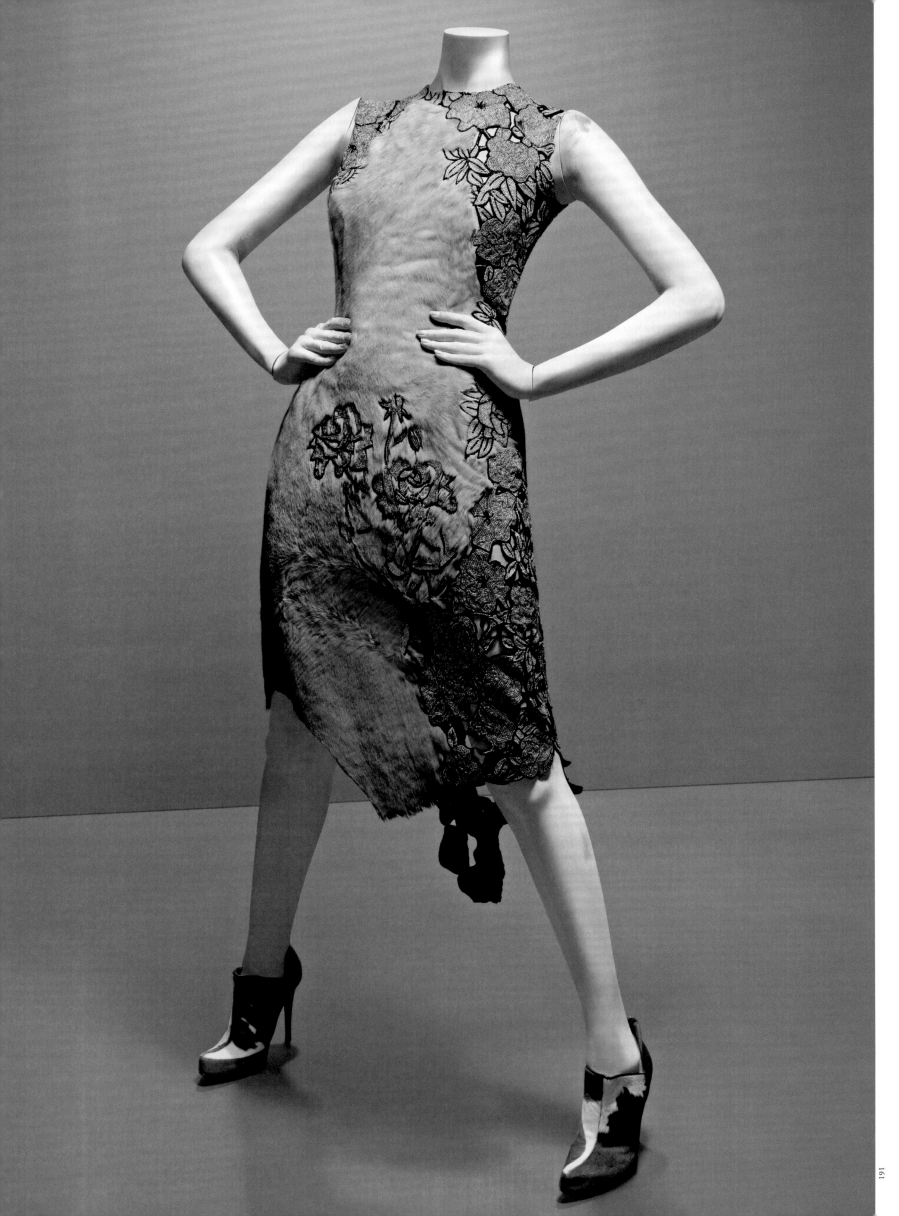

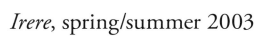

Irere, spring/summer 2003

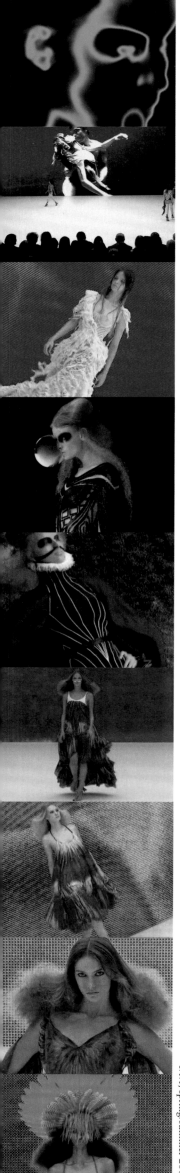

"I'm a romantic schizophrenic. Some people think I've become softer with this spring collection, but it's always been in my work. There may be an Edgar Allan Poe romance to it—it's not a heart-on-your-sleeve type thing—but that's just my personality. I've always been very sensitive, very romantic, but not everyone has seen that."

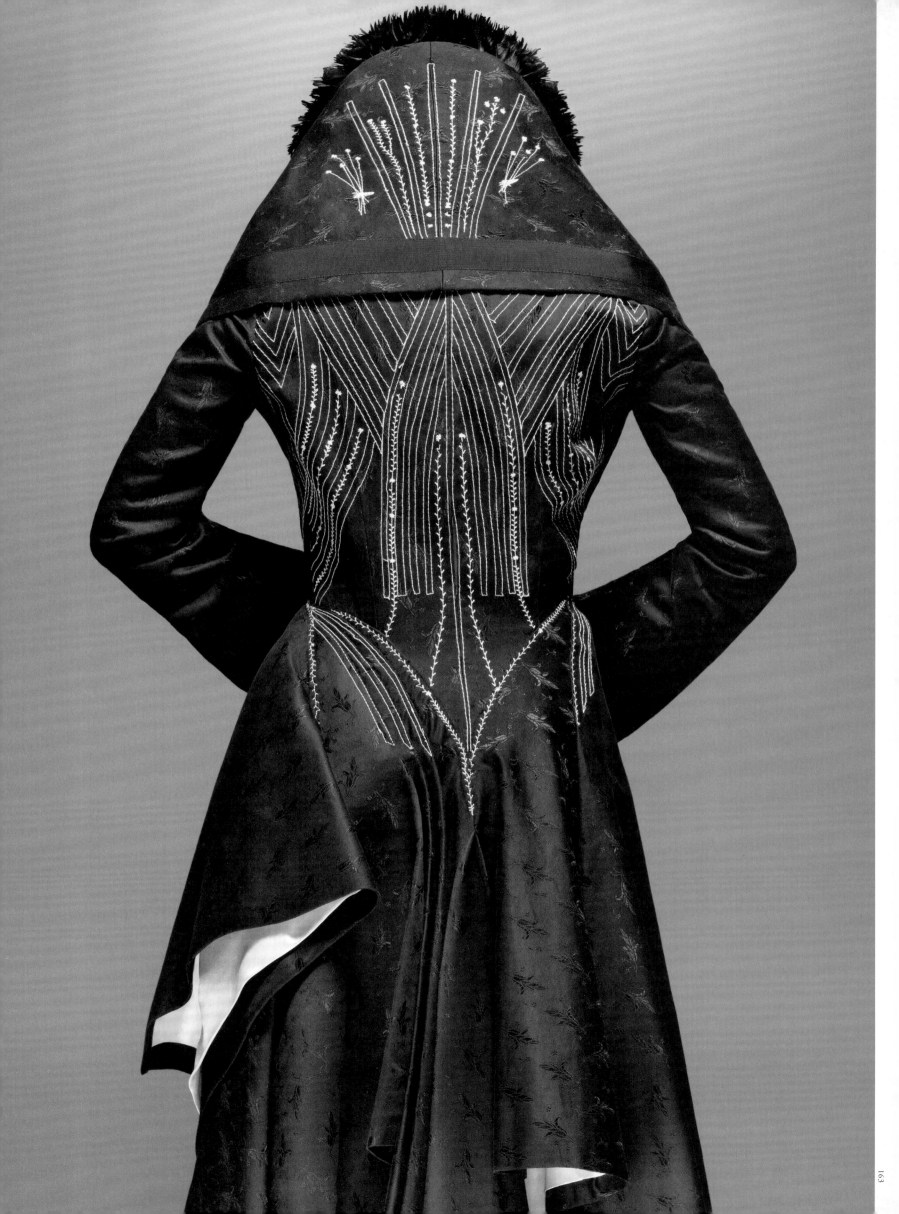

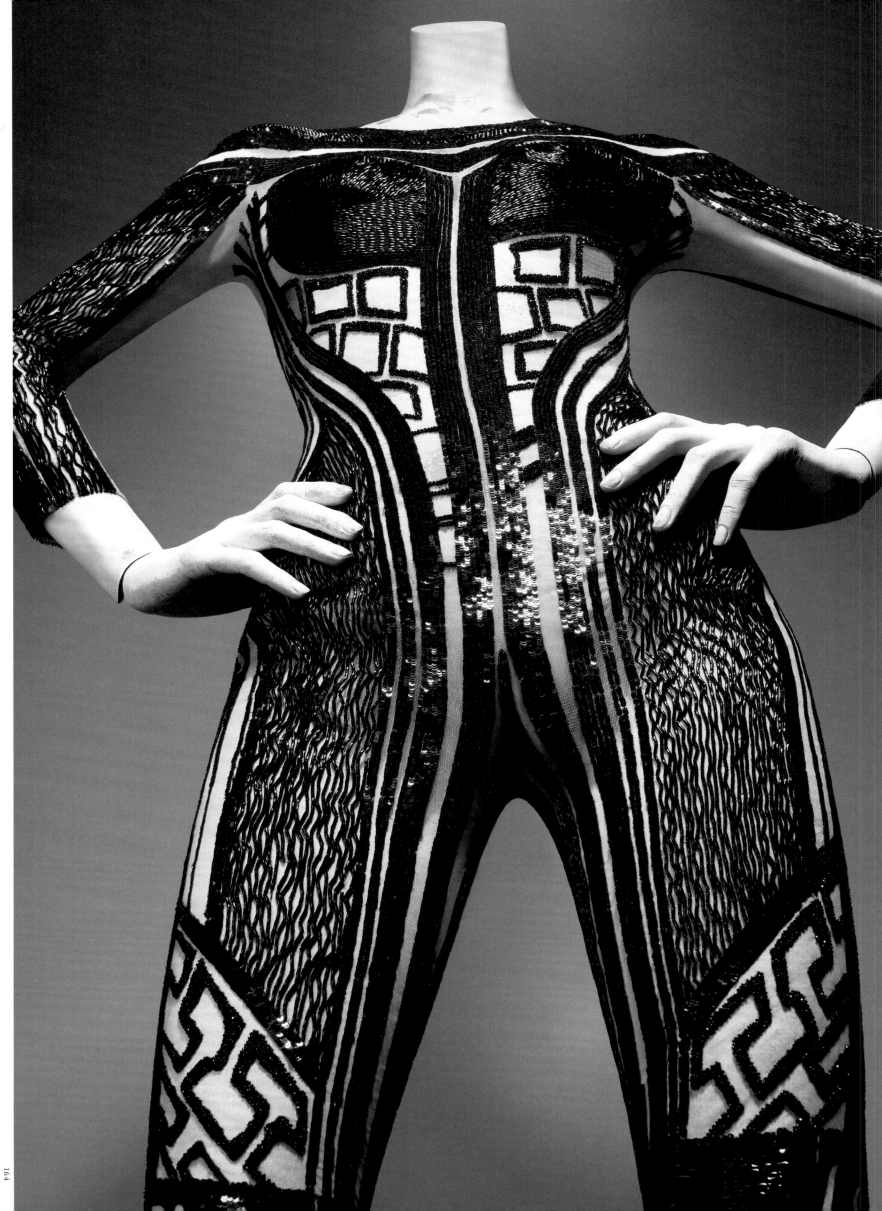

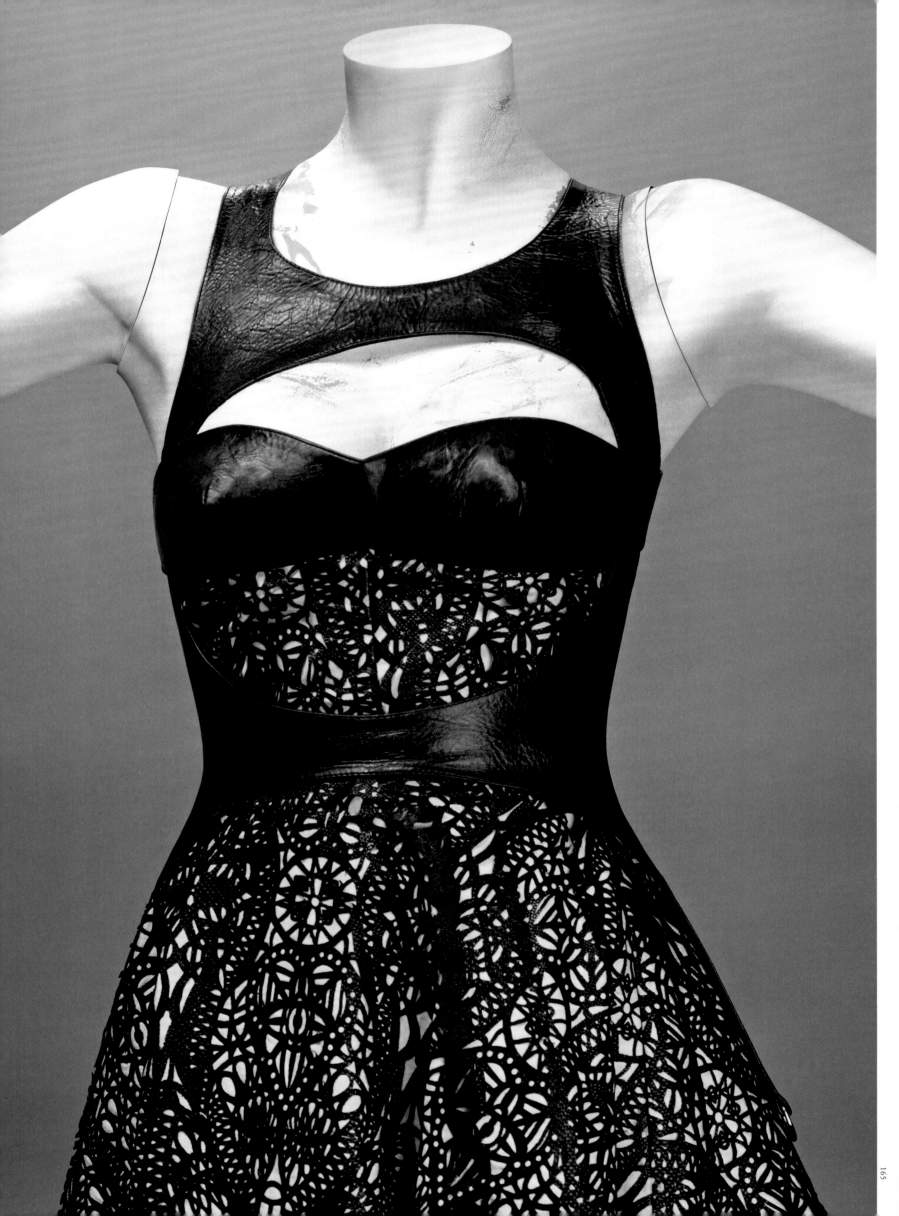

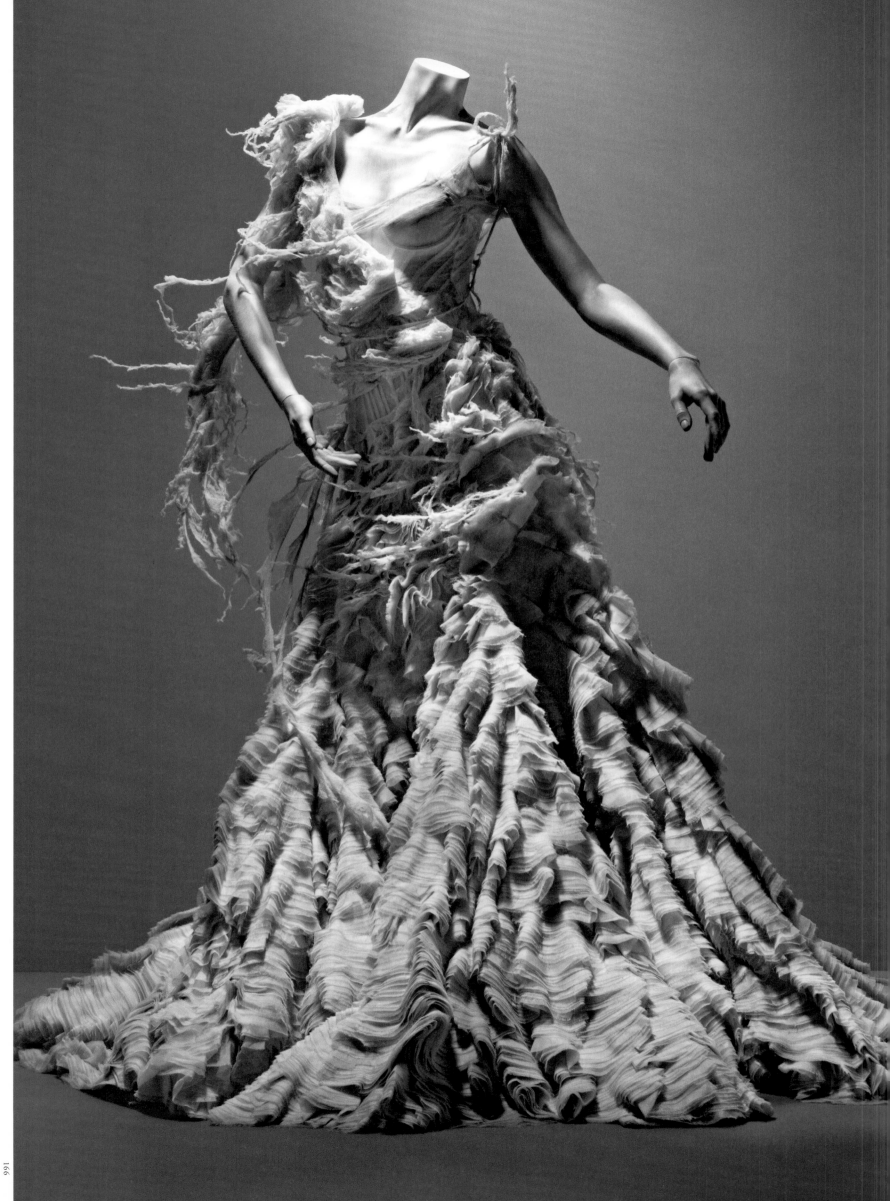

"Working in the atelier [at Givenchy] was fundamental to my career. . . . Because I was a tailor, I didn't totally understand softness, or lightness. I learned lightness at Givenchy. I was a tailor at Savile Row. At Givenchy I learned to soften. For me, it was an education. As a designer I could have left it behind. But working at Givenchy helped me learn my craft."

"I think that couture has complete relevance today. Designer fashion shouldn't be throwaway."

"I've never aspired to mass production. Because of my training as a tailor, my work involves lots of love and care, which is why so many of my clothes are made by hand here in London. Not to wow the crowd during a show, but because I love it."

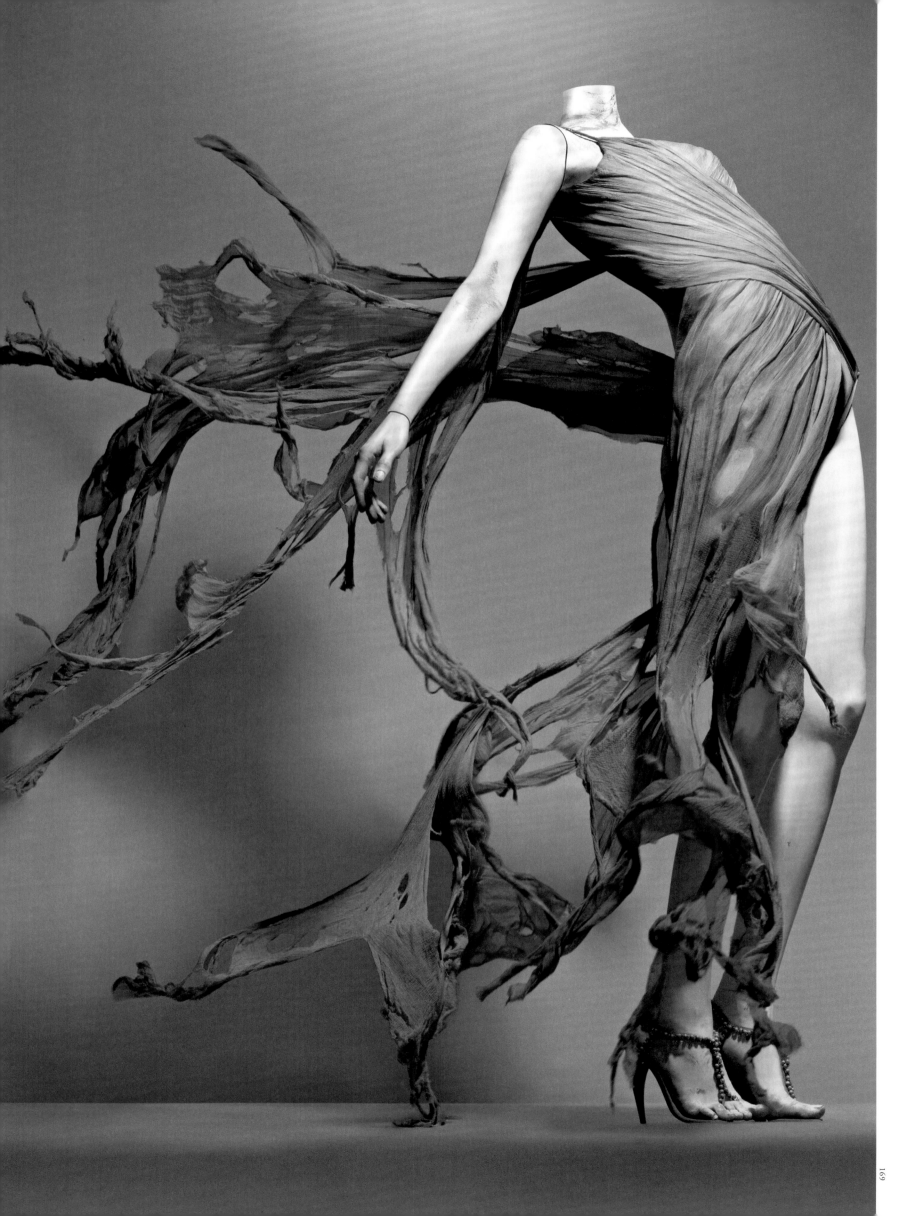

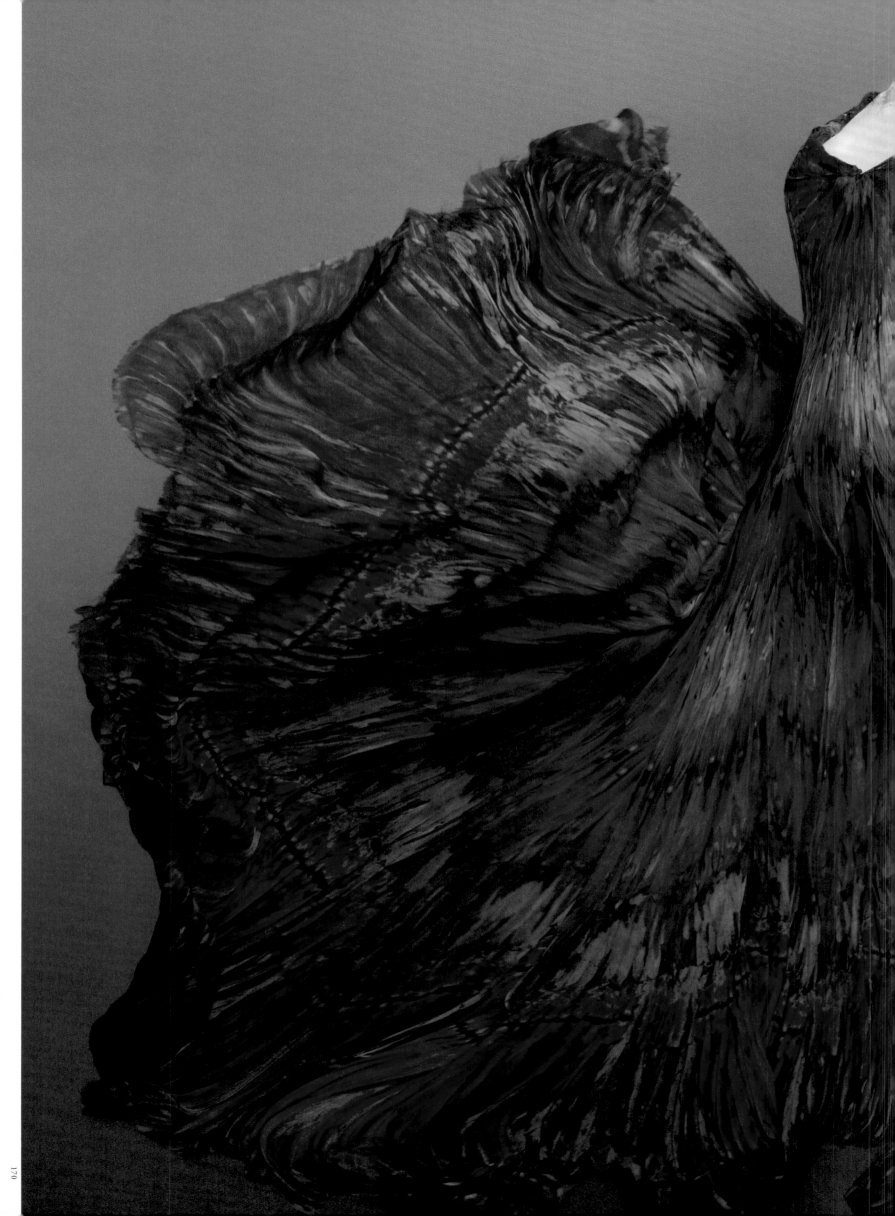

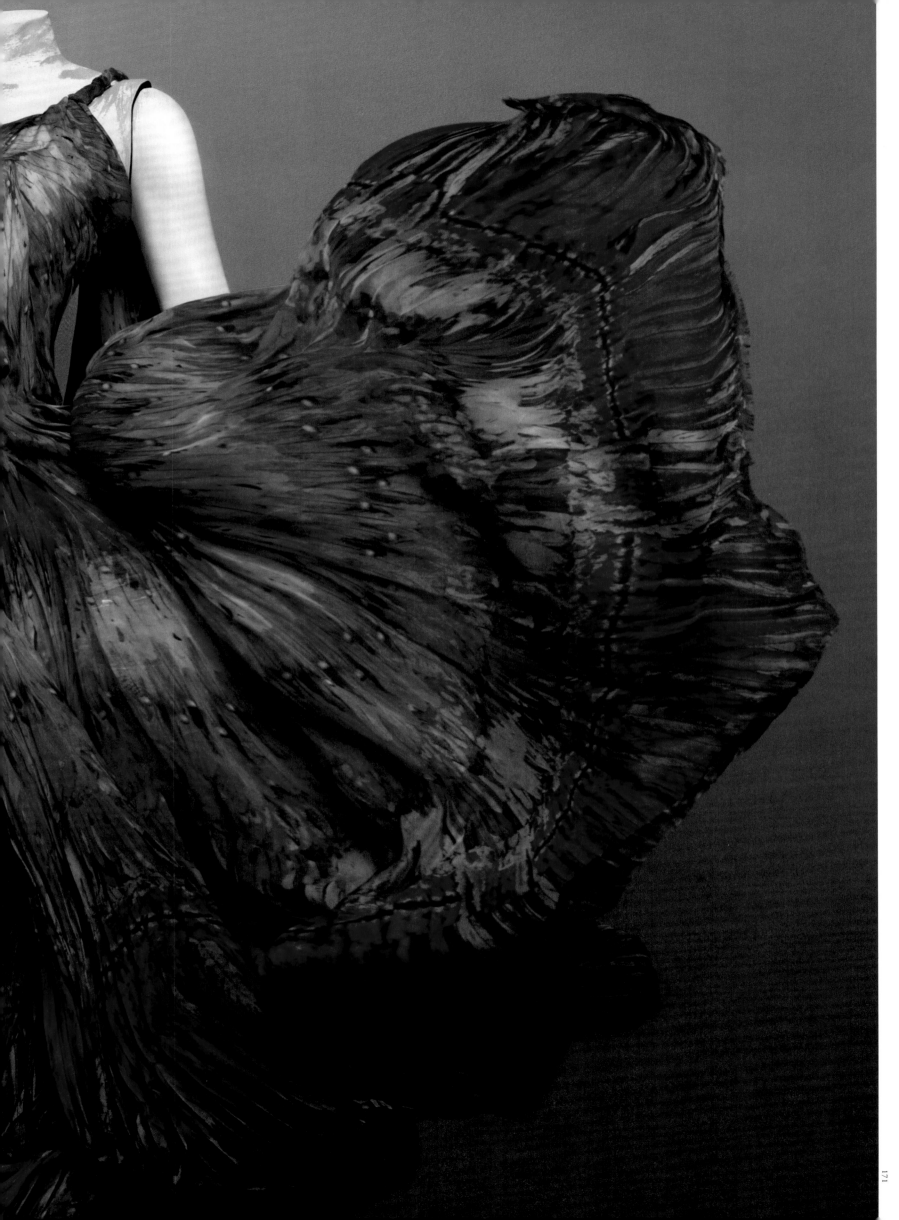

"I have always loved the mechanics of nature and to a greater or lesser extent my work is always informed by that."

"Birds in flight fascinate me. I admire eagles and falcons. I'm inspired by a feather but also its color, its graphics, its weightlessness and its engineering. It's so elaborate. In fact I try and transpose the beauty of a bird to women."

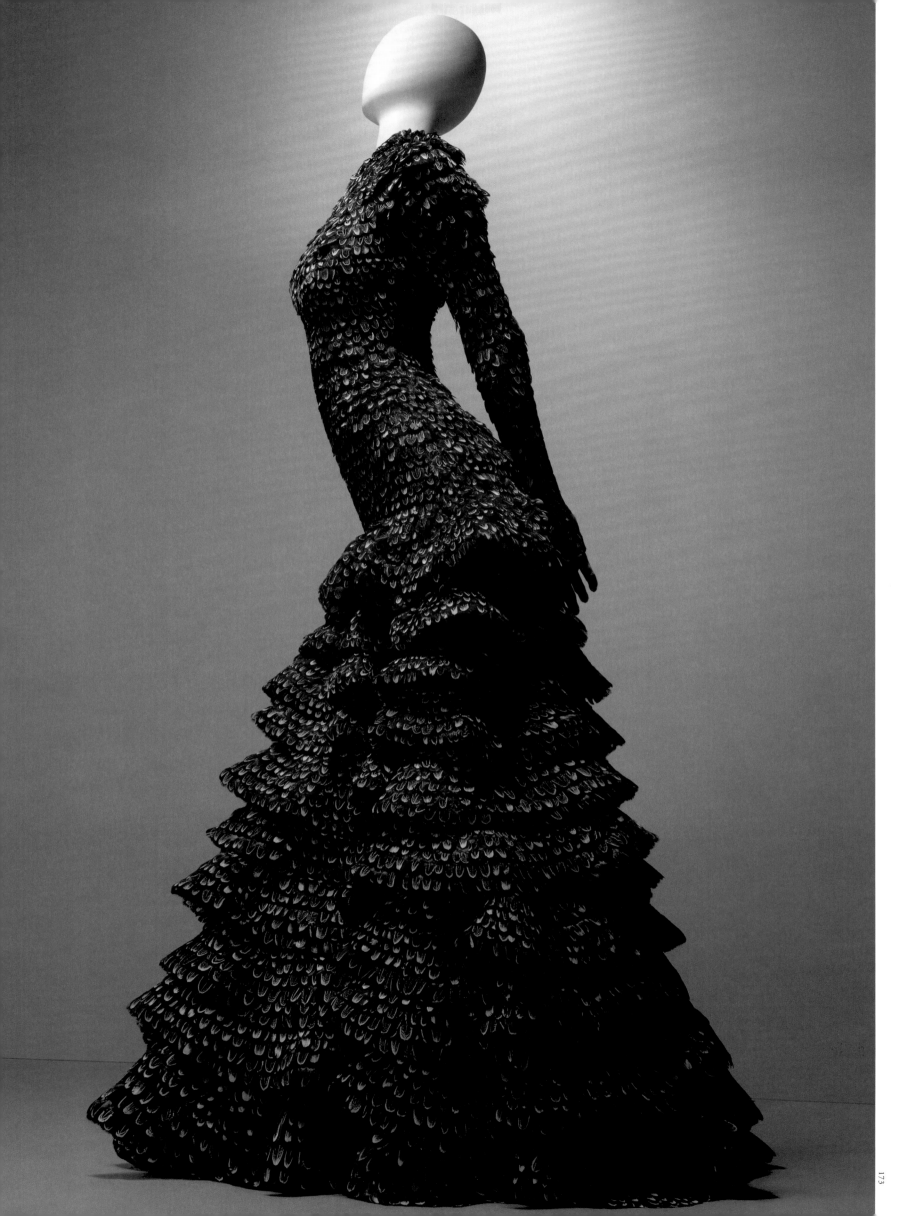

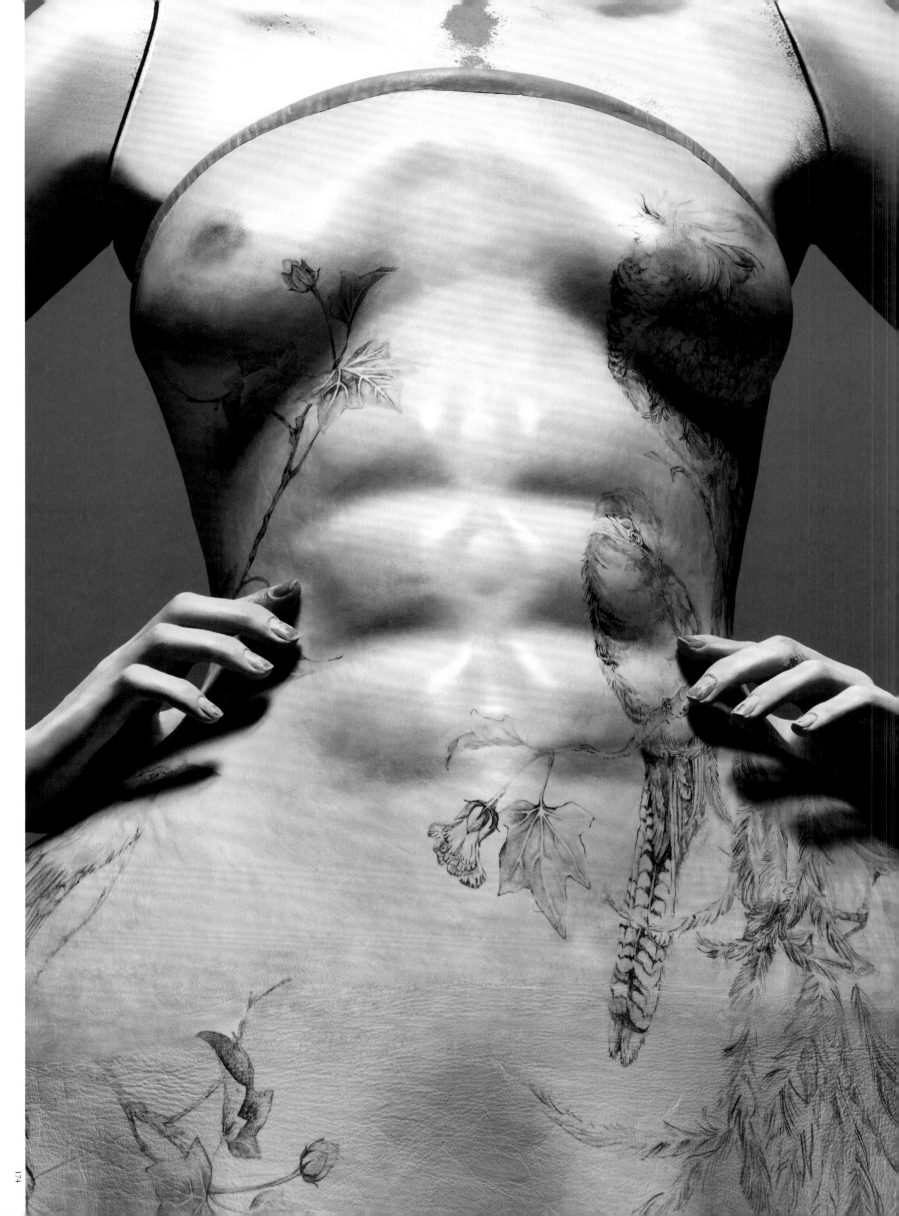

"Women should look like women. A piece of

cardboard has no sexuality."

"I liked the padded hips because they didn't make the [piece] look historical, but . . . more sensual. Like the statue of Diana with breasts and big hips. It's more maternal, more womanly."

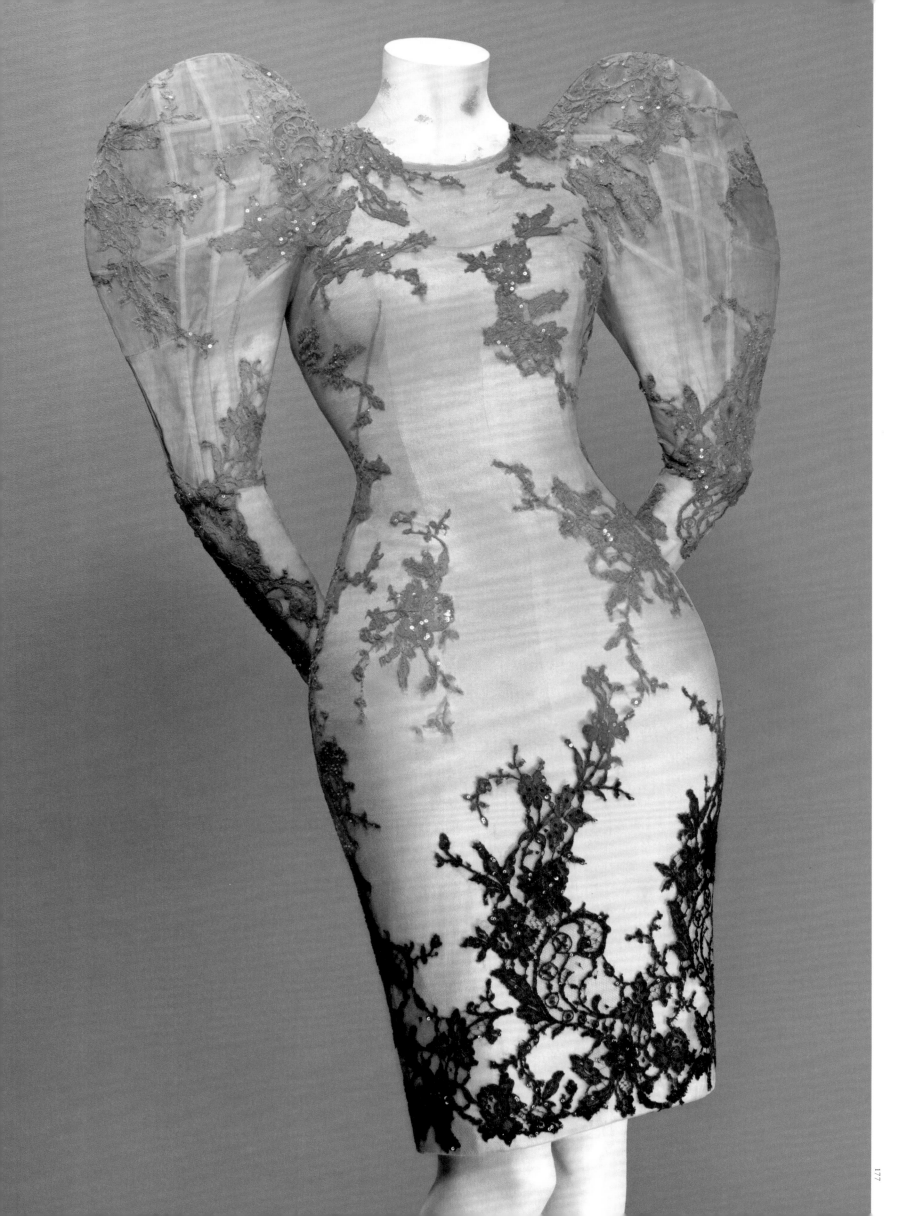

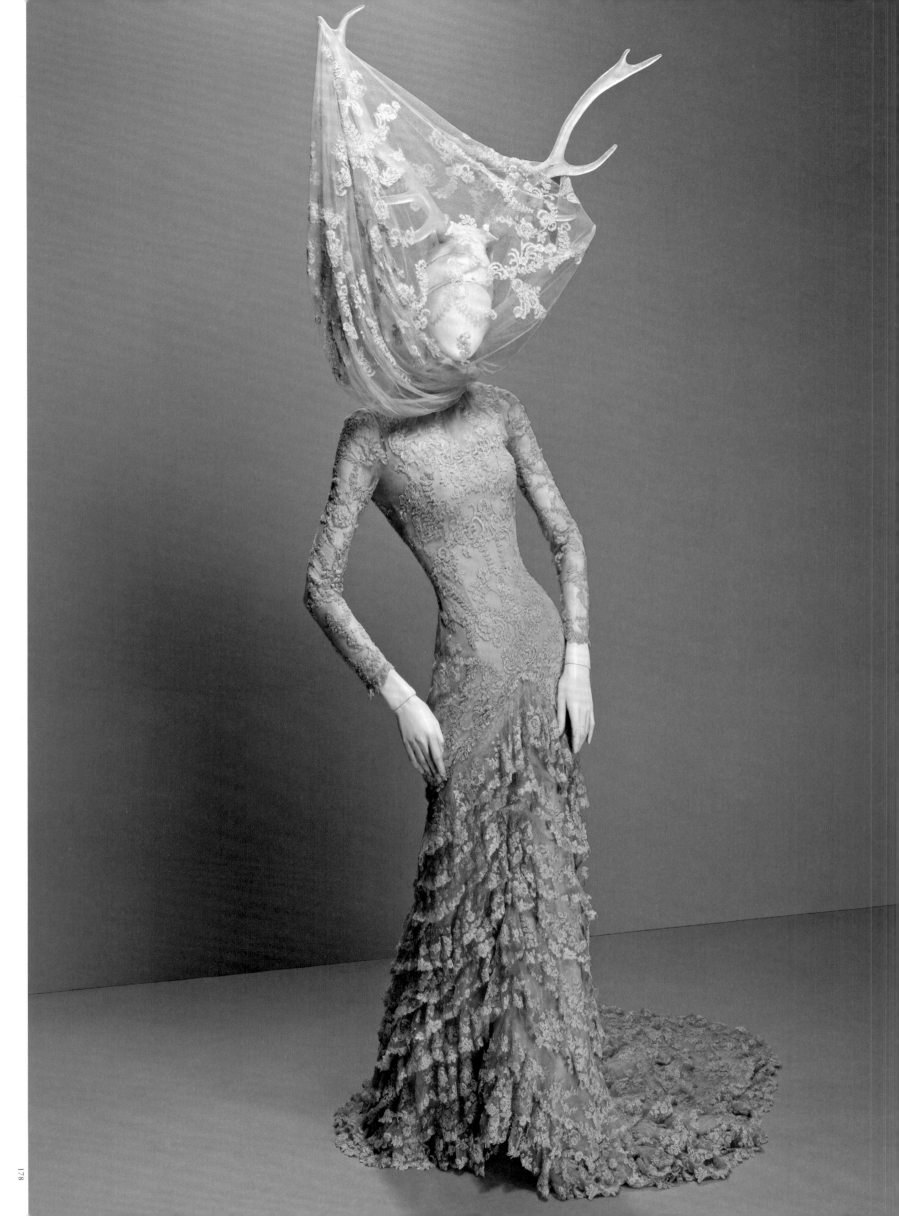

"When we put the antlers on the model and then draped over it the lace embroidery that we had made, we had to poke them through a £2,000 piece of work. But then it worked because it looks like she's rammed the piece of lace with her antlers. There's always spontaneity. You've got to allow for that in my shows."

"[I love the] washed out colors [in this collection].

Julia Margaret Cameron. Hand-painted

Victorian pictures. So, it's not really black, it's

grey. And, it's not really white, it's dirty white.

And, the pink is like the powder on the face."

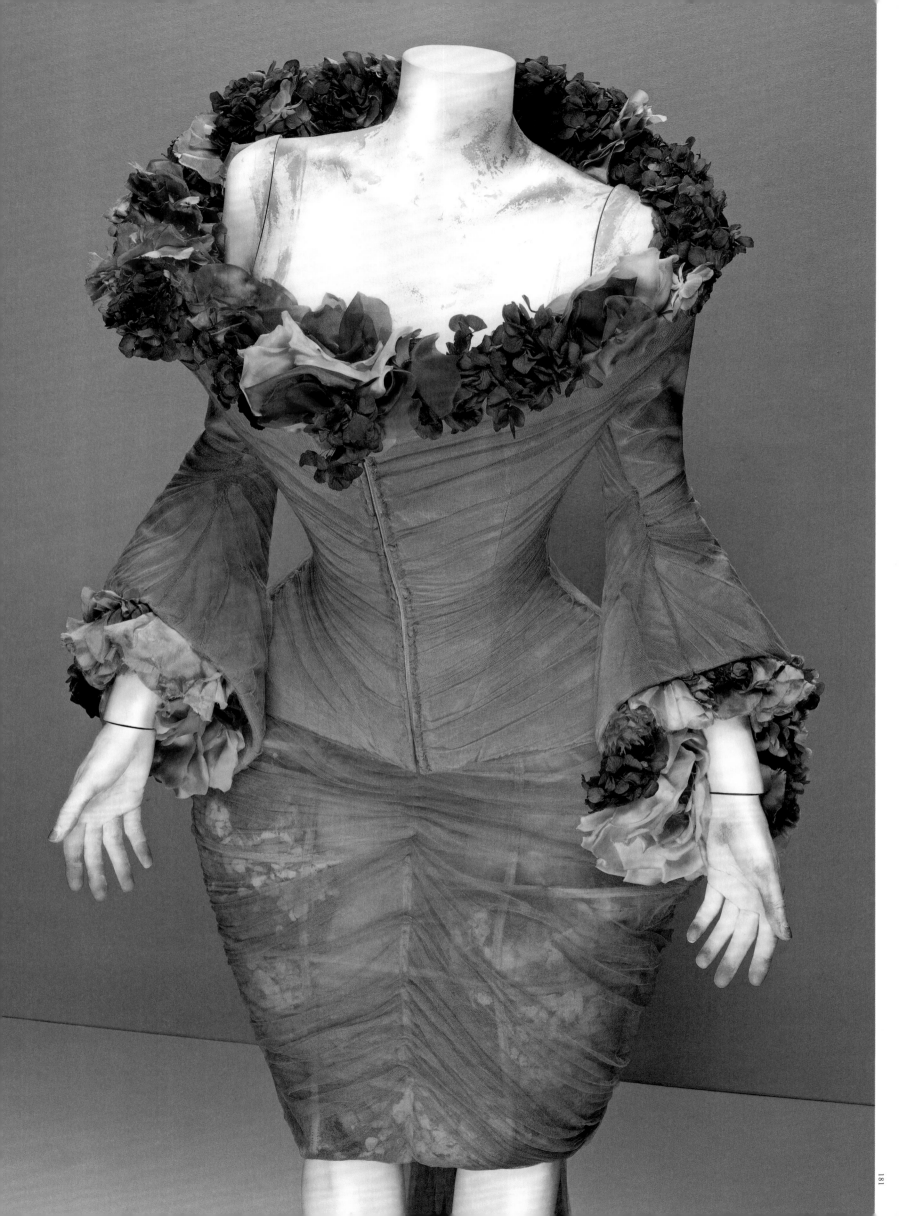

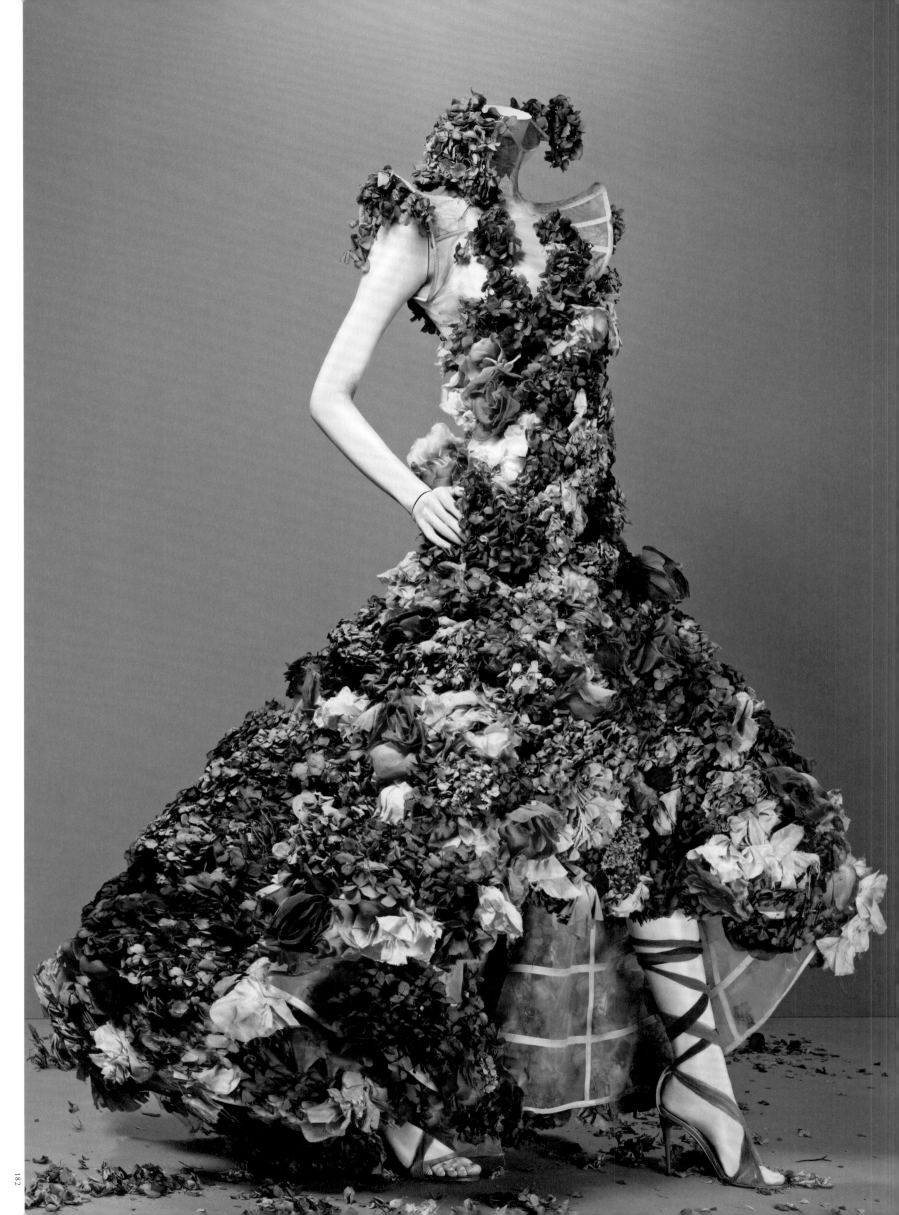

"Remember Sam Taylor-Wood's dying fruit?

Things rot. . . . I used flowers because they die.

My mood was darkly romantic at the time."

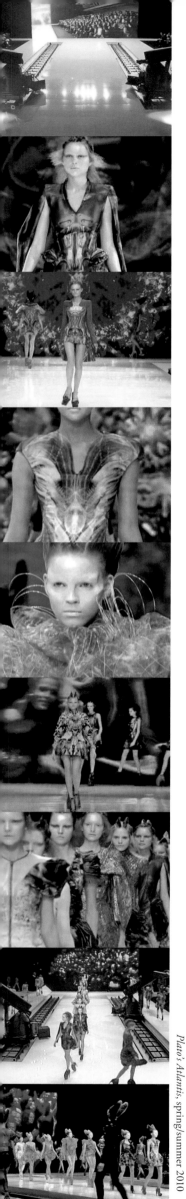

Plato's Atlantis, spring/summer 2010

"[This collection predicted a future in which]
the ice cap would melt . . . the waters would rise
and . . . life on earth would have to evolve in
order to live beneath the sea once more or perish.
. . . Humanity [would] go back to the place from
whence it came."

"There is no way back for me now. I am going
to take you on journeys you've never dreamed
were possible."

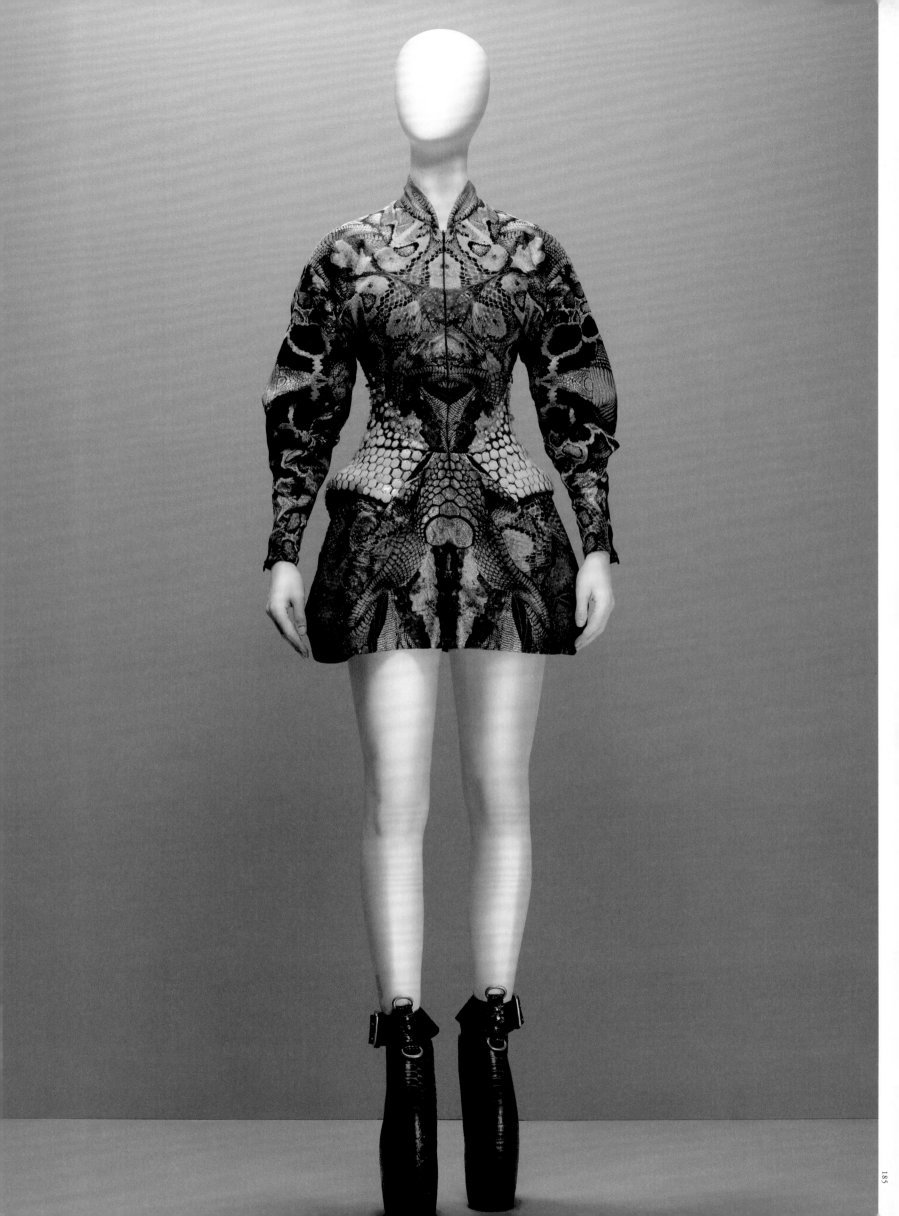

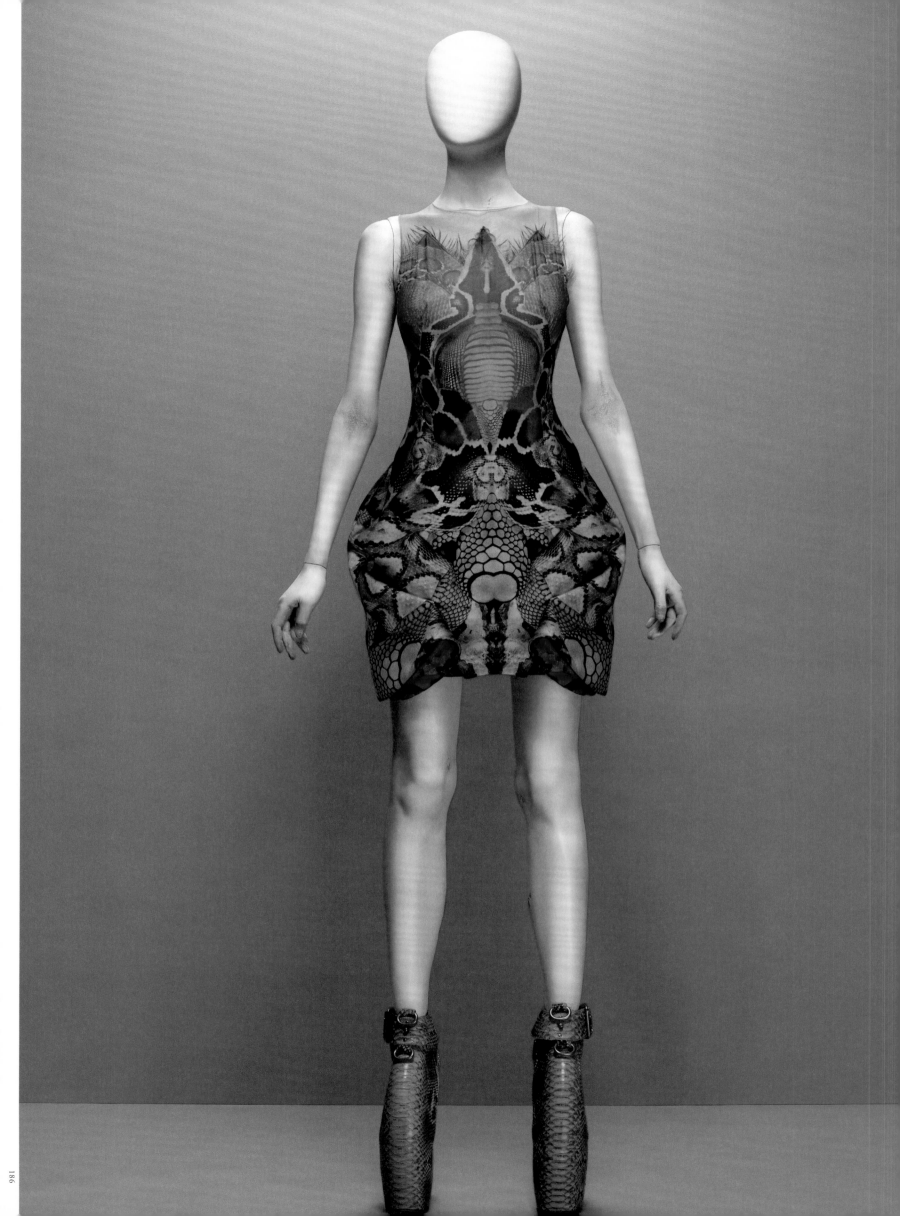

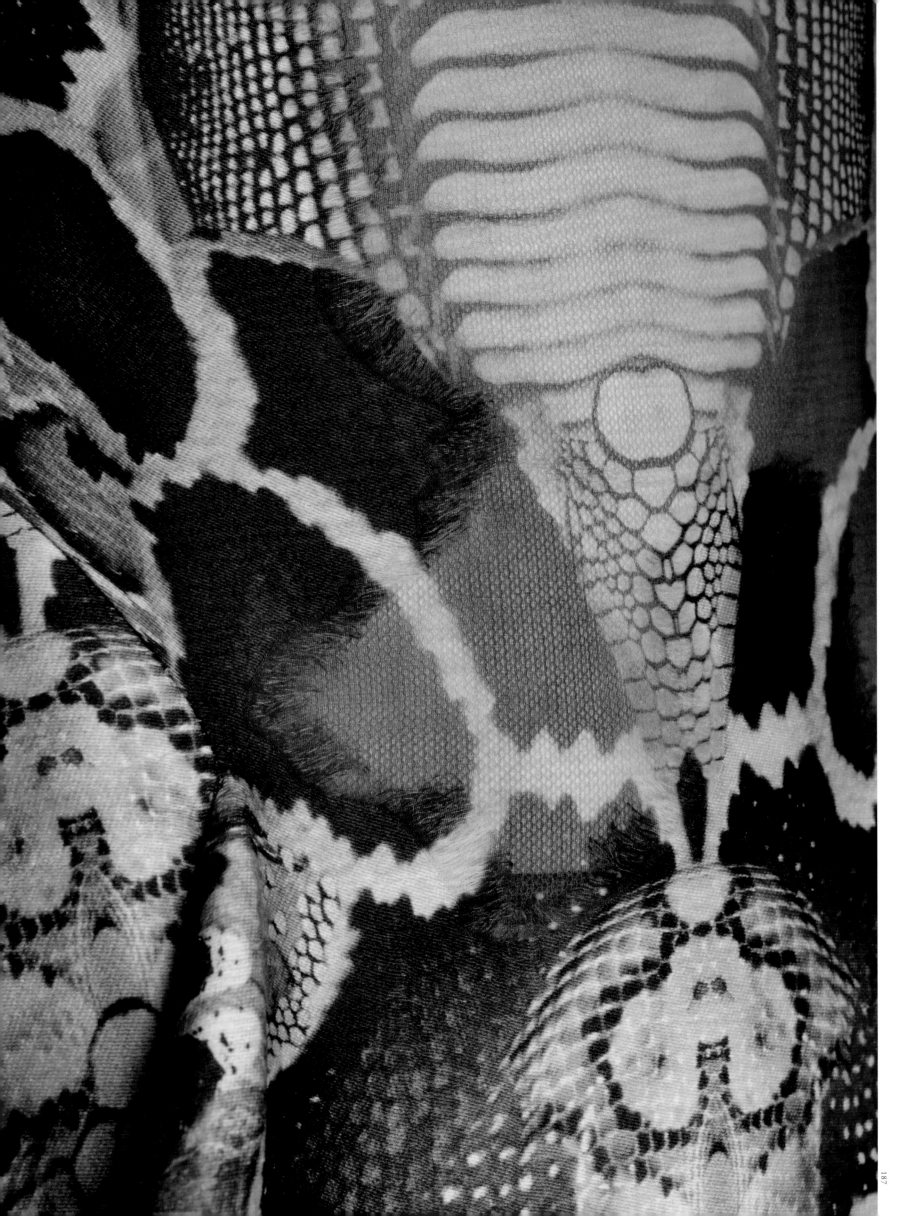

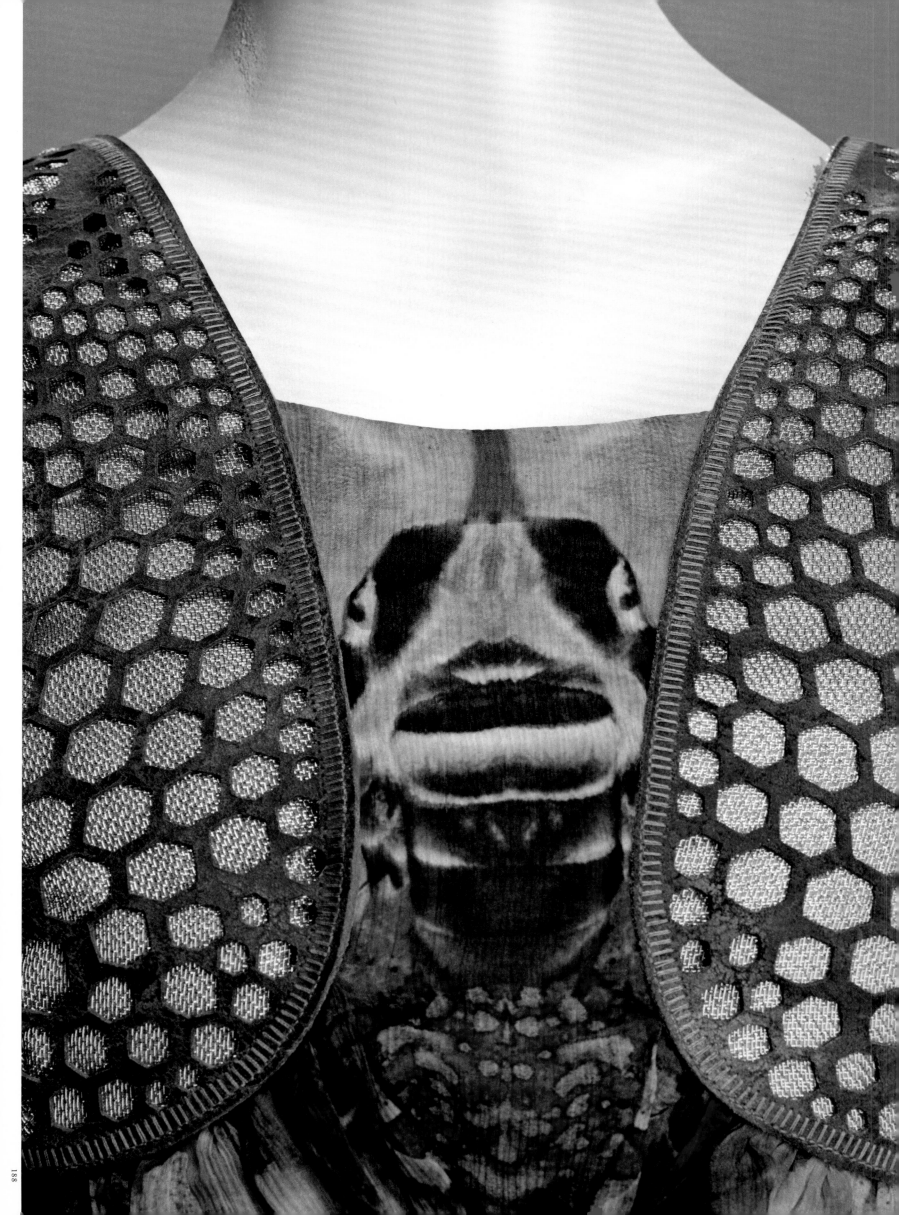

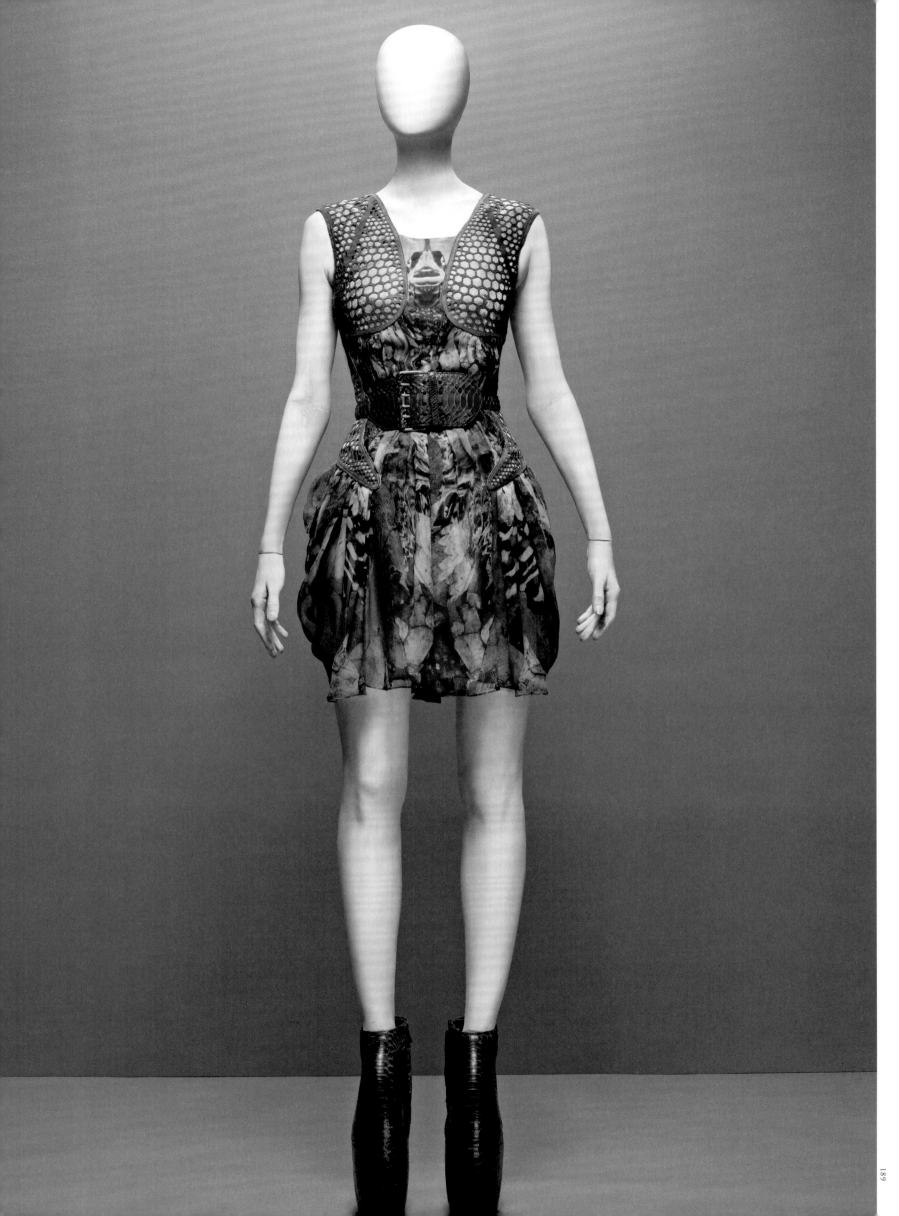

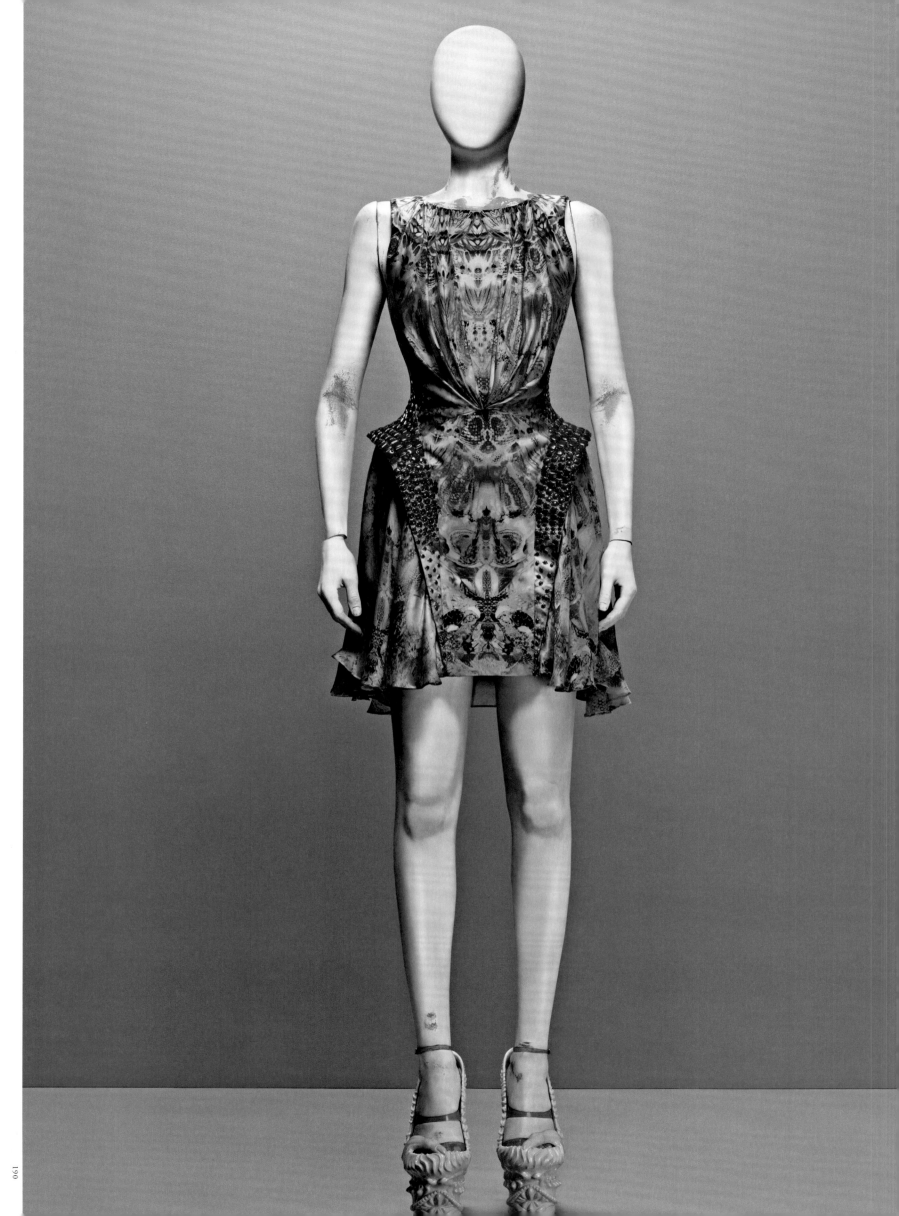

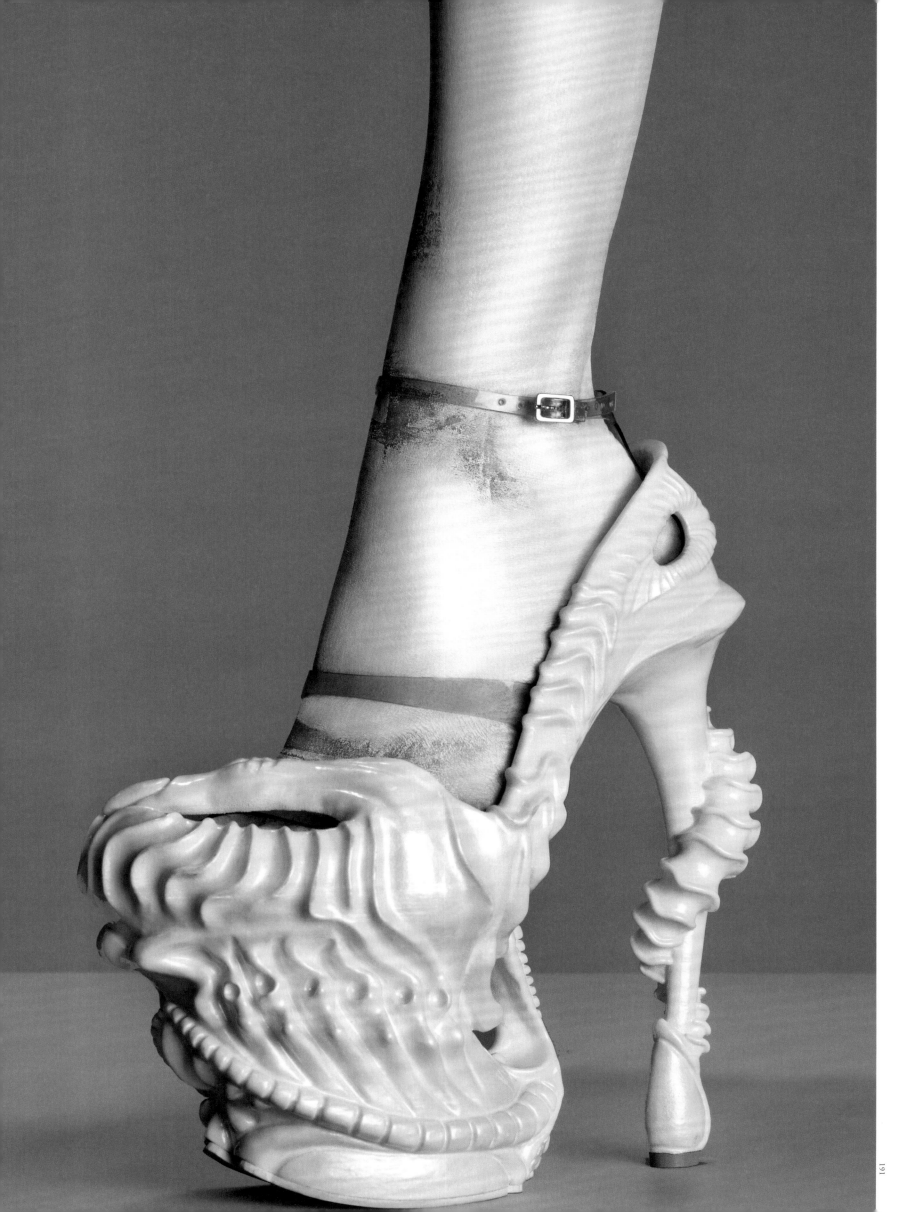

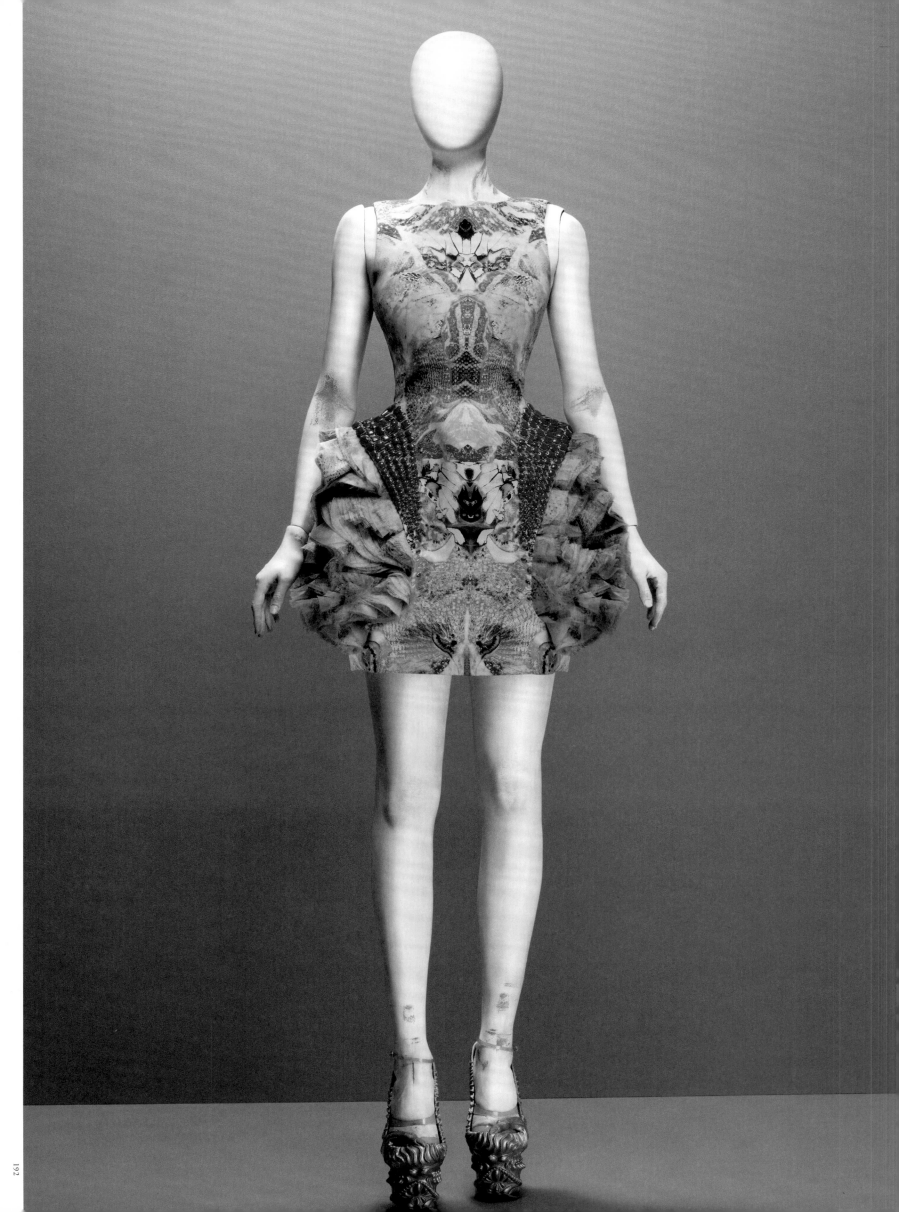

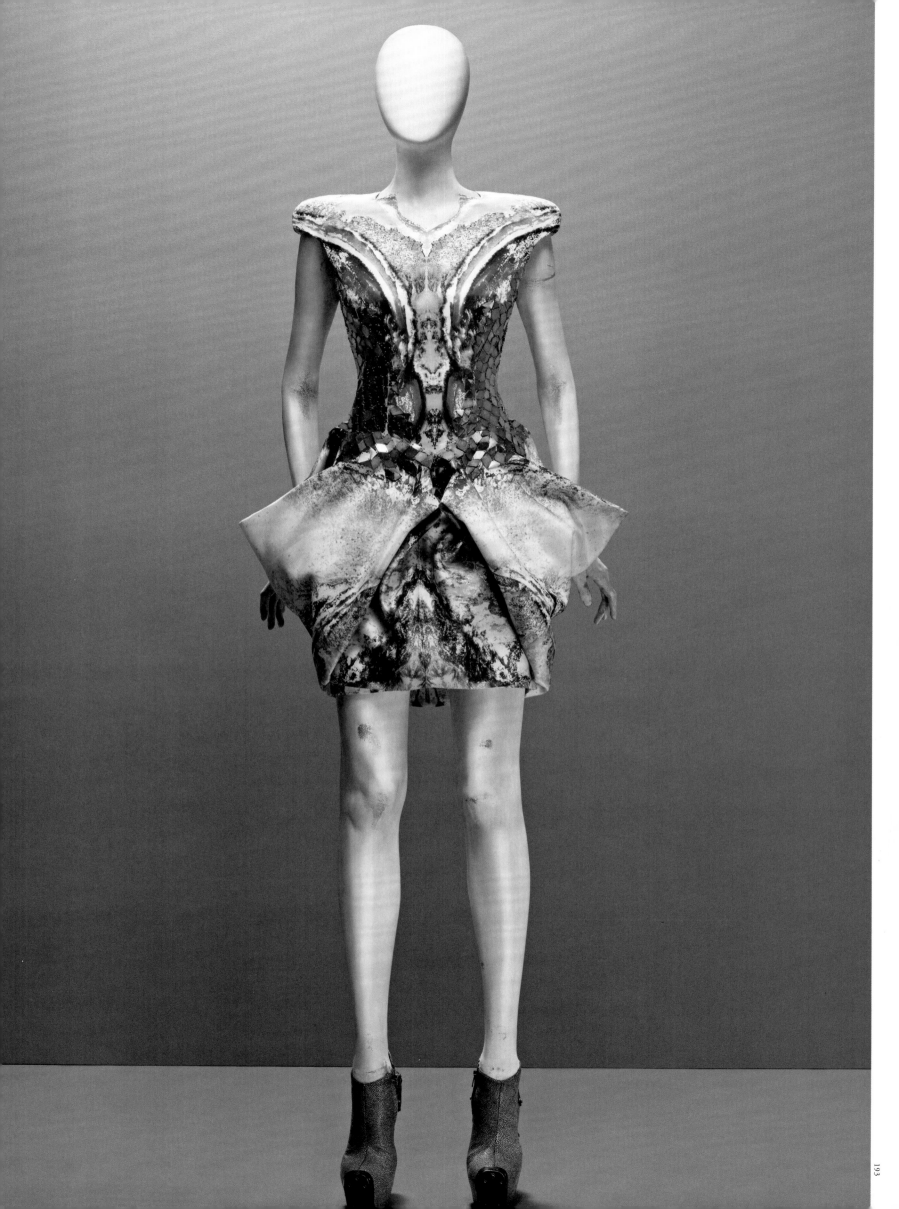

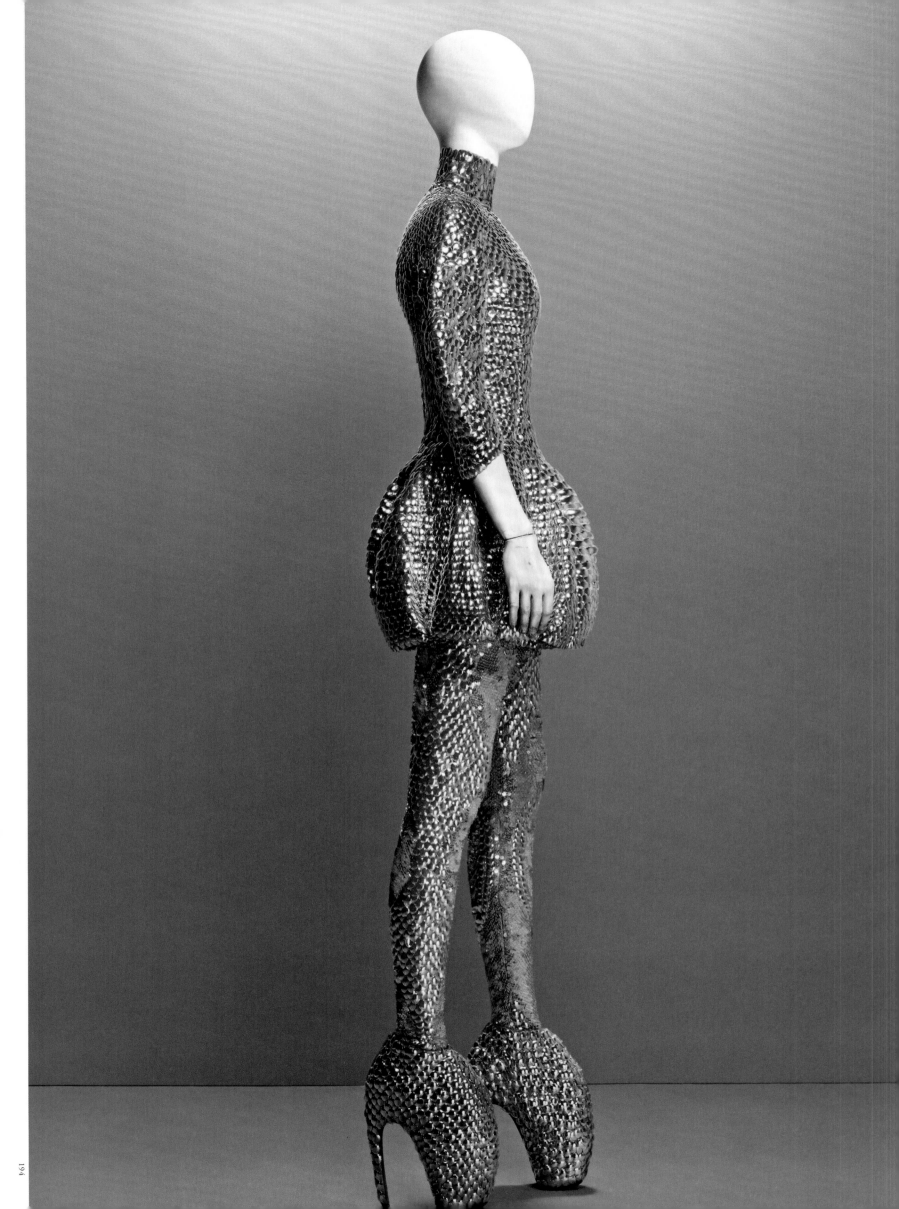

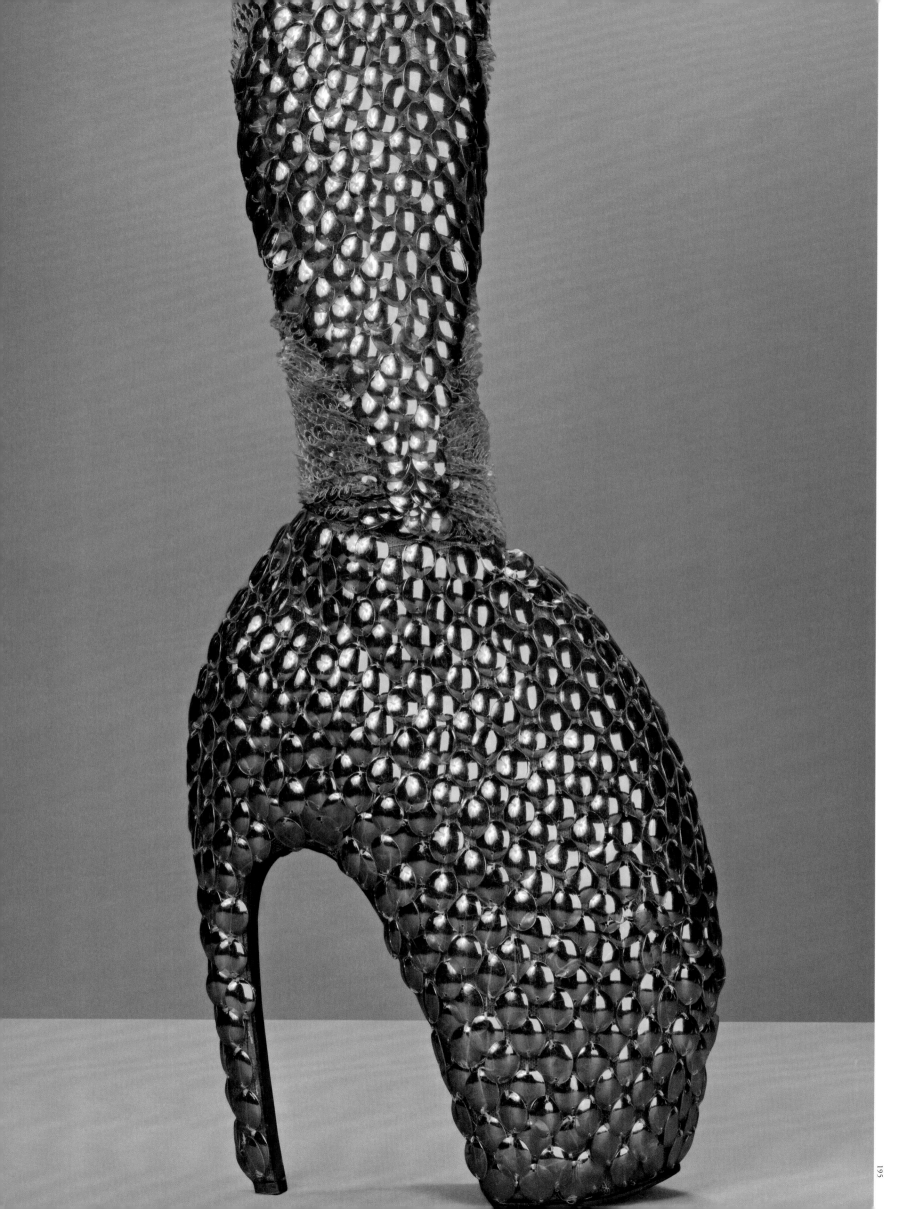

"Beauty can come from the strangest of places,

even the most disgusting of places."

"It's the ugly things I notice more, because

other people tend to ignore the ugly things."

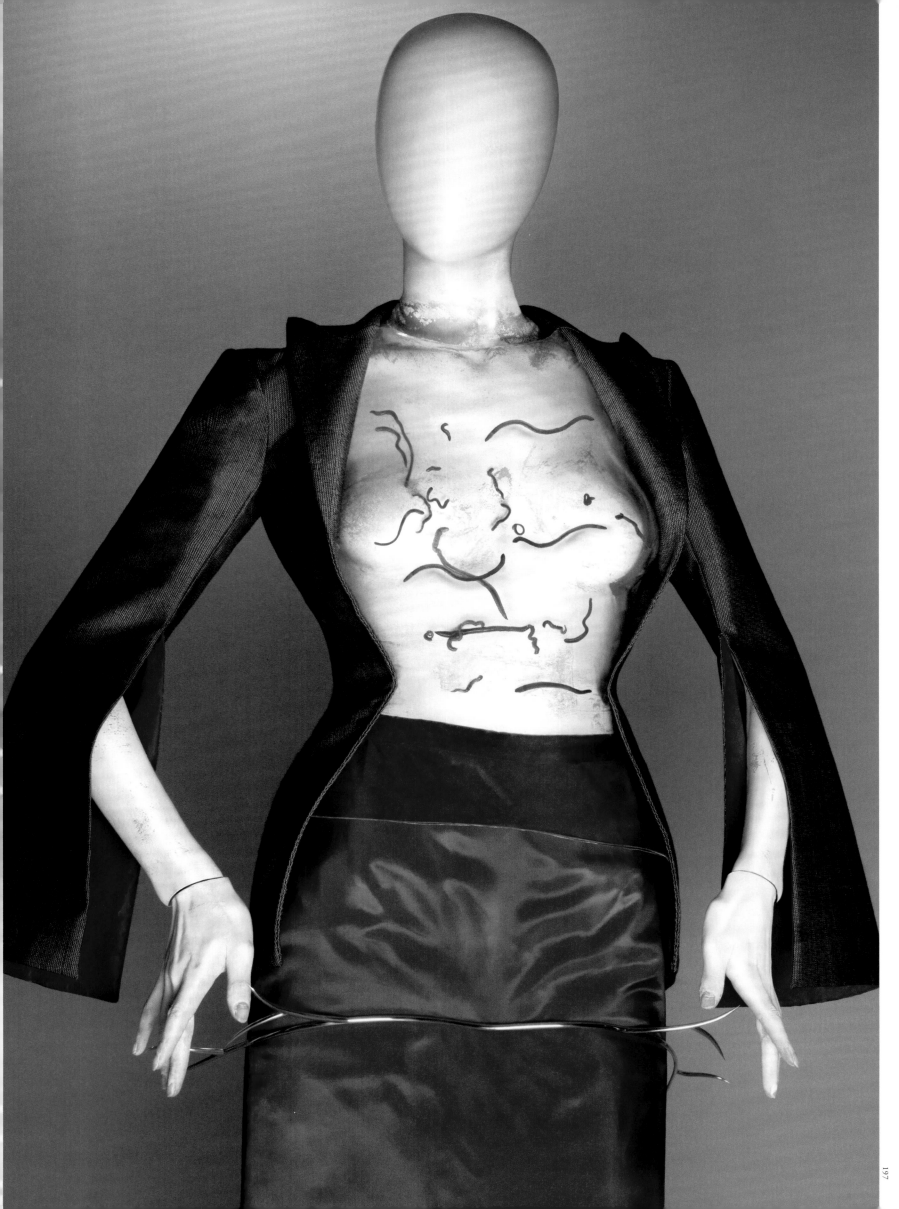

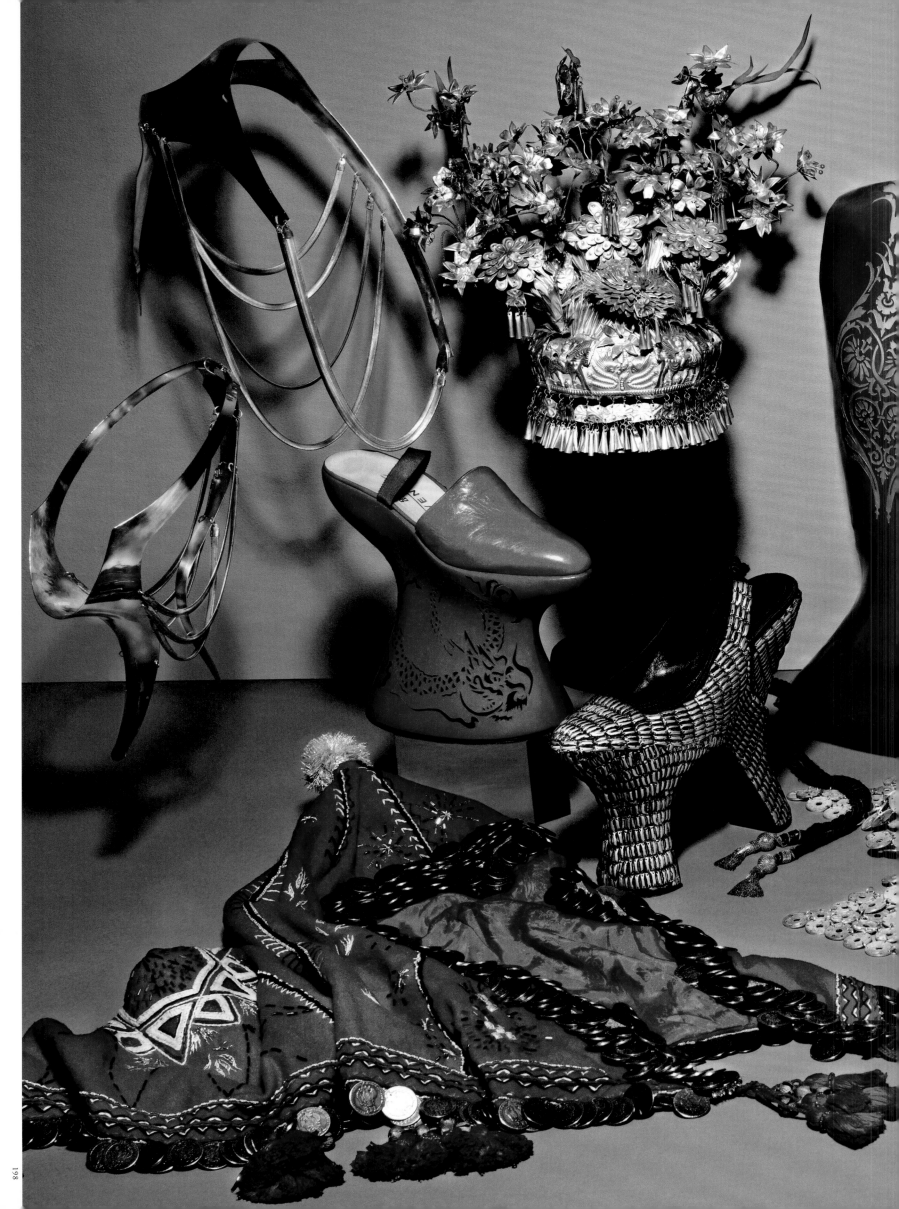

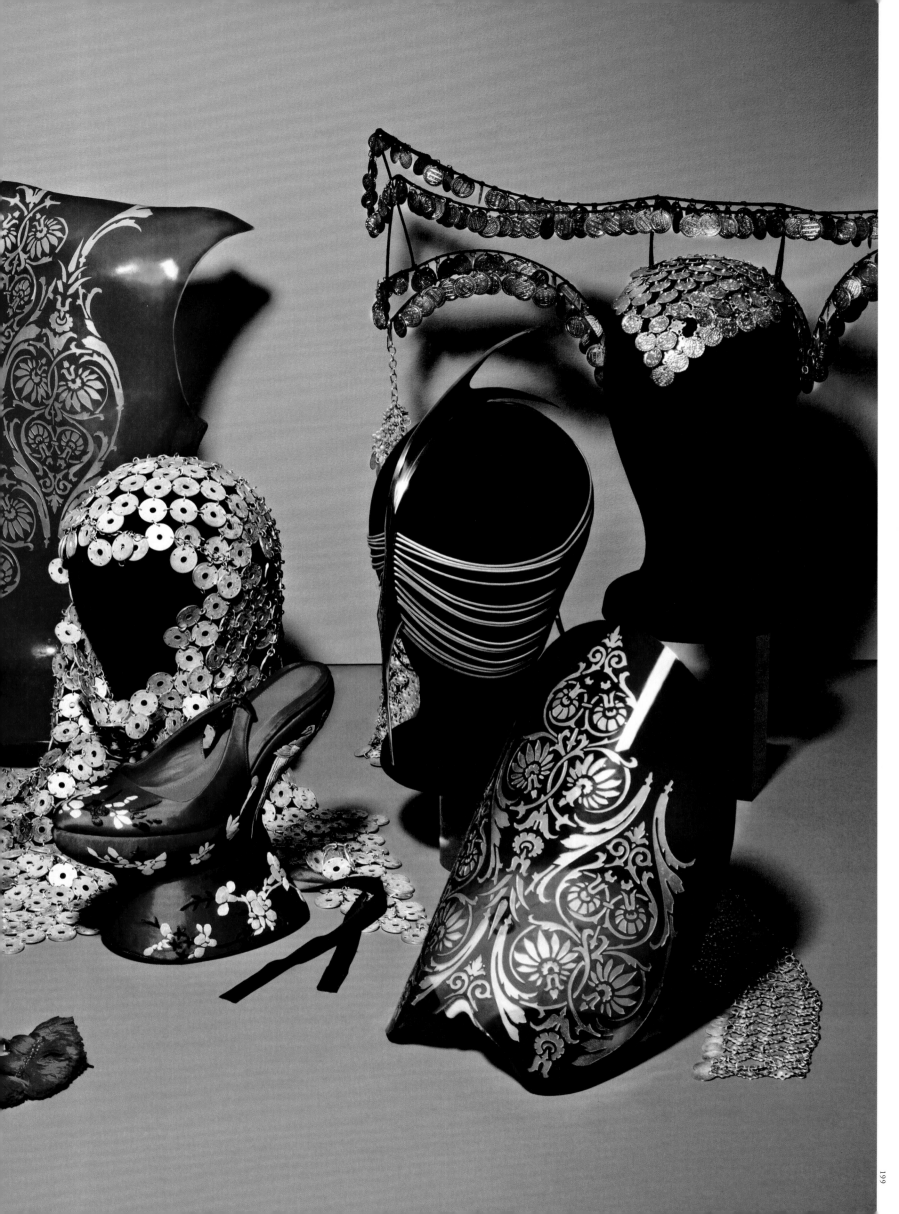

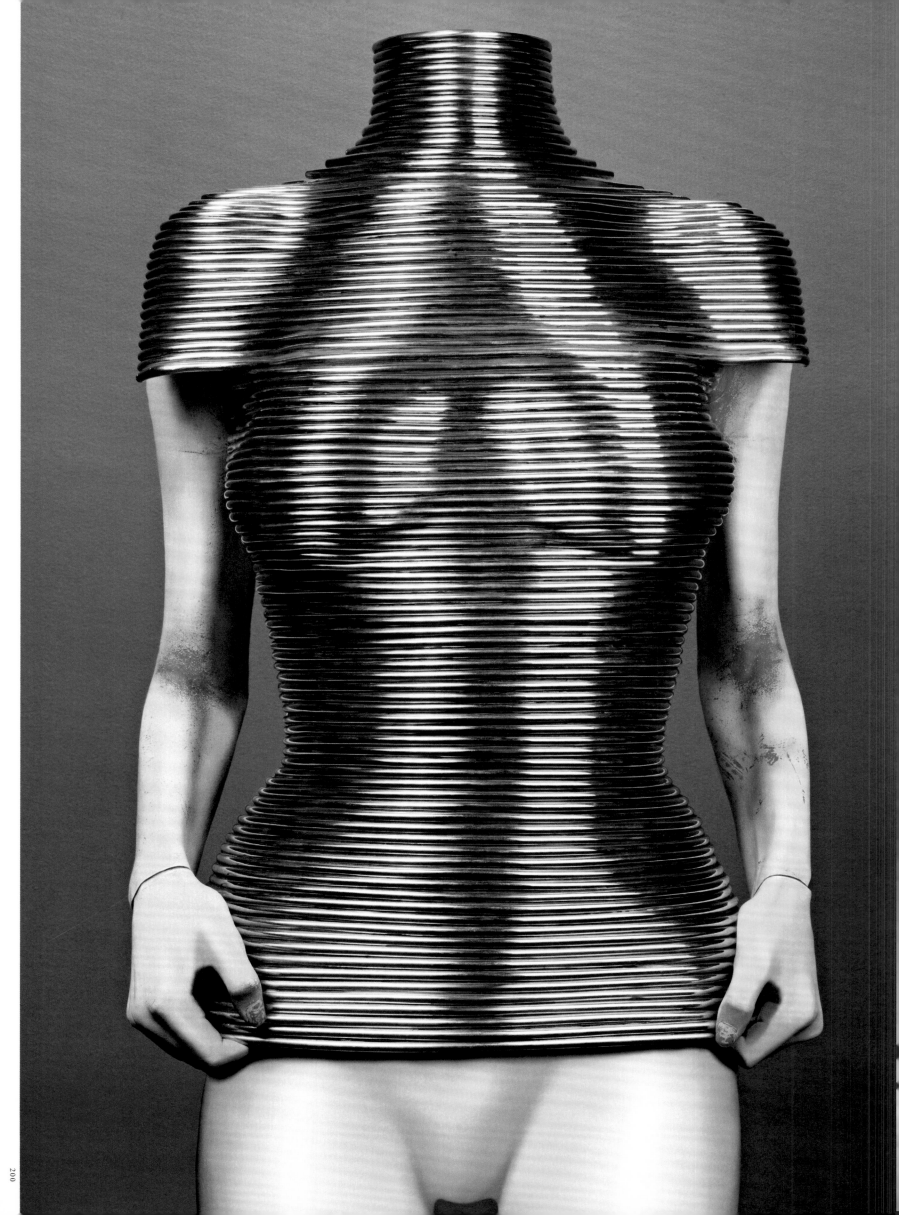

"I especially like the accessory for its

sadomasochistic aspect."

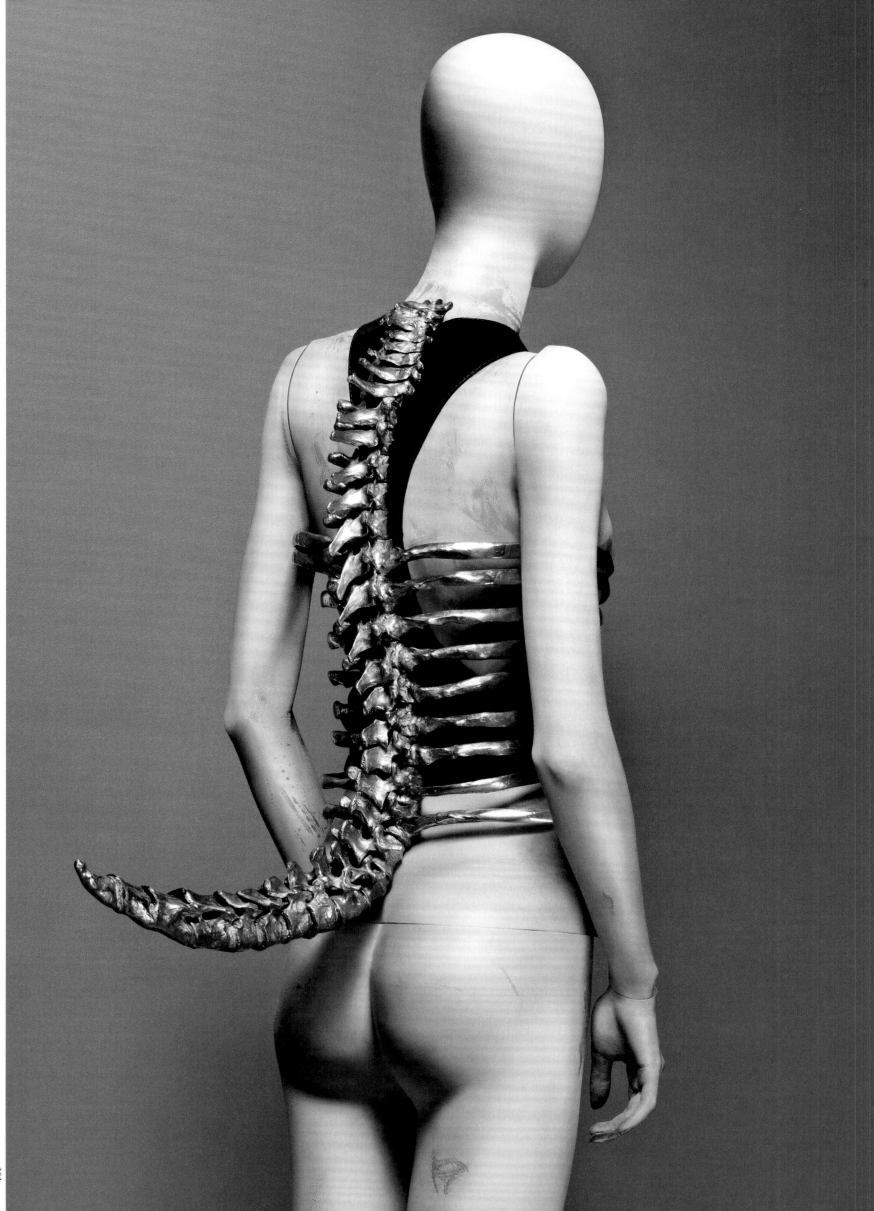

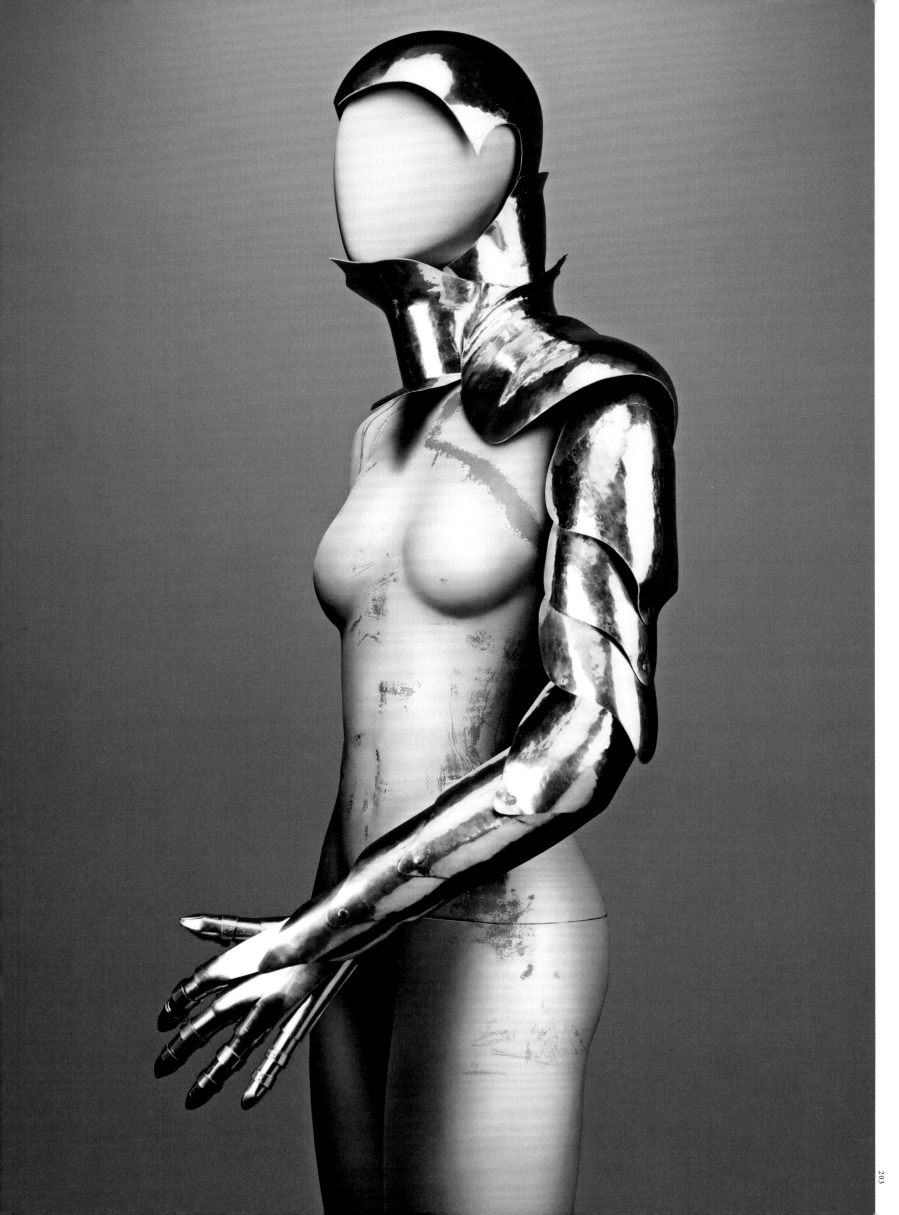

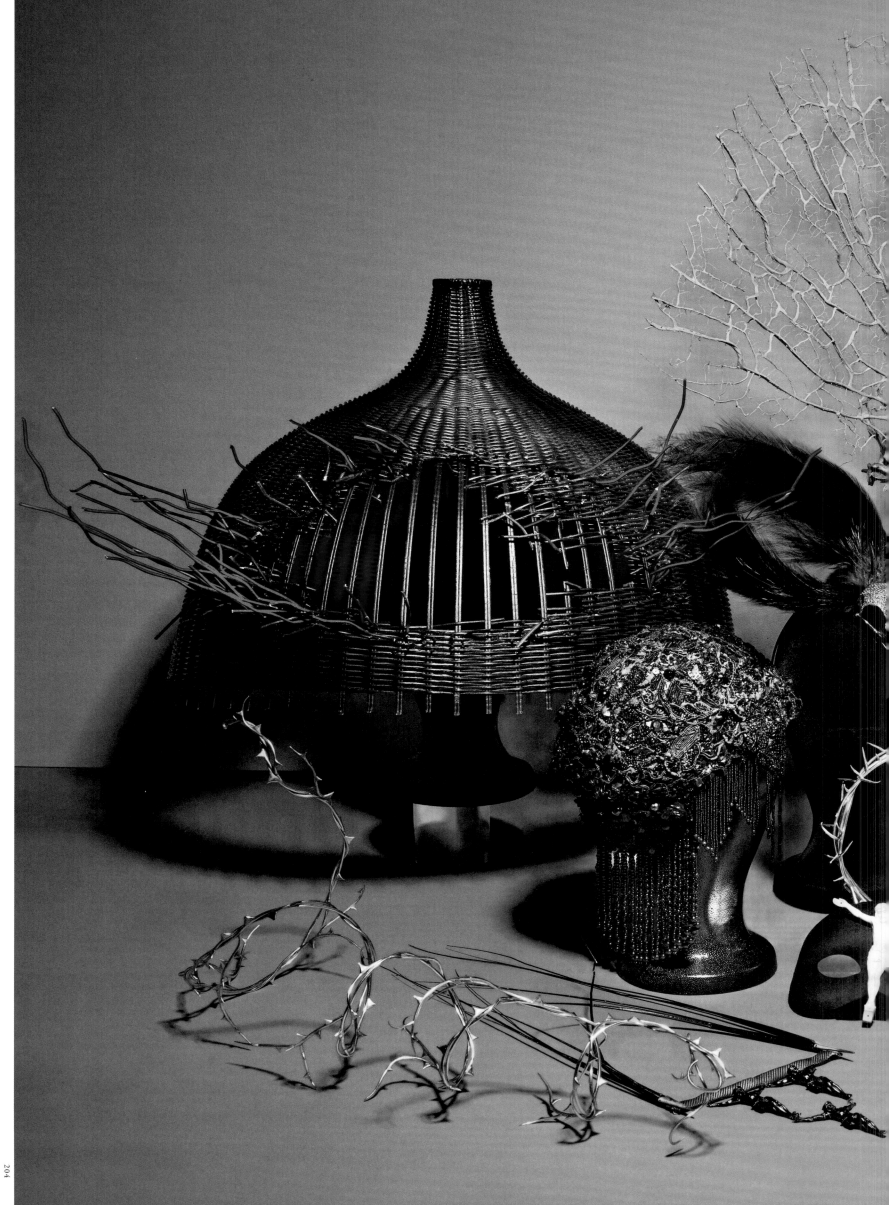

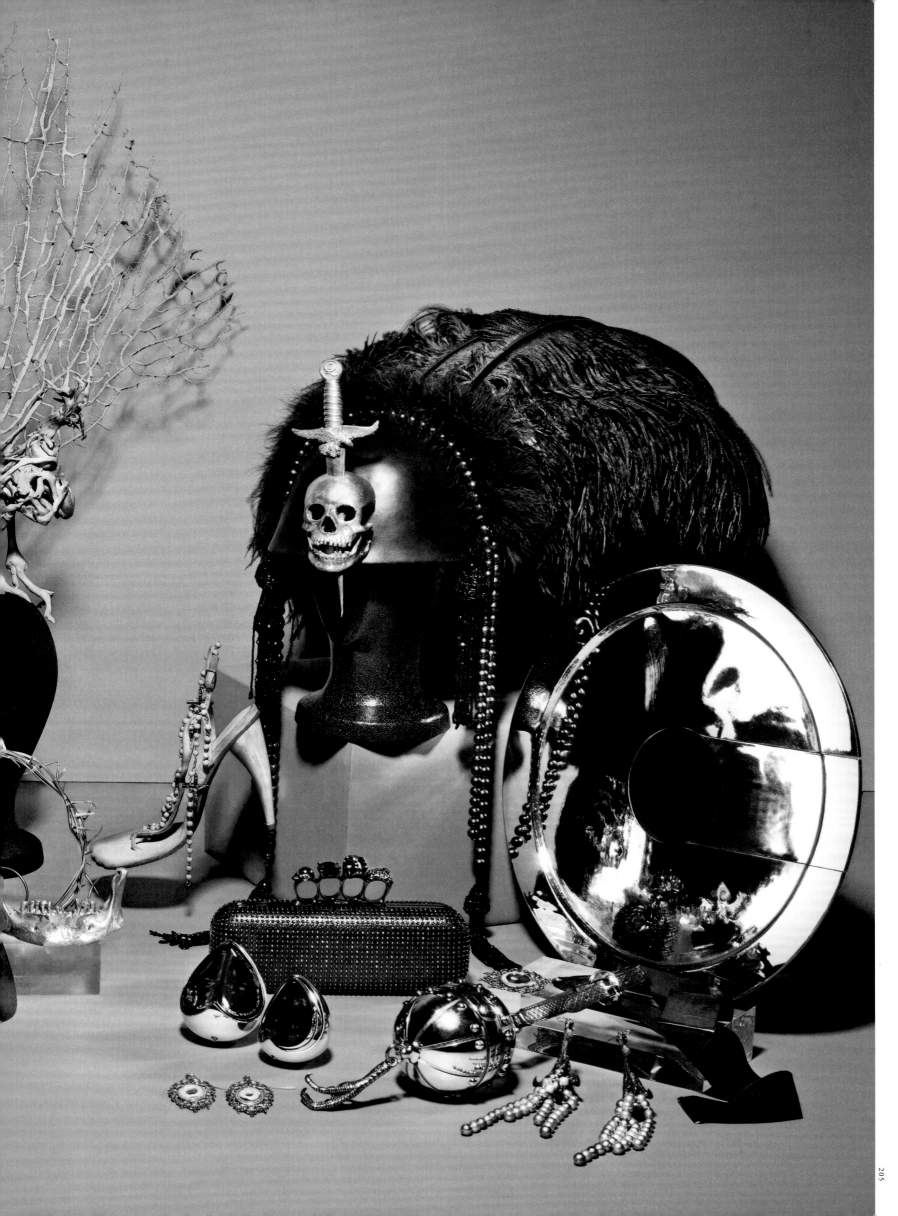

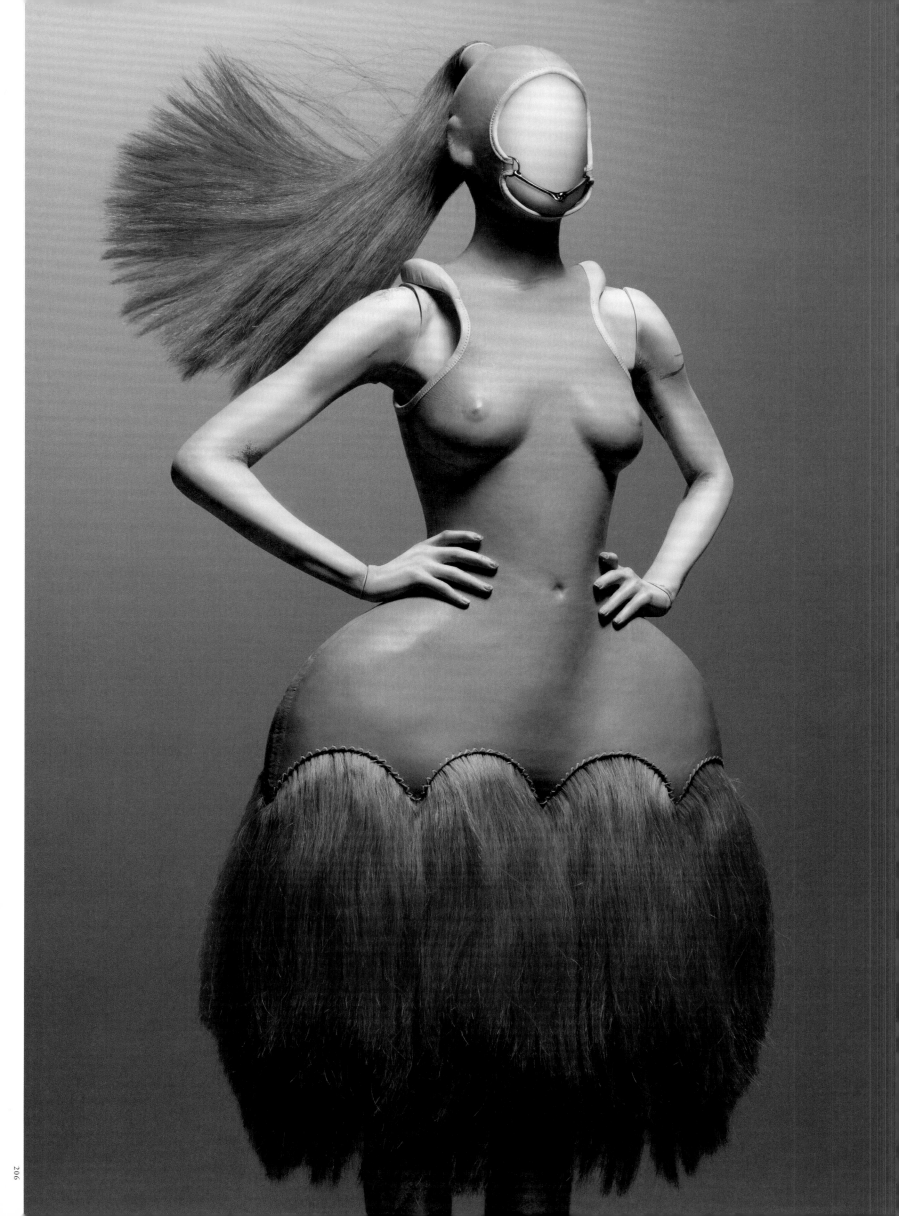

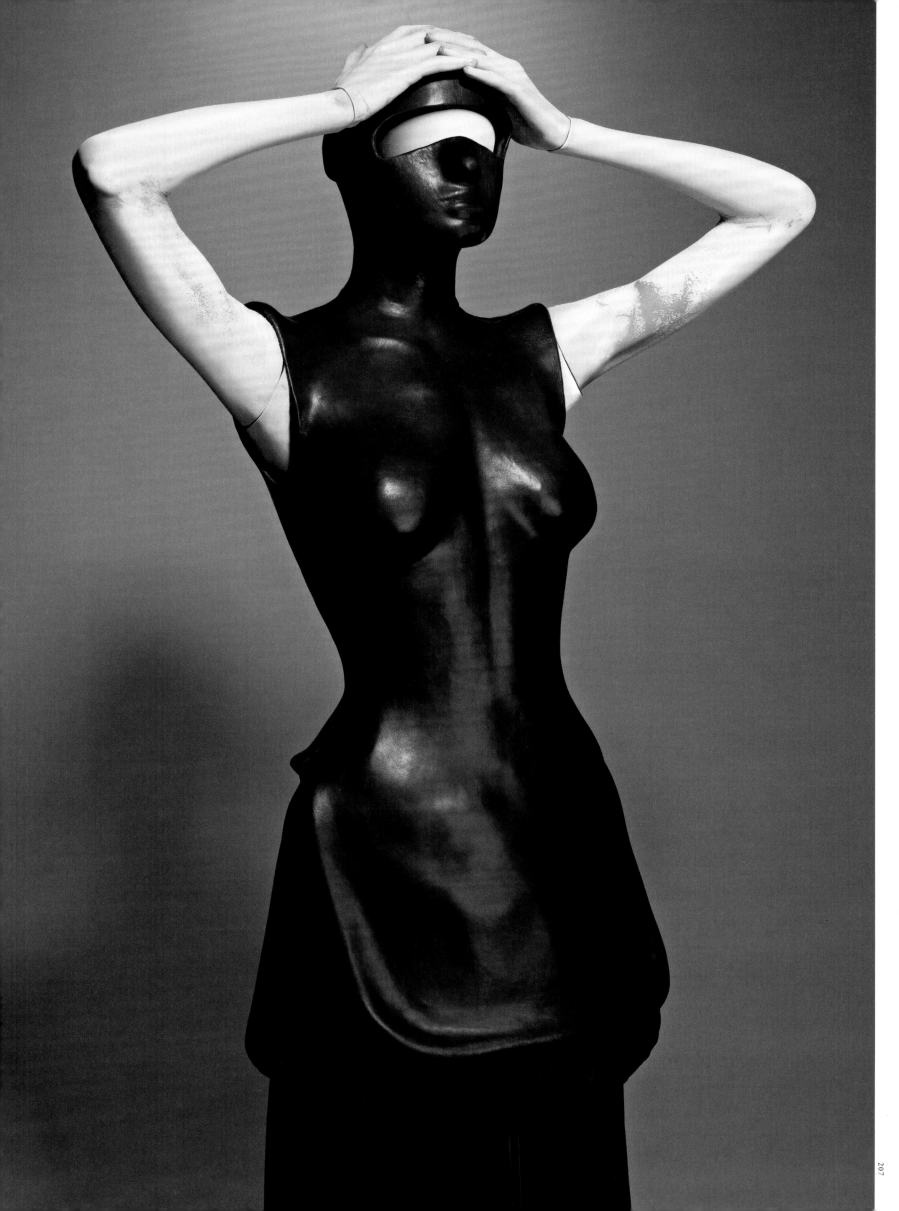

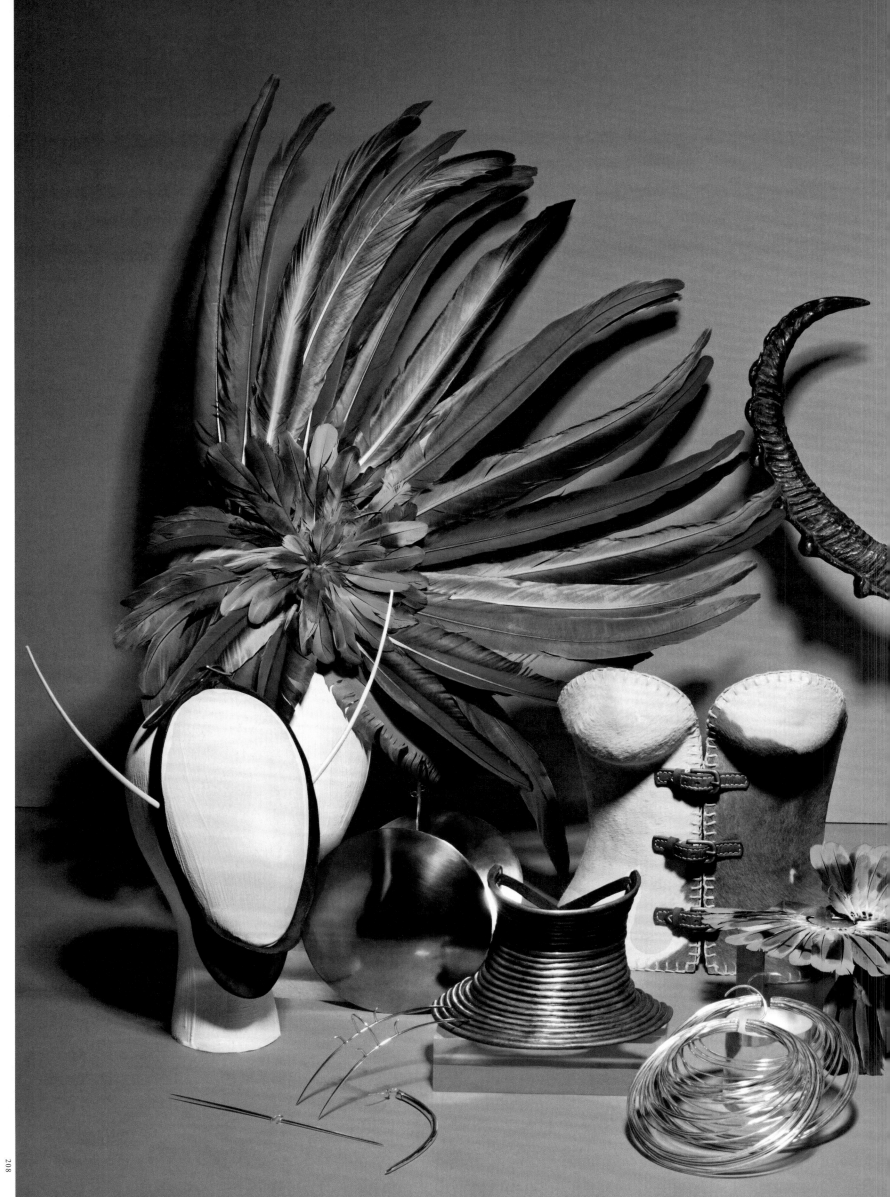

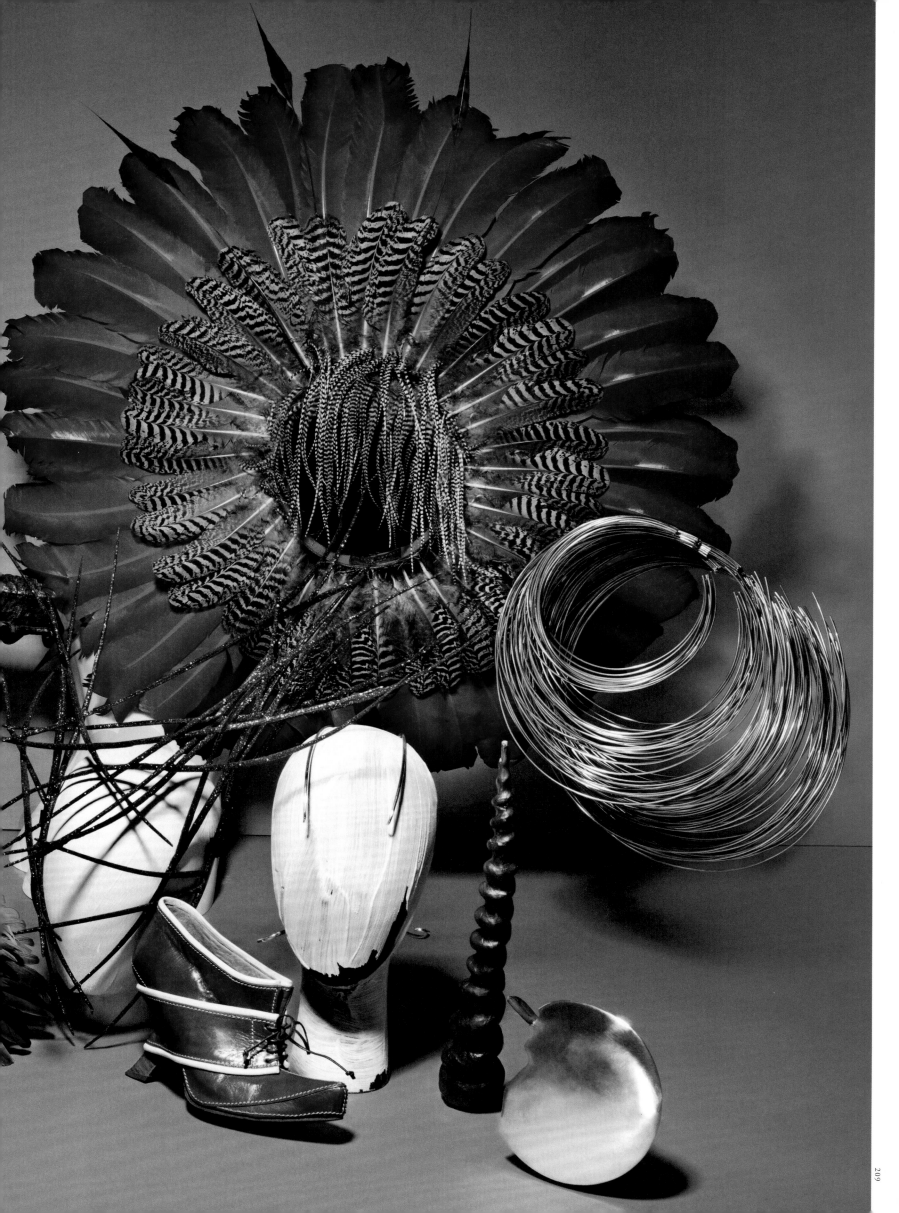

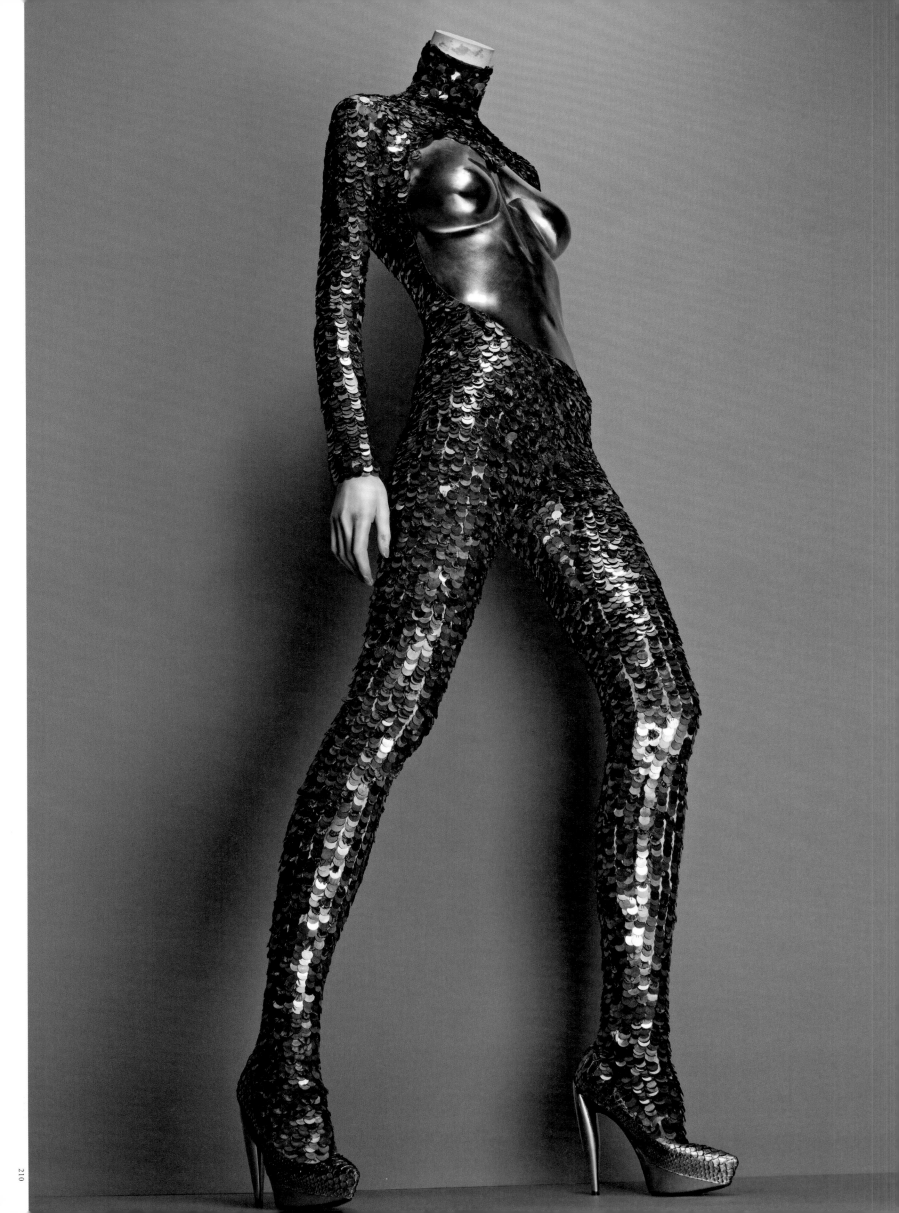

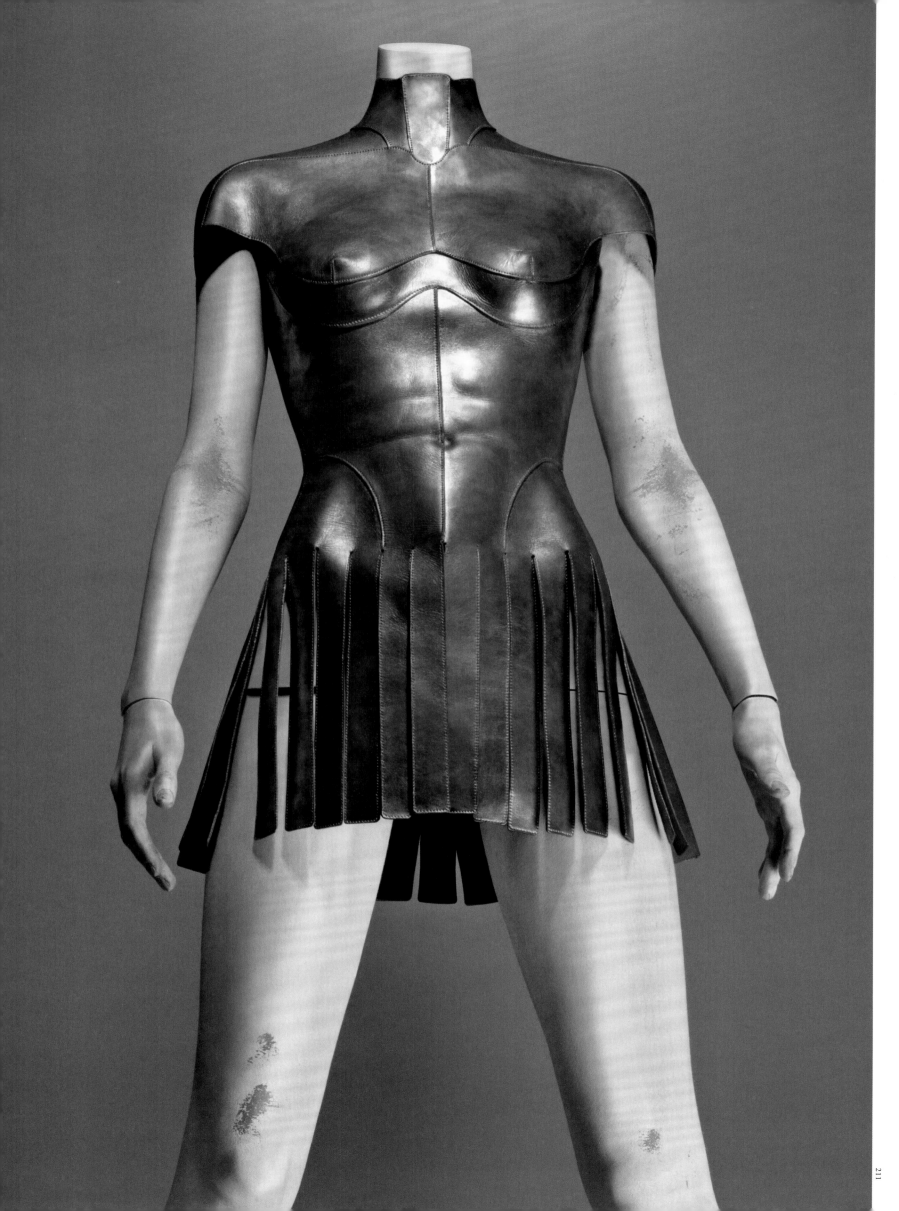

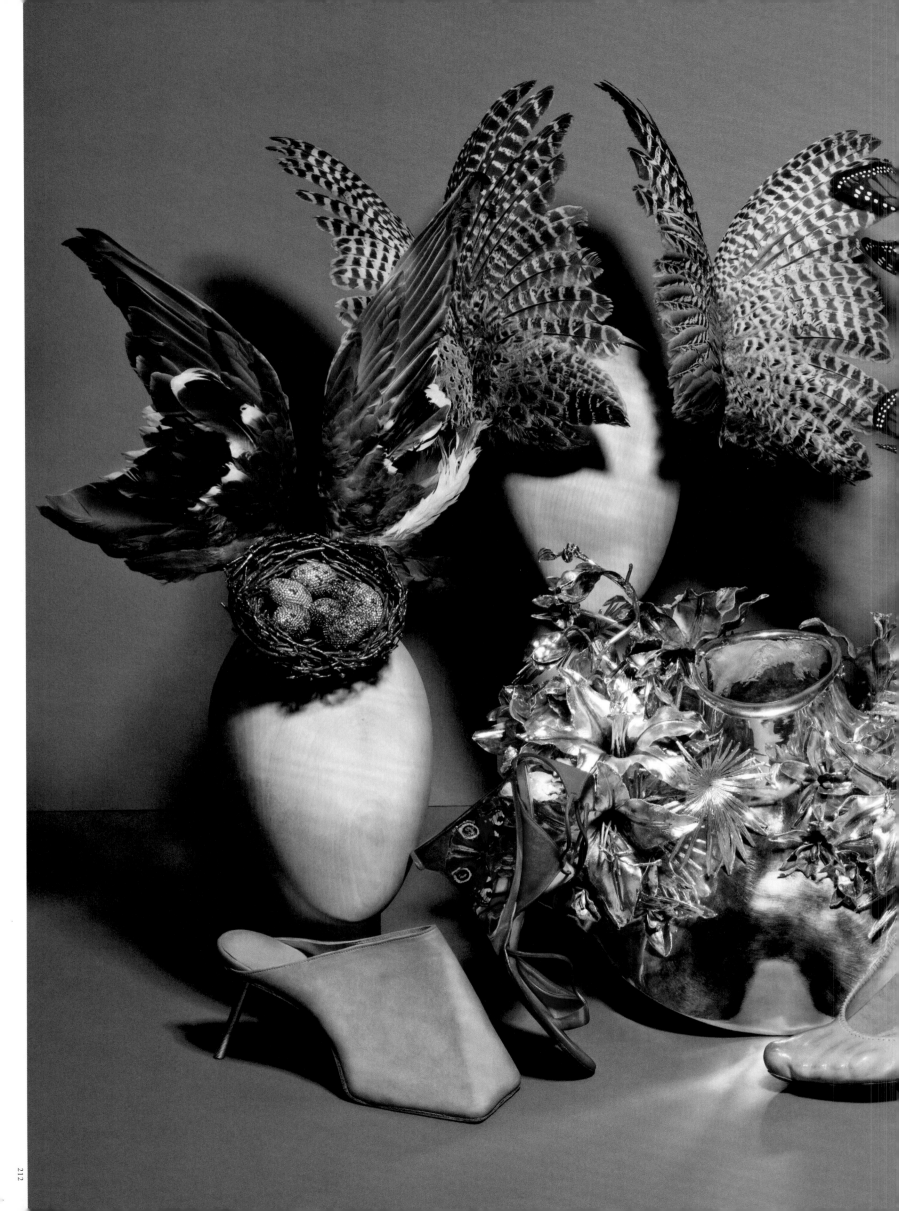

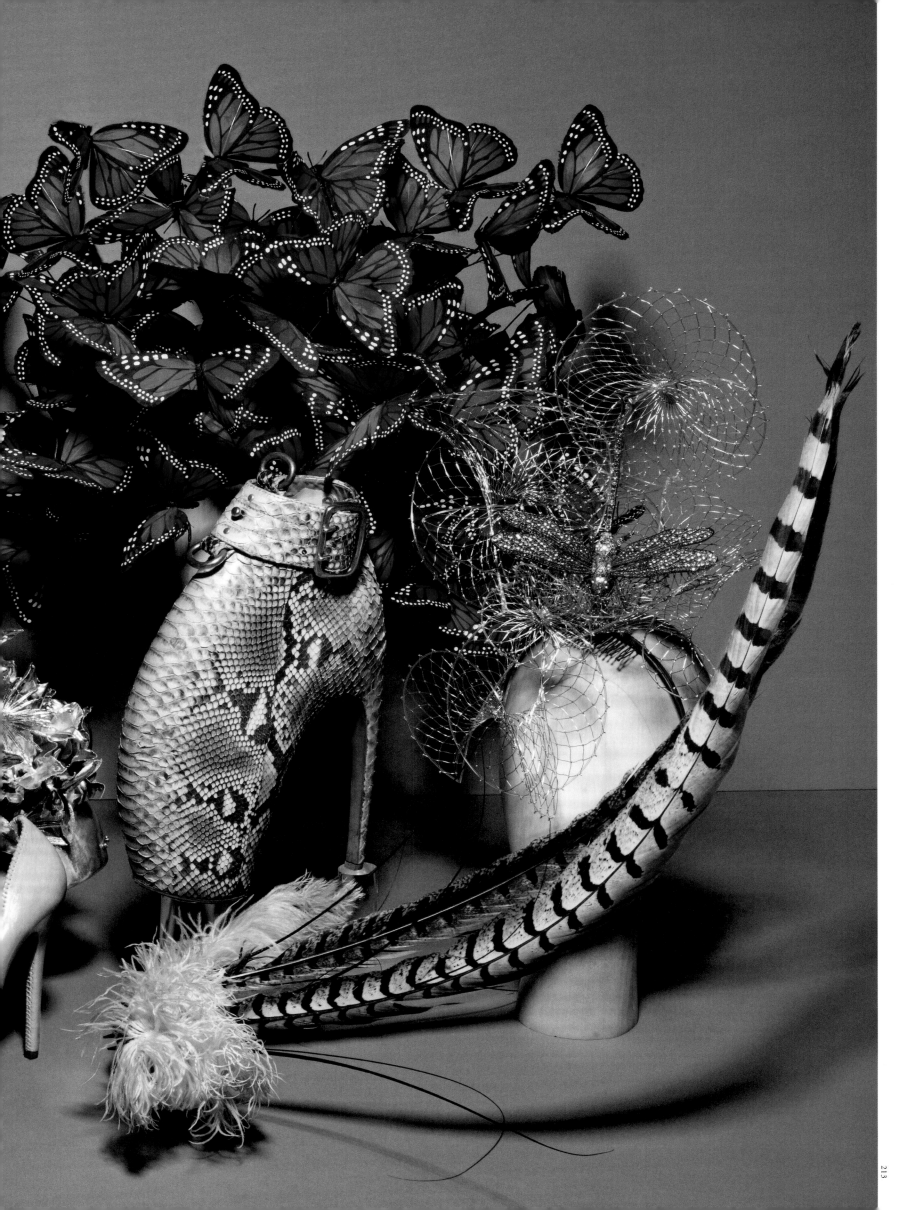

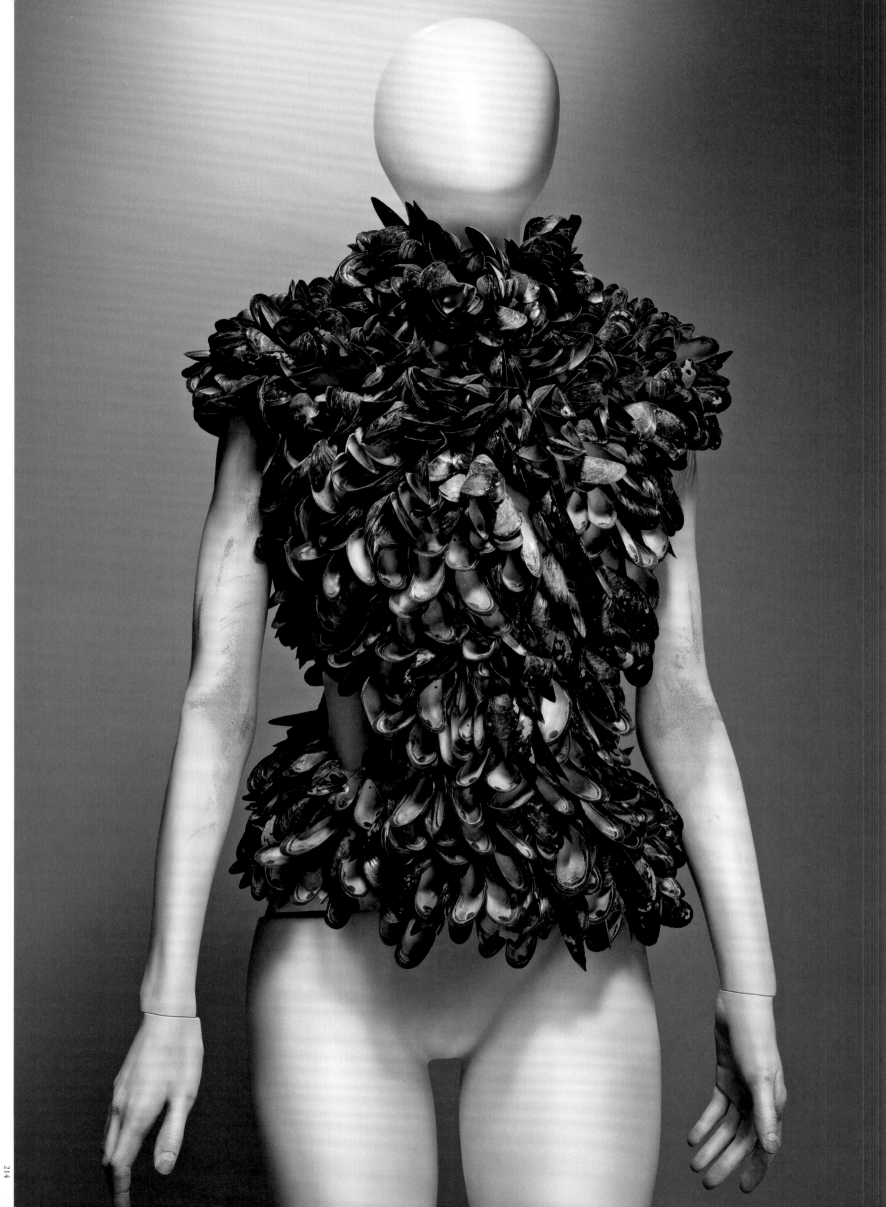

"It needs to connect with the earth. Things that are processed and reprocessed lose their substance."

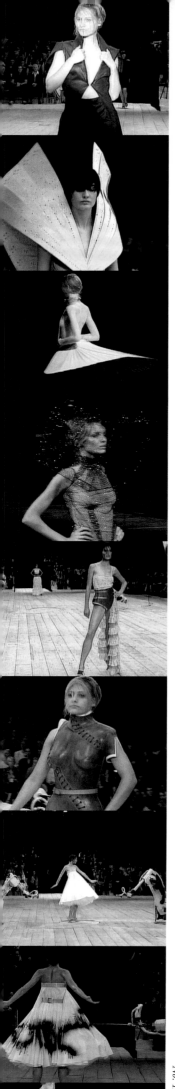

"[The finale of this collection] was inspired by an installation by artist Rebecca Horn of two shotguns firing blood-red paint at each other."

"It was really carefully choreographed. It took a week to program the robots."

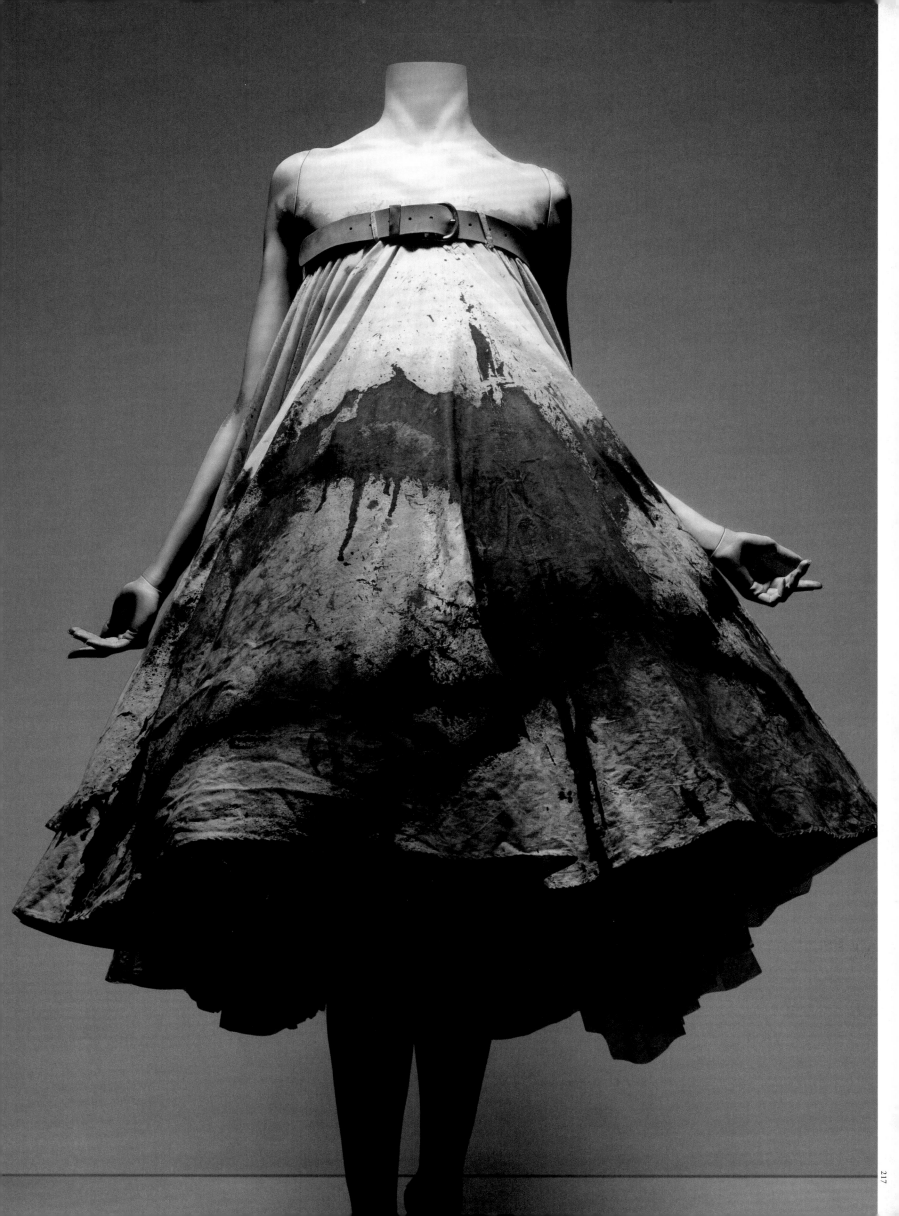

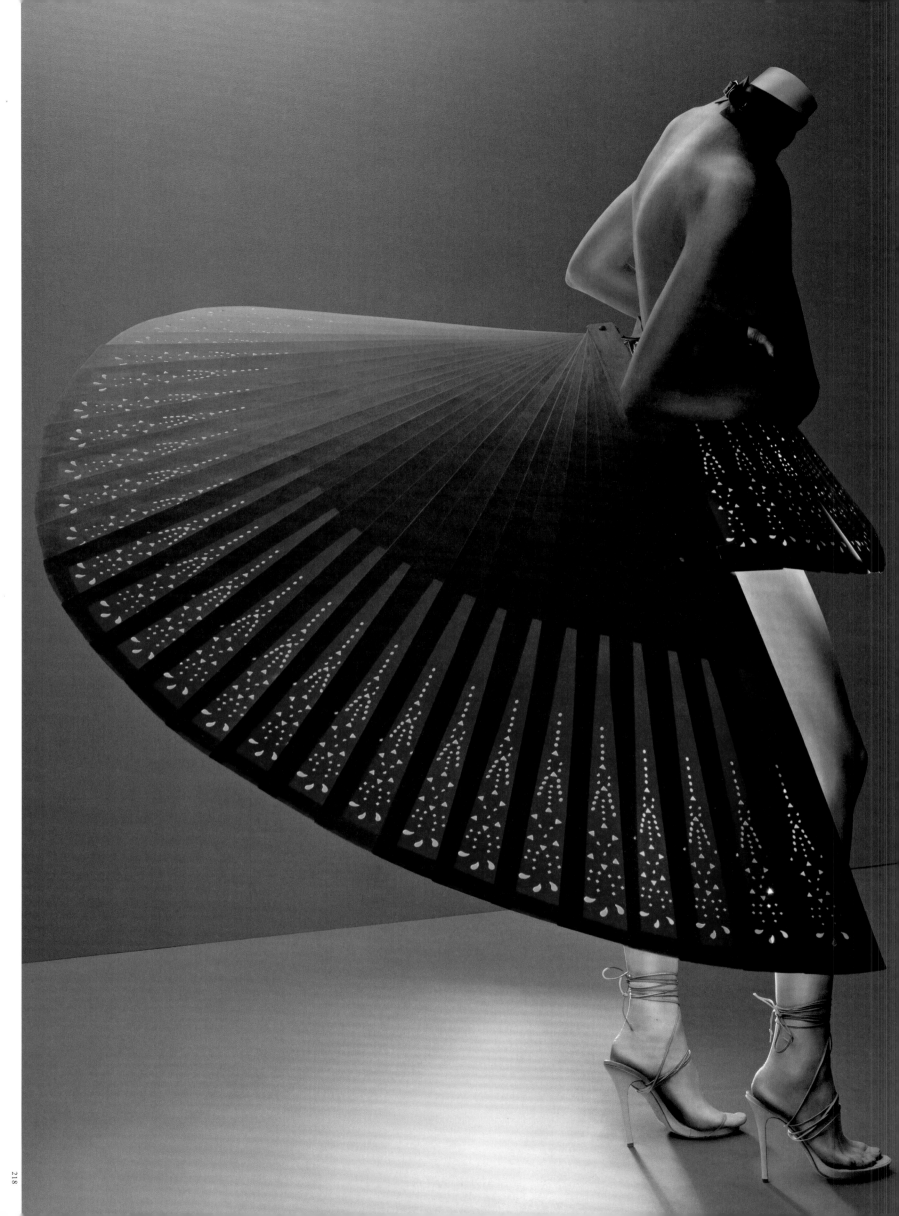

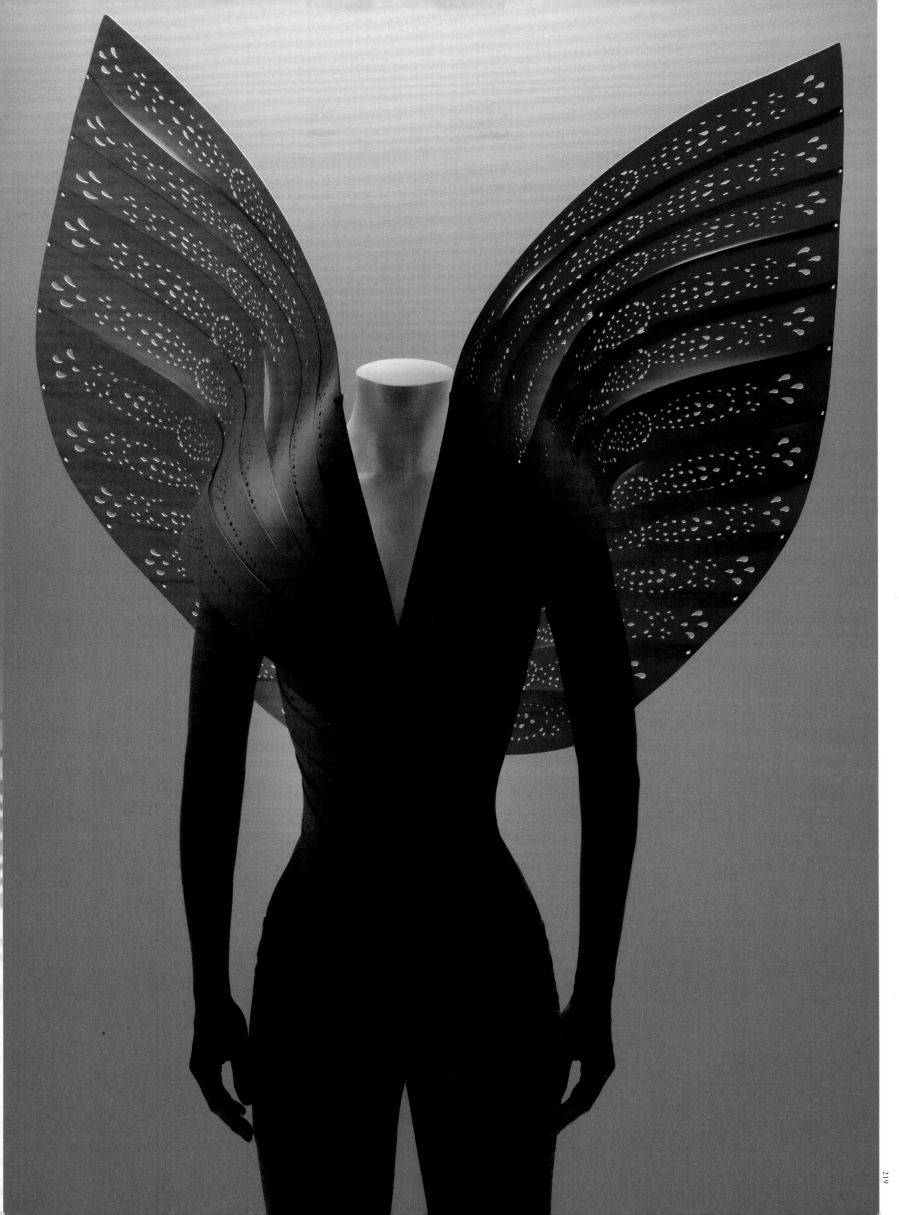

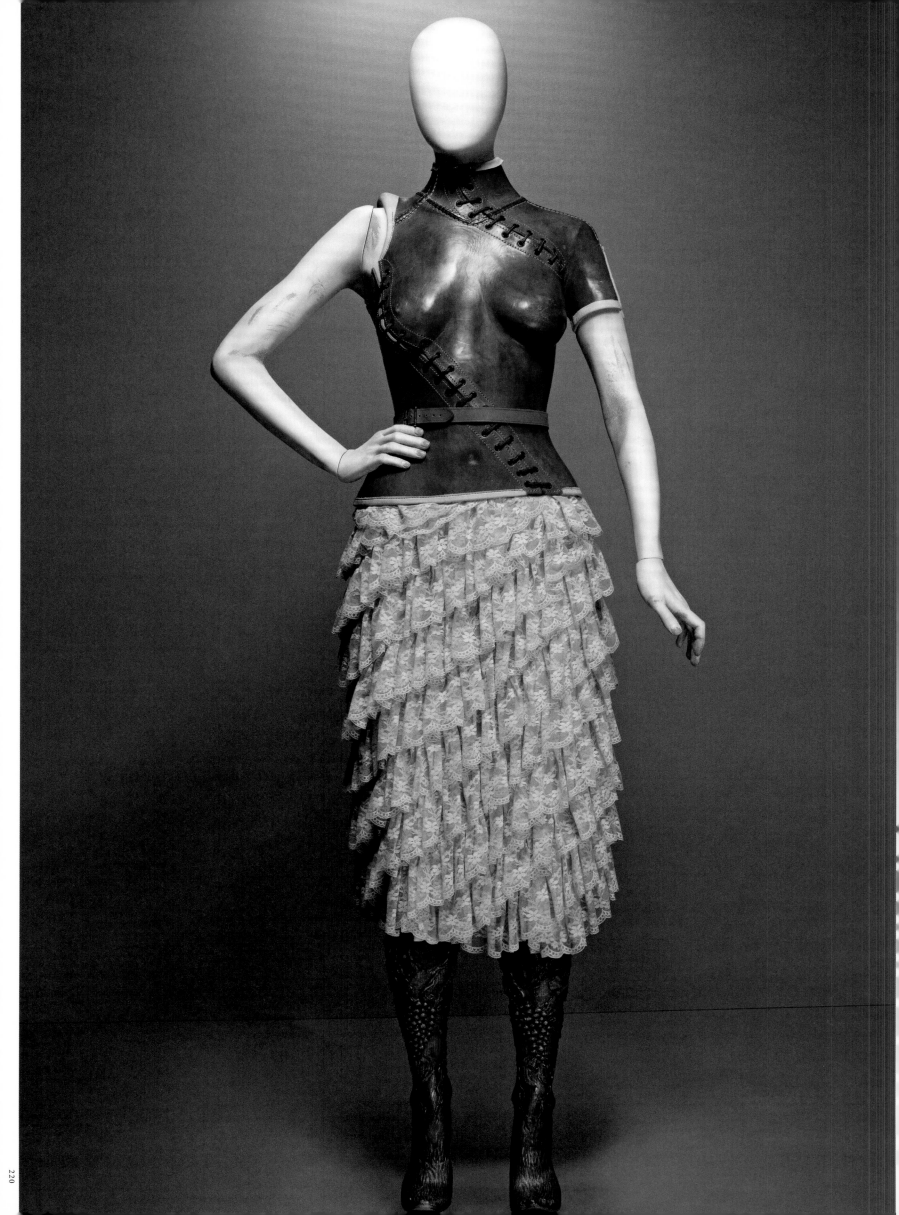

"When I used Aimee [Mullins] for [this collection], I made a point of not putting her in . . . sprinting legs [prostheses for running]. . . . We did try them on but I thought no, that's not the point of this exercise. The point is that she was to mould in with the rest of the girls."

"Let me not forget the use of my own hands,

that of a craftsman with eyes . . . that reflect

the technology around me."

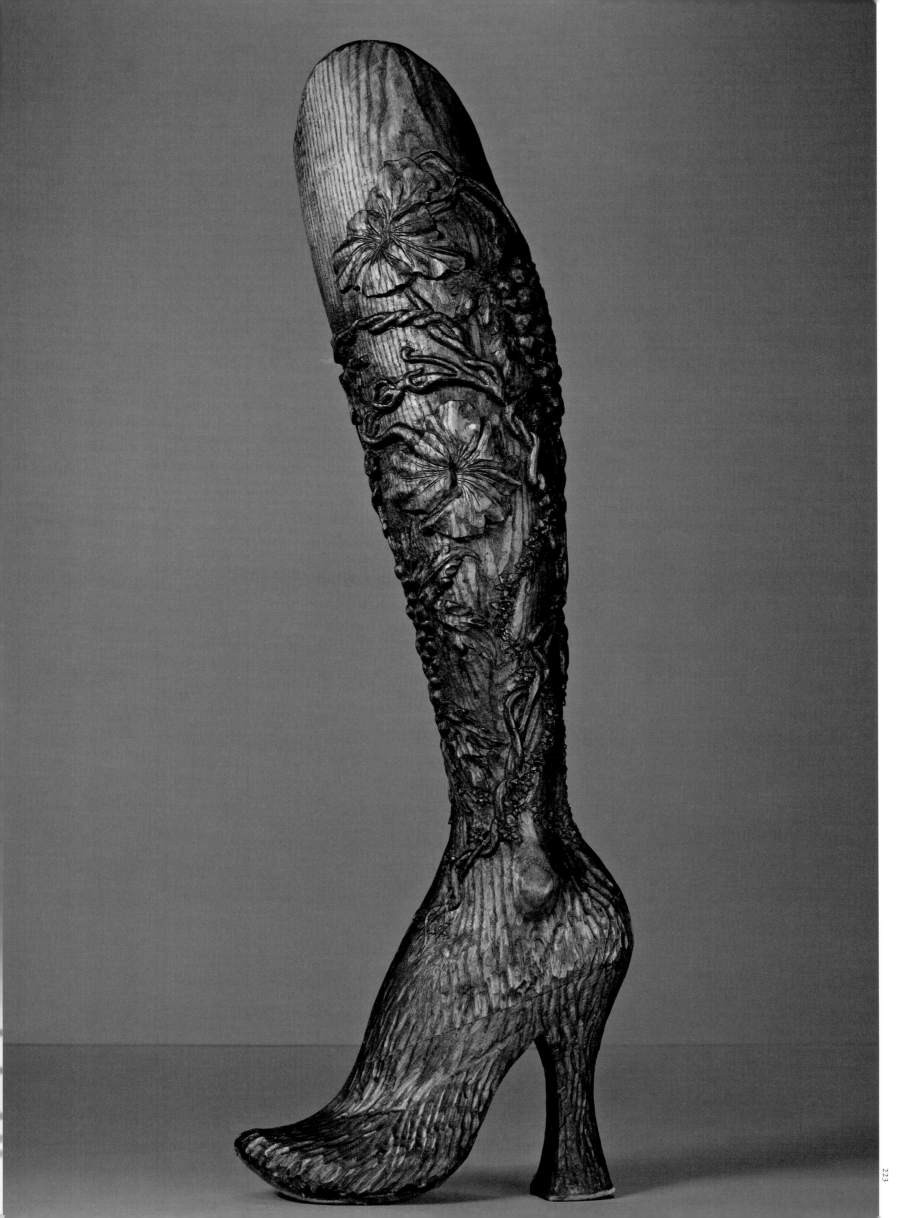

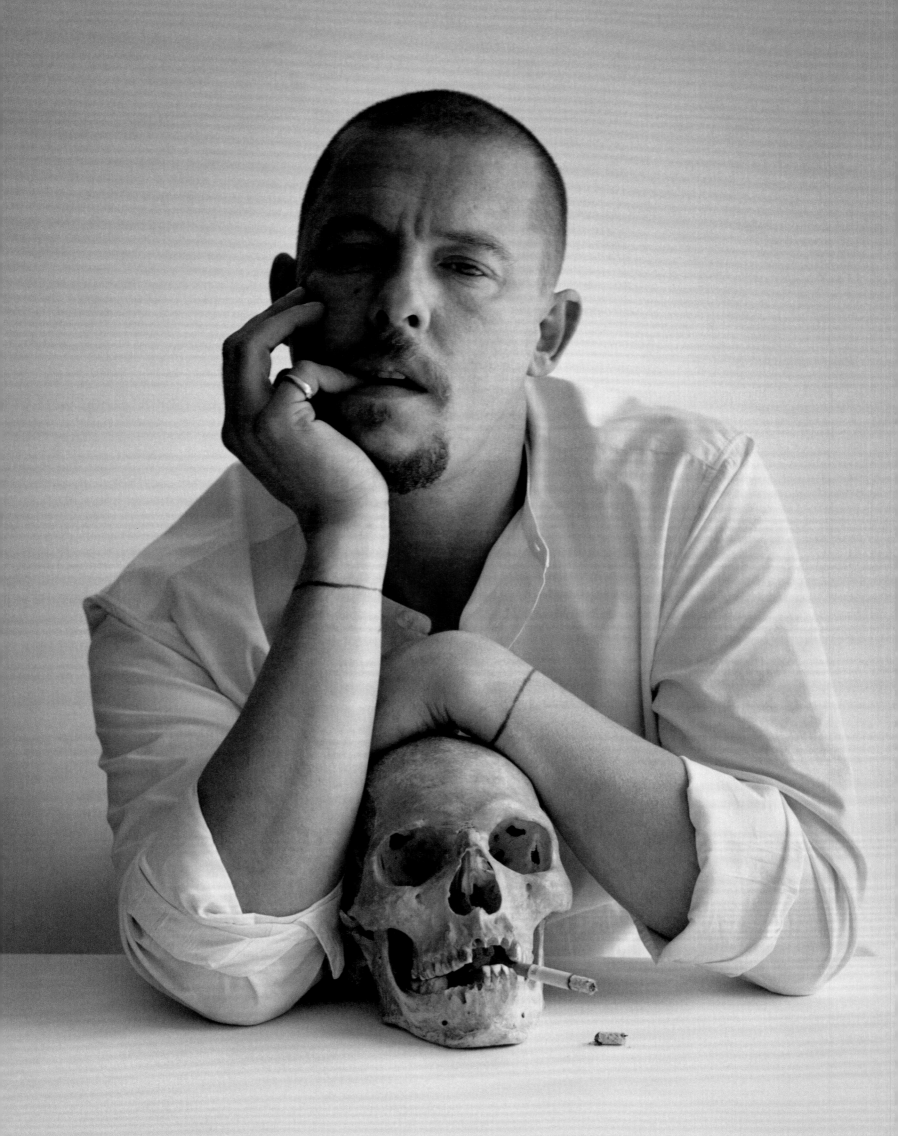

The Alexander McQueen design studio is an airy, skylit space on the top floor of the company headquarters on Clerkenwell Road, London. A new collection is taking shape under the aegis of Sarah Burton, McQueen's design assistant for fifteen years and the natural heir to his legacy.

Lined with display boards and an impressive library of books, the space is probably tidier than when McQueen was in charge. For one thing, his massage chair is gone. So is the dog basket. What has remained unchanged, however, is the breadth and depth of material on the boards. When McQueen was creating a collection, Burton compiled much of this material on his behalf, integrating his past inspirations with his present inclinations. "I'm a hoarder," she says. "I've kept every one of Lee's drawings."

Fortunately, this includes material that predates Burton's arrival in 1996, such as the drawings from his MA graduation collection at Central Saint Martins College of Art and Design in 1992, entitled *Jack the Ripper Stalks His Victims*. These early drawings are a revelation, illustrating signature designs such as a frock coat, signature details such as a peaked shoulder, and signature techniques such as corsetry, slashing, fringing, and featherwork. Everything is rendered with a startling precision. Another student project features a split jacket with a twist in the middle, a detail that resurfaced in McQueen's first couture collection for Givenchy in 1997. According to Burton, McQueen never referred back to these early drawings, proving that his aesthetic operated on a primal, instinctive level. Delicate lacework, the Celtic macabre, classic men's suiting, the severe tailoring of the 1940s, and the films of Alfred Hitchcock—all added a sophisticated gloss to one of the most coherent, persuasive design vocabularies of the past two decades.

Burton pulls from the shelves the book she says was McQueen's favorite—*McDowell's Directory of Twentieth-Century Fashion*, published in 1985. McQueen was still in high school when the book was written, but looking at some of its chapter headings—"Clothes as a Weapon," "Fashion and the Arts," "Creating the Line," "From Salon to Street," "The First Couturier"—one muses that he could have been its consummate subject.

AN INTERVIEW WITH SARAH BURTON, CREATIVE DIRECTOR, ALEXANDER McQUEEN
BY TIM BLANKS

TIM BLANKS: How did you meet Lee McQueen?

SARAH BURTON: My connection to Lee was the textile designer Simon Ungless, a very good friend of Lee's, who did all the early prints. My first collection was *La Poupée* [spring/ summer 1997]. I actually made some of the pieces, though Lee made most of them himself. He taught me how to cut an S-bend in chiffon and how to put in a zip, which I didn't know how to do. In those days, it was Katy England, Trino Verkade, and me. Lee lived upstairs from his Hoxton Square studio. At that time Trino was doing licensing in Japan, and I would go to Japan with her. I remember when he got the call from LVMH, Lee thought he was being given a job to design a handbag for Vuitton—it was around the time that people like Azzedine Alaïa, Vivienne Westwood, and Helmut Lang were doing special-edition bags for Vuitton's anniversary. The deal with Givenchy was done in two weeks, and then he was on the train to Paris. I was meant to go for a placement at Calvin Klein in New York. Lee asked me to stay, and I did. We had one pattern-cutting table, which used to belong to Body Map and Flyte Ostell, with chairs that didn't reach properly. When Lee got the Givenchy job, we got chairs that reached the table. And he was really excited because it meant there was money coming in, and he could do things he'd never done before.

TB: With the resources from Givenchy, did this make Lee more experimental with his collections?

SB: Yes, they definitely helped Lee to push boundaries. I remember one collection—the prêt-à-porter autumn/winter 1999–2000 collection—which involved a model in a Perspex robotic body. The guy who made the robot told us ten minutes before the model walked out, "If she sweats in the suit, she's going to electrocute herself. So tell her not to sweat."

Givenchy was an amazing experience for Lee. He was a superb tailor anyway, and he could cut amazing dresses, but at Givenchy he learned all about couture, especially embroideries.

TB: The boards showing embroidery samples are particularly detailed. With Lee, how much was provided by embroidery companies and how much was specially commissioned?

SB: It was kind of a mixture. First I'd go through the archives. We kept everything from past seasons because Lee had a memory like an elephant. So we'd bring out things that maybe hadn't been used, and then we'd develop new things as well. But every collection began with a show. To start work on designing the collection, he'd have to visualize how it would be seen.

TB: When he was visualizing the show, was he thinking of each look as a character, like he was casting a production?

SB: Each show was very much done as a couture show, in that Lee would have a board numbered, say, one to fifty, and we always had about seventy-five looks. We would edit them in Paris. They were grouped, quite often in three sections, and there was always a story. *Irere* [spring/summer 2003] was the first time we'd ever done a pre-collection, so the whole first group was pre-collection.

Lee always designed each look as a complete look, with shoes, hair, and makeup. Shoes were really important because they anchored the look. The "Armadillo" shoe from *Plato's Atlantis* [spring/summer 2010] was based on a ballet point shoe designed by Allen Jones. They were actually quite comfortable to walk in, but if a girl couldn't walk in them, she wasn't in the show.

The hair was almost the same on everybody. In the lineup for Lee's shows, the identities of the girls were completely blanked out. It was about the clothes and about the show—never about the model. An extreme example of this was in the collection *In Memory of Elizabeth How, Salem 1692* [autumn/winter 2007–8] when one girl wore a leather molded bodice that covered her face entirely.

TB: The shows always seemed to be the result of remarkably stable collaborations.

SB: Lee was amazingly loyal, with a great belief in people. He was very strong in his collaborations. His vision was so pure that he would very much be the director of whatever project he worked on, whether it was a show or a photo shoot. But when he worked with the milliner Philip Treacy, he was very respectful. He'd show him boards and give him key words, and Philip would come up with something. For example, in the collection *The Horn of Plenty* [autumn/winter 2009–10], Lee wanted plastic bags on the heads, like he'd seen in Hendrik Kerstens's photos at the National Portrait Gallery, but it was Philip who came up with the dustbin lid and the exploding wicker basket. Guido Palau's coiffures for *The Horn of Plenty* brought another layer to the collection. For Lee, Philip and Guido really finished off the look. It was the same with the jeweler Shaun Leane. Lee loved his craftsmanship.

When he first started to think about the production of a show, that's when Sam Gainsbury would come in. They'd discuss the venue, the theme. When Lee began to show in Paris, he sometimes chose a venue because of its special atmosphere, such as the Conciergerie, where he staged his collection *Supercalifragilisticexpialidocious* [autumn/winter 2002–3]. Most of the time, however, Lee wanted to create his own environment, so he showed at the Palais Omnisports de Paris-Bercy. For *The Girl Who Lived in the Tree* [autumn/winter 2008–9], which featured a tree wrapped in fabric, Lee looked to the artist Christo for inspiration, then to Sam to make it happen. She had a huge input in things. Joseph Bennett and Simon Kenny worked on the design, and Dan Landin on the lighting. John Gosling always did the music, which was vital, because whatever we played was part of the feeling of the collection. Lee had a very strong point of view on what music he wanted for a show. There were always drums in some way and always an evocative song at the end that made you feel uplifted or sentimental. Lee listened to a lot of classical music over the last three years, especially during fittings—Philip Glass's music from *The Hours* or Michael Nyman's music from *The Piano*. Music seemed more important once we moved to the current studio. I don't remember it playing in the former one on Amwell Street.

TB: Maybe that was because he couldn't see the sky from the other one.

SB: True, he couldn't. One reason he was really excited when we moved here.

TB: What do you think the big spectacles satisfied in Lee?

SB: He really loved the shows. He used to say, "This is the last big one we're doing," but he couldn't help himself. Lee just didn't like doing normal catwalk shows, and so much was expected from him. The nearest he came to a standard runway presentation was for the Hitchcock-inspired *The Man Who Knew Too Much* collection [autumn/winter 2005–6]. The presentation that immediately followed this—the Greek-inspired *Neptune* collection [spring/summer 2006]—was also more conventional.

TB: You talk about Lee having a freakish visual memory. For real?

SB: Completely. He would say, "We're going to work on the 1940s," or whatever the theme was going to be. He'd start with an idea, and we'd prepare boards and boards of research. Then the idea would start to change. He'd add something completely opposite or pull different things he liked. And sometimes you would come in a week later and it would all be down and

something else would be up. He was so fast, and because he could get bored quite easily with things, he just kept coming up with more and more ideas.

Lee got inspiration from anything. "I was walking to work and I saw this poster," or "I was watching *Friends* and Joey was wearing this green shirt." He loved the Discovery Channel and nature books. We all used to get *National Geographic*. It was that disparate. But he had an amazing way of editing. Each day was a different thing. He'd say, "I'd like this as a jacquard," or "I want this damask in a new laminated technique," or "Let's get someone in the sewing room to make this suit." You never said, "No, I can't do that," because either he could do it or you had to learn to do it, and he was always right. I remember one dress from *Scanners* [autumn/winter 2003–4] that was composed of engineered panels of embroidery, and I couldn't get my head round it. He sketched how to work it out. For another dress, he wanted all the lace to be cut by hand and engineered onto circles. Lace can't be cut on the circle, so it had to be cut out flower by flower and reapplied on a tulle circle, which was reembroidered and then placed on the dress. The dress was from *Widows of Culloden* [autumn/winter 2006–7]—it was in gray lace, and the model wore antlers covered with a veil. But Lee always wanted boards featuring a million techniques. Maybe we'd use none of them, but he'd push you to do them in a completely different way than you would do traditionally. I miss that a lot, his modernity.

TB: But it was modernity rooted in an incredible grasp of tradition.

SB: Completely. For example, the shapes in the *Horn of Plenty* collection were a take on Dior's New Look, but the fabrics we used were based on trash luxed up to make couture: bubble wrap made from a silk synthetic mix, bin liners made from silk, heavy bonded neoprene printed with houndstooth. The second look in the show used traditional houndstooth that had been lacquered. Lee cut the jacket himself. He slashed it, cut an asymmetrical kimono sleeve, and took the collar off and recut it. He laid a piece of fabric on the floor and cut it to make just the right collar shape. It was incredible.

What was great about *The Horn of Plenty* was how Lee started with himself, using his own vocabulary. He worked very hard on that collection. The jackets were pure McQueen—he could do them with his eyes shut. In fact, the last couple of collections were almost like a pure concentrate of what Lee did.

TB: Did the research ever involve having an actual vintage piece as a reference?

SB: No, Lee didn't really work like that. He loved Victoriana: Julia Margaret Cameron, Jack the Ripper, and the characters in *Oliver Twist*. He loved the structure of Victorian jackets, with the small shoulder, the short proportion, and especially the tiny waist. Every time we did a fitting, he'd get a piece of grosgrain and pull the girl in, making the waist even tighter. It was always tighter, tighter. Lee was all about a waist. Quite often there were corsets under the garments. And there were always elements of old couture, but we'd never go out and buy vintage to copy. Some of the tailoring he'd start from cutting up jackets or cloth, and a couple of military-influenced pieces were based on vintage, but he'd always cut it up and change it.

He didn't do many research trips either. He didn't like to travel that much. One exception, however, was to Salem, Massachusetts, for the collection *In Memory of Elizabeth How*. His mum was really into genealogy, and she had traced one of their ancestors to the Salem witch trials. We went to the Salem Witch Museum and to the grave where his ancestor Elizabeth How was buried. It was a very personal collection for Lee, but then Lee always used to say that his work was autobiographical.

TB: I always imagined a kind of emotional dialectic to his collections—there would be a thesis, an antithesis, then a kind of synthesis. The way, for instance, that the haute couture traditionalism of his posthumous autumn/winter 2010–11 collection followed on from the avant-garde technology of his spring/summer 2010 collection [*Plato's Atlantis*].

SB: With *Plato's Atlantis*, Lee mastered how to weave, engineer, and print any digital image onto a garment so that all the pattern pieces matched up with the design on every seam. That was the difficulty with the collection that followed. Where do you take it? How do you move forward? I know he would have taken it off on a completely different tangent. He wanted to talk about craftsmanship, about the old techniques that are being lost, and how people don't do things with their hands anymore.

TB: Did Lee ever acknowledge a "McQueen" in his own history? Someone who taught him to put in a zip?

SB: I think he very much did it on his own, although he would talk about Romeo Gigli a lot.

TB: Maybe working with Gigli was his real introduction to the "anything is possible" feeling he himself brought to fashion. Lee was a bit like an artist or writer or musician who goes back and teases out themes from his own past. When someone has

created such a rich body of work to draw on, it's not hard to revisit something and have it look new.

SB: When I went through the archive a while ago, I realized, "God, he actually has done everything." There were so many threads of ideas he started in each show, and then he'd go off in different directions. There were ten shows of ideas in one show; it was endless. Like the *VOSS* collection [spring/summer 2001], his first after leaving Givenchy. He often went back to that one.

TB: What made that one so seminal?

SB: It was at a time when the British art scene was still full of the energy that had been kicked off by *Sensation*, the touring exhibition of Charles Saatchi's collection, and there was a lunacy around collecting. *VOSS* had the real feel of a mind collecting things. Lee wasn't scared of an idea coming from anywhere. One day he came in with handfuls of mussel shells, and he said, "We're going to make a dress out of this." Another day, he said, "Get a student to buy a jigsaw." Then a week later, he went to his house in Fairlight, on the East Sussex coast, and came back with razor-clam shells and said, "We're going to make a dress out of these." Another time he went on a trip to Brighton and brought back some beach mats. The pack of cards, the glass surgical slides we hand-painted, an old screen that he brought back from Givenchy in Paris and tore apart—were all highlights of the *Asylum* collection.

TB: Was *VOSS* the first collection in which he allowed his imagination to go anywhere, to do and to make anything possible?

SB: No. Lee always had a way of bringing ideas from anywhere, but this show to me really seemed like so many completely different juxtapositions that all worked well together. It was about finding beauty in everything. He often challenged people's perceptions of beauty, like in the *No. 13* show [spring/summer 1999]. Lee liked to shock people because he wanted them to feel something.

TB: Let's talk about Lee's process, especially in relation to developing new fabrics. After he'd request a damask, for example—treated like no one had treated that fabric before—it would be the duty of a design assistant to go away and make it happen. How long would that process take?

SB: Lee was immediate. It would have to be quite quick. The studio had a fabric girl, an embroidery girl, and two design assistants on shoes and bags. I'd delegate, and they would immediately go to the mills in Italy to find similar techniques that they could start to develop.

TB: If Lee's idea was the genesis, I'm curious about the rest of the research process.

SB: Lee would sit here and stick Post-its in books from our studio library. For *Plato's Atlantis*, he said, "I want thousands of aerial views." Basically the world's surface from the sky—views of cities, oceans, mountains. I would delegate to each department, and he'd expect the results the next day. It had to be the next day because he was so immediate.

TB: And if it wasn't?

SB: It always was [laughs].

TB: Would Lee look at visual sources all the time, or only if he had to for a collection?

SB: I don't remember him sitting still that much. He'd always be doing something—getting out all the fabrics, all the embroideries, all the leathers, all the furs. There would be all these mounds of things. After an intensive day with him, you'd be left with a list of about fifty themes. He usually worked with that kind of intensity, though there were days when he'd come in and just flip through books or when he'd work three-dimensionally on the stand. He used to love Michel Frizot's *A New History of Photography* in particular. Quite often things would come from this book, normally at the beginning of the season.

TB: Did Lee always work in the studio?

SB: Occasionally, we'd design collections at Lee's house—for instance, *Supercalifragilistic*. He wanted all his books and all his fabrics sent to his home. He had just moved to Aberdeen Road at that point.

TB: Do you think Lee was provoking himself to find different ways to working?

SB: He just wanted to work when he wanted to. Sometimes, we'd go down to his house in the country with bags and bags of fabrics. He was a really good cook. He'd make an amazing roast lunch, then say, "Oh, let's look at everything next week in the office."

TB: Given the historicism in his work, was Lee more inspired by pictures and books or by his raw materials?

SB: With him, it was definitely a case of getting his hands into things, touching them, draping them. When we were working on *Plato's Atlantis*, we turned all the research boards around so that there were just big pieces of printed fabric hanging on the wall. Usually, his research boards consisted of an eclectic mix of images based around a specific theme. These images could reference nature, historical portraits, the works of old masters and modern artists, historical fashions, and traditional and innovative fabric techniques. For *Plato's Atlantis*, he said, "I don't want to look at any shapes, I don't want to reference anything, a picture, a drawing. I want it all to be new." And he was completely right, because he then created something new, without a reference. That's why on those occasions when we hadn't handed in the collection by the deadline he knew it didn't really matter. Sometimes the deadlines were so tight. I'd press him, and he'd give me something, anything, and say, "Just send off the sketches to the factory," because he knew that in the fitting he was completely capable of making a whole collection out of nothing.

TB: How often did he do that?

SB: Oh, once or twice [laughs]. There were situations when, if he didn't have a garment but he had bolts of fabric, Lee could literally create a dress on the spot—embroidery here, fabric there, chop this, and he would completely have it. He would cut on the stand. He spent a lot of the time with mannequins, cutting things. The way he designed was so organic that he didn't really sit and sketch. It was very 3-D, and when he did it three-dimensionally, it was always better because he'd come up with new things. As time went by, we scanned into the computer the patterns of the garments that Lee had draped. Then we would place the artwork onto these pattern pieces. It could be a print or a jacquard. Then we would print out the paper pattern in miniature with the artwork on it and stick it together to make a 3-D garment. Toward the end, we'd have to make paper dolls of each outfit because his patterns were so complex to visualize. I did it so it would be easier for him to see. You had to work in a certain way with him, it was so visual. You had a moment. It had to be immediate or it was gone. We did the fittings for the last couple of collections with all the garments in the real fabric, whereas maybe in the past we might have created the toiles in calico. But Lee was at the point where he wanted to see everything in the right jacquard, the right print.

TB: When was that point actually reached?

SB: We did it for *The Horn of Plenty* and *Plato's Atlantis*. For these collections we had to launch a rough fabric or jacquard for the pattern at the design stage—the stage when Lee was draping on the stand. When the pattern came back from the factory in Italy, or from the atelier downstairs, and Lee fitted it on a mannequin, we had to change the artwork again for the correct pattern. Lee would cut and change the garment on the mannequin, which meant that the print no longer matched at the seams, so we had to go back to the computer and make it match again. Three weeks before the show, we'd hand the fabric to sketching and we'd launch the final fabrics. That is to say, we'd allocate the fabrics to the garments and order the clothes we needed for the show from the factory. This was especially challenging for *Plato's Atlantis* because all the patterns were so precise. After the showpieces were done, I'd go to Italy to check everything. For *Plato's Atlantis* everything was engineered and hand-embroidered, like couture.

TB: It sounds like an incredibly extravagant and challenging way to work, using such expensive fabrics to test out ideas that might not work.

SB: For *Plato's Atlantis*, there were thirty-six prints altogether. They were circle-engineered to the body. By circle-engineered, I mean that the prints were based on a circle shape that sat in the middle of a bolt of fabric. Not only did you have to place the print correctly, but also, for example, if a fabric went from opaque to sheer, Lee had to do that in the fitting. I'd say he cut half of these pieces. His eye was so amazing he could drape an engineered print.

TB: So he'd cut it after he'd draped it, and then, if he didn't like it . . .

SB: He'd throw it away. What was incredible was that it nearly always worked. I tried to do it recently, and I thought, "Oh no, I've cut the wrong bit off." But he discarded hardly anything at all with *Plato's Atlantis*. Of course, there were always pieces that got dropped. But he'd pass them over to the commercial collection. In the show collection, Lee offered looks that combined jersey and tailoring.

TB: How long did the fittings take?

SB: Three days of fitting thirty garments. Fittings were really the

key thing. Lee was very quick. Did you ever see him in a fitting? He came alive when he was fitting clothes. He made you feel like you might as well pack your bags and go home. He could draw a pattern on the floor; he could change things so confidently. He had a very masculine, instinctive way of doing it. He'd get beads of sweat on his head. His knowledge of clothes, of what he wanted, was so black and white. There were no gray areas in anything Lee did. He'd slash the whole thing up, cut bits off, re-create pieces, make sleeves, make trousers.

TB: And how often would he change a whole collection?

SB: He rarely changed whole collections, but a collection would evolve alongside his imagination. *Sarabande* [spring/summer 2007] was quite a different collection before the summer holidays. But we kept many pieces and just reworked them— the tailcoats, for instance. Nobody minded. What Lee instilled in people was his passion. You'd do anything to make him happy. Like the women in the factories who would work late because they were challenged in their own work. Lee had this way of making you challenge yourself. You were always on edge because you had to push yourself. So everybody went above and beyond for him.

TB: I always wondered if, in revering strong, powerful women, Lee had very little empathy for women who weren't.

SB: Lee loved strong women. From my own experience, the minute I started standing up and expressing my own opinion, he respected me more. You had to be brave enough to do it, but he really wanted someone with an opinion. What made it easy to work with Lee was that he was so clear about what he loved. He never *um*-ed and *ah*-ed about anything.

TB: Did you bond over things like movies? They always seemed so important to him. I remember after *The Overlook* [autumn/ winter 1999–2000], which took its title from the name of the hotel in *The Shining*, he was keen to clarify that it was all about Stanley Kubrick's movie and had nothing to do with Stephen King's book.

SB: He didn't really go to the cinema to watch films. He watched DVDs.

TB: I see you've pulled out ten favorites: *Barry Lyndon*; *Death in Venice*; *They Shoot Horses, Don't They?*; *Lady Sings the Blues*; *La Reine Margot*; *Paris, Texas*; *Picnic at Hanging Rock*; Coppola's

Dracula; *The Hunger*; and *The Abyss*. It's easy to match each of those films to a collection.

SB: Yes. *Barry Lyndon* and *Sarabande*, for instance. Or *The Abyss* and *Plato's Atlantis*. And the color scheme of *La Reine Margot* was a constant. Often, Lee would tell me to read books, to look at artists, or to listen to a piece of music. That was the thing about Lee, his mind was so active. Every season, Lee wasn't just designing clothes. He really was an artist. He had to better himself, and it was just relentless. But, in saying that, he loved doing it so much. I'd never see him happier than when he was here, touching things, making things.

TB: Do you think he saw himself as an artist?

SB: I don't know. Lee wanted to go back to art college. He actually got into the Slade School to do art, but he always called himself a designer, not an artist. He was a showman more than anything. Still, when you think about the way he designed, it did feel more about art. It was never, "Oh, is that comfortable?" It was all about the vision and the head-to-toe look of it. When you saw the models lined up, it was so clear and so direct. Lee was a designer who was making a world and telling a story. Sometimes it was on such a level that maybe the fashion audience wasn't the right audience to tell it to, but what audience was right? That's the problem I think he had. The stigma: Is it fashion? Is it art? But if it's not making money, you can't do these amazing shows. Lee did care about the commercial side of the industry, but what most people remember are the shows.

TB: But you said he'd start with the show, so if that's how he was assessed, surely that's what he wanted.

SB: I think you're right. But what I realize as well is that he created a world for himself where he could do anything he wanted to do, with no constraints, no merchandiser coming upstairs and asking, "Where's my three-button jacket?" That's very unusual in fashion.

Unless otherwise acknowledged, all
garments in the catalogue and exhibition
have been lent courtesy of the Alexander
McQueen Archive in London.

Page 6
Dress, *Joan*, autumn/winter 1998–99
Red bugle beads

Page 8
Dress, *Untitled*, spring/summer 1998
Ivory silk

Page 10
Ensemble, *The Dance of the Twisted Bull*,
spring/summer 2002
Jacket of black silk embroidered with black
bullion, and jet and crystal beads; jumpsuit
of black wool; hat of black leather
Hat by Philip Treacy for Alexander
McQueen from the collection of Isabella
Blow courtesy of the Hon. Daphne
Guinness

Page 11
Ensemble, *The Dance of the Twisted Bull*,
spring/summer 2002
Dress of red and ivory silk; spears of wood
and silver-plated metal with red cotton
Spears by Shaun Leane for Alexander
McQueen

THE ROMANTIC MIND

Page 31
Jacket, *Jack the Ripper Stalks His Victims*
(MA Graduation Collection), 1992
Black silk lined in red silk with
encapsulated human hair
From the collection of Isabella Blow
courtesy of the Hon. Daphne Guinness

Pages 32–33
Coat, *Jack the Ripper Stalks His Victims*
(MA Graduation Collection), 1992
Pink silk printed in thorn pattern lined in
white silk with encapsulated human hair
From the collection of Isabella Blow
courtesy of the Hon. Daphne Guinness

Page 34
Trouser Detail, *Nihilism*, spring/summer
1994
Gray silk/wool
Courtesy of Tiina Laakkonen

Page 37
Coat, *Nihilism*, spring/summer 1994
Gray silk/wool
Courtesy of Tiina Laakkonen

Page 38
Jacket, *Nihilism*, spring/summer 1994
Black silk/cotton
Courtesy of Tiina Laakkonen

Pages 40–41
Dress, *No. 13*, spring/summer 1999
Coated black cotton

Page 42
Dress, *Plato's Atlantis*, spring/summer 2010
Gray wool and silk/synthetic printed in
jellyfish pattern

Page 43
Dress, *Plato's Atlantis*, spring/summer 2010
Gray wool and silk/synthetic printed in
jellyfish pattern

Page 45
Jacket, *Dante*, autumn/winter 1996–97
Black cashmere
Courtesy of Samantha Gainsbury

Page 46
Jacket, *Dante*, autumn/winter 1996–97
Black cotton/synthetic

Page 47
Jacket, *Joan*, autumn/winter 1998–99
Black cashmere
Courtesy of Janet Fischgrund

Page 48
Jacket, *La Poupée*, spring/summer 1997
Black wool
Courtesy of Trino Verkade

Page 49
Jacket, *La Poupée*, spring/summer 1997
Black wool
Courtesy of Mira Chai Hyde

Pages 50–51
Jacket, *It's a Jungle Out There*, autumn/
winter 1997–98
Silk and cotton twill printed with an
image from *The Thief to the Left of Christ*
by Robert Campin, ca. 1430

Page 52
"Bumster" Skirt, *Highland Rape*, autumn/
winter 1995–96 (reproduction from
original pattern)
Black silk

Page 55
"Bumster" Trouser, *Highland Rape*,
autumn/winter 1995–96
Black silk/cotton
Courtesy of Mira Chai Hyde

Page 56
Skirt, *Highland Rape*, autumn/winter
1995–96
Black wool with silver metal watch chain
Courtesy of Trino Verkade

Page 58
"Kick-Back" Trouser, *No. 13*, spring/
summer 1999 (reproduction from original
pattern)
Black silk

Page 59
"S-Bend" Trouser, *No. 13*, spring/summer
1999 (reproduction from original pattern)
Black wool

Page 61
Dress, *Untitled*, spring/summer 1998
Black wool
Courtesy of Trino Verkade

Page 62
Jumpsuit, *La Poupée*, spring/summer 1997
Black wool
Courtesy of Trino Verkade

Page 63
Coatdress, *What a Merry-Go-Round*,
autumn/winter 2001–2
Black wool and silk

Page 64
Jacket, *Banshee*, autumn/winter 1994–95
Black wool and silver silk embroidered with
gold military braid
From the collection of Isabella Blow
courtesy of the Hon. Daphne Guinness

Page 65
Jacket, *Highland Rape*, autumn/winter
1995–96
Green wool embroidered with gold military
braid
Courtesy of Mira Chai Hyde

Page 66
Coat, *Dante,* autumn/winter 1996–97
Black wool embroidered with gold bullion
cord
From the collection of Isabella Blow
courtesy of the Hon. Daphne Guinness

Page 67
Jacket, *Banshee*, autumn/winter 1994–95
Gray wool embroidered with gold military
braid
Courtesy of Ruti Danan

Pages 68–69
Wrap, *What a Merry-Go-Round,* autumn/
winter 2001–2
Black silk embroidered with gold military
bullion

ROMANTIC GOTHIC

Page 71
House of Givenchy Haute Couture
Ensemble, *Eclect Dissect*, autumn/winter
1997–98
Black silk with black silk lace and black
horsehair embroidered with jet beads
Courtesy of Givenchy Haute Couture

Page 72
Dress, *The Horn of Plenty*, autumn/winter
2009–10
Black duck feathers

Page 75
Dress, *VOSS*, spring/summer 2001
Red and black ostrich feathers and glass
medical slides painted red

Page 76
House of Givenchy Haute Couture
Ensemble, *Eclect Dissect*, autumn/winter
1997–98
Dress and gloves of black leather
Collar of red pheasant feathers and
resin vulture skulls by Simon Costin
Courtesy of Givenchy Haute Couture

Page 78
Ensemble, *The Horn of Plenty*, autumn/winter 2009–10
Dress of black synthetic; corset of black leather and silver metal

Page 79
Boots, *The Horn of Plenty*, autumn/winter 2009–10
Black leather

Page 81
Ensemble, *The Horn of Plenty*, autumn/winter 2009–10
Jacket of black leather, black fox fur, and silver metal; skirt of black leather

Page 82
Corset, *Dante*, autumn/winter 1996–97
Lilac silk appliquéd with black silk lace and embroidered with jet beads

Page 83
House of Givenchy Haute Couture
Dress, *Eclect Dissect*, autumn/winter 1997–98
Lilac silk with black silk lace, jet beads, black leather, and beige silk inserts
From the collection of Isabella Blow courtesy of the Hon. Daphne Guinness

Page 84
Ensemble, *Supercalifragilisticexpialidocious*, autumn/winter 2002–3
Jacket of black silk; skirt of black silk with jet beads; jabot of black silk/cotton lace
Jacket courtesy of Katy England

Page 86
Dress, *Widows of Culloden*, autumn/winter 2006–7
Black silk

Page 87
Dress, pre-collection autumn/winter 2006–7
Black silk

Pages 88–89
Ensemble, *Supercalifragilisticexpialidocious*, autumn/winter 2002–3
Shirt of black mesh; skirt of black silk
Shirt courtesy of Katy England

Pages 90–91
Ensemble, *Supercalifragilisticexpialidocious*, autumn/winter 2002–3
Coat of black silk; trouser of black synthetic; hat of black silk
Hat by Philip Treacy for Alexander McQueen courtesy of Alister Mackie

Autumn/Winter 2010–11

Page 93
Dress, autumn/winter 2010–11
Bodice of silk jacquard with motifs from paintings by Hieronymus Bosch, including *Garden of Earthly Delights*, *Last Judgment*, and *Temptation of Saint Anthony*, ca. 1500, embroidered with gold sequins; skirt of black silk satin

Page 94
Ensemble, autumn/winter 2010–11
Dress and glove of silk satin printed with an image from the Cologne *Dombild* by Stephan Lochner, ca. 1440; underskirt of duck feathers painted gold

Page 95
Shoe, autumn/winter 2010–11
Nylon composite painted gold, plastic beads, and gemstones

Page 96
Shoe, autumn/winter 2010–11
Nylon composite painted silver and cream leather embroidered in silver thread

Page 97
Dress, autumn/winter 2010–11
Gray and white silk jacquard with an image of Gabriel from the *Annunciation* of the *Portinari Altarpiece* by Hugo van der Goes, ca. 1475

Pages 98–99
Dress, autumn/winter 2010–11
Gray and white silk organza printed in a fil coupé pattern with an image of the Virgin from the *Annunciation* of the *Portinari Altarpiece* by Hugo van der Goes, ca. 1475

Pages 100–101
Ensemble, autumn/winter 2010–11
Coat of duck feathers painted gold; skirt of white silk embroidered with gold thread

ROMANTIC NATIONALISM

Page 103
Ensemble, *Widows of Culloden*, autumn/winter 2006–7
Dress of McQueen tartan; top of nude silk appliquéd with black lace; underskirt of cream silk tulle

Page 104
Dress, *Widows of Culloden*, autumn/winter 2006–7
McQueen tartan appliquéd with black silk lace; underskirt of black silk tulle; faux jabot of black cotton with broderie anglaise

Page 107
Dress, *Widows of Culloden*, autumn/winter 2006–7
McQueen tartan embroidered with jet beads; collar, cuffs, and hem of cream silk tulle

Page 108
Jumpsuit, *Widows of Culloden*, autumn/winter 2006–7
McQueen tartan; ruffled shirt of black cotton with broderie anglaise

Page 109
Dress, *Widows of Culloden*, autumn/winter 2006–7
McQueen tartan with appliquéd black lace; top of white silk embroidered with red bugle beads; underskirt of black silk tulle

Page 110
Dress, *Widows of Culloden*, autumn/winter 2006–7
Ivory silk organza

Page 113
Ensemble, *The Girl Who Lived in the Tree*, autumn/winter 2008–9
Jacket of red silk velvet embroidered with gold bullion and trimmed with white shearling; dress of ivory silk tulle

Page 114
Ensemble, *The Girl Who Lived in the Tree*, autumn/winter 2008–9
Overdress of red silk woven with silver jacquard borders; underdress of ivory silk tulle

Pages 116–17
Ensemble, *The Girl Who Lived in the Tree*, autumn/winter 2008–9
Dress of ivory silk tulle; bolero of red silk velvet embroidered in gold bullion

Pages 118–19
Ensemble, *The Girl Who Lived in the Tree*, autumn/winter 2008–9
Dress of ivory silk tulle embroidered with red glass crystals; bolero of red silk

Pages 120–21
Ensemble, *The Girl Who Lived in the Tree*, autumn/winter 2008–9
Coat of red silk; dress of ivory silk tulle embroidered with crystal beads

Highland Rape

Page 123
Dress, *Highland Rape*, autumn/winter 1995–96
Green leather with silver metal studs

Page 124
Coat, *Highland Rape*, autumn/winter 1995–96
Green silk
From the collection of Isabella Blow courtesy of the Hon. Daphne Guinness

Page 125
Dress, *Highland Rape*, autumn/winter 1995–96
Dress of green and bronze cotton/synthetic lace

Page 126
Suit, *Highland Rape*, autumn/winter 1995–96 (jacket and skirt not worn together on the runway)
Jacket of McQueen tartan with green wool sleeves; skirt of McQueen tartan
From the collection of Isabella Blow courtesy of the Hon. Daphne Guinness

Page 127
Ensemble, *Highland Rape*, autumn/winter 1995–96
Jacket and ruff of McQueen tartan
Jacket courtesy of Ruti Danan

Page 128
Dress, *Highland Rape*, autumn/winter 1995–96
Black silk with gold discharge print
Courtesy of Ruti Danan

ROMANTIC EXOTICISM

Page 131
Ensemble, *VOSS*, spring/summer 2001
Jacket of pink and gray bird's-eye embroidered with silk thread; trouser of pink and gray bird's-eye; hat of pink and gray bird's-eye embroidered with silk thread and decorated with Amaranthus

Pages 132–33
Ensemble, *VOSS*, spring/summer 2001
Overdress of panels from a nineteenth-century Japanese screen; underdress of oyster shells; neckpiece of silver and Tahiti pearls
Neckpiece by Shaun Leane for Alexander McQueen courtesy of Perles de Tahiti

Page 134
Dress, *Scanners*, autumn/winter 2003–4
Brown and gold silk/cotton threads embroidered with gold metal sequins

Page 135
Dress, *Scanners*, autumn/winter 2003–4
Natural jute embroidered with cotton and silk thread with underskirt of gold silk tulle

Pages 136–37
Ensemble, *It's Only a Game*, spring/summer 2005
Dress and obi-style sash of lilac and silver silk; jacket of lilac silk embroidered with silk thread; top of nude synthetic embroidered with silk thread

Page 139
Ensemble, *It's Only a Game*, spring/summer 2005
Bodysuit and obi-style sash of lilac silk embroidered with silk thread; shoulder pads and helmet of fiberglass painted with acrylics

Page 140
Ensemble, *Widows of Culloden*, autumn/winter 2006–7
Coat of ivory silk embroidered with silk thread; dress of lilac silk tulle

Page 141
Ensemble, *It's Only a Game*, spring/summer 2005
Dress of lilac silk appliquéd with silk and embroidered with silk thread; jacket of lilac silk embroidered with silk thread
Courtesy of Basya Lowinger

VOSS

Page 143
Ensemble, *VOSS*, spring/summer 2001
Shirt of light blue silk; skirt of ostrich feathers; taxidermy hawks

Simon Costin for Alexander McQueen
Cap, *Dante*, autumn/winter 1996–97
Black silk/cotton embroidered with jet beads

Mask, *Dante*, autumn/winter 1996–97 (reproduction)
Black synthetic and white enameled metal

Shaun Leane for Alexander McQueen
"Crown of Thorns" Headpiece, *Dante*, autumn/winter 1996–97
Silver
Courtesy of Shaun Leane

Philip Treacy and Shaun Leane for Alexander McQueen
Headpiece, *Widows of Culloden*, autumn/winter 2006–7
Silver, Swarovski gemstones, and black aigrette feathers
Courtesy of Swarovski

Philip Treacy for Alexander McQueen
Headdress, *The Girl Who Lived in the Tree*, autumn/winter 2008–9
Wood and coral
Courtesy of Philip Treacy

Shaun Leane for Alexander McQueen
"Jaw Bone" Mouthpiece, *Untitled*, spring/summer 1998
Aluminum
Courtesy of Shaun Leane

Shoe, *Irere*, spring/summer 2003
Cream leather, metal, wood, and bone

Shaun Leane for Alexander McQueen
Earrings, *Sarabande*, spring/summer 2007
Gold-plated metal, gold-plated silver, mother-of-pearl beads, enamel, and human hair

"Kingdom" Flacon, 2002
Red glass, silver metal, and plastic

"Kingdom" Flacon, 2002
Red glass and silver metal

"Knucklebox" Clutchbag, pre-collection autumn/winter 2010–11
Black leather and silver-plated metal

Philip Treacy for Alexander McQueen
Hat, *What a Merry-Go-Round*, autumn/winter 2001–2
Black leather, black ostrich feathers, silver metal, and black pearls

Bag, *In Memory of Elizabeth How, Salem 1692*, autumn/winter 2007–8
Silver-plated metal and brown leather

Shaun Leane for Alexander McQueen
Locket, *Sarabande*, spring/summer 2007
Black silk ribbon, gold-plated metal, hair, enamel, and mother-of-pearl beads

Shaun Leane for Alexander McQueen
Earrings, *What a Merry-Go-Round*, autumn/winter 2001–2
Silver, pheasant claws, and Tahitian gray pearls
Courtesy of Shaun Leane

Neckpiece, *Eshu*, autumn/winter 2000–2001
Silver-plated metal over resin

Page 206
Dress, *It's Only a Game*, spring/summer 2005
Lilac leather and cream horsehair

Page 207
Ensemble, *In Memory of Elizabeth How, Salem 1692*, autumn/winter 2007–8
Bodice of burgundy molded leather; skirt of burgundy silk chiffon

Pages 208–9, left to right:

Dai Rees for Alexander McQueen
Headpiece, *La Poupée*, spring/summer 1997
Brown leather and porcupine quills
Courtesy of Dai Rees

Philip Treacy for Alexander McQueen
Headdress, *Irere*, spring/summer 2003
Parrot feathers

Shaun Leane for Alexander McQueen
Nose Bar, *Eshu*, autumn/winter 2000–2001
Silver

Shaun Leane for Alexander McQueen
Tusk Mouthpiece, *Eshu*, autumn/winter 2000–2001
Silver
Courtesy of Shaun Leane

Shaun Leane for Alexander McQueen
Tusk Earring, *The Hunger*, spring/summer 1996
Silver
Courtesy of Shaun Leane

Shaun Leane for Alexander McQueen
Disc Earrings, *Pantheon Ad Lucem*, autumn/winter 2004–5
Copper

Shaun Leane for Alexander McQueen
Coiled Neckpiece, *It's a Jungle Out There*, autumn/winter 1997–98
Brass

Corset, *Sarabande*, spring/summer 2007
Tan and white pony skin

Shaun Leane for Alexander McQueen
Hooped Earrings, *Eshu*, autumn/winter 2000–2001
Silver
Courtesy of Shaun Leane

Shaun Leane for Alexander McQueen
Fan Earrings, *Irere*, spring/summer 2003
Silver and macaw feathers

Dai Rees for Alexander McQueen
Headpiece, *La Poupée*, spring/summer 1997
Porcupine quills painted black and sprayed silver, and leather
Courtesy of Dai Rees

Backpiece, *Dante*, autumn/winter 1996–97
Resin horn

Philip Treacy for Alexander McQueen
Headdress, *Irere*, spring/summer 2003
Parrot feathers and turkey feathers

Shoe, *No. 13*, spring/summer 1999
Brown and white leather

Shaun Leane for Alexander McQueen
Face Clamp, *Untitled*, spring/summer 1998
Silver
Courtesy of Shaun Leane

Headpiece, *Dante*, autumn/winter 1996–97
Resin horn and metal wire

Shaun Leane for Alexander McQueen
Face Disc, *Irere*, spring/summer 2003
Silver

Shaun Leane for Alexander McQueen
Hooped Neckpiece, *Eshu*, autumn/winter 2000–2001
Silver

Page 210
Bodysuit, *In Memory of Elizabeth How, Salem 1692*, autumn/winter 2007–8
Gold plastic bodice with gold paillettes and peacock feathers

Page 211
House of Givenchy Haute Couture
Dress, *The Search for the Golden Fleece*, spring/summer 1997
Gold leather
Courtesy of Givenchy Haute Couture

Pages 212–13, left to right:

Benoît Méléard for Alexander McQueen
Shoe, *VOSS*, spring/summer 2001
Tan leather and metal
From the collection of Isabella Blow courtesy of the Hon. Daphne Guinness

Shaun Leane and Philip Treacy for Alexander McQueen
Headpiece, *Widows of Culloden*, autumn/winter 2006–7
Silver, Swarovski gemstones, and gull feathers
Courtesy of Swarovski

Shoe, *Irere*, spring/summer 2003
Red silk and leather with butterfly encased in Lucite heel

Philip Treacy for Alexander McQueen
Headpiece, *Widows of Culloden*, autumn/winter 2006–7
Woodcock wings
Courtesy of Philip Treacy

Shaun Leane for Alexander McQueen
"Orchid" Shoulderpiece, *Pantheon Ad Lucem*, autumn/winter 2004–5
Silver-plated metal

Shoe, *NATURAL DIS-TINCTION UN-NATURAL SELECTION*, spring/summer 2009
Tan leather

Erik Halley for Alexander McQueen
Neckpiece, *Dante*, autumn/winter 1996–97
Pheasant feathers and ostrich feathers

"Armadillo" Boot, *Plato's Atlantis*, spring/summer 2010
Python snakeskin

Philip Treacy for Alexander McQueen
Hat, *La Dame Bleue*, spring/summer 2008
Turkey feathers painted and shaped as butterflies

Philip Treacy for Alexander McQueen
Hat, *La Dame Bleue*, spring/summer 2008
Silk net with Swarovski dragonfly

Page 214
Bodice, *VOSS*, spring/summer 2001
Mussel shells

No. 13

Page 217
Dress, *No. 13*, spring/summer 1999
White cotton spray-painted black and yellow with underskirt of white silk

Page 218
Ensemble, *No. 13*, spring/summer 1999
Halter shirt of tan leather; skirt of balsa wood (reproduction)

Page 219
Ensemble, *No. 13*, spring/summer 1999
Winged bodice of balsa wood (reproduction); trouser of cream wool and cream silk lace

Page 220
Ensemble, *No. 13*, spring/summer 1999
Corset of brown leather; skirt of cream silk lace; prosthetic legs of carved elm wood

Page 223
Prosthetic Leg, *No. 13*, spring/summer 1999
Carved elm wood

PREFACE BY ANDREW BOLTON

The quotations from the following sources were compiled by the author from clippings in the press books at the Alexander McQueen Studio. Unless otherwise noted, the quotations are from Alexander McQueen.

1. *The Guardian*, April 20, 2004.
2. *Harper's Bazaar*, April 2007.
3. *Pirus*, no. 8, June 1996.
4. *The Guardian*, October 6, 2007.
5. Isabella Blow, quoted in British *Vogue*, July 1996, catwalk report supplement.
6. *Time Out* (London), September 24–October 1, 1997.
7. *Big*, Autumn/Winter 2007.
8. Suzy Menkes, *International Herald Tribune*, October 1, 1996.
9. *L'Officiel*, February 2010.
10. American *Vogue*, June 2000.
11. *ISIS*, Spring 2005.
12. *L'Officiel*, February 2010.
13. *Guardian*, April 20, 2004.
14. *WWD: The Magazine*, July 2006.
15. *Big*, Autumn/Winter 2006.
16. *Independent Magazine: Fashion*, Autumn/Winter 1999.
17. *Times* (London), January 31, 2000.
18. *W*, June 2008.
19. *TJF Magazine*, June/September 2006.
20. *Time Out* (London), September 24–October 1, 1997.
21. *Harper's Bazaar*, August 2004.
22. *Plato's Atlantis* (spring/summer 2010) program notes.
23. *International Herald Tribune*, October 8, 2009.
24. Alexander Fury, quoted on *SHOWstudio.com*.
25. *W*, September 1999.

INTRODUCTION BY SUSANNAH FRANKEL

1. Alexander McQueen, quoted in Susannah Frankel, "The Real McQueen," *Independent Magazine: Fashion*, Autumn/Winter 1999, 11.
2. Ibid.
3. Alix Sharkey, "The Real McQueen," *Guardian Weekend*, July 6, 1996, 39.
4. McQueen, quoted in Frankel, "The Real McQueen," 12.
5. Ibid.
6. McQueen, quoted in Sharkey, "The Real McQueen," 40.
7. McQueen, quoted in Frankel, "The Real McQueen," 12.
8. Bobby Hillson, quoted in Sharkey, "The Real McQueen," 40.
9. Louise Wilson, interview with author, November 2010.
10. McQueen, quoted in Sharkey, "The Real McQueen," 41.
11. McQueen, quoted in Frankel, "The Real McQueen," 15.
12. Fay Cattini, letter to the editor, *Guardian Weekend*, July 20, 1996.
13. Trino Verkade, interview with author, December 2010.
14. Ibid.
15. Katell Le Bourhis, quoted in Susannah Frankel, "Bull in a Fashion Shop," *Guardian*, G2, October 15, 1996, 8.
16. Katy England, quoted in Susannah Frankel, "Forever England," *Independent Magazine*, September 8, 2001, 10.
17. Alexander McQueen, quoted in Susannah Frankel, "Wings of Desire," *Guardian Weekend*, January 25, 1997, 16.
18. Alexander McQueen, quoted in Susannah Frankel, "Body Beautiful," *Guardian Weekend*, August 29, 1998, 15, 19.
19. Alexander McQueen, quoted in Susannah Frankel, "Collections Report," *Another Magazine*, Spring/Summer 2002, 200.
20. Sylvie Guillem, quoted in Susannah Frankel, "Genius in Motion," *Harper's Bazaar* (UK), August 2010.
21. Janet Fischgrund, interview with author, December 2010.
22. Sam Gainsbury, interview with author, December 2010.
23. Alexander McQueen, quoted in profile by Susannah Frankel, *Neiman Marcus Magazine*, Autumn/Winter 2003.
24. Alexander McQueen, quoted in Susannah Frankel, "Collections Report," *Another Magazine*, Spring/Summer 2004, 184.
25. Alexander McQueen, quoted in Susannah Frankel, "Collections Report," *Another Magazine*, Autumn/Winter 2005, 181.
26. Fischgrund, interview with author.
27. Katy England, quoted in Susannah Frankel, "The Real McQueen," *Harper's Bazaar* (US), April 2007, 202.
28. Verkade, interview with author.
29. Alexander McQueen, interview with author, February 2009.
30. Alexander McQueen, quoted in Susannah Frankel, "Collection Report," *Another Magazine*, Spring/Summer 2008, 222.
31. McQueen, interview with author, February 2009.
32. Alexander McQueen, quoted in Susannah Frankel, Alexander McQueen show notes, Spring/Summer 2010.
33. Alexander McQueen, interview with author, September 2009.

QUOTATIONS BY LEE ALEXANDER McQUEEN

These quotations were compiled by Andrew Bolton and were drawn primarily from clippings in the press books at the Alexander McQueen Studio.

Page 16: British *Vogue*, October 2002.

Page 30: *GQ*, May 2004; *Self Service*, Spring/Summer 2002; *New York Times*, March 8, 2004.

Page 35: *Time Out* (London), September 24–October 1, 1997.

Page 36: *Domus*, December 2003.

Page 39: *Self Service*, Spring/Summer 2002; *Muse*, December 2008.

Page 44: *Wynn*, Winter 2007–8; *Numéro*, December 2007.

Page 53: *Guardian Weekend*, July 6, 1996.

Page 54: *Stella*, September 10, 2006.

Page 57: *Domus*, December 2003.

Page 60: American *Vogue*, April 2010; *Guardian*, September 19, 2005; *Purple Fashion*, Summer 2007.

Page 70: *W*, July 2002; *Numéro*, December 2007; *Time Out* (London), September 24–October 1, 1997.

Page 73: *Drapers*, February 20 2010.

Page 74: *Observer Magazine*, October 7, 2001.

Page 77: *Numéro*, July/August 2002; *Dazed & Confused*, September 1998.

Page 80: *Purple Fashion*, Summer 2007.

Page 85: *Numéro*, July/August 2002; Reuters, February 2001.

Page 92: *Harper's & Queen*, April 2003; *Muse*, December 2008.

Page 102: *Independent Magazine: Fashion*, Autumn/Winter 1999.

Page 105: *Another Magazine*, Autumn/Winter 2006.

Page 106: *Another Magazine*, Autumn/Winter 2006.

Page 111: *WWD: The Magazine*, July 2006.

Page 112: *Dazed & Confused*, September 1998; *Numéro*, July/August 2002.

Page 115: *Corriere della Sera*, July 14, 2003; *Interview*, September 2008; *Purple Fashion*, Summer 2007.

Page 122: *Time Out* (London), September 24–October 1, 1997.

Page 129: *WWD: The Magazine*, July 2006.

Page 130: *Nylon*, February 2004.

Page 138: *Another Magazine*, Spring/Summer 2005.

Page 142: *The Fashion*, Spring/Summer 2001; *20/20 Europe*, January/February 2001; *WWD*, September 28, 2000.

Page 146: *WWD*, September 28, 2000.

Page 150: *Purple Fashion*, Summer 2007.

Page 155: *Harper's Bazaar*, April 2003; British *Vogue*, October 2002.

Page 156: *L'Officiel*, February 2010.

Page 159: McQueen, quoted in Caroline Evans, *Fashion at the Edge: Spectacle, Modernity and Deathliness* (New Haven, Conn.: Yale University Press, 2002).

Page 160: *FQ Magazine*, Holiday 2004.

Page 162: *Harper's & Queen*, April 2003.

Page 167: *Purple Fashion*, Summer 2007.

Page 168: *Another Magazine*, Autumn/Winter 2006; *Numéro*, March 2002.

Page 172: *NATURAL DIS-TINCTION UN-NATURAL SELECTION* (spring/summer 2009) program notes; *Numéro*, December 2007.

Page 175: *W*, April 2007.

Page 176: *Purple Fashion*, Summer 2007.

Page 179: *Big*, Autumn/Winter 2006.

Page 180: *Purple Fashion*, Summer 2007.

Page 183: *Harper's Bazaar* (US), April 2007.

Page 184: *Plato's Atlantis* (spring/summer 2010) program notes; *WWD*, February 12, 2010.

Page 196: *Times* (London), February 12, 2010; *The Face*, November 1996.

Page 201: *L'Officiel*, February 2010.

Page 215: *Index Magazine*, September/October 2003.

Page 216: "Style," *South China Morning Post*, September 2007; *ArtReview*, September 2003.

Page 221: *i-D*, July 2000.

Page 222: *i-D*, January/February 1999.

Page 240: *Harper's Bazaar* (US), April 2007.

ACKNOWLEDGMENTS

I am grateful to the many people who provided generous support for the exhibition "Alexander McQueen: Savage Beauty" and this associated publication. In particular I am fortunate to have had the advice and encouragement of Thomas P. Campbell, Director of The Metropolitan Museum of Art; Emily K. Rafferty, President of The Metropolitan Museum of Art; Nina McN. Diefenbach, Vice President for Development and Membership; Harold Koda, Curator in Charge of The Costume Institute; Anna Wintour, Editor in Chief of American *Vogue*; and the house of Alexander McQueen, which generously underwrote the exhibition and this publication, especially Jonathan Akeroyd, Chief Executive Officer; Sarah Burton, Creative Director; and Trino Verkade, Creative Coordinator. I would also like to thank American Express and Condé Nast for providing additional support for both projects. I am also indebted to Colin Firth, Stella McCartney, François-Henri Pinault, and Salma Hayek.

My sincerest appreciation goes to Sam Gainsbury and Joseph Bennett, respectively the creative director and the production designer of the exhibition. Special thanks also to John Gosling, the musical director of the exhibition, and to Anna Whiting and Stefania Farah of Gainsbury and Whiting. I would like to express my deepest gratitude to Guido Palau, who created the remarkable masks and head treatments for the mannequins. Special thanks also to Sandy Hullett and the team of Teddi Cranford, Tomas DeLucia, Jared Glaze, Jarrett Iovinella, Tony Kelley, Adam Markarian, Matthew Monzon, Desi Santiago, and Helen Woolfenden.

Sincerest appreciation also goes to Jennifer Russell, Associate Director for Exhibitions; Linda Sylling, Manager for Special Exhibitions, Gallery Installations, and Design; Taylor Miller, Associate Buildings Manager, Exhibitions; Daniel Kershaw, Brian Cha, and Sue Koch of the Design Department; and Christopher A. Noey, Paul Caro, and Robin Schwalb of Digital Media.

I am extremely grateful to the lenders. My thanks go to Ruti Danan, Katy England, Janet Fischgrund, Samantha Gainsbury, House of Givenchy (Caroline Deroche Pasquier, Laure Aillagon), Daphne Guinness (Kate Ledlie, Primrose Dixon), Mira Chai Hyde, Maison de La Perle (Jonathan Sayeb), Tiina Laakkonen, Shaun Leane (Nancy Wong), Basya Lowinger, Alister Mackie, Dai Rees, Swarovski (Jessica Nagel, Brianne Walker), Philip Treacy (Stefan Bartlett), and Trino Verkade.

My deepest gratitude goes to Sølve Sundsbø, who created the extraordinary photographs for this publication. Special thanks also to Paula Ekenger, Sally Dawson, Alex Waitt, Karina Twiss, Ashley Reynolds, Myro Wulff, Dan Moloney, Phil Crisp, Jayden Tang, Patrick Horgan, Jim Alexandrou, and Jake Hickman.

The Editorial Department of The Metropolitan Museum of Art, under the direction of Mark Polizzotti, Publisher and Editor in Chief, provided the expertise to realize this book. Sincere thanks go to Gwen Roginsky, Michael Sittenfeld, Peter Antony, Chris Zichello, and Mary Jo Mace. For her advice, knowledge, and notable patience, I would like to thank my editor, Elisa Urbanelli. I would also like to thank Tim Blanks and Susannah Frankel for their insightful contributions. Special thanks also to Takaaki Matsumoto for his beautiful book design, and to Amy Wilkins.

I am especially grateful to the house of Alexander McQueen and its collaborators, particularly: Lara Alexander, Carolina Antinori, Christina Astolfi, Sidonie Barton, Natalya Bezborodova, Klaus Bierbrauer, Björk, Nicola Borras, Will Bowen, Lorenzo Brasca, Alessandro Canu, Michael Clark, Kathryn Dale, Duncan Dow, Olaf Fernandez, Judy Halil, Sofia K. A. Hedman, Jeannette Kenny, Simon Kenny, Laura Kiefer, Ronald Kim, Steven Klein, Nick Knight, Masako Kumakura, Chi Lael, Daniel Landin, Sarah Leech, Andrea Lattuada, Paul Little, Shonagh Marshall, John Maybury, Karen Mengers, Stephen Metcalf, Chiara Monteleone, Kate Moss, Torrunn Myklebust, Christine Nielsen, Laurent Paoli, Dee Patel, Gaetano Perrone, Maria Claudia Pieri, Benoît Sackebandt, Christian Sampaolo, Ambrita Shahani, Simon Simonton, David Sims, Kevin Stenning, Dick Straker, Sam Taylor-Wood, Charlie Thomas, Francesca Tratto, Malin Troll, Loredana di Tucci, Olivier Van de

Velde, Rachael J. Vick, Baillie Walsh, Gemma A. Williams, and Kerry Youmans.

My colleagues in The Costume Institute have been invaluable every step of the way. I extend my deepest gratitude to Elizabeth Abbarno, Elizabeth Bryan, Julie Burnsides, Michael Downer, Joyce Fung, Amanda Garfinkel, Cassandra Gero, Jessica Glasscock, Jennifer Holley, Mark Joseph, Julie Lê, Meghan Lee, Bethany Matia, Brigid Merriman, Marci Morimoto, Won Ng, Chris Paulocik, Shannon Price, Elizabeth Randolph, Jan Reeder, Anne Reilly, Suzanne Shapiro, Kristen Stewart, and Lalena Vellanoweth.

I would also like to express my sincere appreciation to the docents, interns, and volunteers of The Costume Institute, including Sarah Altman, Marie Arnold, Kitty Benton, Clara Berg, Lauren Bradley, Jane Hays Butler, Patricia Corbin, Katherine Dean, Eileen Ekstract, Michel Fox, Arianna Funk, Katherine Gregory, Madeline Haddon, Ruth Henderson, Jennifer Hart Iacovelli, Alison Johnson, Silvia Kemp, Susan Klein, Lucie-Marie Cecelia Jespersdatter Layers, Rena Lustberg, Marcella Milio, Butzi Moffitt, Ellen Needham, Wendy Nolan, Ryan O'Conner, Rebecca Perry, Patricia Peterson, Victoria Rogers, Lisa Santandrea, Gina Scalise, Rena Schklowsky, Eleanore Schloss, Bernice Shaftan, Nancy Silbert, Judith Sommer, Chandler Sterling, DJ White, and Arielle Winnick.

For the ongoing support of Friends of The Costume Institute, chaired by Lizzie Tisch, and the Visiting Committee of The Costume Institute, I am especially grateful.

I would also like to thank colleagues from various other departments at the Museum for their assistance, including Pamela T. Barr, Warren Bennett, Nancy Chilton, Jennie Choi, Aileen K. Chuk, Meryl Cohen, Clint Coller, Willa M. Cox, Mathew Cumbie, Martha Deese, Cristina Del Valle, Aimee Dixon, Lisa Musco Doyle, Peggy Fogelman, Debra Garrin, Patricia Gilkison, Jessica Glass, Christopher Gorman, Nadja Hansen, Sarah Higby, Katie Holden, Harold Holzer, Kirstie Howard, Marilyn Jensen, Brad Kauffman, Will Lach, Christine Larusso, Richard Lichte, Joseph Loh, Ruben Luna, Kristin M. MacDonald, Ann Matson, Rebecca McGinnis, Missy McHugh, Mary McNamara, Katherine Merrill, Melissa Oliver-Janiak, Stella Paul, Ashley Potter Bruynes, Frederick Sager, Tom Scally, Alice Schwarz, Amy Silva, Ron Street, Jane Tai, Elyse Topalian, Valerie Troyansky, Jenna Wainwright, Sandy Walcott, David Wargo, and Donna Williams.

I would also like to thank the following agencies and individuals for providing photographs for the exhibition and this publication: David Bailey (Danielle Edwards), Don McCullin (Jeffrey Smith, Contact Press Images), Gary James McQueen, Chris Moore (Zoë Roberts, Catwalking), The Fashion Institute of Technology Library (Juliet Jacobson), and Tim Walker (Myles Ashby, Art + Commerce).

Special thanks also to Byron Austin, Hamish Bowles, Sid Bryant, Giovanna Campagna, Judith Clark, Grace Coddington, Frances Corner, Oriole Cullen, Ellie Grace Cumming, Antonia D'Marco, Amy de la Haye, Sylvana Durrett, Caroline Evans, Linda Fargo, Kyle Farmer, Paula Fitzherbert, Sally-Ann Fordham, Shelley Fox, Danny Hall, John Hitchcock, David Hoey, Elizabeth Hsieh, Stephane Jaspar, Gina Kane, Polina Kasina, Nicole Lepage, Penny Martin, Johanne Mills, Misaki, Kaori Mitsuyasu, Sarah Mower, Kate and Laura Mulleavy, Aimee Mullins, Michael Nyman, Lyza Onysko, Clare Read, Anda Rowland, Neal Rosenberg, Caroline Roux, Megan Salt, Ivan Shaw, Katerina Smutok, Sonnet Stanfill, Tavi, Uliana Tikhova, Derek Tomlinson, Claire Wilcox, Amie Witton, and Yumiko Yamamoto.

For their ongoing support, I would like to extend my heartfelt thanks to Paul Austin, Alex Barlow, Harry and Marion Bolton, Ben and Miranda Carr, Randall Cochrell, Christine Coulson, Alice Fleet, Chris Galiardo, Tina Hammond, Teresa Lai, Alexandra Lewis, Benoît Missolin, Clare and Jack Penate, Sabine Rewald, Fernando and Soumaya Romero, Lita Semerad, Anna Sui, Rebecca Ward, and especially David Vincent.

"I find beauty in the grotesque, like most artists.

I have to force people to look at things."

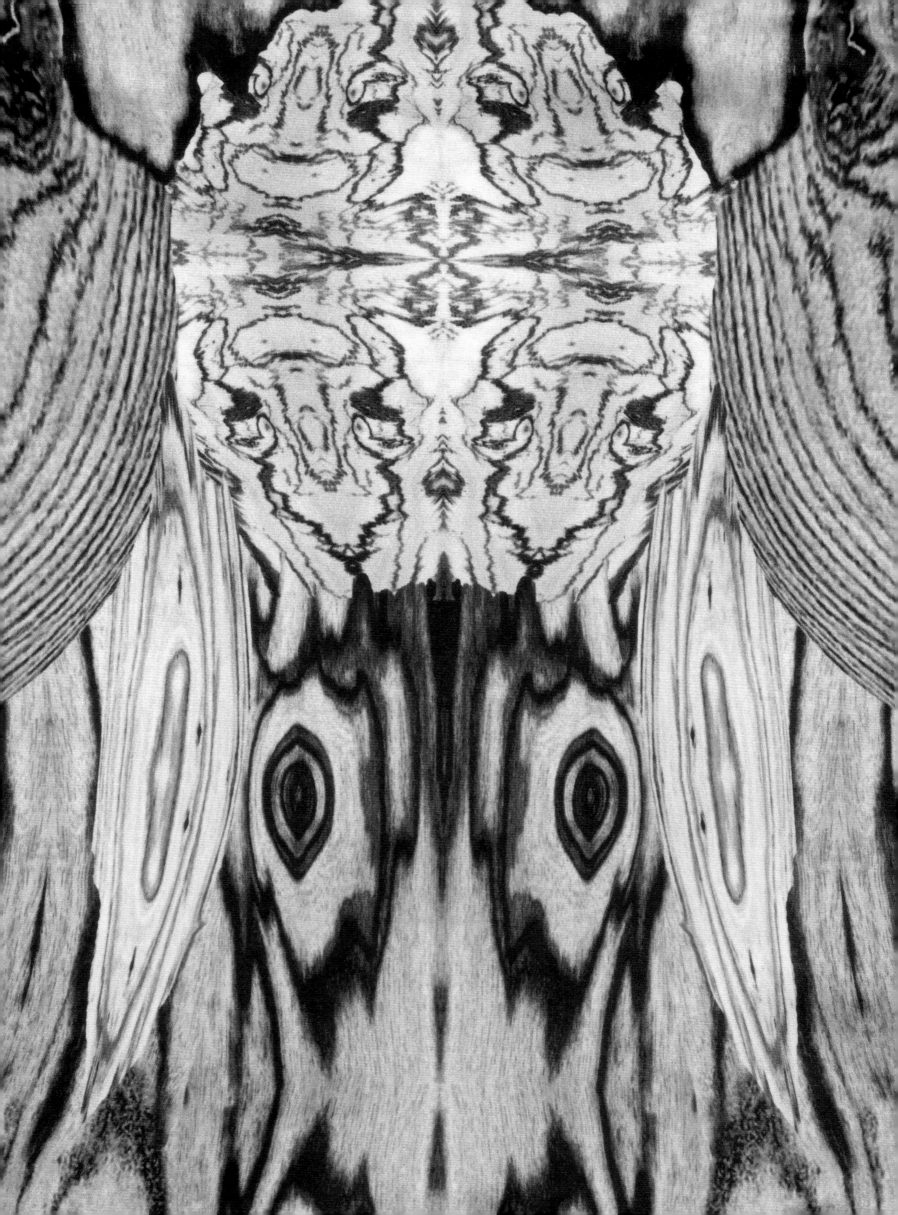

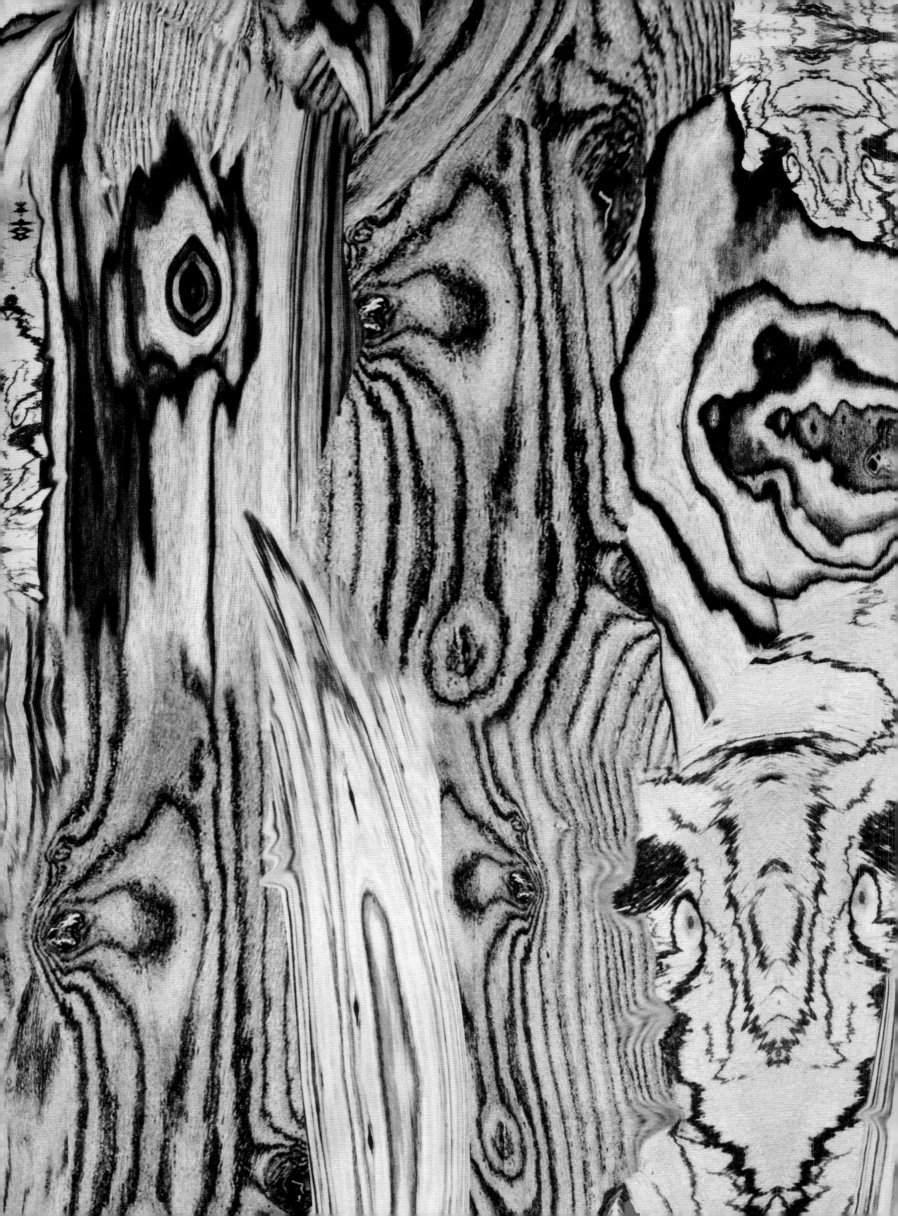